AF271123

THE HOGLES

THE HOGLES

By Gerald M. McDonough

A McMurrin–Henriksen Book

Salt Lake City — 1988

Copyright © 1988 by Hogle Associates, Inc.

Published by McMurrin–Henriksen Books

1260 East Stratford Avenue
Salt Lake City, Utah 84106-2727
(801) 484-8273

Distributed by Western Epics

254 South Main Street
Salt Lake City, Utah 84101
(801) 328-2586

ISBN 0-914740-33-4

Library of Congress Cataloguing-in-Publication Data

McDonough, Gerald M., 1945–
  The Hogles.

    Bibliography: p.
    Includes index.
    1. Hogle family. 2. United States — Biography.
3. Pioneers — West (U.S.) — Biography. 4. Business-
men — Utah — Biography. 5. Utah — Biography. 6. Utah —
Genealogy. I. Title.
CT274.H64M33 1988   929'.2'0973   88-23045
ISBN 0-914740-33-4 (alk. paper)

To Bonnie Hogle

Beloved wife, mother, grandmother of twenty-three,
great-grandmother of seven, constant and creative —
and to her four sons, who are almost as devoted as their father —
this first book is dedicated.

Foreword

In the center of our condominium in Oak Hills Gardens in Salt Lake City is an atrium, glass-enclosed on all four sides. Within this atrium, designed and installed by our son Donald Michael, is a small flowing brook. Amid the brook and foliage stands a magnificent bronze statue of St. Francis of Assisi which we acquired on a trip to Florence in 1964.

I had long intended the statue of that gentle saint to become the central element of a family memorial. But the more I thought about it, and about the seven generations that have borne the Hogle name, the more evident it became that something was missing. What would the future generations know about their forebears? The first generation left behind little of their own lives and nothing of those who went before them. The third generation, composed solely of my parents, intentionally neglected to record the family's past out of a conviction that a shadow of doubt might be cast on the honor and integrity of the name.

It became clear to me that if a history of the Hogle family were ever to be written, it had to be started now, before memory fails and the passage of time obliterates all knowledge.

The chronicle of the Hogle family is intended to portray both the strength and weakness, the happiness and sorrow of our family's background and heritage. It is also a saga which so far proclaims a resounding victory for the attributes of steadfastness and joy.

In the coming years some members of the sixth or seventh generation will determine that it is timely to continue this saga and tell the story of their own time — and so the work will carry on until the library is full.

James E. Hogle
Salt Lake City, Utah
October 15, 1980

Contents

Part III. Mary Cecilia Copley

Part IV. J. A. Hogle & Co.

Part V. Affliction, Struggle, & Triumph

Introduction

LEGEND, MYTH, & REALITY
Salmon River Mountains — October 1870

ON A BOULDER-STREWN RIDGE high above the tumbling waters of Panther Creek, the watcher braced himself against the trunk of a giant lodgepole pine and peered intently through the trees at the snow-covered ribbon of path far below — the trail winding back to Loon Creek.

Above the timberline, earth-drawn clouds hung along the saddle of a rocky peak looming thousands of feet over the Salmon River. Somewhere in the basin directly below, his pursuers were closing.

At first the watcher had welcomed the pre-dawn snow. If it had continued, his tracks would have been obliterated as quickly as he made them, and his escape would have been clean. On that chance he had left the main trail to Leesburg and made for the old William's Lake trail to Salmon City. But the light storm had lasted for only two hours, and the new snow neither hid where he had been nor obscured where he was going. There was one certainty: if he ventured onto the open snow field above the tree line, his tracks could be plainly seen from the basin below. There was no way he could outrun his pursuers. He was on foot and his trackers were mounted. So unless the clouds that hovered above the saddle moved lower down the slope, he was stuck where he was — and so he watched and waited.

Less than a mile to the northwest, at the mouth of a narrow gulch on Panther Creek, Jem Guiraud and Jake Painter were making their way steadily along the Prairie Basin Trail, which connected the tiny camp of Oro Grande on Loon Creek to Leesburg City on the Napias. They had set out the previous morning and had little trouble following their quarry; but shortly before dawn a sudden snow squall had passed through, and for the last two hours the track of the fleeing man had been lost. The gray morning light made no shadows, and picking up the half-buried footprints wasn't going to be easy.

Guiraud had dismounted and was leading his big bay. For some time he had walked parallel to his companion, thirty to fifty yards southeast of the trail. Guiraud knew that if the German was going to make a break for it, that's the way he'd go.

Near a small rill that joined Panther Creek at the foot of Porphyry Ridge, Guiraud went to one knee to examine a slight depression in the snow. He backtracked a few feet and found another. Craning his neck, Guiraud strained to see up the ragged little canyon to the high peak and rounded shoulder of the mountain in the distance. The snow field above the timberline was undisturbed. He peered intently at the tangle of pines in the bowl far below the ridge. Motionless, he listened. It was several minutes before his companion rode slowly up behind him.

"It's him, all right," Guiraud said. "He's either trying to double back on us or he's headed for Salmon City."

Painter glanced up the canyon for a moment and gestured the direction with a slight nod of his head. "Are we going up there?"

Guiraud took his time tightening the cinch on his horse's belly before replying. "It's your money too, Jake."

Painter stood up slightly in his stirrups to survey the trail ahead. "It's just that this plug ain't much of a climber."

Guiraud drew the reins over the bay's head, grabbed the horn, and swung easily into the saddle. "Just stay as close as you can. It looks like a dandy place for a bushwhacking."

As Guiraud spurred his horse up the steep embankment at the mouth of the canyon, Painter eased the hammer strap off his holster and slid the Colt Double Action .38 from its leather sleeve. He fumbled in the pockets of his long coat for the cartridges, loaded each cylinder, holstered the weapon, and slipped on the retaining strap.

A slight breeze came up from the west, and wind-blown snow drifted down from the ridges above. The sudden cold on Painter's neck sent a shiver through him, and he pulled up his coat collar and clenched it tight around his neck. He leaned forward in the saddle, whipping the flanks of the old plug, who reluctantly began to struggle up the slippery, rocky slope. Guiraud was already some distance ahead on the narrow trail.

From the basin below, the snow that blew from the leeward ridge line of the Salmon River Mountains was a delicate whiff of fleece. On the ridge line itself it was a blizzard, and in the trees at the edge of the snow field, a sudden flurry of tiny flakes that danced in the cold morning air.

At first, the man huddled at the base of the pine thought that the storm was finally moving in and he could safely move out over the open ground above the timberline. But a quick glance back toward the mountain peak told him it was just the wind. He shivered as he folded his arms across his chest, resuming his anxious watch.

The cold breeze stirred other feelings in him. Long-dormant instincts came alive. All his senses, like those of a hunted animal, were keyed to signs of danger; and there was something in the wind that drew his entire being sharply into focus. He could neither see nor hear them, but he sensed the presence of horse and rider. He could feel their hearts pounding as sharply as he felt his own.

Suddenly on the trail below, not two hundred yards away, appeared the big bay and her stocky rider. Guiraud! Painter was nowhere to be seen. The old nag Jake was riding must have given out on him. It was even odds now — time to finish this business once and for all. The watcher moved silently down the slope.

Jem Guiraud leaned from the saddle to better see the tracks in the snow as the horse plodded its way up the narrow path. The prints were sharp and deep and had been made since the snow stopped at dawn.

"The German must be about an hour ahead," he figured, unless, of course, he had stopped . . . No sooner had Guiraud realized his mistake than he was aware that he was being watched. He pulled gently on the reins and brought his mount to a stop. The trees ahead betrayed no movement. He could hear nothing but the even breathing of his horse and the creaking of the saddle as he shifted his weight to look around him. He nudged the bay slowly forward up the steep trail.

As he rounded a sharp switchback he was suddenly confronted by the looming figure of the man himself, standing on the trail cut five feet above the rocky path, not twenty yards off.

Guiraud was startled as much by the attitude of the man as by his sudden appearance. He was anything but threatening. He seemed tired, cold, and weary of the chase. His head was bowed and he offered no sign of resistance. It seemed clear that the German was sullenly accepting his capture. So convincing was the trap that Guiraud quite forgot the old adage about a cornered animal being the most dangerous and gently guided his mount directly toward the silent figure.

They were no more than ten feet apart when the man on the embankment suddenly hurled a fist full of coins at the head of the horseman. The sharp, shiny metal fragments slashed across Giraud's face with such force that he reeled in the saddle.

The horse reared and spun. Guiraud's foot lost the stirrup, and the man above sprang from the embankment and knocked him clean off the saddle. The two men crashed into the rocks and snow at the side of the trail as the horse bolted and ran back down the hillside.

For an instant Guiraud was stunned by the fall, but instinctively he struggled with his attacker, who seemed to be trying to punch him through his heavy coat. It was then that he saw the dagger.

Guiraud held the German's wrist and tried to fend off the stabbing blows as the two men rolled among the snow-covered rocks already splattered with Guiraud's blood, but the hand and its weapon kept twisting free and slashing ever higher. He crossed his arms in front of his face to ward off the ugly razor-sharp blade.

The German had the opening he needed. He seized the stocky man's hair with his left hand, jerked back the head, and plunged the dagger deep into the exposed throat. Guiraud frantically grabbed the blade lodged in his windpipe. The German was trying to twist it, but Guiraud's hands were now locked vise-tight on the blade just below the handle. The German yanked the blade up through the clutching, bleeding fingers of his victim and plunged it back down again toward the heaving chest.

Jem Guiraud stared helplessly up into the pitiless eyes of his attacker. He was strangely detached from the events around him — a spectator at his own murder, examining the most minute and meaningless details with unimagined clarity. He noted a button missing from the German's coat, a large bloodstain on his sleeve. Everything was moving so slowly now that he could count the hairs on the man's bulging neck or describe the weave of threads in the collar of his shirt. As the man raised his dagger high in the air with both hands, Jem Guiraud looked beyond the knife and saw the low clouds and the flakes of white. It was snowing again. From the corner of his eye he imagined he saw the face of Jake Painter standing over them. It was contorted in anger and he seemed to be shouting something, but the voice was far off — as if it came from a distant prospect in a wide canyon. He saw the hand and the holster, and the gun-blue barrel of the D.A. .38 Colt.

"For God's sake shoot him!"

The knife plunged toward his chest and there was a horrible roaring noise. The sky and snow were smothered in the dark wet wool of the German's coat, and there was a ringing in his ears which trailed off to silence.

Jake Painter pulled the German off Guiraud and rolled him face up on the snow. The bullet had crashed into the man's skull behind the right ear, making a frightful hole.

Painter listened at the chest of his badly wounded friend. Guiraud was still alive. He seemed to be breathing through the hole in his neck. During the war he had seen surgeons make just such incisions at the field hospitals. Perhaps if he could dress the wound and get him back to Oro Grande, Guiraud would live.

It was several hours before the German came to. His head reeled from the dull pain and stinging cold throbbing behind his ear. He lightly touched the oozing wound and was startled to find that part of his skull was missing. He was nauseated and dizzy from loss of blood, but he was alive.

He staggered to his feet and peered down the canyon. On the trail he could plainly see the pole marks of the Indian travois Painter had built to take Guiraud away. They disappeared beyond the bowl far below him. He was alone once more, and the snow clouds had settled low over the mountain's ridge and tree line. It was time to move out toward the distant peak.

In the weeks and months that followed, stories of the bloody encounter above Panther Creek circulated in the mining camps of Oro Grande, Leesburg, and Salmon, Idaho. Deputy Sheriff Reyney tried to check Painter's account of the incident. There was certainly a lot of blood up above Panther Creek. Something violent had occurred there, but there was no sign of the German. In the distant communities of Idaho City, Idaho, and Shelby, Montana, official inquiries were ordered, but nothing ever came of them.

In the half century which followed, "The Incident" became confused with other violent episodes of the period, including the killing of a man in front of Guiraud's saloon in Salmon, Idaho, and a massacre of Chinese miners in Iron Creek. The location of the incident was variously ascribed to Challis and Yellow Jacket, communities not yet in existence in 1870. Gradually the facts of the case were lost altogether and folklore took over entirely. Even so, the incident left its mark on the map of Idaho, on a city over three hundred miles away, and on the family whose history is the subject of this narrative.

The Hogle family has been prominent in Salt Lake City for well over a hundred years. The name is as familiar as any in the valley. The Hogles have contributed enormously to the growth and development of the Intermountain West. The name graces the city's zoological gardens, and the family's business and real estate interests are well known, as are their many charitable contributions. The Hogles legitimately rank among the great empire builders. They played such an important part in the development of the west that their story is by extension a history of the region as well.

It is therefore most surprising that the history of the Hogle family has remained something of a mystery. Indeed, the strange tale of the stabbing and shooting in the Salmon River Mountains in the fall of 1870 is in large measure responsible.

A family as distinguished as the Hogles deserves extensive and exhaustive treatment. As individuals, the principal characters in this book are such interesting people that each merits a complete biography; of necessity, this is something less. What follows is neither pure biography nor general history, but an amalgam of both.

Nor does this work make any pretense of being complete. It ends with the death of James Albert Hogle in 1955. The history of the Hogle family since that time is as fascinating and as worthy of study as anything that went before, and there are many who will no doubt fault the early termination of the story. This volume is intended as a long-overdue start. It was crucial that this first attempt be as accurate and detailed as possible, but later historians will no doubt uncover even more information.

What follows is neither folklore nor fiction. Every detail contained in this narrative was painstakingly researched. It is a complicated tale full of names that appear again and again and of facts and incidents that only become meaningful in the context of the whole. It is also a tale full of surprises, not the least of which is the true identity of the first James Hogle. For the origins of the Hogles are not to be found in the genealogical records of any family named "Hogle," but rather in the lineage of the Clan MacGiolla Mhuire O'Morna of Armagh County, Ireland, where the first James "Hogle" was born James Gilmore, on October 15, 1838.

Gerald M. McDonough
Salt Lake City, Utah
March 25, 1988

Part I

ORIGINS

CHAPTER ONE

The Gilmores

THE IRISH FAMILY SEPT MAC GIOLLA MHUIRE were a branch of the family O'Morna and took their name from the great thirteenth-century Lord of Lecale. Mac Giolla Mhuire O'Morna, who died in 1276, was the principle chief of northeast Ulster and ruled a large portion of what later became Down, Armagh, and Antrim counties. He was a strong political leader, famous enough to have been listed in the Annals of the Four Masters, the first authoritative history of Ireland. His descendants were chiefs of the "Ui Derca Cein" at Castlereagh and continued to hold sway in mid-Ulster through the next century, until incursions by other Irish septs, including the powerful O'Neills, and later the Anglo-Norman invaders, greatly reduced their territory.

The Mac Giolla Mhuires and the O'Neills were among the most consistent opponents of English aggression in Ulster up through the end of the fifteenth century.

The success of the English invasions, the concurrent growth of bilingualism, and the gradual destruction of the Irish aristocracy had lasting effects on Irish society, one of which was the anglicization of Irish Gaelic names. By the sixteenth century the family name, which in Gaelic had literally meant "Son of the Servant of Mary" had been anglicized to MacGilmore. The "Mac" too was soon dropped, and the modern version of the name, now simply "Gilmore," shows little evidence of its ancient Irish Gaelic origins. But the Gilmore sept continued to play a leading role in the turbulent history of Ireland for many generations to come, and the name figures prominently in the early records.

[3]

In 1593 the Gilmores joined a confederation of Irish chiefs under "Red Hugh" O'Neill, the Earl of Tyrone. In 1595 the Gilmores were included in the English lists of rebels who participated in Red O'Neill's open revolt against the English Crown. Following O'Neill's defeat at the battle of Kinsale in 1601, the Irish aristocracy fled to the Continent, and their self-imposed exile became known as the "Flight of the Earls."

The lands of the departed aristocrats were divided and given to the English officers who had fought in the recent campaigns. The English then systematically confiscated the remaining Irish estates of Ulster. The Gilmore family had not fled Ireland, but they were quickly dispossessed.

It wasn't the Irish landowners alone who suffered losses when the old estates were confiscated. More than 7,000 English and 13,000 Scottish settlers were brought to Ulster in the two decades following "Flight" to replace the Irish peasantry.

In October 1641 rebellion broke out again, this time led by Sir Phelim O'Neill and Owen Roe O'Neill. The Gilmores enlisted in Owen Roe's army. Owen was the nephew of the exiled Earl of Tyrone and an officer in the Spanish army. By the fall of 1642, Owen O'Neill's forces controlled all of Ireland except Dublin and some well-fortified towns in Ulster and Leinster. "Owen" has been a popular Gilmore family name ever since.

In May of 1642 Irish leaders met under the direction of the Catholic Primate of Ireland, Archbishop O'Reilly of Armagh, to form a government. A prominent leader of the native Irish in the "Confederation of Kilkenny" was a Charles Gilmore.

King James II landed in Kinsale with a French army in March of 1689. Although he was an English king, he was universally acclaimed as the champion of the Irish Catholic cause, and the people flocked to his banner. The name "James" has been another prominent Gilmore family name since that time. James's "Irish Army" included the regiment of Col. Felix O'Neill, yet another of that famous clan, one of whose chief officers was Captain Daniel Gilmore.

In May of 1689 James convened his "Patriot Parliament" in Dublin. Among the 224 Catholic M.P.'s was a John Gilmore. This

Irish parliament was the last under British rule to permit Catholic representation.

On July 1, 1690, the forces of James II met those of William of Orange on the banks of the Boyne River. James was defeated and fled to France while his Irish armies fought on under the leadership of General Patrick Sarsfield. Sarsfield and more than 11,000 of his Irish officers and men eventually left Ireland forever to become the "Wild Geese" who would staff European armies as officers from Spain to Russia through much of the century. Among the Wild Geese was Captain Daniel Gilmore, later a general in the French army.

The Gilmores who remained in Ireland continued to honor the memory of their fallen and exiled Irish leaders. In the nineteenth century, one of Ireland's most celebrated composers was Patrick Sarsfield Gilmore, named for the general who had led James II's Irish army into exile. The name "Patrick" too is closely associated with the Gilmore family's early history and has been passed along to members of each succeeding generation.

Members of the Gilmore family had participated in every major rebellion and campaign against the English since the days of Lord Mac Giolla Mhuire O'Morna. They must have been a special target of punitive interest, for by 1770 not a single Gilmore was listed as a property owner in Ulster.

During the sixteenth century, members of the sept began moving west into the baronies of O'Neilland East and O'Neilland West, in what is now northeastern County Armagh. During the seventeenth century the name was firmly established in Armagh.

One area in particular where the Gilmores remained in the nineteenth century was the eastern border of County Armagh. There, in Orica Barony in the parish of Jonesborough and several miles to the north in the town of Lurgan in the parish of Shankill, are the first tangible links to this family history.

In Jonesborough, two brothers, Owen and James Gilmore, owned thirty-four acres in the townland of Edenappa in 1834, and in Lurgan lived another brother, Patrick Gilmore, a central character of this narrative, who was born on March 12, 1810.

Every property owner, whether Catholic or Protestant, was

tithed to support the Protestant Church of Ireland. Records of the Tithe Composition Applotments for 1834 show that Patrick Gilmore owed 1 shilling 7 pence on the tiny peck of land he owned in the seventy-two-acre Townland of Tiersogue, Shankill Parish, Armagh.

Little is known of Patrick Gilmore's early life in Ireland. Tax and parish church records provide only the barest of facts. In 1830 he married Mary Boyle, daughter of John Boyle and Mary Liviston. Six children were born of this union: Arthur, John (1832), Catherine (1833), Margaret (1835, died in infancy), Margaret (1837), and James, born October 15, 1838.

The records also show that Patrick lost his land to the tax collector in 1838. The family then moved to Armagh City, fourteen miles to the southwest. Armagh City had been the ecclesiastical center of Catholicism in Ireland since its establishment by St. Patrick in the fifth century. It was from here that missionaries had spread the Faith to much of Western Europe, including Britain.

Since the sixteenth century Armagh has also been an important administrative center for mid-Ulster. A painting by Thomas Black in 1810, the year of Patrick Gilmore's birth, portrays a community set amid low rolling hills and surrounded by farmlands. Atop a hill in the center of the town is the imposing Protestant cathedral. A Catholic cathedral was later constructed on an opposite hill, but through the first half of the nineteenth century, the only structure to rival the Protestant edifice was the town jail, a large, grim block-like building with slit windows and high-walled yards.

It was in Armagh City that James was born, the last of the children of Patrick Gilmore and Mary Boyle. She died less than a year later, and Patrick's five surviving children were sent to live with his brother James. With the exception of the youngest child, their fate is unknown.

The Flight from Ireland

There were many reasons why the Irish fled their homeland in the nineteenth century, but all of them had their roots in British political and religious oppression. It had been going on for hundreds of years, but the social effects of that history were cumulative: the invasions, the English colonization, the Scottish plantation of the north, the confiscation of Irish Catholic estates, the brutal penal laws, the oppressive tax acts, and the tithe all combined to make the lot of the average Irish Catholic among the poorest in Europe. But no one in the government anticipated anything as disastrous as the potato blight and famine which would strike Ireland in the mid-1840's. In 1839 that unprecedented disaster was still six years off, but Patrick Gilmore didn't have to be a prophet to see that there was no future for him in Ireland. In the summer of that year, at the age of twenty-nine, he booked passage on a ship bound for Canada, leaving his children behind.

It was a pattern to be repeated by hundreds of thousands of Irish over the next half century. The father or sometimes the older brother would sail first. When he had earned enough in the new country to pay passage for other family members he would send for them. If luck was with them, they in turn would send for others. For the poorest Irish families, emigration was a piecemeal process.

Atlantic voyages of this period took from fifty to eighty days, depending on the weather. The sailing vessels were slow wooden-hulled square riggers and clippers. Passenger berths were rough, wooden-slatted bunk-like beds often stacked in tiers in the holds of converted cargo ships. Steerage passengers were little more than cattle, and the voyages were later remembered as hellish experiences by most emigrants. Of Patrick Gilmore's own voyage nothing is known beyond his destination.

Patrick's decision to head for Canada was one that was favored by many nineteenth-century Irish. Canada was also a British province, and all one needed to emigrate was a boat ticket. As early as 1825 the British government in Canada had assisted the Irish in emigrating to the province, encouraging them to colonize the backwoods and frontier outposts of the Canadian wilderness. Free homesteads were offered to promote settlement on the Canadian frontier, and boat passage was paid for many thousands who would agree to push into the interior. So many Irish emigrated to Canada in the nineteenth century that today a quarter of the population claims Irish ancestry.

St. John's was the first port of call after the long Atlantic passage, and during much of the last century was one of the continent's busiest ports. Ships stopped at St. John's to refit, take on additional supplies, or make repairs before continuing to Boston, New York, or Quebec, and many thousands of Irish disembarked there. Patrick Gilmore's first view of the New World was of St. John's. It was crowded, dirty, and rough, and though choked with commerce, suffered from high unemployment. After a short stay in St. John's, Patrick set sail for Quebec, the richest province in Canada.

Quebec boasted the country's principal port and was a major center of Canadian commerce. But perhaps just as important to Irish Catholics was the fact that French Catholic Quebec enjoyed a degree of religious freedom unknown in their homeland.

The language barrier, however, served to push the Irish into their own separate districts or townships. Some of the province's communities, such as Tinguick, were populated almost entirely by refugees from the Emerald Isle. In such places it was not French but Irish which was the common language of trade and commerce.

Patrick held a number of jobs in Canada, first as a barkeeper, then as a laborer, and finally as a teamster. He earned enough money in his first year there to start a second family, and in 1840 he married twenty-year-old Ellen Tammary. The register of Notre Dame de Luc Parish in Montreal recorded the baptism of their first child, Owen Gilmore, on April 18, 1841. The godparents were Patrick Donnelly and Mary McCarthy. Two years later Ann Ellen (always called Anna) was born to this union, and Mary Ellen (Molly) would be born in 1851.

Shortly after the birth of Ann, Patrick's brother James and James's wife arrived, bringing with them little James, Patrick's five-year-old son by Mary Boyle. They had left Ireland just in time, for the year was 1844 and the Great Famine was beginning. Records show that during this period James operated a saloon in Quebec City.

Little James Gilmore became a part of his father's second family. Owen was only three years younger than James, and the half-brothers began a close association that would last throughout their lives. In 1845 James was enrolled in a school operated by the Sisters of Charity, and he would spend eight years under the watch-

Portrait believed to be of the Gilmore family in Illinois, about 1855. Patrick Gilmore is flanked by two women believed to be his sisters. Patrick's wife Mary Ellen stands behind him, her hand on his shoulder. James stands in the center, with Owen at the far right. The two girls are probably Margaret Gilmore and Anne Ellen (Anna) or possibly Mary Ellen (Molly). The eyes of all the figures have been retouched. Courtesy Mary Anne Tanselle, great-granddaughter of Patrick Gilmore.

ful eyes of the French nuns. During his formal education in Quebec
James would learn two skills which he would later put to good use,
bookkeeping and French. In 1854 the Gilmore family left Quebec
for Illinois.

THE AMERICAN FRONTIER

Illinois was still considered a frontier state, but it was a rich land
and its commercial importance as a strategic trade center was just
emerging. During the 1850's the new railroads pushed their lines
farther into the wilderness. The railroads augmented the rivers and
existing canal systems and opened up new lands to settlement. From
the railheads, freight and stage roads crisscrossed the state and the
economy flourished.

Patrick Gilmore and his family moved to the small farming
town of Middleport (now Watseka), not far from the Illinois–
Indiana border. The town was near the Iroquois River on the main
road which then connected Peoria with Logansport, Indiana. Here,
in 1856, Patrick Gilmore opened a saloon.

On August 11, 1857, twins Patrick Albert (Ab) and Michael
Henry (Henny) were born to the Gilmores, bringing Patrick's total
to ten living children. The twins were identical and Patrick never
could tell them apart. He later took to calling them both "Henny-
Aby" or "Aby Henny." He did so without discrimination and used
the names interchangeably, a confusion he mischievously continued
to foster long after the boys were grown.

Patrick's saloon in Old Middleport was an unusual establishment. The county newspaper, *The Iroquois County Republican*,
was strongly Prohibitionist. Editorials frequently demanded that
the Iroquois County Board of Supervisors shut down the town's
saloons, where there had been frequent brawls and gunfights. After
many months of lobbying, the board finally acquiesced to the
paper's demands. On January 21, 1858, the paper printed the
following editorial:

> It is a matter of warm congratulations on the part of the
> citizens of this county that the Board of Supervisors at its last ses-
> sion took such prompt and efficient measures for the supression
> of the illegal trafficking of spiritous liquors. They not only

revoked all of the licenses which had been issued, but have determined to prosecute to the utmost all who sell liquors contrary to the law.

We want to say for the benefit of those who may be disposed to cavil at and find fault with the action of the board in revoking the licenses, that they have not done so without deliberate and mature consideration and after having become entirely satisfied, upon the testimony of numerous witnesses, that the vendors had violated the conditions upon which the licenses were issued. However we believe there is one exception, in the case of Patrick Gilmore, who voluntarily agreed to give up his license upon having his money refunded, deducting for the time he had the use of it. Every true friend of temperance reforms must rejoice at this action.

In closing his saloon Patrick Gilmore was playing a shrewd game of politics, for in February of 1859 that same Board of Supervisors appointed the honest saloon keeper to the post of Deputy Sheriff and Jailer for Iroquois County. Over the next three years the *Iroquois County Republican* routinely reported various payments made to the deputy by the Board of Supervisors. His stipend was $22.00 a month for guarding prisoners, with additional fees for transporting prisoners to district court. The paper also reported that Gilmore frequently submitted bills to the county "for expenses."

The register of St. John the Baptist Catholic Church in L'Erable, Illinois, records that Ellen Gilmore, Patrick's second wife, died March 31, 1860, at the age of forty. Her youngest children, the twins Henry and Albert, were only two and a half.

Patrick Gilmore was an imperfect practitioner of the Catholic faith, and the priest officiating at Ellen's funeral chose this inopportune occasion to chastise Patrick for his lack of religious zeal. In the aftermath of the row which followed, Patrick and his children left the church. Anna, then fifteen, tried Christian Science for a while, but her belief had been shattered. As a granddaughter later commented, "The other Gilmore children could find no substitute religion."

During the 1860's, Patrick was employed as the stagecoach driver on the regular mail run between Peoria and Logansport — a distance of some 165 miles. The route passed through Middleport, but the duties of the stage driver included punctuality, and his visits with his family, though frequent, were brief.

Patrick drove the stage until the completion of the Toledo, Peoria and Western Rail Road in 1869, when he was hired by the T.P.&W. as "foreman of the road," the crew chief for that section of the line. His job, and that of his section hands, was to maintain the roadbed, to periodically repair and replace track and ties. To better accommodate his new situation, he moved his family to Sheldon, Illinois. Patrick worked for the T.P.&W. until his retirement in 1879.

CHAPTER TWO

The Fortune-seekers, 1859–1863

THE TARIFF OF 1857, PASSED BY THE DEMOCRATIC-CONTROLLED CONGRESS, was the lowest since 1790. It was intended to assist the "Cotton States" in increasing their share of the European market, but the threatened influx of foreign goods, particularly British iron, caused a financial panic in the North. Prices plummeted, factories closed, unemployment soared, and banks failed.

> The panic of 1857 swept over the country like a tornado, uprooting, leveling and scattering the systems built upon state banks, reckless credit and mistaken theories of government. Our manufacturing industries fell in common ruin. Innumerable depositories of public and private funds went down, taking with them the savings of the poor and the modest middle class. Millions of notes became waste paper.

Though the Panic of 1857 was short-lived, the low prices and unemployment which followed plagued the country for several years and the general distrust of "Paper" dried up investment and credit. But the Panic was as much a spiritual sickness as a banking disaster. It was observed that "The energy and power of the young Republic seemed paralyzed by the fearful crash." What was needed then was not so much a return to high tariffs or a protectionist monetary policy, but a restoration of faith. The Pikes Peak Gold Rush was intimately linked to the Panic of '57 and contributed more to the country's spiritual recovery than to its financial well-being.

In the fall of 1858, when the news began to circulate in the east that gold had been discovered at Pikes Peak, the event was seen as a panacea for the nation's economic troubles. The days of gloom and uncertainty were drawing to a close. There were fabulous riches just over the horizon and recovery was just around the corner. Horace Greeley, editor-columnist for the *New York Tribune*, who had advised the unemployed workers in the eastern cities to "Go west young man, go west!," jumped on the Pikes Peak discovery as proof and vindication for his advice. But the actual proof was hard in coming. There was indeed "gold in them thar hills" — trappers had found small quantities of the metal on Clear Creek as early as 1832 — but it wasn't until the strikes made by Green Russell and George A. Jackson in 1858 that the country took any notice.

In 1859 the American people needed something to shake them from the general malaise which had dominated the scene since the Panic of '57. The Pikes Peak Gold Rush was an answer to a prayer, a sign of divine Providence, and those who braved the trek across the plains to the mountains were performing an act of faith. Compared to later strikes, the quantity discovered was pitifully small, but by the time the stories and rumors had made their way to St. Louis and Kansas City, the gold had multiplied and divided a hundred-fold. Newspapers were hounded for copy on the distant Pikes Peak region, and enterprising publishers printed guide books to lead would-be prospectors across the plains.

It is little wonder that the tales from Pikes Peak took on a fantastic and even mystical dimension. Illinois, in particular, was vulnerable to the "Pikes Peak Hysteria." The number of bank failures had been high and the young men had little prospect for steady employment. Even the most outrageous exaggerations of the Pikes Peak strike reinforced the belief that there had to be something substantial behind all the rumors. In Middleport, the *Iroquois County Republican*, edited by Michael Hogle, faithfully reported the "News From the Peak." This gem from the March 17 issue was typical:

> A marvel has come to light which even to us dwellers in the gold land is a marvel! . . . It is so strange that men can scarcely credit their own senses and yet this every word is true. The waters of Cherry Creek convert everything of a metallic nature submerged in them for twenty four hours into the finest gold.
>
> A thorough test has been made and there is no doubt about the genuineness of the metal . . . . The report spread like wild

fire . . . . Every Gun and pistol, every stew kettle and pot in our city has been placed in the stream by the watchful owners who even now are squatting over the waters watching them as you would sometimes see a frog watch a fly. There is one blacksmith here who has taken the implements of his trade and converted them all into solid gold. It is clear that the very air has an auraferrous influence. Tell everyone to come and tell them to bring all the old iron they can find.

Although it is unlikely that this tall tale inspired anyone in Middleport to haul wagonloads of anvils across the plains, there was no shortage of gullible readers whose expectations exceeded all possible reality. One paper commented: "No story, from whatever source it may have come, or however stamped with falsehood or humbug upon its face, regarding the gold discovery at Pikes Peak, not to mention ridiculous, is believed by a certain portion of the people."

In the spring of 1859 Pikes Peak was the promised land. The Panic of 1857 still cast its shadow, and the country was more than willing to believe in anything. Among the believers was Patrick Gilmore's twenty-one-year-old son James.

The Trek Across the Plains

In the five years since the move to Illinois, James Gilmore had assisted his father in raising his second family. The stage line kept Patrick away most of the time, and so it fell to James as the eldest to look after things in his father's absence. During this period Owen, Mary, and Anna attended school in Middleport. James helped his stepmother with the family's small farm and took odd jobs to supplement their income.

With unemployment running high, the young men of Iroquois County needed few inducements to join the gold rush. James Gilmore and two companions, names unknown, loaded all their worldly possessions into a "Murphy Wagon," also known as a "Prairie Schooner," and with a yoke of oxen and a mule set off for Pikes Peak some time in early March of 1859. Leander M. Hogle, a Middleport wagon builder, was making a small fortune building wagons for the Pikes Peak migration, and it seems altogether likely that young Gilmore and his friends were traveling in one of Mr.

Hogle's rigs. Yet another Hogle, George, was selling provisions to the goldseekers through his store. In Middleport, the rush to Pikes Peak was stimulating the local economy.

The large train of emigrants that Gilmore and his friends joined was ill-prepared for the arduous journey that awaited them. The weather that spring had been unusually wet and the dirt roads quickly became rutted quagmires. The heavy wagons, loaded down with supplies, sank to their axles in thick mud, and the men had to pry them out of the ruts repeatedly. The mud was described as being "like sticky dough that clung with tenacity to the wheels and spokes and piled up on the under carriages." On some days the train managed to muck its way westward a total of four miles. They were still in Illinois, and many turned back before they had barely started.

A weekly Illinois newspaper, *The Bloomington Pantagraph*, kept tabs on the comings and goings of the Pikes Peakers and reported in the spring of 1859 that the roads west of Bloomington were impassable and that many western-bound emigrants were stranded in that city.

Before a traveler could actually join the Pikes Peak rush he had to get to one of the starting points. There were three principal routes to the Pikes Peak region, the southern, or Arkansas River route, which started at Kansas City; the northern, or Platte River route from Omaha; and the central route out of Leavenworth, Kansas. There were numerous alternate routes (such as the Smoky Hills Trail), but these were all variations on the three principal themes.

For many, the first goal was St. Joseph, Missouri, since from here a "Peaker" had his choice of all three trails. When James Gilmore's train reached St. Joseph, discouraging reports about the road ahead convinced even more men to turn back. In March the *Bloomington Pantagraph* reported on their dilemma:

> An intelligent resident of this city who just returned from a journey into western Missouri, informs us that 30 or 40 men, immigrants to Pikes Peak from Illinois, are laid up in St. Joseph

James's train had been on the trail for a month when it reached Lawrence, KS. Denver was forty-six days away. Distances shown on this map are approximate.

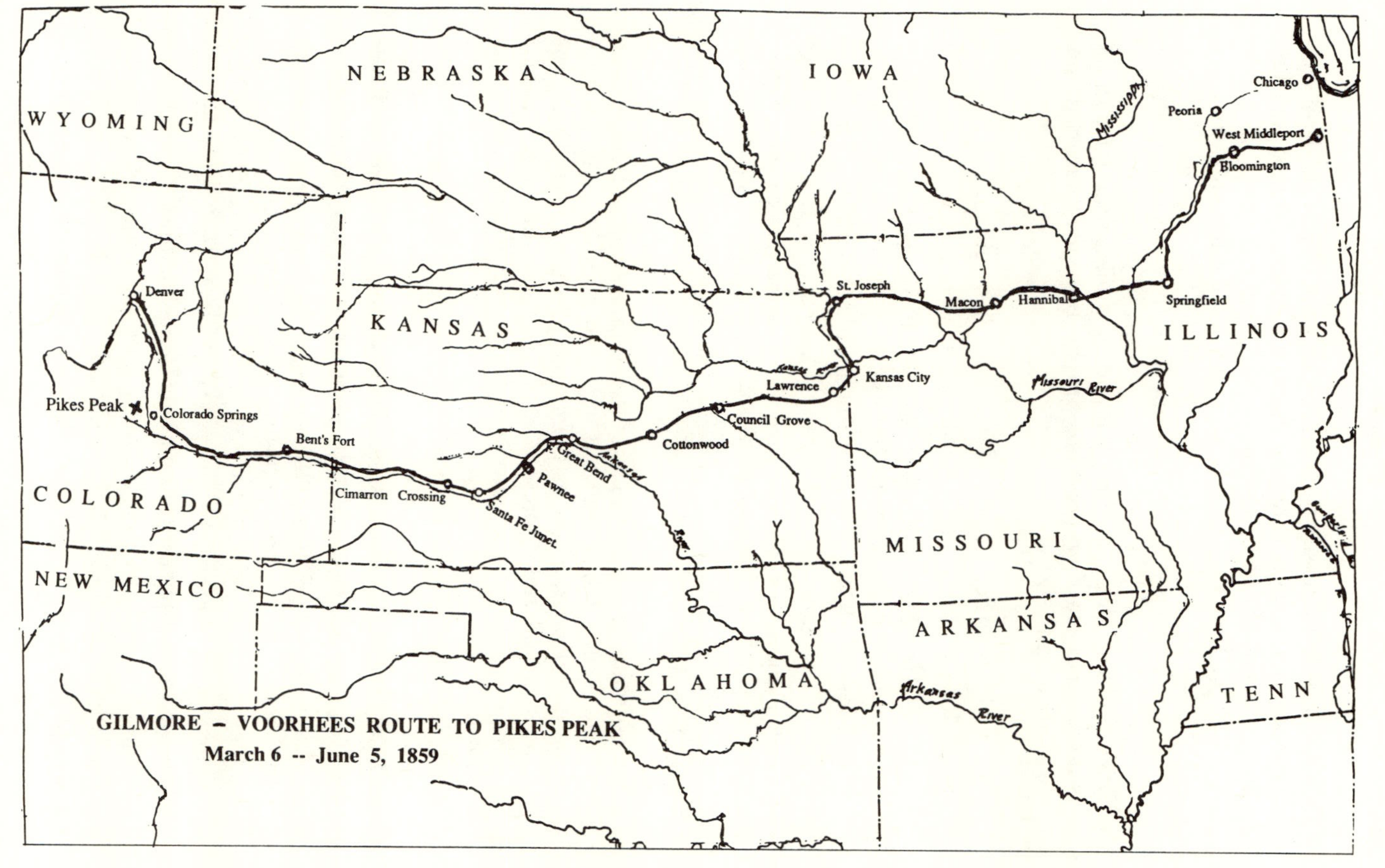

NEBRASKA
IOWA
WYOMING
Chicago
Peoria
West Middleport
Bloomington
Denver
St. Joseph
Macon
Hannibal
Springfield
ILLINOIS
KANSAS
Lawrence
Kansas City
Missouri River
Pikes Peak
Colorado Springs
Council Grove
Bent's Fort
Cottonwood
Great Bend
Cimarron Crossing
Pawnee
Santa Fe Junct.
Arkansas
COLORADO
MISSOURI
NEW MEXICO
ARKANSAS
OKLAHOMA
Arkansas River
TENN
Mississippi
GILMORE – VOORHEES ROUTE TO PIKES PEAK
March 6 -- June 5, 1859

being unable to pursue their travel for want of any mode of conveyance. He says that the routes are not open or that if they are, they are not stocked. Living at St. Joseph is dear . . . . The weather in that part of Missouri has been unusually cold and scores of oxen and mules have perished from starvation.

If these things are true it is important that they be given attention to. It would be better for persons intending on going to Pikes Peak to delay starting a few days until a little later in the season, than starting now only to be impeded, harassed and fleeced along the way.

When the weather cleared, James and his companions took the Arkansas River route to the gold fields. It was the first of the trails that opened that year, and although the weather continued to be wet, the roads were in excellent condition.

On April 20, 1859, a man named Luke Voorhees joined Gilmore's train at Lawrence, Kansas. Lawrence, a frontier village thirty-seven miles west of Kansas City, was the last eastern supply point on the Arkansas River Trail. Voorhees later wrote his recollections of the abundance of game on the plains that year, particularly the buffalo:

To estimate or comprehend their numbers would have been entirely futile. I had traveled over two hundred miles, buffalo being on all sides, as far as the eye could see. To say there was millions would not express it. . . . [O]n coming over Pawnee Butte, was a most magnificent sight. It was the thickest of the great herds.

There was plenty of game and the roads were good, but the news from the Peak turned sour. Travelers on the Arkansas River route were suddenly confronted by hundreds of bitterly disappointed prospectors who were returning to "The States." The waters of Cherry Creek weren't "auraferrous" after all and now, metaphorically, they were dragging their anvils back to Illinois. The bubble had burst, and the eastern newspapers which had been in part responsible for the boom were now peddling the bust.

After leaving Lawrence, Kansas, Gilmore's train had headed southwest to Council Grove, Cottonwood, Great Bend of the Arkansas River, and then turned sharply south through Pawnee. It was near the junction of the Santa Fe Trail, at the future site of Dodge City, that Gilmore's group first encountered the hordes of returning prospectors. The large number of bitter men screaming "fraud" had a predictable effect. Since leaving Illinois the company had traveled over 400 miles and endured many hardships, but the angry men with their tales of failure were convincing, and the new panic was infectious.

Of the large number of men from the original Illinois party, only James Gilmore and his two companions decided to push on with Voorhees and the other true believers. From the Santa Fe junction, the trail turned north to a place called Cimarron Crossing and then west to Bent's Fort, Colorado Springs, and finally Denver. The company arrived at Auraria, just outside of Denver, on June 3, 1859. The trip from Kansas City to Denver via the Arkansas River Trail had taken fifty hard days of travel. They arrived just in time to hear the remarkable news that gold had just been discovered at a place called Gregory's Gulch.

DENVER

James Gilmore arrived in Denver during the first week of June 1859. He described the future capital of Colorado as "A cluster of roughly built houses. No one living there at the time had any idea that the little settlement was the beginning of a great city."

On June tenth, Denver's *Rocky Mountain News* reported the sudden arrival of enormous numbers of immigrants from the east, about 600 a day. The paper also made brief mention of those who fled the "Pikes Peak Fraud" and had returned to the States. There followed a list of more than 200 names, with a partial listing of the various companies and the number of men who arrived with them. Among those who came through Denver that first week in June were several who would later figure prominently in the career of James Gilmore, including Luke Voorhees, Alva P. Challis, A. C. Smith, and George Shoup. Later that summer, Enos A. Wall, Fred Phillips, and Alexander Toponce arrived in Denver. They too would play significant roles in the life of James Gilmore.

On the evening of June 6, 1859, Denver played host to a famous visitor from the east. Horace Greeley was no criminal, but if he had arrived a few weeks earlier, before the gold discoveries at Gregory's Gulch and before the departure of the malcontents, he might very well have been lynched. James Gilmore, Luke Voorhees, and the other arrivals did not stay in Denver. They pushed on to the great discovery on the Clear Creek River near Black Hawk, Colorado, then called Gregory's Diggings, and Mr. Greeley pushed on too.

LESSONS OF THE GOLD CAMPS

When Greeley arrived at the Gregory's Gulch Diggings he found a community unlike any other on the face of the earth. In the narrow canyon there were hundreds of tents, lean-to's, cabins, and other hastily constructed shelters. The men were working at fever pitch, digging up entire hillsides, constructing sluices, hauling lumber, building "rockers and shakers," and everywhere the journalist looked men were shoveling dirt and hauling sacks of ore. On the road there was a traffic jam of monumental proportions — wagons and horses, oxen, mules, an unbelievable tangle of men, animals, and wheeled conveyances. And still they came. This was something to write home about.

The faith of true believers had been rewarded. Horace Greeley could report to the nation that the Pikes Peak Gold Rush was real. For James Gilmore, Luke Voorhees, and thousands of others, however, the riches of Pikes Peak would prove elusive. There was gold in Gregory's Gulch, numerous rich deposits, but these had already been taken. Hundreds of men pushed on to California Gulch, where another lode had been discovered.

Prospectors were everywhere and every inch of ground for miles was staked by someone. A week or two was all that separated the fabulously rich from the destitute. The rights of discovery went to the first on the scene, and the fates served latecomers a sour dish of envy and regret. The men who arrived too late to stake a claim were now forced by necessity to work for their more fortunate brethren. The wages were low, $1.00 to $1.50 a day. The shifts were fourteen hours long and most worked seven days a week. These were bitter lessons, but there were other lessons equally instructive and more rewarding.

As everyone in the Gulch was acutely aware, the mine owners weren't the only ones getting rich. Flour was selling for $44 a 100-lb. sack. Sugar, coffee, bacon, beans, and other staples, all in short supply, sold at outrageously inflated prices. Tools of all kinds were sold as if they were made of the precious metal itself. Blacksmiths charged lawyers' fees to sharpen spades and axes, and even bad whiskey sold for 50 cents a glass.

James Gilmore, like many others, briefly tried his hand at prospecting until his meager supplies were exhausted. He could have gone to work in Gregory's Gulch, but digging other people's gold for them was not James Gilmore's idea of success. If he had to work for wages, it wouldn't be with a pick and shovel.

In the late summer of 1859, James returned to Denver. Luke Voorhees, who returned about the same time, went into partnership with a man named Lavin and opened a small grocery store on McGan Street. James was to find a good use for the French education he had received in Quebec.

A Member of the Family

One day James Gilmore noticed a French name on a newly constructed building at the corner of F Street and McGan, two doors down from the Voorhees grocery. The sign read "Guiraud's Dry Goods." Guiraud was a familiar name to the young out-of-work Pikes Peaker. He had known some Guirauds in Quebec and some in Illinois. On the chance that "G. Guiraud" might need some help in the store, he entered and inquired after the owner. Although Gurston Guiraud and his family had made their way to Colorado from Ohio, they were distant relatives of the Quebec Guirauds James Gilmore had known.

The Guirauds were still struggling with the English language, and James got a chance to demonstrate his mastery of the conversational French he had learned from the nuns in Quebec. The personable and eager young man must have seemed a godsend to the store owner. Not only could he speak French and English, but he had had some training in bookkeeping as well. He was exactly what the Guiraud family had been looking for, and James Gilmore was hired on the spot.

Mr. and Mrs. Guiraud and their two young children lived in a house behind the store. It was a family business in the old tradition, with everyone in the household contributing to the success of the venture. When the Guirauds learned that James was also looking for lodging, it was only natural that they would invite him to move in with them.

For the rough frontier town of Denver, the store was a curiosity. Guiraud's was not just a general store but a quality import house which featured a unique line of specialty items. Ads for the establishment in the *Rocky Mountain News* suggest that Guiraud's was a frontier combination clothier, jeweler, vegetable stand, and liquor store. The May 16, 1860, issue of that paper carried the following ad:

G. Guiraud's

Corner of McGan and F. Streets. Denver, C. Ter. Dealer in all kinds of FRENCH GOODS. For Gents: Clothing, workman's undershirts, all furnishing goods and french soft hats. For Ladies: An assortment of rich dress patterns, embroidery, Broche and Chenile Shawls, Chintzes and furniture. Jewelry for Christmas Presents, Fresh French Vegetables, Imported Champagne and Swiss Absinthe.

James would work for and live with the Guirauds for almost four years. Many who knew him during this period mistakenly thought that "Jimmy" at Guiraud's was in fact "Jimmy Guiraud." It was a natural mistake; the young man did speak fluent French and the Guirauds treated him as a member of the family. It was a confusion, however, that would haunt Jimmy Gilmore for many years to come.

Denver in the early 1860's was a far cry from Paris, or for that matter, Montreal. The Champagne, absinthe, and vegetables sold well enough, but the other items featured at Guiraud's were not particularly useful to the frontier miners. There were few women in the entire territory. Fine French lace and jewelry might have been prized by a portion of the newly rich, but there was not sufficient business to justify a continued emphasis on these items. Guiraud's was failing, and a new tack had to be taken.

By the fall of 1862, Guiraud's specialty import dry goods store was a memory. A man by the name of Lambrech had arrived in Denver that year with experience in operating restaurants, and Guiraud had made Lambrech his partner. Jimmy Gilmore would stay on as a bookkeeper and bartender for the new business, an exclusive French restaurant in the same location, F Street and McGan. In March of 1863 ads for this establishment appeared in the *Rocky Mountain News.*

Guiraud & Lambrech's Star Restaurant

F Street and McGan, Denver, Col. Territory Having remodeled and refurbished in the most superb style of anything in this country, our well known restaurant and ladies saloon having the best cook that could be obtained from New Orleans to attend to the kitchen, we solicit the patronage of ladies and gentlemen at all hours, day or evening, assuring patrons that they may be politely cared for with the luxuries and delicacies of the season at our cafe. Respectfully, G. Guiraud and A. Lambrech.

Guiraud and Lambrech's Star Restaurant may have been the Antoine's of pioneer Denver, but a month later it too was gone, and with it James Gilmore's career as a bookkeeper, his association with the Guiraud family, and his life in Denver, Colorado.

CHAPTER THREE

The Rebellion in the Gold Camps, 1863–1865

IN THE LATE SPRING OF 1861, when the mining activity at Gregory's and California Gulch was at its height, news reached Denver that Fort Sumter had been fired on and the long-dreaded conflict between the North and the South was at hand. Although the great battles seethed around Washington and Richmond, the war was a national calamity and the westerner was not immune to its tragedy. A slim majority of the men who joined the Pikes Peak Rush were Unionists; the rest were southerners strong in their allegiance to the new Confederacy.

The Civil War in the American west was not characterized by large troop movements, pitched battles, or the studied practice of drill and maneuver. But a war, of sorts, was waged and what it lacked in scale it often made up for in brutality. In some places it was as vicious and ugly as anything seen in the east.

BRIGANDS, RENEGADES & REFUGEES

The manner in which the Civil War was to be fought in the west was accurately described in a proposal submitted to John B. Gordon, the Confederate Secretary of War, in the summer of 1861. The proposal described the formation of "Volunteer companies of freebooters which would make war at no cost to the Confederacy, supporting themselves by the seizure of Yankee goods and chattels. Such companies propose going and fighting without restraint and without orders and conveying the property captured to their own uses, thereby benefiting their own pecuniary circumstance as well as doing their country Good by crippling the enemy."

At this early stage of the war, Secretary Gordon was horrified by the proposal and rejected it outright. Later, however, the Confederacy would authorize the use of privateers, commissioned and built in England, which would do much the same thing on the high seas. Even some "official" Confederate units such as Colonel John Singleton Mosby's 43rd Virginia Cavalry, otherwise known as "Mosby's Rangers," would operate in the Shenandoah Valley using many of the tactics described in the letter Gordon had earlier found so abhorrent.

In Kansas and Missouri irregular bands of "border ruffians" like Quantrill's guerillas robbed banks, looted and burned towns, and shot and executed civilians — all in the name of the Confederacy. They did so with the aid of such patriotic recruits as the Younger brothers and Frank and Jesse James.

In Kansas, James H. Lane's fiercely abolitionist "Jayhawkers" raided town after town looking for Confederate sympathizers. Outlaw and renegade bands like the "Bob Black Gang" preyed on both sides. Black, a deserter from the Confederate Navy whose real name was John Keene, would have a fateful encounter with James Gilmore and some of his friends in Montana several years later. Other armed gangs of enterprising marauders preyed upon the country from Missouri to the Rockies, from the Gulf of Mexico to the Canadian border.

As time went on, the gold fields of Colorado, Idaho, and Montana saw increasing numbers of refugees fleeing the war-torn east. Some had been burned out of their homes and were forced to find new lives in the west. Many were draft-dodgers, and a good many were deserters.

The renegades and freebooters, deserters and draft-dodgers, brigands and refugees, Confederates and Unionists combined to make the western gold camps of the early 1860's volatile places indeed. With the element of gold fever added to this mixture, it is easy to see how the camps became the most dangerous and violent communities in the history of the American continent.

The war's outbreak electrified Denver, and large groups of anxious men gathered at the newspaper office. The transcontinental telegraph line would not reach Denver until October, and war dispatches had to be brought from St. Louis by special courier at a maddeningly slow pace. Denver was strongly Unionist, but Confederate sympathizers managed to hoist the Stars and Bars over a prominent building. Hoping to avoid bloodshed, the authorities allowed the flag to fly for a day, on the stipulation that when it was taken down at nightfall it would never be raised again.

A Sudden Conflagration

During the early weeks of April 1863, brothers Joseph C. and A. M. Walker were trying to induce friends in Denver to join them on a trip to a new strike near Bannack City, Montana. Stories of the "Grasshopper" and "Beaverhead" diggings had been floating around Denver for months. One large party of Denverites, which included Alexander Toponce and Enos A. Wall, had left for Montana back in February, but no word from this group had come back to either verify or debunk the "Great Grasshopper Strike." Some said it was the strike of the century and would make Gregory's Gulch but a faded memory. The Walkers were certain that the stories were true, but they had a hard time convincing others. By mid-April they had given up looking for traveling companions, and on Saturday, April 19, they purchased four mules, a wagon, and sufficient supplies for their journey. The prospect of two men attempting the dangerous 800-mile trek into the unmapped wilderness could not have been a very happy one.

Denver was now the unquestioned queen of the Plains, a city without rival on the eastern slope of the Rockies. Many of the Pikes Peak miners who had watched Denver grow from a small cluster of cabins to a great mercantile center had no thought of abandoning their comfortable new city to join the Grasshopper dig. At least they were content to wait and see if the new strikes had any "color." That Saturday in April almost the only thing that was moving out of Denver was the Walkers' wagon. But in forty-eight hours unexpected things can happen, and by Tuesday morning much of Denver was packing for Montana.

What changed the minds of the seemingly complacent Denverites occurred at 1:15 A.M. the morning of April 20, 1863, in or about the rear of the Cherokee House. Within minutes the fire had engulfed all the wooden structures in the immediate vicinity.

The *Rocky Mountain News* described what happened next: "A sharp breeze was blowing from the South and rapidly blew the fire northward, but it spread also in every other direction where the buildings were contiguous. The alarm was soon spread and the City aroused but all efforts to confine the conflagration to the neighborhood of its source were unavailing."

Seeing that the blaze was unstoppable, a large body of men frantically tried to save the contents of the doomed buildings. Guiraud and Lambrech's Star Restaurant at F Street and McGan was one of the buildings "contiguous" with the Cherokee House. The occupants had no time to save anything. In a matter of minutes the Star Restaurant was an inferno and James Gilmore was lucky to have escaped with his life. So intense was the fire at Guiraud's that it leaped F Street and "seized upon Chessman's Drug Store on Blake St. That block quickly suffered the same fate as the fire roared down a row of wooden framed buildings."

If that were the end of the story, subsequent history might have been significantly different, but the fire had barely started. Four city blocks were completely destroyed that night, along with half the goods in the city. Every hardware store and stove store was lost in the fire, and in all, more than seventy businesses. Included in the inventory of ruin were Voorhees Grocery, Kiskadden & Co. stores, W. D. Arnett's store, A. C. Edwards Co., A. A. Mayfield Cigars, and George Shoup's hardware company. Remarkably, only one fatality was reported the following morning, a man who had slipped and fallen from a roof while trying to douse a blaze at one of the warehouses.

On the morning of April 22, James Gilmore registered at the Fremont Hotel. Everything he had worked for — the home he had lived in, the business he had hoped to advance in, three years of effort — was gone. It was time to look for something new.

The Race for Bannack

Rebuilding after a fire is not something that can be done easily, and many of the men who had been burned out were busily outfitting for the trail. The *Rocky Mountain News* reported on April 23 that "Large numbers of men had started for the Beaverhead mines." As with the Walker party, most of the men left with a wagon or two, but gradually they met and joined others en route until increasingly larger companies were formed.

Luke Voorhees later reminisced that the trip from Denver to Bannack was far more exciting and eventful than his previous journey across the Plains to Pikes Peak, "what with the Indians and the high waters that had to be crossed in some improvised way as there were no ferry boats or bridges." There was the usual sense of urgency among the men bound for the new digs, but date of departure and mode of transport notwithstanding, Luke Voorhees, James Gilmore, the Walkers, Adolphus Fisher, Alva Challis, and the rest all arrived in Bannack the morning of June 4, 1863. This historic party now included "X" Beidler, who would play an important role in the life of James Gilmore.

Rumors of gold strikes were flying in all directions, and it was difficult for the new arrivals to distinguish tall tales from factual accounts. New strikes were being reported at Cottonwood, Deer Lodge, Prickly Pear, Stinking Water Spring, and a place called Alder Gulch. This latter site was the most recent discovery, and many of the former Pikes Peak men set off immediately for Alder Gulch. By June 16 several hundred men were working rich claims up and down the gulch, and gold was already being shipped out in large quantities. On that day a townsite company was formed and 320 acres of land were laid out for the new town of "Varnia."

VARNIA

The "Left Wing of General Price's Army" (so-called because they had "Left it") had come to Montana with the Denver and Pikes Peak refugees. Varnia was the name of Jefferson Davis's wife, and they intended to honor the president of the Confederacy. But when Judge Bissel drew up the articles of incorporation for the new community he flatly refused to accept the name. "Damned if my name is going to be on any document with Jeff Davis's wife. It's going to be Virginia and that's that." The fact that there already was a Virginia City in Nevada apparently was never brought to his attention, and the confusion of the two communities played havoc with the mails for years to come.

During the summer and fall of 1863, Virginia City, Montana, grew rapidly into the largest and most productive mining camp the country had yet seen. James Gilmore could not have been one of the lucky miners, for in September he was looking for work in the infant town that sprawled and spilled its way along the Alder Gulch drainage.

Virginia City was built by many of the men who had fled Denver following the fire. William Kiskadden and W. S. Pfouts opened general stores in the fall of 1863. Sam Greer and B. F. Crocker went back into the saloon business, and Adolphus Fisher started a brewery. Pioneer James Granville Stuart described the camp's phenomenal growth:

> The winter of 1863–64 was a mild one and building was carried on without interruption. . . . Before spring every branch of business was represented . . . saloons, gambling houses, public dance halls (hurdy gurdies), freight offices, stage lines, stores, newspapers, hotels, and restaurants. . . . But most of the miners built their own cabins and did their own cooking.

The California Exchange Saloon was the largest and best-stocked of Virginia City's many watering holes. It had been built and was run by Nathan Thompson, who had made his way to Montana from Walla Walla, Washington.

In early October of 1863 Thompson was approached by a twenty-four-year-old placer miner who was down on his luck and needed a job. Upon making discreet inquiries, Thompson learned that the young man was both honest and hard-working. He had been employed by a prominent Denver importer who had unfortunately been wiped out in the great fire the previous spring. The young man was known to the men from Denver as "Jem" or "Jimmy Guiraud." James Gilmore had little choice but to accept the tag with the job. Thompson hired him as a bartender and "Jimmy Guiraud" would work for him in that capacity through

October of 1864, when Thompson sold his interest in the Exchange and moved back to Walla Walla.

That same October a general election was held in Virginia City. The official election register preserves the names of those residents who voted in the election held on the twenty-fourth. The roll does not contain the name of Jimmy Guiraud — or James Gilmore. It does list a certain Mr. Hogle, the first and only such listing of the name Hogle under any spelling to appear in the official records of Virginia City. While it can not be established with any certainty that James Gilmore was the "Mr. Hogle" listed in the Virginia City election register, the chances are very good that he was indeed this man. By the spring of 1865 James Gilmore was known as James Hogle. There are many reasons why someone with something to hide might want to change his name. But in the early years of the gold rush in Montana, there were also good reasons why an honest, hard-working young man might want to keep his identity to himself.

Early photo of Wallace St., Virginia City, Montana. Courtesy Montana Historical Society.

The Democrats of Confederate Gulch

Judge Bissel may have prevented Rebel sympathizers from giving the name "Varnia" to Alder Gulch's principal settlement, but the number of "Johnny Rebs" in the gold fields was large, and as new strikes were located, the southern patriots succeeded in honoring their cause with place names that included Varney, Dixie, Confederate Gulch, Jackson (for Stonewall Jackson), and Jeffers and Jeff Davis Gulch for the Rebel president himself.

N. P. Langford, the Internal Revenue collector for the Territory, wrote: "I was in a Territory more disloyal as a whole than Tennessee or Kentucky ever were. Four fifths of our citizens were openly declared secessionists. . . . In our local matters we were completely under Rebel rule."

Col. William Fisk Sanders, an Alder Gulch Unionist leader, wrote years later: "Any attempt to describe those times which omitted reference to the political situation would be very faulty. . . . The Civil War was at its height, and a very large majority of the immigrants were in sympathy with the Rebellion. . . . [They] seized upon the Democratic Party as their . . . organ. And although their platforms went no further than insisting on the cessation of hostilities . . . , that was simply a matter upon which adroitness had seized to permit the Rebellion to succeed."

During the time that Jimmy Guiraud tended bar for Nathan Thompson, the Exchange Saloon was the very hub of Virginia City's turbulent social life. It was the camp's most popular "den of iniquity," never closed, always crowded, and thus often the setting for violent confrontations.

"Incidents" at the establishment were frequently reported in *The Montana Post.* In his official capacity, Guiraud got to know everyone of any consequence in town. It was during this time that he became acquainted with men like "X" Beidler, Col. W. F. Sanders, George Shoup, Fred Phillips, and James Williams. Frequent guests at the Exchange Saloon also included Sheriff Henry Plummer and his deputies Ned Ray and Buck Stinson.

Henry Plummer was a handsome man. He was tall and distinguished looking, and compared with the ragged appearance of the general placer miner, well groomed. In speech and manners Plummer was a gentleman, a friendly and outgoing westerner who was popular with everyone. He was well educated and had that certain quality that made him a natural leader. Back in 1856 he had been elected Marshal of Nevada City, California, re-elected in 1857, and then nominated by the Democratic Party for the State Assembly in 1858.

Plummer had arrived in Montana in October of 1862, accompanied by several men who would do much to mold the early history of the Territory. Plummer was a sure shot, and it was generally conceded that he was the fastest gun in Virginia City. He once boasted that he could slap leather and get five shots into his target in three seconds. Whether this was true or not, he was undisputably an expert with a gun. In the spring of 1863, Plummer was elected sheriff of Bannack County, and his term of office would coincide with the most violent and disturbing period in the history of Montana.

For the successful miner who wanted to bank his "poke," as the miner's personal fortune was usually called, there were two routes out of the gold fields. One was by way of Fort Benton, Montana, and then down the Missouri River by steamboat. The other was over the old trail to Salt Lake City. Both had their disadvantages. The Ft. Benton–Missouri River route was long and entailed a good month of travel. The Salt Lake route was shorter but was regularly plagued by murderous road agents lying in ambush. During this period Alder Gulch produced over sixteen million dollars' worth of gold, and shipments of $20,000 or more were common. From July of 1863 to January of 1864, hardly a day went by that someone wasn't robbed on the Virginia City–Salt Lake road. During this short period an incredible 102 men were known to have been murdered by highwaymen.

The identity of the robbers was unknown, but there was a rough element in Virginia City that brazenly threatened and bullied the citizenry, and these men were generally suspected of being members of the outlaw band. Sometime during late 1863, a secret society known as the Vigilance Committee was organized to fight the tight-knit band of outlaws.

Clasbey House, Virginia City, Montana, operated by James T. Clasbey, James Hogle's future saloon chain partner. X Beidler stands third from left. Courtesy Montana Historical Society.

The leaders of this group included "X" Beidler, James Williams, and Col. W. F. Sanders. Though the Committee numbered in the hundreds, the identities of fewer than a score were ever known. Secrecy was the hallmark of the organization, and its members adopted aliases both to mask their activities and to protect themselves and their families from later reprisals.

Just sorting out the good guys from the bad guys was a major problem. Sheriff Plummer had all his men fashion their ties in sailors' knots so they could recognize each other on the road. A secret oath was taken and a password adopted to insure that proper security was maintained. Even so, mistakes were sometimes made. After an infamous series of crimes, sometimes followed by equally infamous examples of frontier justice, an outlaw named Red Yeager revealed that the chief and supreme leader of the outlaw band was none other than the principal law enforcement officer of the county, that impeccable gentleman Sheriff Henry Plummer.

Yeager revealed the password ("Innocent") and also supplied the Vigilantes with detailed accounts of numerous stage robberies, ambushes, and murders of which he had first-hand knowledge, as well as the burial locations of a number of victims. His evidence was checked and proved to be grimly accurate.

Henry Plummer and his deputies Buck Stinson and Ned Ray were surprised and captured by Vigilantes from Bannack and Virginia City on the night of January 9, 1864. They were then taken to a gallows which they themselves had erected in their capacity as law officers for the county and summarily hanged.

Over the next thirty days the Vigilantes systematically hunted down and executed seventeen members of Plummer's band. Many of these men were still convinced that they were fighting for a cause. At his execution in Virginia City a desperado named Boone Helm shouted from the scaffold, "Every man for his principles — Hurrah for Jeff Davis and let her rip!" The sound of his words echoed through the streets with the accompanying twang of the hangman's rope.

In the months that followed, the Vigilantes captured and executed twelve more murderers. In addition to those executed, a number of minor associates of the gang were banished from the Territory forever, under pain of death. Included were Judge "Rab" Smith, the founder of Leesburg, J. Thurmond, an attorney, and a man named [George?] Moyer, who was said to have provided Plummer's gang with a meeting room and lodgings in Bannack.

The Exchange Saloon had played host to many of the events surrounding the conflict between the "Innocents" and their adversaries. Its owner Nathan Thompson was at one time suspected of being a member of the Plummer gang, primarily because of his frequent trips to Walla Walla, a known outlaw destination. Whether he was or not, the Exchange was frequently the scene of both armed arrests and impromptu Vigilante trials. As bartender, the man known as Jimmy Guiraud witnessed that frontier justice at close hand.

CHAPTER FOUR

The Good Work Continues
Helena, Montana, 1865–1870

Luke Voorhees was getting anxious. He was twenty-six years old and he wasn't rich yet. His placer claim in Alder Gulch was producing gold but "not the volume of the stuff he hankered after." In early March of 1864 he met some French Indian trappers from British Columbia who showed him large nuggets of pure gold they had found in the extreme northwestern part of Montana. When the men agreed to lead Voorhees back to the source — where they said there was "Heap Gold" — Voorhees attempted to induce some of his friends to accompany him. Among those he approached was James Hogle, but Hogle did not join the Voorhees expedition. He had prospected with Voorhees before without success. His job with Nathan Thompson at the Exchange Saloon was secure and paid well — well enough at least that he must have felt another long journey to an unknown destination could not be worth the effort. If so, he was mistaken:

> We outfitted with provisions, ammunition and two good cayuses each, leaving Alder Gulch at the last of March, 1864. Although there were deep snows to encounter, we successfully made the trip. On the fourth of April we camped on a creek which emptied into the Kootenai River. Although we had about two days travel to make the stream the "half breeds" were leading us to, I liked the appearance of the wash of the gravel, although ice still covered the creek.
>
> I managed by building a fire to thaw the ice and warm some water in which I put a shovelful of gravel, which I panned and washed and found much gold. That of course made me the discoverer of the "Kootenai Diggings." After working there during the summer and late into the fall, I returned to Virginia City.

The opportunity James Hogle had passed up made Luke Voorhees a wealthy man. In December of 1866, a little over a year and a half after making the Kootenai discovery, Voorhees took the stagecoach from Helena to Salt Lake City with "About 200 lbs. of gold dust which I was anxious to get run into ingots and bars to sell for currency."

Voorhees was not the only man in Montana who preferred spending his winters and his money in Salt Lake City. Alexander Toponce and Enos A. Wall went to Salt Lake often and had been robbed twice on the trail by the Plummer gang. Vigilante leaders Colonel W. F. Sanders and X Beidler made frequent trips to Salt Lake, sometimes on "Official business." That fall Virginia City's newspaper, *The Montana Post*, reported that "Daily we see teams loaded with men that have made their pile leaving the country for Salt Lake and other parts, some to return in the spring and some never to see this fair territory any more."

In October of 1864 Nathan Thompson sold his Virginia City saloon and moved for a time back to Walla Walla. It was shortly after this that James Hogle made his first visit to "Zion," the Mormons' term for their western refuge. Two other Montanans of note visited Salt Lake City during the winter of 1864–65, but these men were neither merchants nor vigilantes, saloonkeepers, or placer miners. Their names were John Keene and Harry Slater and they were killers.

BAD BLOOD

Salt Lake City was the first metropolis of the Intermountain West. By 1864 it was a major crossroads for both east–west and north–south traffic. In April of 1862 the final link in the transcontinental telegraph was completed there and Fort Douglas, which overlooked the "Mormon Mecca" from the east bench, was the principal military base between California and the Plains.

Most of the goods bound for the mining camps in Idaho and Montana were shipped through Salt Lake City, and freighters and merchants of all kinds used the city as their supply point. The likes of Fred Auerbach, William S. Godbe, the Siegal brothers, George and Sam Teasdel, Kimball and Lawrence, and the Walker brothers headquartered in Salt Lake. The gold fields of the north were also turning the town into a banking and financial center as miners traveled to Zion for the sole purpose of caching their "poke." Many miners naturally preferred to spend their winters in Salt Lake, escaping the cabin fever and rough life of the boom towns.

Salt Lake had several fine hotels, including the Salt Lake House, the Mansion House, and the California Hotel. A large proportion of the guests were boarders or long-term residents. It was no wonder that the men who came to Salt Lake brought with them the problems usually associated with the wild west mining camps. During James Hogle's first winter in Salt Lake, the community was as "wild" as any in the region.

On October 5, 1864, the *Deseret News* reported that two killings had occurred on East Temple Street during the previous week: one at Moore's Saloon, one at the Bank Exchange Saloon. The paper reported that there had been a knife fight at the Greenback Saloon, a fistfight in front of Sholes Saloon, and an armed robbery as well.

Soon J. Thurmond, who had been banished by the Vigilantes of Virginia City, showed up in Salt Lake, and finding that a certain Mr. Fox, a member of the Vigilance Committee, was in town, promptly took him to court and sued the man for assisting in his banishment. Thurmond won his case and was awarded a judgment of $8,000 by a Salt Lake jury. This, coupled with the fact that many well-known desperadoes like John Keene and Harry Slater were wintering in the town, convinced some Vigilantes that the Mormons were in cahoots with the road agents.

John Keene was a Confederate deserter, murderer, and all-around renegade who had eventually made his way to the Montana Territory, where his talents were put to use by Henry Plummer.

Harry Slater was a professional gambler and gunman with a wicked temper and mean disposition. He too had been associated with Plummer's gang and in fact had narrowly escaped lynching by the Virginia City Vigilantes. During the winter he attempted to assassinate the Vigilante leader, Col. W. F. Sanders, on a Salt Lake City street but was restrained by companions.

There was bad blood between Keene and Slater, the exact cause of which is unknown. On a spring day in 1865 Slater got the drop on Keene in a Salt Lake City saloon. Slater shoved his derringer into Keene's mouth and threatened to blow the back of his head off. He disarmed Keene and heaped insults on him, calling him an Irish pig and a damn Vigilante, and a number of other unpleasant things. In the end, Slater was satisfied with running Keene out of town. The insults and humiliation weighed heavily on John Keene, and he could think of nothing but revenge.

A MURDER IN LAST CHANCE GULCH

In the fall of 1864 a small party of former Coloradans had set out for Luke Voorhees' new strike on the Kootenai but had ended up tired and discouraged in the Prickly Pear Valley. Their disappointment was brief because they discovered gold at a place they called Last Chance Gulch. News quickly spread to all parts that this strike might be even richer than Alder Gulch, and so it wasn't long before a full-scale rush was in progress.

In addition to gold, Last Chance Gulch had other advantages that attracted the merchant, the tradesman, and the freighter. The place was accessible. It was closer to Ft. Benton and still within reach of Salt Lake. The terrain was better for wagons; there were wide grasslands for stock and water was plentiful. By spring a number of Virginia City businessmen had taken down their establishments and moved lock, stock, and barrel to Last Chance Gulch, where Helena was born. Among those "Virginians" who moved to the new town were the saloon keepers Sam Greer, B. F. Crocker, C. W. Mathers, John Mahan, G. Jules Germain, and numerous merchants — Kiskadden, Pfouts, Hauser, and Auerbach among them.

Many of the men who had spent the winter in Salt Lake City, including James Hogle, Luke Voorhees, Alexander Toponce, Col. Sanders, and Harry Slater, went to Helena instead of returning to Virginia City. They must have been surprised to find the new community so strikingly familiar, even down to the names on the store fronts.

On June 7, 1865, the mining camp was basking quietly in the late afternoon sun. Men strolled down Main Street or talked with each other on the wooden sidewalks. In the doorway of Sam Greer's Saloon a man slumped in a chair, his wide-brimmed hat shielding his face from the glare of the sun, his hands folded in his lap, his legs, crossed at the ankles, stretched out onto the boardwalk.

In the street slightly below Greer's Saloon a man named Kelley was sitting on a pile of logs idly whittling away at a stick. Across the street James Binns was reading the bill of fare in the window of a restaurant. In Greer's itself the owner stood at the end of the bar near the door polishing a glass with a towel. His brother Charles was serving two customers at a table near the open doorway. At the table the customers, Mr. Fred Phillips and Mr. James Hogle, were engaged in casual conversation.

Three doors up the street a barber named Tom Lyon was in the act of putting a straight razor to the whiskers of a skittish customer. Another man, Charles French, had just passed Lyon's Barber Shop and was walking down Main St. headed for Sam Greer's. He was exactly in front of the door to Bernard's Clothing Store, two doors above Greer's Saloon, when he saw the man sitting slouched at the doorway and, behind him on the boardwalk in front of the saloon, two men who had just stepped up from the street and were also walking toward Greer's entrance.

John Keene had arrived in Helena just that morning. He had overtaken a man named James Parker near the summit of MacDonald Pass southwest of the town. As the men rode together Keene inquired if Parker had seen Slater in Helena. He told Parker how Slater had thrust a derringer into his mouth in a Salt Lake City saloon that spring and run him out of town. The two men arrived in Helena shortly before noon and went their separate ways.

On the street about half a block below Greer's Saloon, John Keene met a man named Boyden. Boyden had known Keene since childhood, but he had not seen him in many years and did not recognize him at first. As Boyden and Keene walked up the street together, Keene told Boyden that he was looking for a gentleman who had "done an act of kindness for him." In the street near Greer's Saloon Keene stopped to shake hands and exchange a few words with Mr. Kelley, the man who was sitting on the logs. The two then mounted the sidewalk. Keene was a little ahead of Boyden by the time they reached the saloon entrance.

John Keene recognized the man sitting in the doorway immediately. Without saying a word, he drew his revolver and squeezed off two shots, point-blank range, at the squinting face of the man seated in the chair. The first bullet crashed into the man's head near the temple over the right eye. The second was ugly but unnecessary; Harry Slater was already dead.

Between the first and second shots Keene managed to shout at his victim: "You son of a bitch! You ruined me in Salt Lake." By this time there was no shortage of witnesses. Keene then put up his revolver, turned, and ran from the scene of the murder. He ducked down an alley off Main Street where he was immediately captured by X Beidler and a man named Curtis who had heard the shots and were rushing to the scene of the shooting. They had just happened to turn up the other end of the same alley.

Keene was held briefly by Sheriff Wood, but the Vigilantes quickly relieved the sheriff of his prisoner and "a Committee was formed to give the murderer a hasty trial." A courtroom was improvised in a lumber yard adjacent to the sheriff's office. The trial started immediately and without formality.

The town doctor was called, but before he could testify the accused stood up and launched into a lengthy oration in his own behalf. He said he had acted in self-defense, that Slater had run him out of Salt Lake, had threatened his life, had slapped him in the face, and was in the act of rising with his hand on his pistol.

A number of witnesses were then called and the events reconstructed. A reporter from the *Montana Post* covering the trial correctly identified the next witness. Although the spelling was phonetic, subsequent events leave no doubt as to his identity: "James Geero was called for and sworn." He described how Slater was sitting when he was shot and the effects of the shooting on the victim, and also that Slater had neither struck nor spoken to the defendant prior to the murder. He also testified that he knew nothing about the cause of the shooting.

At this juncture something happened in the crowd. Whether it was an attempt to rescue or rush the prisoner is unknown, but the guards quickly closed around the prisoner and the trial continued.

Fred Phillips was called next. He corroborated "Geero's" testimony, saying: "I don't know anything about the affair but I heard the shots and saw Slater fall. I know what Jem Geero says is true. I saw Slater sit in this position . . . ." The prisoner interrupted here and asked for a number of witnesses to be called and then asked Phillips to give additional testimony bearing on the character of Slater. The crowd became increasingly restless. A motion to guard the prisoner until morning was made and after some discussion carried with the proviso that the prisoner's guard be increased.

The trial was resumed shortly after eight A.M. the next day at the California Exchange Saloon, and a number of witnesses were called. The examination was then closed and the jury retired to consider the evidence. At 9:50 they returned and the prisoner was sent for. At 10:00 the prisoner was escorted into the Exchange surrounded by fifty armed men. The foreman of the jury then delivered the verdict: "We, the jury in the case of the people of Montana vs John Keene, find him guilty of murder in the first degree." Thomas Dimsdale described Keene's execution in *Vigilantes of Montana*:

> At 11:00 crowds of people could be seen ascending the Hill North of Helena. The place of execution was chosen with due regard for convenience, a large pine tree with stout limbs, stand-

Nathan Thompson's Exchange Saloon in Helena, Montana, forty years after James Hogle testified here against John Keene at Keene's murder trial in 1865. Owen Hogle tended bar here from 1865 to 1871. Courtesy Montana Historical Society.

ing almost alone in a shallow ravine. . . . The execution was conducted by "X" Beidler and everything went off in a quiet and orderly manner. Many familiar faces, known in Virginia City in the trying times of the winter of 64 were visible in the crowd.

At four minutes to twelve the prisoner's arms were pinioned and he was assisted to mount the wagon. Standing on the rail platform he said, in a loud and distinct voice: "What I have done my honor compelled me to do. Slater run me from Salt Lake City to Virginia and from there to this country. . . . If I was to live until tomorrow, I would do the same thing again. I'm ready, jerk the cart as soon as you please."

At 12:07 the wagon started, the trap fell, and John Keene, deserter, renegade, highwayman, murderer, and veteran seaman of the Confederate navy was "Launched into eternity."

The execution of John Keene was intended as a warning to any would-be desperadoes that in the town of Helena justice was going to be swift and efficient. Thomas Dimsdale reported that the effect of the execution on the "Rough element" in Helena was "electrical": "Cayuses began to rise rapidly in demand and price and men went prospecting who had never been accused of such an act before."

Corporal Owen Gilmore

Following the trial and execution of John Keene, Helena settled down to the business of becoming the most important mining and commercial center in the Territory. The town was already beginning to challenge Virginia City for the title of territorial capital, and the feud between the rival camps sparked bitter debate.

The Civil War had ended in April of 1865, and in the months since the new community had received a fresh influx of citizens recently discharged from the Union and Confederate armies. In that number was a twenty-five-year-old veteran of the Conflict, James's younger brother Owen.

When James had left home to join the Pikes Peak Rush, Owen Gilmore was sixteen years old. He too wanted to join the great exodus, but he was badly needed at home. The departure of James must have placed a special burden of responsibility on Owen. There were four younger Gilmore children; the twins, Albert and Henry, were only two years old at the time and his mother needed all the help she could get.

But on June 6, 1861, Owen Gilmore enlisted in the Union Army at Urbana, Illinois, the day following the death of Senator Stephen Douglas, another famous citizen of that state, and the opponent of Lincoln in the famous debates of 1858. Owen was mustered into the 25th Illinois Infantry on August 21. Owen had special gifts, and he was not enlisted as just another foot soldier. His musical talent was to be put to good use, and he was made a musician in the 25th Infantry's regimental band, serving in that capacity until he was discharged on December 18, 1861.

On May 14, 1864, Owen re-enlisted in a Chicago unit, Company B of the 134th Illinois Infantry. His enlistment was for a short 100-day tour of duty, and he was mustered into the army on May 31, 1864. Because of his prior service Owen was given the rank of corporal. He was discharged from the Union army on October 25, 1864. Corporal Owen Gilmore, veteran of the Grand Army of the Republic, was now private citizen Owen Hogle.

A Matter of Identity

True mysteries are hard to solve. For the Hogle family, the mystery turns on the last week in October 1864. It was the week following the departure of Nathan Thompson for Walla Walla, and James Gilmore, known to Thompson as Jimmy Guiraud, registered as Mr. Hogle for the upcoming Virginia City election. From that date on Hogle was the family name; this was true not only for James but also for other members of the family who were to come west later on.

Nathan Thompson, the man who had employed "Jimmy Guiraud" in Virginia City, dated the name change to his own movements during 1864 and 1865. In a sworn deposition taken many years later he recalled the sequence of events.

In October of 1865, Thompson returned to Montana from Walla Walla, Washington, after a year's absence. In early November he went into partnership with D. A. G. Fleury and A. P. Carter in the operation of a new Exchange Saloon in Helena. This second Exchange was already prospering when Thompson entered the business. It stood at the corner of Main and Wood streets and was large enough to have doubled as an impromptu courtroom for the trial of John Keene the previous summer.

Thompson soon found that his former barkeeper in Virginia City was now living in Helena, where he was known as Jimmy Hogle. But some men from Denver and Virginia City still called him by the former name.

James Hogle explained to Thompson that he had received the name "Guiraud" while working behind the counter at Guiraud's Store and later for Guiraud's Star Restaurant in Denver. Like the Guirauds he spoke French, and he had lived with the Guirauds as a member of their family. It was little wonder that many men just assumed he was a Guiraud. Whether nickname or alias, the tag stuck and the man found himself saddled with it. He did not tell Thompson about the name Gilmore, and this left his employer with the impression that Hogle was his real name. While the use of the name Guiraud seems to have come about through a misunderstanding, the adoption of the name Hogle was intentional, and the link connecting Hogle to the James Gilmore who had left Iroquois County, Illinois, in 1859 was now lost.

If the double name change was taken to hide the person called James Gilmore from prosecution for some offense or criminal activity, that offense has never been determined despite energetic and thorough research, and no record of a James Gilmore being wanted for anything has ever come to light. On the other hand, the man known as Jimmy Guiraud had what was known as a "colorful history," and perhaps he thought it better forgotten.

A specific reason for James's name change is impossible to pinpoint. His taking of the name Hogle is easier to understand. The Hogles were, without question, the most prominent family in West Middleport, Illinois. Members of the Hogle family owned the town's newspaper, blacksmith shop, saddle shop, general store, and hotel. The Hogles had moved to Iroquois County from Ohio in 1838, and since that time they had been prominent farmers in the county and owned large tracts of land. The 1860 Census listed fifty-four Hogles in Iroquois County. Leander M. Hogle had served two terms as county sheriff. James Gilmore's father, Patrick, had served for a time as his deputy. George Hogle served on the county board of commissioners, and Abraham and Michael Hogle had served on the Middleport city council.

The Gilmore children had grown up with the Hogles, and it seems likely that some of the Hogle family (Caroline, Horatio, John, Michael, Margaret, and Elizabeth Hogle) had gone to school with James, Owen, Anna, and Mary Gilmore. They were all about the same age. If there was a good reason to adopt a new name, Hogle was as good as any and perhaps better than most — a name that James respected and one that would provide a worthy incentive. Family tradition has it that James Gilmore wrote to one of the senior Hogles back in Middleport (probably Abraham) for permission to use the name and the request was granted. No documents or records have come to light which might verify this, and no formal court hearings on the matter are known.

In November of 1865 Owen Hogle was hired as a bartender by Nathan Thompson, a position that he would occupy at the Exchange Saloon until 1871. James Hogle's occupation during his residency in Helena is unknown. The names Hogle and Guiraud seem to have been used interchangeably and even simultaneously when James was in Idaho. Col. George Shoup, who operated a wholesale grocery, storage, and commission house in Virginia City in 1865, and later the general store in Salmon, Idaho, knew Hogle to use the name Guiraud in Idaho as late as 1870 and was well aware of his dual identity.

The man known as James Guiraud was indeed colorful. He was not the kind to run from a fight, and the *Montana Post* records several instances when he was involved in dangerous engagements. One such incident occurred on Christmas Eve of 1865. A man variously reported as either Thomas Gooms or Mr. Conley was sitting on one of the Phelan Pool Tables at the Exchange. Sitting on a pool table is considered a great sin in the west, and signs were usually posted to discourage such ungentlemanly behavior. There were, however, other methods of persuasion: "Guiraud walked up to a man sitting on a table and after saying two or three words, drew his revolver and struck him over the head, knocking him off the table, cutting an artery and making a severe wound."

This was the very sort of behavior that usually brought its performer to the hangman's tree in Helena or, at the very least, banishment from the Territory. Vigilante X Beidler, Montana's most efficient and experienced executioner, was right on the scene to dispense justice. The *Montana Post* noted what followed with some surprise:

> X Beidler was speedily on the ground and carried the wounded man to the "International Hotel." He then summoned a physician who dressed the wound. Guiraud said it was all a mistake and paid the physician fee and made so many protestations of good behavior in the future that "X" took a different course from usual and let the fellow go.

This was unusual treatment indeed. Guiraud and Beidler may have had an understanding, but the *Montana Post* added an editorial warning to Guiraud on its own: "Such men must go slow with their revolvers or men will take retribution into their own hands."

To make it doubly clear to the readers who the principals in the incident were, the *Post* printed a brief account of the story at the bottom of the page on which the longer story appeared with the name "Hogle" used in place of Guiraud. The wounded man preferred no charges against Guiraud and so the matter was dropped.

Considering the level of Vigilante activity, and the warnings that he had already received, Guiraud's next "incident" was especially risky. On March 1, 1866, a war party of Blackfeet Indians and white settlers had fought an engagement at a place called Sun River Bridge, near the Sun River settlement between Helena and Ft. Benton. One settler was wounded, one Indian killed, and three Indians hanged, an action presumably in retaliation for the killing of four white men and the stealing of twenty head of horses the week before.

Near Helena there was a large encampment of Flathead and Pen d'Oreilles Indians who had no connection to the Sun River troubles. The *Post* reported that there were more than 300 lodges and that "Many of the redskins are in town, parading in the streets, peering in windows, leaning against the doors . . . and greeting everyone with 'hows.' "

On Saturday night, March 3, 1866, Guiraud and one George Perkins, who the *Post* described as "two men who are supposed to get their living by fingering the pasteboards," had a difference of opinion. Perkins was from Sun River, and when an Indian appeared on the street in front of Billy Mather's Billiard Saloon, Perkins resolved to scalp him on the spot.

Guiraud stopped the fun and stepped between Perkins and his intended victim. The Indian managed to escape unharmed, but the enraged Perkins drew his revolver on Guiraud, fired, and hit the latter in the arm above the elbow. Guiraud retreated to the doorway of Mather's Saloon and returned Perkins' fire. In the crowded saloon and the street outside, men dove for cover as the gun battle erupted. Six or seven shots were fired in all, but luckily none of the scattering bystanders were hit. Mr. Perkins too escaped injury. Beidler was promptly on the scene and arrested both Perkins and Guiraud. The *Post* correspondent commended Beidler's quick action, saying, "X deserves a promotion from Collector Langford for his promptness in suppressing a shooting gallery that was running without a license."

The *Post* roundly condemned the "parties who had so recklessly imperilled the lives of their fellow citizens." The Vigilance Committee had thrown "necktie parties" for citizens who had done less. They had executed J. A. Slade for shooting up the ceiling of a Virginia City saloon. They had banished attorneys for defending criminals and householders for renting rooms to the wrong sorts of people but, once again, Guiraud's charmed relationship with Beidler held. The Vigilantes looked the other way and Guiraud was released.

If the gambler Jimmy Guiraud went unpunished for his errant behavior, it may have been because he was one of the town's more reliable citizens, or perhaps it was because the man known as James Hogle was earnestly seeking a new line of work. In the summer of 1866, ads began appearing in the Helena papers which touted the special talents of a certain young man: "Wanted — a situation as salesman or bookkeeper in either a dry goods, clothing or grocery house. Talks french and english. Can furnish letters of recommendation if required."

Directly below this ad in Helena's tri-weekly paper *The Herald* on July 26, 1866, was a fan letter which praised the singing talents of a Miss Flora Bray, who had appeared at the Helena Theatre the week before. Signing the testimonial was a list of appreciative Helena gentlemen. The admirers included the Vigilante chiefs James Williams and Nathan Langford, the hotel owner, G. Julius Germain, the saloon keeper, Sam Greer, and the bookkeeper who talked French, James Hogle.

It is not known how well Hogle spoke French. He spoke at least well enough to lend convincing evidence as to the origins of the man everyone knew as Guiraud. It also would have obscured the slight brogue James Gilmore had brought with him from his native Ireland. There is even some evidence hinting that Hogle affected a French accent for a time.

Further notice of James Hogle's activities was published in the *Montana Post* on December 1, 1866, and once again the paper took pains to reveal the subject's "true" identity:

> His Honor, Judge McCarty, has been engaged for two days, Tuesday and Wednesday, in hearing the testimony of a large number of witnesses in the case wherein James Hogle, alias "Gero," is the plaintiff and Trinidad Orlin, alias "Sailor Jack" is the defendant. To give the whole of the evidence is impossible, owing to its length, but we extract the following:
>
> James Gero had a watch taken from him at dusk on Tuesday night by two "Nymphs du Pave" while walking on Bridge Street, which timepiece has ever since been "Non est" both ladies denying knowledge of the whereabouts of the same. The County building on Bridge Street, too small to hold the large crowd of spectators, was abandoned and the District Court Room was taken for the place of preliminary examination.
>
> No Criminal Event in the annals of our local Police Court was characterized by so large an interest manifested by a majority of the outsiders than this. And we are at a loss to say for what reason. Unless it was the extraordinary beauty of the defendant, which seemed to elicit the sympathy of outsiders.
>
> All that law or lawyers could do was done for her, but his Honor, McCarty, untouched by those seductive charms, bound

her over to appear at the next session of the District Court, in the sum of $1,000.00 to answer to the charge of larceny. The bail was forthcoming and we shall hear no more of it until the District Court meets. Meanwhile Jimmy Gero is out a gold watch, for the recovery of which he offers $250.00.

During their stay in Helena, the Hogle brothers were resident boarders of G. Julius Germain at the International Hotel, a three-story wood structure at the corner of Main and Bridge streets. The International was Helena's premier hotel and a favorite haunt of successful miners and merchants. Other residents and guests whose names appear in the register include X Beidler, Nathan Thompson, Luke Voorhees, Col. Wilber Fisk Sanders, Enos A. Wall, and Alexander Toponce. Another guest was a man whose influence on the Hogle family would be more profound and lasting than that of any of the gamblers, vigilantes, or desperadoes the brothers encountered there. His name was Daniel S. Tuttle.

Bishop Tuttle's Helena, 1867–1869

Episcopal Bishop Daniel S. Tuttle was something of a circuit preacher. He spent his time traveling and ministering to seven mining camps in Montana and three in Idaho. As an epistlist and diarist he kept accurate notes and descriptions of his impressions which he later published as *Reminiscences*. The volume contains some of the best descriptions of Montana and its early mining camps. Particularly interesting were his first impressions of Helena.

[From Virginia City] I went by stage to Helena making the distance of 125 miles in twenty hours. . . . Helena is a town of about four thousand inhabitants pitched, as you might expect, in the bottom of a dirty mining gulch. There are fewer log cabins and more frame houses here than at Virginia City; and this Hotel, the International, is really quite comfortable and even genteel in its appointments. . . . We have a room with a double bed just off the parlor, with a door window opening out upon a pleasant balcony. As I sit here writing there comes a confused din of auctioneers and teamsters shouting from the street below. Helena August 6, 7 1867.

Anything but Sunday seems this to me as I sit down and hear feet moving, chains clanking, and teamsters shouting more noisily than on other days because the miners from the gulches come in today. A stalwart negro, ringing a large hand bell, is shouting in front of this Hotel: "Now, gentlemen, now's your chance there's a large stock of goods to be sold just below in Bridge Street: picks, shovels, dry goods, mountain trout, salmon, Now's your chance!" A half dozen teamsters are yelling together, like demons, at their oxen. Anything but a calm, quiet Sunday is this!

Before breakfast I went up to the post office and out of the two hundred stores and businesses along the streets only one was closed. That was the First National Bank!

Bridge Street in Helena, Montana, near the spot where "Mr. Geero" lost his watch. The trial of the beauteous Trinidad Orlin, which followed, created a local sensation. Courtesy Montana Historical Society.

Another Sunday entry from Bishop Tuttle's diary a year later shows that conditions in Helena had changed little in the intervening months:

> The First National Bank is closed today but nine out of ten stores are open. While I write, the shouts of five or six auctioneers are dinning in my ears. They are selling goods and the Streets are filled with hundreds, even thousands of men. There are scores of wagons and hundreds of ox teams. It is a perfect Babel here, and no Sunday at all. The town has greatly grown since I was here last. I think it must have in it five or six thousand inhabitants.

During the late 1860's, Helena was the quintessential mining camp, a wide-open and sometimes violent frontier town whose principal attraction and most common amusement was vice. It was an unlikely location to find an Episcopal Bishop. But Daniel S. Tuttle was an unusual minister, and Helena soon became his headquarters. The good Bishop had an enormous capacity for tolerance, and while he did not sanction or condone the activities of his parishioners, neither did he judge them too severely. He came to recognize that life in the western mining camps was hard and that a softer touch was needed. Tuttle's approach to his ministry was based on the Christian tenets of forgiveness and charity. He did not chastise his wayward flock for their sins as much as he praised and encouraged them for their generosity. Selections from Bishop Tuttle's diary give a clear description of his congregation in Helena and his attitude toward them.

> Here public opinion is universally in favor of the innocence, harmlessness and morality of such amusements as dancing and card playing. . . . Were you to venture to suggest here, or anywhere in the west, it seems to me, that it is wrong to dance, people look at you with mingled feelings of amusement and pity.
>
> It astounds me to think of and realize the breadth and depth of wickedness and vice in which this whole community is steeped. . . . I hear of one Vestryman as having been in a gambling den all day long yesterday and another who is drinking desperately. . . .
>
> Nothing but God's almighty power . . . restrains me from giving up in despair and fleeing Eastward across the mountains,

scarcely daring to look behind me, any more than Lot upon the cities of the plain.

In spite of the wickedness of the people, their personal kindnesses to me were unceasing and overwhelming. . . . Two men, hard drinkers both, one day came to my cabin and brought me $106.00 for charity. When I saw my way to build a church, the people gathered to my help with abounding generosity.

From what we know of Jimmy Guiraud, we would not be shocked to learn that he had spent a day in a gambling hall. But anyone who knew him only through the pages of the *Montana Post* might be surprised to learn that he, as James Hogle, was one of Bishop Tuttle's Montana parishioners.

FIRE AND ICE

On April 28, 1869, yet another of those most common calamities to visit the mining camps of the west occurred in Helena. Like the fire that had wiped out the central business district of Denver six years earlier, the Great Helena Fire took place on a cold April night. Like the Denver fire, the alarm was sounded between the hours of midnight and one o'clock. Like the Denver fire, the blaze was nearly unstoppable. Many of the fire's victims were even the same— William Kiskadden's store, Pfouts and Russell's, Walker Brothers', Sam Greer's saloon, Crocker's billiard hall — all were facing the same hellish test again. Since Owen Hogle was now a Helena resident, the two brothers would have some tales to swap on the relative intensity of the two great fires. Bishop Tuttle recalled the fire in his diary.

The alarm was given soon after midnight and I dressed hastily and ran to the scene to offer any service possible. There was no engine, no fire department, no organization, so the fire had every advantage. The buildings were erected of pine and fir lumber, pitchy at that and exceedingly inflammable. The utmost that could be done was to tear down buildings in the track of the fire. Haul off all the debris and, if possible, stop the progress of the flames. But the fire spread too rapidly for us, the wind speeding it. A little before daylight, the flames caught the International Hotel, a three story wooden structure, and were consuming it with frightful rapidity.

The fire was finally checked by coming against two good buildings of brick. When I went home at eight or nine in the morning, Mrs. Tuttle made gallons of coffee to distribute to the men who had been fighting the Conflagration. By noon she and I went down the street where we took note of the wonderful pluck and grit and force of the mountain people. Everywhere were smoking ruins; and yet draymen were hauling lumber and mechanics were clearing away debris and laying beams for the foundations of new buildings. In less than a week not a few buildings were up all along the street and active business was going on inside them.

Years later an account of the Helena fire was published in the *St. Louis Globe Democrat* which gave special praise to the heroes of the disaster.

When it had been realized that to save much of the town was going to be impossible, every energy was bent to saving the magazine of provisions and a few brave spirits had organized a defense and gathered the populace for the last struggle. A few daring men maintained themselves on the rooftops while others passed up unceasingly, buckets of water and masses of ice cut from the streams and huge balls of snow. The men on the roofs braved fire, smoke and freezing wind. . . . There was no faltering in the desperate struggle and finally the battle was won.

Morning had come, and with it the sun, which as it rose over a shoulder of the mountain, gilded the forms of three men who stood high on the parapet of the building where the fire had been stopped.

These three, with their visages begrimed and black with smoke, their hair and beards singed, their hands torn and bloody . . . looked at the smoking ruins and then at the people below. It was at this moment that the multitude below gave a great shout, recognizing as it were, their deliverers.

Who were these men? They were well known in the mountains if not immediately recognized in the disfigurement of battle. One was Bitter Root Bill, a noted desperado. The second was Joseph Floweree a leading gambler . . . and the third was no less than Dan Tuttle, Bishop of Montana and the Northwest. In the desperate turmoil these three men had gravitated to each other and had risen to leadership.

Bishop Tuttle had won the respect if not necessarily the hearts and souls of the people of Helena. As Bitter Root Bill was said to have commented: "He's the biggest and best bishop to ever wear a black gown."

For all the progress Bishop Tuttle may have made toward converting the heathen of Helena, in the summer of 1869 he decided to move his diocesan headquarters to Salt Lake City. By that time Helena had been rebuilt. Owen was once again a resident of the International Hotel — a new one, this time constructed of fireproof brick — and his brother was prospecting for gold in a place called Loon Creek, Idaho.

CHAPTER FIVE

Prospecting in Idaho, 1866–1870

IN THE SPRING OF 1866 five men formed a partnership to explore the Indian-occupied lands lying between Bannock, Florence, Warren, and Ely City in the Idaho Territory. This was a vast unexplored primitive area, a true wilderness of deep pine forests, impassable ravines, and towering mountains. Hundreds of unnamed streams wound their way through the tangle of basins and valleys; eventually they all poured into the fabled "River of No Return," the Salmon, which circled the entire drainage like a sickle. The Indians in the area were known to be hostile to any intrusion on their traditional salmon-fishing grounds. It was not a journey for the faint of heart.

The men — Barney Sharkey, Bill Smith, Lige Mulkey, Joe Rabb, and Ward Gurdon — purchased their supplies at a trading post called Cottonwood, near Deer Lodge, Montana, and set off for Idaho in early June. Their destination was the Lemhi River, a tributary of the Salmon in the rugged mountains of east central Idaho.

At Elk Creek, Montana, the expedition turned southwest through Big Hole, crossing the Continental Divide into Idaho at Lost Trail Pass on the north fork of the Salmon River. The party followed the north fork to the Salmon and then proceeded upstream, arriving at the present site of Salmon City on July 1, 1866. Here they camped for four days while they constructed a boat for crossing the torrent.

After a successful crossing, the party hid the boat and proceeded up the west bank of the river to William's Creek. They followed this stream past William's Lake and then pushed over the top of the

[56]

jagged Salmon River Mountains and into the next drainage. It was here that they began prospecting in earnest, first on Phelan Creek and then on a small river which was called by the local Indians Napias Creek. Barney Sharkey and Bill Smith sank the first prospect hole at the mouth of Ward's Gulch on July 9, 1866. What they found was beyond their wildest expectations, gold worth $1.20 per pan of dirt!

During the next month the party located ten claims (two each under the law then in force), five by right of discovery and five by right of location. After locating and securing the vital water requirements, the men decided to return to Montana for supplies. Soon after they started, Lige Mulkey became gravely ill. Barney Sharkey decided to stay behind and care for him; the others would make the supply run back to Montana and promised to return within the month.

The following day a war party of thirty-eight Indians arrived at the camp. They had been following the prospectors' trail for several days. The leader demanded to know if they had found "Napias." Not knowing the Indian word, Sharkey replied "No." The leader became furious and called him a liar. He told Sharkey how they had taken dirt from their prospect holes, washed the dirt, and found "Napias." The Indians were not interested in the gold, but they knew that knowledge of its presence would bring hordes of white men to the Salmon River and their traditional fishing grounds would be lost. In spite of this, no violence came to Sharkey and his sick partner. The Indians rode off. Perhaps they knew that the secret of Napias Creek had already slipped out of the mountains.

Rumors of Gold

If the men who made the initial discovery on Napias Creek were to make it through the coming winter, they would have to get their food, clothing, and equipment packed in before the first snow. The problem was that these supplies had to be purchased with the very commodity they were trying to keep secret, gold dust. Store keepers were uniquely situated to learn first-hand of any discovery.

A clever merchant not only knew when a strike had been made; he was often able to judge the quality and size of the claim as well.

The purity and gauge of the gold were a tip-off, but there were other more subtle tricks of the trade. How much a lowly prospector was willing to invest in his claim was one. The sheer volume of supplies purchased was another, for it told the merchant how long the miner thought he would be working the discovery. Most importantly, the types of purchases made were a sure indication when something substantial had been found. The equipment needed to develop a placer claim was different from the equipment needed to locate it. A prospector does not haul into the hills heavy pumps, hoses, or dredging equipment without a good reason.

From the prospectors' standpoint, there were two schools of thought on how to keep the secret secret. Neither of them worked. The first was to purchase all your supplies from one merchant and swear him to secrecy. But this ordinarily necessitated making the man a partner, and there was no guarantee that he wouldn't spill the beans anyway. Merchants were known to spread word of discoveries to promote their own sales, and as Pikes Peak had demonstrated, a rush was a rush whether the gold had been discovered yet or not. The second stratagem was to make several smaller, more discreet purchases from different merchants in the hope that the nature of the discovery would be minimized. It was this technique that Bill Smith, Joe Rabb, and Ward Gurdon used when they returned to Montana for supplies in August of 1866.

How the news got out is uncertain. It is known that each of the men informed "Just a relative or a friend or two," and that was probably enough. The "friends," though sworn to secrecy, swore their friends to secrecy and they in turn swore others. By the end of August the "faithful" numbered in the hundreds.

The rumor mill was working overtime, and the hush hush nature of the rumors did nothing but draw more attention to the strike. Unlike Pikes Peak, there was something else to fuel the imagination: the merchants in Deer Lodge had evidence, $18.00-grade gold dust and coarse gold assaying out from $5.00 to $50.00 a nugget. The shopkeepers, their suppliers, and the freighters knew that a major strike had been made. Though Smith, Rabb, and Gurdon may have been discreet, their friends were not.

The Secret Keepers and their faithful followers began arriving on the banks of the Salmon River by September of 1866. The exact number that came in the first month is unknown, but the little boat the prospectors had fashioned to cross the river was quickly turned into a commercial ferry. Barney Sharkey charged $2.50 a head to take new arrivals to the western bank of the river. "They kept coming thick and fast for about two weeks," he wrote. In that short time Sharkey realized a profit of $585.00.

Lige Mulkey had recovered by this time, and the two men were anxious to join their partners at the diggings. Sharkey sold his boat to a man named Vandruff, then he and Mulkey hit the trail for Napias Creek. When they came over the top of "Phelan Mountain" they were met with a sight which neither could believe.

Six weeks earlier there hadn't been a single cabin in the entire basin. Now there was a sprawling city with a population of well over a thousand people. There were saloons, stores, livery stables, blacksmith shops, restaurants, and a French bakery. The place even had a name: "Leesburg."

Some of the early arrivals were Confederate veterans, refugees from General Price's "left wing" and the "Confederate Army of Western Texas." They named the town in honor of Robert E. Lee. Union veterans were there too, and a distinct suburb called "Grantsville" had been constructed.

In the fall and winter of 1866 James and Owen Hogle were still living in Helena. Owen was tending bar for Dan Furry and Nathan Thompson at the Exchange Saloon, and James was holding forth two blocks away at the International Hotel.

When James learned of the Napias Creek strike is unknown. Word had certainly reached Helena by September, and some of his acquaintances, including Fred Phillips, were already at the scene of the discovery. Phillips had opened Leesburg's first general store in August and had hired as clerk a man named James Glendenning.

In Helena, everyone knew that something was happening somewhere. At first it was just a few faces that disappeared, then small circles of friends, then, suddenly, certain whole saloons and billiard halls began emptying. What started as a trickle was soon a flood. One man was said to have remarked as he galloped out of Helena, "It's south'a here a ways."

James Hogle knew exactly what he wanted to do. The trouble was that his plan required a certain amount of financial backing, so he spent the winter raising the necessary capital for his venture. Some of the money he may have won "fingering the pasteboards." Some probably came from Owen. But other investors were also intrigued by the proposition, including his former employer Nathan Thompson and Julius Germain and Luke Voorhees.

Eventually the precious supplies he needed for the enterprise were acquired and safely packed away in an ox-drawn freight wagon. Hogle and his team then joined a wagon train bound for Napias Creek. The 200-mile trek was slow and tedious, the cargo he carried fragile. James Hogle was opening his own saloon.

George Shoup was also on the trail that fall, his wagons filled with merchandise from his general store in Virginia City. Edgar Edwards, A. A. Mayfield, and Alva P. Challis were headed for Leesburg, as was William Hart Richardson, the operator of the hardware store in Deer Lodge where the discovery party had purchased their supplies. His wagon was filled with hydraulic pipe and equipment for repairing placer machinery. He too had a fair notion of how to get rich in a gold rush.

The Leesburg Stampede

The California Gold Rush of 1849 produced more gold. The Pikes Peak Rush of 1859 produced less gold but was more famous. The Comstock Lode and the Cripple Creek Strike contributed more western lore. The rich strikes at Alder Gulch and Last Chance Gulch, and at Bingham and Park City, Utah, had more lasting economic impact, and the uranium boom of the 1950's more lunatic frenzy. But even so, in the history of the intermountain west there is nothing that quite compares with what has come to be known as "The Leesburg Stampede."

Leesburg will be remembered for the physical hardships endured by those who went there, the fabulous riches that the camp produced, and the brevity of its glory. Like the later Dawson City Stampede in the Yukon Territory of 1896 to 1902, the event known as the Leesburg Stampede was something more than a gold rush.

Just getting there was a memorable adventure. By October of 1866 early snows had already blocked the mountain passes. Many of the prospectors who set off for the new strike were ill-equipped for a winter expedition and were forced to turn back. One man, Eli Minert, got as close as what is now Salmon, Idaho, on October 30. He found there a lone cabin and mountain passes blocked by ten-foot snowdrifts. Minert was forced to return to Montana. The decision to turn back must have been painful as he had traveled over 200 miles, the last fifty in a snowstorm. He had come to within twenty miles of his goal but had started his journey too late. Minert would have to return when the passes were clear in the spring.

A man named John David Wood was in Deer Lodge when the discovery party departed from there for the Lemhi River in the spring of 1866, and by coincidence he was in Elk Creek, Montana, in August when the prospectors passed through on their return to Montana for supplies. But he didn't hear about the stampede until October and didn't manage to join it until December.

Wood and his partner Chester Davis started out on a winter expedition, and for this reason they were better equipped for the weather than the men who had set off in late September. They arrived in Leesburg the first week of January 1867. While most of the men in Leesburg huddled about their fires waiting for the spring thaw, Wood and Davis managed to stake out a dozen claims as they traversed the Leesburg Basin several times.

They accomplished all this with the help of "Norwegian snow shoes, toboggans, blankets, tents and plenty of grub." Even so, the two men barely escaped with their lives when they exhausted their food supply and got caught in the open during a blinding April blizzard that lasted five days. They arrived, more or less by accident, at the infant town of Salmon City on April 15.

We know that James Hogle was still in Helena in December of '66 when "Sailor Jack" lifted his gold watch, so it is not likely that he could have arrived in Leesburg before April of 1867. That month Lorenzo Falls arrived at Salmon City from Helena and found there "A large number of snow bound gold seekers headed for Leesburg." It seems likely that James Hogle was in this group.

The same snows which had stopped Eli Minert in October had

stopped these men as well, but instead of turning back they had decided to stick it out. At the first break in the weather they would chance an assault on the snow-covered peaks which rose over a thousand feet above the Salmon River canyon. But the hoped-for thaw was long in coming. January, February, and March of 1867 produced nothing but more snow. As the "Stampeders" continued to pour in, the temporary layover quickly grew into the most permanent community of the region, and Salmon City was born.

The new town was one of the oddest communities ever to grace the mountain west. That first winter, the east bank of the Salmon River was crowded with a strange collection of log cabins, tent buildings, lean-to's, mud adobes, and Indian tipis. These structures housed restaurants, butcher shops, stores, and saloons. It is probable that James Hogle's first saloon was opened in Salmon during the winter layover.

Col. George Shoup saw that the location of the community was well suited as a supply depot for the surrounding area. He therefore decided to make the town his base of operations and spent the winter cutting and framing timber for the construction of his store. Others engaged in the lumber business, getting as much as twenty cents a board foot. The general shortage of lumber that winter was the reason for Salmon City's peculiar architecture. Lumber was too precious to use for roofing or floors, so the Salmon City buildings of 1866–67 had earthen floors covered in animal hides and roofs of sod, thatch, and branches.

As the long winter dragged on, the population of Salmon City continued to grow. By April the men were low on supplies and growing impatient. And so with "Nothing much more than their hands," a hundred men clawed and shoveled a trail over the Salmon River Mountains. They then formed a human chain to pass supplies over the top. This was the "Leesburg Toll Road" and like "Sharkey's Ferry" before it, the builders charged dearly for its use. Lorenzo Falls and hundreds of others paid their fees to enter the promised land of Napias. Leesburg now had a population of 2,500.

In addition to Hogle and Falls, newcomers that spring included Alva Challis, John Noble, Michael Boyle, Bat Doodey, A. A. Mayfield, Lorton Prince, and the Frank Hagenbarth family.

The placer claims in the immediate vicinity of Leesburg on Napias and Panther creeks had all been taken. So like the late arrivals at Gregory's Gulch and Alder Gulch, many went to work for their predecessors. The pay averaged seven dollars a day, an extravagant wage by mining standards of the nineteenth century. Others prospected the dozens of small tributary streams in the Leesburg Basin, many of which had placer gold deposits, though none as rich as the initial discoveries.

By June a number of freighters were serving Leesburg and they brought in anything they thought might sell. Those engaging in this profitable enterprise in addition to Col. Shoup included John David Wood, Eli Minert, and James Hayden. These men took considerable risk and faced no little danger in hauling in the precious supplies. It was 415 miles to Salt Lake City, 400 miles to Ft. Benton, Montana, 350 miles to Boise City, and more than 700 miles to Walla Walla — the principal supply points for the Leesburg Stampede.

With the enormous distances involved, it might be assumed that the men who brought cargo to Leesburg would concentrate on the

Leesburg, Idaho, in 1870, where James Hogle operated a "Guiraud" saloon. Courtesy Idaho State Historical Society.

vital necessities, but nothing could be further from the truth. Some of the claims on Napias Creek were producing many thousands of dollars in gold. These men were not about to waste that good money on salt pork, hard tack, and beans, though even these items were selling for exorbitant sums.

One freighter, Thomas Pope, charged the following prices for items he brought into Leesburg in 1867: butter $1.25 per pound, tea $3.50 per pound, syrup $6.00 per gallon, cans of tomatoes or corn $1.50 each, soap $.75 a bar.

Excavations of mining camps of this period indicate that although life in the boom towns was often hard, the men endured their hardships in style. The Leesburg placer miner had a remarkable penchant for luxury. Foodstuffs packed into Leesburg included tins of imported sausages, specialty meats, pickles, confections and imported cheeses, sardines, candy of all kinds, fruit preserves, and caviar.

An unusual Christmas tradition in the intermountain mining camps was the importation of oysters on ice for "Christmas Eve Oyster Stew." The arrival of the Christmas Oyster Wagon was a much-anticipated event frequently reported in the camp newspapers in December.

If the miner's taste in cuisine tended toward the epicurean, his taste in spirits was that of the true connoisseur. Bottle collectors have found that at least one Leesburg saloon had a stock which would have rivaled many a Parisian cellar. Included in its bottle inventory were an assortment of French wines, brandies, and fine Champagnes. We do not know much about James Hogle's saloon in Leesburg; however, it is safe to assume that it wasn't just another beer hall. Records of James's later establishments show that he specialized in "Fine Imported Wines and Brandies." Nor do we know the specifics of his arrangement with his silent partners and investors back in Helena. As with the saloons he would later open in Salmon and Oro Grande, Idaho, the establishment was called "Guiraud's." But by this time we know that he was personally going under the name of Hogle. The use of the name Guiraud was probably an attempt to capitalize on the reputation of Denver's Guiraud's, as there were many former Pikes Peakers in the mining camp.

The Leesburg Stampede would peak in 1871. When the census was taken in 1870 there were more than 3,000 people living in Leesburg proper and more than 7,000 in the surrounding basin. There was never before, nor has there been since, a city of that size in Lemhi County. Leesburg reached its zenith before the arrival of the railroad, before the existence of graded roads, even before that part of the country was accurately mapped. As long as the gold held out the place not only boomed, it roared. When the placer deposits were exhausted, the people left. It was all very brief and glorious.

THE SALOON ON GUIRAUD'S CORNER

James Hogle conducted his saloon business in Leesburg through the summer and fall of 1867. The miners were hard-drinking men, and frequent supply runs had to be made to Helena to keep them happy. The riches that had eluded him at Pikes Peak and Alder Gulch were now within his grasp. That first summer he realized a substantial profit, for in the winter of 1868 he purchased, from a man named Heap, a large saloon and gambling house in Salmon City.

This second Guiraud's was at the corner of Terrace Street and North Main. We do know something about this establishment and the buildings that directly adjoined it. The original structure, built by a man named Hughey, was adobe, but Mr. Heap had adorned it with a lumber façade and an elaborate wooden balustrade. A large wooden porch ran the entire length of the structure along the Main Street frontage. The "Heap Building" was something of a Salmon City landmark and was large enough to house the saloon, a restaurant — also operated by Hogle — and several offices.

Across the street from the saloon, on the west corner of Main and Terrace streets was Wilson Ellis's butcher shop, and on the south corner Michael Spahn's brewery and saloon. Directly east was the Haines Andrews Hotel, which would be purchased in turn by Leesburg pioneer Eli Mulkey and later E. S. Edwards. Next to this was the William Orcot Saloon and then Col. Shoup's store. This was the central business district of Salmon, Idaho, in 1868, and Guiraud's Saloon commanded the intersection of Salmon City's principal streets.

A Touch of Gold Fever

James Hogle operated his Leesburg and Salmon City saloons through the winter of 1868–69. But in the spring he resolved to do some prospecting of his own. Whether it was the constant stream of successful placer miners that had infected him or just cabin fever from the long harsh winter, the saloon keeper was hanging up his apron and heading for the hills.

The Leesburg Basin had been thoroughly located during the previous two years of the Stampede. If there were any new claims to be discovered they had to be someplace else. Hogle headed southwest farther into the primitive wilderness of Idaho's Salmon River Mountains. He would eventually push more than fifty miles into the rugged back country.

This expedition was both hard and dangerous. Dangerous because any incursion on Indian-occupied lands was dangerous, and hard because of the terrain. There was, as yet, no established path through this country, and he had to scout and feel his way through the unexplored mountain passes which entailed many false starts and much back-tracking. The meandering trail which now leads into this section of the Salmon River Mountains was established by the wanderings of prospectors like Hogle. The original name given the route, "the Old William's Lake, Iron Creek and Prairie Basin Trail," reflects the tortuous nature of its origin. Eventually it became known as The Loon Creek Trail.

Hogle arrived on the banks of Loon Creek in June of 1869. Earlier that spring a prospector named Nate Smith had located rich placer deposits on the wild little river. Smith had been grubstaked by several Leesburg residents, and since Hogle arrived soon after the discovery, it is possible that he was one of Smith's backers. Whether he was or not, it is known that James was one of the first men at the Loon Creek Diggings. He located two claims that June and worked them through the summer. Others who found their way to Loon Creek that first season were Fred Phillips, A. A. Mayfield, Murdoch McPherson, Lawrence Phelan, and Frank Hagenbarth.

Placer mining, whether at Alder Gulch, Leesburg, or Loon Creek, was much the same. Water was used to wash the loose earth from the ore-bearing gravels shoveled from sand bars or dug from the ground near the streambeds. At first individual miners worked their claims by carefully washing the sands in oversized pie tins. The technique was not easy to master. A circular motion of the pan was maintained to wash the lighter material over the lip while the heavier precious metal stayed on the bottom and sides. It took coordination and a delicate touch to pan without losing significant quantities of dust.

The second step in the development of a placer deposit was the construction of wooden flumes and sluices into which small teams of men would shovel ore-bearing earth. Again the lighter material was washed off, leaving the gold behind. The third step was the wholesale washing away of ore-bearing banks and sand bars with high-pressure hydraulic hoses. In the early days these were gravity-fed from small reservoirs, while later stream-driven pumps were introduced.

The final step in the development of many western placer areas was the use of stream-driven dredges to tear the very bottoms out of the rivers. This accelerated "erosion" process left the landscape permanently rutted and denuded of foliage. From an ecological standpoint, placer mining was a disaster, and the men who mined in the Salmon River Mountains in the nineteenth century were not insensitive to its effect on the landscape. In a poem entitled "The Grave of Lizzie King," Idaho placer miner Clarence E. Eddie wrote:

> Through the Lovely, Lonely Valley far below her grave,
> Winds a river once like crystal, pure and clear,
> But relentless man has marred it, and polluted its fair wave
> Seeking gold beside its waters many a year.
>
> Like the life of her now lying in the grave upon the hill,
> The stream might still be sparkling pure and fair,
> But the wiles of men have marred it, marred the
>   pure sweet mountain rill,
> And marred the life of her that slumbers there.

"Big Gold"

Word of the new strike at Loon Creek spread quickly. By the fall of 1869, the placer deposits along the stream had all been claimed. Other prospectors were seeking quartz deposits in the nearby mountains. Another new town, spread out all along the floor of the Loon Creek drainage near the small tributary stream of Grouse Creek, sprang up almost overnight to supply the miners.

By October the camp had a hotel, a general store, a freight office, a blacksmith shop, a Chinese laundry, two restaurants, and a saloon named Guiraud's. James Hogle had put down his shovel and was once again in the liquor business.

The gold nuggets found at Loon Creek were unusual. Unlike the irregular nuggets of Napias Creek, many of these seemed to come in a standard size and shape. They were oval and slightly flattened and were known as "pumpkin seed gold." These unusual nuggets helped give the new town a name, Oro Grande from the Spanish, meaning "big gold."

Oro Grande was a far cry from the cosmopolitan metropolis of Leesburg. In 1869–70 it was a camp in every sense of the word. While Leesburg gave every indication of being a permanent community, the little settlement on Loon Creek had all the markings of the temporary. Most of the miners were living in tents, and few bothered to build the sturdy log cabins that were the hallmark of the Napias Creek settlement. Oro Grande was a fair-weather town, and when the winter snows threatened, the miners retreated to Leesburg or Salmon City. During the winter the isolated little camp they left behind disappeared beneath the snows.

James Hogle returned to Leesburg during the winter of 1869–70. But with the spring thaw and the return of the miners, Guiraud's Saloon in Oro Grande was once again open for business. There was a new stampede in progress and Loon Creek was the new destination.

1870 was the year of the census, and on August 19 in Oro Grande, in the mining district of Loon Creek, the census takers found James Hogle. The listing, which was on page 24 of the Lemhi County Census Record, is as follows: "James Hogle: 27, Saloon Keeper, born in Ireland parents Irish/$5000.00 real estate/ $5,000.00 personal property."

But James Gilmore was born in 1838. A true accounting of his age would have made him thirty-one years old on the day of the census taker's visit. The census also showed that he had done very well for himself. In the entire Loon Creek district there were only four merchants who could boast greater assets.

The census of Loon Creek provides us with an interesting glimpse of the makeup of the community. The tables list more than 300 placer miners, 9 saloon keepers, 8 mule packers, 6 merchants, 5 hotel keepers, 5 disreputable ladies, 4 dance hall girls, or "Hurdy Gurdys" as they were known to the census taker, 4 blacksmiths, 2 brewers, 2 butchers, 2 sawmill operators, 2 lawyers, 2 livery men, 1 doctor, 4 musicians, and 6 actors.

The musicians and actors were members of C. B. Plummer's Theatrical Troupe out of Vancouver, B.C. They had been touring "The Gold Circuit" since the summer of 1867 and had made a small fortune bringing Shakespeare to the hinterlands.

Virtually absent from the census were women and children. Only five families were listed as residents of the camp. Frank Hagenbarth's was one of these. Hagenbarth, who at this time anglicized his name to Hagert, his wife Catherine, and their two children, Frank Jr., and an infant daughter, had moved to the new diggings after selling their Leesburg hotel. The census listed Frank's occupation as "brewer," but they were opening a new hotel in Oro Grande at a location later called Casto. Catherine Hagenbarth would play a crucial role in an incident which would change James Hogle's life. James Horton, one of the livery stable operators, would eventually bring the incident to light. More prominent in the casual tragedy were two other Loon Creek residents listed in the same census: John Painter, a blacksmith, and a placer miner named George Moyer.

The Blacksmith and the Placer Miner

The blacksmith was an indispensable tradesman in the western mining camps. He not only fashioned and fitted the shoes of the camp's horses, but fixed the harnesses, bridles, wagon wheels, and axles of the freight and mine wagons as well. When mine machinery broke down, it was often the blacksmith who was called upon to fix it. In the placer camps he had to have the additional skills of a tinsmith, for nineteenth-century hose clamps and nozzle fittings were made of tinplate. The blacksmith's special skills put him a cut above the ordinary miner, and he enjoyed a close and profitable relationship with the mine owners who were dependent upon him. A good blacksmith sometimes became a mining engineer, and some made enough to buy the very mines they worked for.

John Painter, known as Jake, had learned his trade from his father, who had operated a blacksmith shop and mill in New York state. At the age of twenty-two he set off to make his fortune, arriving in Virginia City in 1866. In 1869 he moved to Helena, and in the spring of 1870 he was residing at the recently rebuilt International Hotel. But in the summer the thirty-year-old Painter made his way to the camp of Oro Grande on Loon Creek.

George Moyer, the placer miner in question, is something of an enigma. We know that he was born to German immigrant parents in Pennsylvania in 1825, and that although he was a natural-born American citizen, he spoke with a German accent and was generally assumed to be a German. The census fails to record either personal or real property, and it can safely be assumed that he had none. We do not know much more, but being treated as an alien in his native country must have made Moyer bitter. It is certain that he had a short temper, but whatever his faults, the time would come when this unlikely man would have a river, a valley, and a high peak in the Salmon River Mountains named for him.

The Loon Creek Incident

In October of 1870 the first snows had already dusted the highest peaks overlooking the Loon Creek Mining District. A. F. Thrasher, a reporter from a Deer Lodge newspaper, *The New Northwest*, reported from Loon Creek that most of the mining had stopped in the camp and the men were packing it up for the winter. He went on to say that, "Some ten claims have paid well this summer, the others poorly. James Guiraud, James Hayden and Mr. Clitus Barbour, well known Montanians, will be over in the next two or three weeks."

The saloons in Oro Grande that October were filled with men intent on having one final fling together before the cold blasts of winter scattered them to warmer locations. Gambling was particularly heavy, and the autumn "clean up" had filled the pockets of miners and merchants alike with pumpkin seed gold and bags of high-grade dust.

Miners who had hoarded their poke though the summer were throwing much of it away on "inside straights" and "kickers." Gamblers who had lost money during the summer were anxious to recoup their losses. Miners who had not done well were interested in a fair share of the profits. The table stakes were high and the betting wild, and the pots that fall were the biggest Oro Grande would ever see.

At a table in Guiraud's Saloon, James Hogle, Jake Painter, George Moyer, James Hayden, and James Horton, the livery stable owner, were playing cards with several other men. The cards weren't falling right for George Moyer that evening. In the early going Moyer was forced to draw light on several hands, and he quickly became heavily indebted to Hogle, Hayden, and Painter. But during the course of the long evening, Moyer's luck appeared to change. Perhaps it was just bluster or bluff, but the men at the table supposed that Moyer was winning. Somehow or other Moyer managed to leave the game without ever settling up with Hogle or Painter. The men at the table believed that Moyer's departure was temporary. It was not. When the creditors sought him the following morning, "The German came up missing."

In the western mining camps "chiseling" was a serious offense, and the chances of getting away with the crime were almost nil. As we have seen, the mining population was fluid, and a man's reputation followed him from camp to camp. Chiselers were marked for life and eventually were caught up with.

Hogle and Painter didn't believe at first that Moyer had really run off; they thought he had just gone to his cabin, some distance up Grouse Creek. But when they learned that he had taken the Old William's Lake Trail, which led in the opposite direction, they realized that the "German" was skipping the country.

The trail out of Loon Creek wound up the rocky stream bed of

Cabin Creek and over the top of Sleeping Deer Mountain, a distance of some seven miles. From here the Loon Creek Trail descended into the Silver Creek drainage and followed that stream another twenty-two miles until it joined with Panther Creek, a major tributary of the Salmon River. Seven miles downstream from this point, the trail split, one fork following Panther Creek to Leesburg and the other following a small stream up to its origin near the saddle which separates the Panther Creek and Iron Creek drainages. This latter fork, the original William's Lake Trail, eventually wound its way to Salmon City and was George Moyer's route in his flight from Loon Creek.

Moyer had twelve hours' head start. He was traveling light and fast, but he was on foot. Hogle and Painter got horses from Horton's livery stable and set off in pursuit. That evening a light snow fell, and the following morning the trackers picked up Moyer's trail. In the afternoon they caught up with him four miles short of the top of the Salmon River Range.

Moyer knew why he was being followed and resolved to settle the matter then and there. As Hogle and Painter rode up, Moyer stood waiting for them at the side of the path. Hogle dismounted and approached the glowering man, but before any words were exchanged, Moyer threw a handful of money in Hogle's face, at the same time pulling a short dagger, or dirk, from under his coat. Moyer then lunged at Hogle, plunging the dagger into his throat, and bore him to the ground. As the two men struggled, Painter dismounted. The badly wounded Hogle was unable to fend off his attacker, and as Moyer raised the knife to stab him again, Hogle shouted frantically, "For God's sake shoot him!" Painter quickly drew his revolver from its holster and put the barrel to Moyer's head as he squeezed the trigger. The gun discharged as Moyer's knife was driving toward Hogle's chest, and Moyer pitched forward over his intended victim.

Painter pulled the motionless Moyer off Hogle. The puncture wound near the trachea was ragged and bleeding profusely, but Painter succeeded in stopping the bleeding. After Hogle was bandaged, Painter searched Moyer and found no money on him. He collected the money that Moyer had thrown at Hogle, which came to less than twenty-five dollars. George Moyer had not been a winner after all.

Painter and Hogle made their way back to Loon Creek. Hogle was left in the care of Catherine Hagenbarth at the hotel, and Painter went to report the killing to John Reyney, the county sheriff. Reyney and his deputy John Snook returned with Painter to the scene of the shooting to retrieve Moyer's body. There was no question that they had come to the right place; the area was covered with blood. But to Painter's astonishment, Moyer was nowhere to be found. They searched the area for a time and then returned to Oro Grande. Their conclusion was that "Moyer had played possum."

George Moyer, though badly wounded, had managed to struggle another four miles toward Salmon City. He was just short of the summit of a peak which rose above the saddle between the Panther Creek and Iron Creek drainages when he died. His body was found by a party of Leesburg-bound miners the following day. They buried him where he fell — on the trail just below the summit — and marked his grave with a wooden cross.

Several years later the U.S. Army was mapping the area for the Geological Survey. The 9,085-foot peak was named for the man who was buried there, as was the valley to the west of the peak and the stream which drains it. Moyer Peak, Moyer Basin, and Moyer Creek have ever since honored the memory of George Moyer, the placer miner. As Malcolm said of the Thane of Cawdor in Shakespeare's *Macbeth*, "Nothing in his life ever became him like the leaving it."

RECOVERY

James Hogle had found his fortune but was in grave danger of losing his life. The stab wound was severe enough to immobilize him completely, and in his weakened state he was susceptible to pneumonia. Reflecting on his fate at this time, he might have taken some consolation in his travels and experiences. He had had adventures enough to fill a score of lifetimes and could look back on Ireland, Canada, Illinois, Pikes Peak, Alder Gulch, Helena, and the Leesburg Stampede. On October fourteenth he had celebrated his thirty-second birthday.

But James Hogle's life was not over. His wound was long in healing, his recuperation slow; but his recovery was complete. He later credited the care he received from Mrs. Hagenbarth as having saved his life.

When James was well enough to travel, he went first to Salmon and then to Helena and stayed for a time with his brother. But in the spring of 1871 James moved to Salt Lake City. Despite the presence of a rougher element, his visit to the orderly Mormon capital in 1864 had impressed him. Having survived the often-violent gold rushes and boom camps of Colorado, Montana, and Idaho, he decided that he had pressed his luck far enough. It was time for Mr. Hogle to settle down, and the name "Jimmy Guiraud" was buried with George Moyer at the Loon Creek summit.

Grave marker of placer miner George Moyer on Moyer Peak in the Salmon River Wilderness. The original wooden cross was replaced by this elaborately carved tree trunk in 1922. Courtesy United States Forest Service, Salmon, Idaho.

CHAPTER SIX

Gentiles in the Promised Land, 1847–1877

FROM THE BEGINNING OF THE MORMON COLONY there had been "Gentiles," non-Mormons, in Utah. It had been, after all, a Gentile, Jim Bridger, who had advised Brigham Young on the suitability of the Great Salt Lake Valley for settlement and directed him to the location. Two Gentile companies from Missouri bound for California had accompanied the Mormon pioneers on part of their trek westward, and non-Mormon trappers were trading with the Mormons by the spring of 1848.

After the discovery of gold in California in 1849, Salt Lake City saw a steady stream of wagon trains pass through the community bound for the rush. It was inevitable that enterprising merchants would seize upon the location, 1,500 miles from the States, as a supply depot, and by 1850 Gentile merchants were trading to gold seekers and Mormons alike. The Mormon Zion had become the "half-way house of the nation."

Early Utah Gentiles were tolerated by the Mormons. The goods and services they provided to the struggling pioneer community were badly needed. But the Mormons had followed Brigham Young west to escape persecution. They had seen their previous settlements destroyed by the Gentiles, their Prophet Joseph Smith murdered, and they had suffered enormously at the hands of disbelievers. Persecution does not engender tolerance in the persecuted, and beneath a façade of acceptance seethed suspicion and hostility.

During the 1850's the government in Washington was under increasing pressure to do something about the Mormons. Brigham Young's territorial claims, "The Polygamy Question," and the refusal of Utah authorities to accept the federal judges appointed for the Territory finally forced President Buchanan into action.

In 1857 the Utah Expeditionary Force was organized under General Albert Sidney Johnston to put down the "Mormon Rebellion" or Utah War, as the conflict was usually called. Johnston was a professional soldier. West Point–trained and highly regarded, he would find that the "Saints" were well protected in their mountain stronghold and that Brigham Young was a formidable adversary.

As the Mormons in the north fought a guerrilla action against the invaders, a wagon train from Missouri, bound for California, was attacked by Mormons in southern Utah and, with the exception of a few very young children and infants, was wiped out. Accounts of this outrage, since known as the Mountain Meadows Massacre, would fuel Gentile hatred of the Mormons through the next four decades.

Meanwhile Johnston's Army was harassed by irregular Mormon detachments under the command of Lot Smith and Orrin Porter Rockwell. Alexander Majors of the firm Russel, Majors and Waddell held the freight contract for the U.S. Army's campaign, and in his memoirs he described the crucial engagement of the "war."

> A party of Mormons under Lot Smith had been sent out by Mormon authorities in the rear of Johnston's army to cut off supplies. They captured and burned three of our trains, two on the Sandy just east of Green River and one on the west bank of the Green River. . . . The loss to the army was about five hundred thousand pounds of government supplies. This loss put the army on short rations until . . . they could be reached with new supplies in the spring of 1858.

This represented a kind of victory for Brigham Young. Alexander Toponce, who was employed at the time as a wagon master for General Johnston, described in his reminiscences the effect that the loss of the supply trains had on the Army.

> What Lot Smith and his Mormon Cowboys did to the wagon trains on the Sandy put a crimp on our trip to Utah. For the first time Johnston and his West Pointers woke up to the fact that they were engaged in a real war. Their scouts and spies brought them the news that the Utah Militia . . . had 6,008 men under arms to oppose his 3,000 and all the mountain passes were fortified and mined.

Fort Bridger was not exactly a Winter Resort, but Johnston decided to winter there while he sent back east for more men and supplies. We spent a miserable winter. We had insufficient shelter and nearly froze. Then too we were short of grub and short of rations. Even what grub we had we were compelled to eat without salt as our salt was burnt up. There was some salt that came from the valley but the officers would not allow us to use it for fear it was poisoned.

The next spring 3,000 more soldiers arrived and plenty of supplies and in late May of 1858 we began to advance.

During this winter a treaty, of sorts, was worked out between Brigham Young and the federal authorities. Johnston did not enter the Salt Lake Valley until the summer of 1858. He was required by the agreement of the peace commission to quarter some distance south of the city. Albert Sidney Johnston was in no position to argue the arrangements. Although he had avoided defeat, he had not really won a victory. Alexander Toponce recorded the reaction of General Johnston when he learned that a settlement had been reached.

When General McCulloch, or someone, arrived from Washington with a special message that there was to be no real fighting, Johnston and Smith, his chief of staff were furious. Johnston took off his hat with the insignia of a general on it, threw it on the ground, stamped on it and said, "Damn such a government. Here we have starved and froze all winter, and now that we have these fellows right where we want them they are going to get off without shedding so much as one drop of blood. Damn such a government!"

Federal judges were in place in Salt Lake City and the U.S. Army was at "Camp Floyd," forty miles south of the city and west of Utah Lake. The Gentiles had come to Utah in force and that force was resented.

In November of 1859 Johnston received reinforcements from Ft. Leavenworth, Kansas. With this later detachment arrived a large number of civilian tradesmen, merchants, saloon keepers, and army suppliers, and his garrison now numbered more than 3,000. The civilian population of nearby Fairfield soared to 4,000; the majority of these were Gentiles. A clever merchant could make as much money selling to the Army as he could selling to placer miners. Then as now, a government voucher was as good as gold.

Joseph Robinson Walker and his brother David Frederick were two of the merchants who struck the motherlode at Camp Floyd. They had acquired from their former employer, Salt Lake merchant William Nixon, $15,000 worth of goods. With this stake they opened a general store at Camp Floyd. Walker Brothers', a mercantile name as famous as any in the west, was born.

The American Civil War was fast approaching and the government recalled the Utah Expeditionary Force. Ironically, many of the men who had put down the "Mormon Rebellion," including their commander, were southerners who would soon join the Confederate armies in the east and participate in a rebellion of their own. General Johnston was considered at the time "the ablest of all the professional soldiers who had joined the Confederacy." He was an early casualty of the war, falling at the battle of Shiloh.

An Era Begins

After every war someone makes a fortune in war surplus. It was no different following the Utah War. When Camp Floyd was abandoned in the spring of 1861, large stores of surplus government matériel were up for grabs. Alexander Toponce watched first-hand as the government stores were liquidated at pennies on the dollar: "I saw big government Wagons, complete with bows, covers, neck yoke, double trees, stretchers and chains for six mules sold at $6.50 each. . . ." The enterprising young man took advantage of the opportunity to set himself up handsomely in the freighting business.

Ben Holladay, the stage line operator, bought government mules at less than ten cents on the dollar. The enterprising Walker brothers bought large lots of the surplus and removed the goods to Salt Lake City. Here they had recently opened Walker Brothers' Store, which presently became the city's center of commerce, "Walker Brothers' Corner."

The federal government continued to be wary of Mormon intentions, and so a force of 750 volunteers from California and Nevada was sent to Utah. This detachment, under the command of Col. Patrick Edward Connor, anticipated trouble. Reports that the

Saints were fortifying positions along the Jordan River led Connor to remark with grim determination, "I will cross the river Jordan if Hell yawns before me."

Connor and his men entered Salt Lake City without opposition on October 20, 1862. Although there were no hostilities, his reception was cold. A correspondent of the *San Francisco Bulletin* who accompanied the troops wrote: "Every crossing was occupied by spectators and every window door and roof had their gazers, Not a cheer, not a jeer greeted us. . . . There were none of the manifestations of loyalty that any other city in a loyal territory would have made."

Connor's assignment was ostensibly to guard the central Overland Trail from Indian attack, but his real job was to keep an eye on the Mormons. Connor's fort was not built forty miles from the city as Johnston's had been; it was built on the high east bench overlooking the Mormon capital. On this strategic position, later known as Federal Heights, Patrick Connor placed his artillery. A cannon was kept trained on Brigham Young's own residence.

This was how Brigadier General Patrick E. Connor (who had been promoted in the spring of 1863) chose to defend the Overland Trail from Indian attack. Connor wrote back to his superiors in Washington that the Mormons "were a community of traitors, murderers, fanatics and whores." He accused Brigham Young of preaching treason and claimed that Brother Brigham murdered those who disobeyed his commands. Needless to say, General Connor and Brigham Young were at odds with each other from the start.

Connor had extensive experience with mining, geology, and assaying. He quickly had his troops scouring the Territory prospecting for mineral deposits, and he allowed his men to keep any claims they found. Connor wanted a stampede. He openly vowed to attract enough Gentiles to Utah to outnumber the Mormons and overthrow the Mormon theocracy.

In July of 1864 he outlined his policy in a letter to his superior, Adj. General R. C. Drum in San Francisco.

> My policy in this Territory has been to invite hither a large Gentile and loyal population, sufficient by peaceful means and through the ballot box to overwhelm the Mormons by mere

force of numbers, and thus wrest from the church, disloyal and traitorous to the core, the absolute and tyrannical control of temporal and civil affairs, or at least a population numerous enough to put a check on Mormon authorities. . . . With this view, I have bent every energy and means of which I was possessed both personal and official, toward the discovery and development of the mining resources of the Territory. . . . The number of miners is steadily and rapidly increasing, with them, and to supply their wants, merchants and traders are flocking to Great Salt Lake City, which by its activity, increased number of Gentile stores and workshops, and the appearance of its thronged and busy streets, presents a most remarkable contrast to the Salt Lake of one year ago.

Rich ore discoveries did attract many thousands of Gentiles to Utah, but never as many as Brigham Young feared or General Connor hoped for.

When the Civil War ended most of the California Volunteers went home. Connor stayed on, and for his efforts history has rewarded him with the title "Father of Utah Mining."

THE RIGHT PLACE

James Hogle arrived in Great Salt Lake City in the summer of 1871. The dusty pioneer community had undergone enormous changes since he had first visited the city back in 1864. What had been a fairly rough provincial capital was now a mercantile and manufacturing center with more than 20,000 inhabitants. What had been predominantly Mormon was taking on a more cosmopolitan character. The Gentile population of the city had more than tripled since 1867, and there was spirited opposition to local Mormon rule.

James Hogle noted the changes, the most striking of which was in the general appearance of the residents themselves. When Hogle had been in Salt Lake in 1864, most of the clothing worn by Salt Lakers was of home manufacture. The shortage of material and the isolation of the city had made clothing standardized, practical, and drab. But in 1871, residents were wearing the very latest fashions from the east.

The reason for this transformation was the completion of the transcontinental railroad on May 10, 1869, and the completion of the Utah Central Railroad, which connected Salt Lake to the railhead in Ogden, on January 10, 1870. Brigham Young himself drove the last spike for the Utah Central.

The effect that the railroads had on Utah was sudden and dramatic. Large sections of the Mormon economy were threatened by the sudden flood of goods from the east, and some local enterprises, such as the Mormons' infant cotton and wine industries, were crippled. The railroad gave other Mormons access to new markets. Fresh fruit, vegetables, and beef were shipped to San Francisco for large profits. The railroad ruined some and showered others with wealth. Some of the effects were temporary and others permanent.

The arrival of the railroad led to the founding of Zion's Cooperative Mercantile Institution, Z.C.M.I. The store was conceived as a protectionist measure to help support the local "Valley Tan" (home-made) economy. For a time Mormons were forbidden to do business with Gentiles and were also instructed not to engage in the mining industry. Z.C.M.I. handled both imported and local goods, and in this way Brigham Young hoped to manage and control the financial affairs of the Territory. It was something he had longed to do for years, and the target of this enterprise was the Gentile merchant.

The combination of boycott and monopoly, which had been practiced as early as 1865, was deeply resented by the Gentiles. Many Mormon merchants also objected to the attempt of the church leadership to control their economic life. William S. Godbe, John Chislett, Henry Lawrence, W. H. Shearman, E. L. T. Harrison, E. B. Kelsey, and a number of other intellectual Mormons with business or mining interests, openly defied the church's intrusion into commercial matters. In *The Utah Magazine*, a publication edited by Godbe, they boldly declared: "The prophet, seer, and revelator of the Lord had power and rightful authority to direct and dictate in spiritual matters. But in business matters it was not competent for him so to direct and to dictate, and that in these things the people had a right to judge and act for themselves."

The questioning of the authority of the Prophet was, from the

Prophet's standpoint, blasphemy, and the apostates were not to be coddled or reasoned with. The church leadership reacted quickly to the challenge and published the following answer to William S. Godbe's editorial comment: "To whom it may concern: This certifies that W. S. Godbe, E. L. T. Harrison and Eli B. Kelsey were excommunicated from the Church of Jesus Christ of Latter-day Saints on Monday the 25th day of October 1869 by the High Council meeting in Salt Lake."

On leaving the church, these men took with them a number of other malcontents. They banded together in an association called The Liberal Institute, which quickly attracted disaffected Mormons and Gentiles alike.

Although the "Godbeite Schism" did not endure as a religious movement, it had lasting effects on the state of Utah, including the creation of the anti-Mormon Liberal Party and the founding of the *Salt Lake Tribune*. This newspaper became the champion of the Gentile cause and conducted a protracted war of words with the church-owned *Deseret News*.

Salt Lake was changing and it was not long before other churches were established in Salt Lake to minister to the non-Mormon population. The new state of affairs was what induced Daniel S. Tuttle, the Episcopal Bishop of Montana, Idaho, and Utah, to move his diocesan headquarters from Helena to Salt Lake City in the summer of 1869. Others from the northern mining camps would soon follow his example.

The coming of the railroad brought many changes and a fresh supply of cheap labor. When the Golden Spike was driven into the polished laurel rail at Promontory, Utah, on May 10, 1869, several thousand Irish and Chinese tracklayers were simultaneously and unceremoniously fired. The unemployed immigrants flooded into Utah's infant mining camps, providing much-needed labor for their development. The Utah mining boom which General Connor had long dreamed of was finally a reality.

This was heavy industrial mining, and Salt Lake City was at the very hub of the new boom. Once again, James Hogle was at the right place at the right time. The Gentiles who came to Utah with the mining industry were his closest friends and associates.

The railroad had made possible the importation of many different kinds of goods. An entrepreneur with a little capital to invest could become a licensed agent for almost anything. James Hogle's line was liquor, and so he went into the wholesale liquor trade. By the sumer of 1872 James had become the licensed agent for several brands. He also acquired at this time an exclusive distributorship for a small St. Louis brewery which was interested in expanding into the western markets. Beer, because of its volume, presented special problems in shipping, handling, and warehousing. In addition, because it was perishable, it had to be stored in a cool place. So James leased the cellar of the Walkers' store for his new business, The Anheuser Brewing Association.

WALL, DALY, TOPONCE, AND HEARST

James Hogle came to Salt Lake City at a time of major Gentile migration to the new mercantile capital. Other men who had made the trek to Pikes Peak in '59 and had then gone on to Virginia City, Helena, and Idaho were now living in the city. Among this early group were Luke Voorhees, Alexander Toponce, and Col. Enos A. Wall. Toponce had been Wall's partner in a freighting company in Montana and Idaho, but in 1871 he had gone into the boot business with a former Helena cobbler, William Sloan. Their shop at 90 South East Temple was right next to Walker Brothers' and sported a giant boot sign which Sloan had brought with him from Helena.

Enos A. Wall, who had been Toponce's partner in a number of joint ventures in mining, freighting, and cattle ranching, was now in Utah and would soon make a major discovery at Silver Reef.

Luke Voorhees moved to Salt Lake in 1870. The money he had made placer mining the Kootenai he had invested in several businesses, including a freight line and later the Black Hills Stage, Mail and Express Company. Voorhees became a prominent spokesman for the Gentile business community and frequently petitioned the city fathers for improved services.

It seems probable that it was Rob Walker who first introduced James Hogle to Marcus Daly. In any event, they met sometime in

1871 when Daly was employed by the Walkers and Hogle was warehousing his goods in the basement of the Walker brothers' store. The two men had much in common and they took an immediate liking to each other. The friendship that developed between them would last through the rest of their lives.

Marcus Daly was also an Irishman. He had been born in County Cavin, the county adjacent to Armagh, in 1841. The severe deprivations of the potato famine had forced his immigration to America when he was fifteen years old. Daly had prospected and mined in Calaveras County and Grass Valley, California (1861–65), and Virginia City and White Pine, Nevada (1865–69). In Virginia City he became a seasoned miner working the famous Comstock Lode. The Comstock was a virtual school of mining engineering, and during his employment there he so mastered the trade that he rose to the position of mine foreman. Daly had no formal education, but he studied mining and geology with such intensity that he soon had an enviable reputation as a prospect geologist. He was said to have "a nose for ore," and his advice was sought by mine owners and speculators alike.

West side of Second South and East Temple (Main) streets in Great Salt Lake City, 1870. Note the boot hanging in front of Alexander Toponce's Mammoth Boot and Leather shop — soon to house Clasbey and Hogle's Saloon. Courtesy Utah State Historical Society.

Little Cottonwood Canyon is the most rugged and scenically spectacular of the five deep canyon passages through the towering Wasatch Range above Salt Lake City. When the Walker brothers acquired their interest in Little Cottonwood's Emma Mine in 1870, Marcus Daly was hired as mine superintendent. During the eighteen months he managed the property the Emma produced earnings in excess of $2,000,000.

Daly also directed operations at the Walker brothers' Ophir mine and the construction of the Pioneer Mill. In his role as prospect geologist and investment counselor he inspected a number of mining properties for the Walker brothers. In August of 1872 he visited a property near Park City, Utah, called the Ontario and recommended its purchase. When his employers rejected the recommendation he informed George Hearst (father of William Randolph), who was in Utah at the time. He told Hearst, "There's a little hole in the ground over near Park City called the Ontario. It looked good to me and I recommended it to Walker Brothers, my employers, but they turned it down. Seems to me it's worth further examination. If you get up there, stop and see what you think of it."

Hearst looked and had his own mining engineer, R. C. Chambers, look too. Chambers didn't have to look long. He recognized immediately the mine's potential and George Hearst purchased the property for $27,000. In the next thirteen years alone, the Ontario would yield up more than $17,000,000 worth of silver. The Ontario became an important cornerstone of the Hearst family's financial empire, and George Hearst would not soon forget Marcus Daly.

In 1880, when Daly needed capital to develop his Anaconda Mine in Butte, Montana, he turned to Hearst and the Walker brothers to help finance the venture. The Anaconda would eventually become the world's largest copper mine and the uneducated Irish immigrant one of the world's richest men.

In the years ahead, Daly would try repeatedly to get James Hogle to move to Butte, but without success. Hogle would visit his friend in Montana often, but Salt Lake City was his home and he intended to stay.

The Landlady's Lovely Daughter

When James Hogle arrived in Salt Lake City, he took up residence at a boarding house operated by Elizabeth King. The home had been constructed by her husband, who was widely regarded as the city's foremost carpenter. Charles King had constructed many of the city's commercial buildings, including the Walker Brothers' Store and the Town Clock Store. He was also responsible for designing and constructing a number of prominent residences.

Elizabeth King's boarding house was located on the south side of Third South between East Temple (now Main St.) and First East (now State) streets. Living with Mrs. King were her two sons, Sidney and Charles, Jr., and her seventeen-year-old daughter, Ida Elizabeth. Ida was a pretty young girl with long brown hair framing her oval face. Her features were full, her eyes expressive. James Hogle was immediately taken with the charming young lady and began to court her. It is not known how Mrs. King felt about one of her boarders courting her daughter. But then, Mr. Hogle was a man of means. The courtship would last two years.

The King Family

Charles H. King was born on October 29, 1816, in Canterbury, Kent, England. His wife Elizabeth was born April 23, 1821, in the same city. On Charles King's thirty-second birthday they sailed from England for America. The Kings resided briefly in New York, then made their way west, living for a time on a farm outside of St. Louis, Missouri.

In June of 1852 the Kings decided to move to California. By early July they had joined a Mormon wagon train formed in Kanesville, Ohio, and bound for Salt Lake City. Trouble plagued Captain Eli B. Kelsey's 19th Company from the start. Oxen died, wagons broke down and had to be abandoned, summer rains mired the train in thick mud, and foodstuffs intended to last the entire journey were lost to spoilage in the first few weeks. The trek was well over a thousand miles, and the 19th Company was falling behind schedule.

It was near Ft. Bridger, Wyoming, that the Kings' arduous journey west nearly came to disaster. A heavy September snowstorm, not uncommon on the plains, struck without warning. The Kelsey Train was utterly stranded and close to starvation. A messenger was sent ahead to Salt Lake City for help.

On hearing the plight of the 19th Company, Brigham Young immediately dispatched food, clothing, blankets, and other provisions to the stranded immigrants. The rescue party, led by Elders Joseph Horne and Abraham Smoot, guided the exhausted 19th Company into the Salt Lake Valley on October 16, 1852. As it was too late in the season to push on to California, the Kings would stay on in Salt Lake City.

Charles King was a skilled carpenter and architect. These talents were much needed in the new city and there was no shortage of work. He was given substantial contracts by the Mormon church, and his fortune was as good as made.

On February 9, 1855, their first child, Ida Elizabeth, was born to Charles and Elizabeth King. Records show that while Ida was "Blessed" in the Mormon faith, and for a time attended the old Eighth Ward, she was never actually baptized. Later events may help to explain this anomaly. Also born to the union of Charles and Elizabeth King were Charles Orson, on December 15, 1856, and Sidney B., on February 15, 1859.

The Convert Takes a Wife

The oral history of any family will contain elements not supported by documents on record. Family tradition relates, for instance, that the King family joined the Mormon church out of gratitude after their ordeal with the 19th Company. But Mormon church records show that Charles had actually been baptized by a Mormon missionary while still in England in 1848. It therefore seems more likely that the King family came to Utah as part of the general Mormon migration. It is certain that whether out of gratitude or conviction, the Kings were practicing Mormons during the 1850's. In December 1859, when their third child, Sidney, was less than a year old, Mrs. King's union with the church and her husband came to an abrupt end.

Back in 1852 thirteen-year-old Louisa Larkin was traveling with her parents to Zion. The Larkins were members of the same ill-fated 19th Company that had brought the Kings to Utah. In 1859 Louisa was twenty-one years old, and Charles had wholeheartedly embraced the principal tenets of Mormonism, including polygamy. One day he brought Louisa Larkin home as his second wife. Whether Charles had first obtained her permission in the prescribed manner or not, Elizabeth was outraged at this development and is reported to have said, "Take her out of here and get out yourself. I'm staying here with the baby."

In December of 1859 Johnston's Army of Occupation was still in Utah. It took a good deal of courage to break with the church at this time. Elizabeth King, in defying her husband and rejecting the doctrine of polygamy, was, in the eyes of her neighbors, "harboring the spirit of apostasy." There is no record that she was formally excommunicated, but it is not known with certainty if she was ever admitted to full membership in the church. Whatever her religious status, her defiance had predictable results. She was ostracized by Mormon society. Elizabeth had cast her lot with the Gentiles. Soon afterward she turned her home into a boarding house, and the circumstances dictated that it would cater to the Gentile segment of the community.

Documents of Record

Records show that while Elizabeth operated her boarding house on Third South, Charles and Louisa King were living in a home on First South between East and West Temple streets. Out of their union were born Eleone, October 1860; Howard, May 21, 1865; and Mattie, July 29, 1869. Another child, Samuel T., was born to Charles on November 7, 1869. The date of birth indicates that this child was by another wife.

Elizabeth King knew that raising her children as non-Mormons in Salt Lake City was going to be a difficult task. Since all their friends and peers were Mormons, the chances of their escaping re-conversion were slim. In the mid 1860's, Elizabeth decided to take her children to San Francisco for a time, where perhaps they could acquire an independent view of Zion and polygamy. It could not have been an easy journey for a woman with three minor children. The overland stage route west from Salt Lake City crossed some of the roughest terrain in the country, including the Great Salt Lake Desert and the Sierra Nevada.

The arduous journey appears to have accomplished its purpose, however. The register of Saint James Episcopal Church in San Francisco records that on November 7, 1867, Elizabeth King and her three children, Ida, Charles, and Sidney, were baptized into the Episcopal faith. They received their first communion and were confirmed on the same day.

A glimpse into that time was recorded by eleven-year-old Ida Elizabeth, who attended school in San Francisco during the family's stay there. One of her homework assignments was the writing of an essay on the subject of Christmas. "Composition #8" clearly reveals the carrot and stick approach used by her mother in bringing up her children, the veiled threat and the desired reward. It tells a story that should be familiar to anyone who has had children. It also reveals how important Ida's mother thought education. The essay was written in the third week of December 1867.

> Christmas, the Anniversary of the birth of Christ, is a time of rejoicing amongst every community except the Jews. Christmas is a day of rejoicing among old and young. We expect Santa Claus to come down the chimney, with a good many presents for us. If we are not good and do not study our lessons, he will not give us any presents. Santa Claus is a little fat man with long gray whiskers. He smokes a little short pipe, and he is very jovial. We expect for our Christmas dinner Turkey, plum pudding and mince pie. After dinner we expect to have a nice Christmas tree, then some romping.
>
> Christmas we go to bed earlier than usual, then we hang up our stockings. In the morning we find our stockings full of candies, nuts and raisins.
>
> How nice it is to take a walk down Montgomery and Kearney Streets to see the toys in the windows fixed so nicely.
>
> People think me a great baby, I am so fond of dolls. Ma says she will not tell Santa Claus to bring me or my brothers a present if we do not get promoted. The little girls think Santa Claus is a good man. Every one you meet talks about Christmas. I heard one little girl say she would kiss Santa Claus if only he would bring her a large doll.

It is not known how long Mrs. King and her children resided in San Francisco, but by 1870 the boarding house in Salt Lake City was again in operation. Bishop Daniel S. Tuttle recorded that year that Elizabeth and her children were among the first parishioners of St. Mark's Episcopal Cathedral.

A Time to Mourn

The weather in December of 1872 had been unusual. The month had started with a bitterly cold blast which blanketed the valley with a foot of snow and piled many more feet on the mountains east of the city. Then the temperature rose, so that by mid-month it was said to be "quite balmy." Then on Christmas Eve a heavy rainstorm struck the city, followed by a similar storm on the evening of the twenty-sixth. Snow depth in the mountains frequently exceeded 300 inches, and the Christmas rainstorm in the city meant many more feet of heavy wet snow in the Wasatch Range which rises 7,000 feet above the high valley floor.

In Little Cottonwood Canyon, some fifteen miles from the city, the new snow did not bind to the earlier pack, and on the morning of December 27 a "Horrific snow slide tore down the North face of the Canyon." Caught in the slide were several freight teams. The *Deseret News* reported on the twenty-eighth that one man had been killed and at least six others were missing, and that a number of horses were lost and others had to be destroyed.

December had been an unusually busy month for the sexton of Salt Lake City's cemetery. He reported that there had been 58 burials in December, 25 males and 23 females; 29 were adults and 19 were children. The mortality tables for December were published in the *Deseret News* on January 8: 10 died of pneumonia, 6 of typhoid fever, 3 of inflammation of the bowel, 3 of consumption, 3 of old age, 2 each of strangulation, croup, measles, diphtheria, and "child bed death"; and one each of accident, shooting, suicide, heart disease, "maramus," cancer, convulsions, spinal disease, liver complaint, paralysis, erysipelas, childbirth, and teething.

Elizabeth King was among those buried that fateful December. She died of pneumonia at her home on December 27, the day of the

Alta snow slide, at the age of fifty-one. No obituary or notice of death was published in either paper. The register of St. Mark's Episcopal Cathedral records that she was buried from there on the morning of December 28, the Rev. R. M. Kirby officiating. At the time of her mother's death Ida was seventeen years old, Charles was sixteen, and Sidney was twelve. On the day of Elizabeth's burial at the Salt Lake City Cemetery, Ida cut a lock of her mother's dark brown hair and folded it in a flower-patterned napkin.

Following the death of their mother the King children moved into the home of their father, his wife Louisa, and their children Eleone, Howard, Mattie, and Samuel. The arrangement was anything but satisfactory, and by spring Elizabeth had had enough of her father's second family. She moved back to her mother's boarding house, resolved to go it alone. She would not be alone for long.

On the evening of Thursday, September 4, 1873, nine months after the death of her mother, Ida Elizabeth King married James Hogle at St. Mark's Cathedral. Officiating at the ceremony was The Rt. Rev. Daniel S. Tuttle, D.D., Bishop of Montana, Idaho, and Utah, and "Hero of the Great Helena Fire." James Hogle's best man was the pioneer diarist of Pikes Peak, Denver, Alder Gulch, and Helena, and discoverer of the Kootenai placer deposit, Luke Voorhees. The maid of honor was one Lumeul (?) Colbath.

Prior to May of 1871, Episcopal services in Salt Lake City had been held at the Independence Hall, located on Third South, across the street from Mrs. King's boarding house. This building had been constructed by a Gentile organization called The Young Men's Literary Association, which had held its earlier meetings on the second floor of Daft's Store on East Temple. Independence Hall was a large adobe structure which could hold more than two hundred people. The hall had been used by various Protestant groups, and for several years it was the only Episcopal church in the city.

On May 21, 1871, Bishop Tuttle had moved his congregation to the basement of a new church which was then under construction on First South. The Bishop had laid the cornerstone for St. Mark's Cathedral on July 30, 1870. Services were held in the basement of the building until September 5, 1871, when they were moved upstairs into the church proper.

James (Gilmore) Hogle and Ida Elizabeth King Hogle shortly after their marriage. James, photographed in 1874, is thirty-four, and Ida, photographed in 1875, is twenty.

In September of 1873, when James Hogle and his young bride exchanged vows at St. Mark's, the building was far from completed. Dedication of St. Mark's Cathedral would not come until May 14, 1874. The Hogle wedding, which was held on a Thursday evening, was the first evening service in the church, and it was only the tenth wedding in the church proper.

The record shows that Ida Elizabeth wrote on the marriage certificate that she was nineteen years old. She was in fact eighteen. It is said that a woman's age is her own business. But then James Hogle wrote that he was twenty-nine. In September of 1873 he was almost thirty-four.

Three years later, on October 12, 1876, Ida gave birth to the couple's only child. On Sunday, New Year's Eve, 1876, the boy was baptized in the Episcopal faith and christened James Albert Hogle. St. Mark's Cathedral was the site of the baptism, R. M. Kirby officiating. Luke Voorhees was the child's godfather and June K. Daggett his godmother.

After their marriage, James and Ida Elizabeth Hogle lived at the boarding house, which was returned to its original function as a single-family dwelling. Ida considered the property her mother's.

Charles King, however, was the owner of record, and the property rights of women were not automatically recognized by nineteenth-century courts. No deed of gift or bill of sale was ever given by Charles to Ida's mother and so the property legally belonged to Mr. King.

To complicate matters further, Ida's brothers had moved out of Louisa's home and in with the Hogles shortly after Ida's marriage. It is clear that there was some friction between Charles's two families, and it was inevitable that misunderstandings would arise. The dispute which finally did develop must have seemed, at the time, very ugly.

In 1876, shortly after the birth of James Albert, Charles King suddenly demanded that the Hogles pay back rent on the Third South home. Mr. King also wanted returned certain pieces of furniture that he said were his. His daughter insisted that they had belonged to her mother. The Hogles pointed out to Mr. King that for the past two years they had been boarding, without compensation, Charles and Sidney King, a responsibility which clearly should have been Charles's. It was only after protracted squabbling that James Hogle and his father-in-law came to a formal written agreement. The document reveals the hand of an unknown seasoned negotiator, someone with a straightforward approach to problems and a mastery of nineteenth-century legalese. The settlement was as follows:

Agreement Made January 26th 1877, by and between James Hogle and Charles King, both of Salt Lake City, Utah. Whereas the parties have claims and demands against each other and differences have arisen between them in regard to the same: Know this agreement witnesseth: That the parties hereto have compromised and settled all such claims and differences on the following terms: That said King gives to the said Hogle two promissory notes for three hundred dollars each, without interest until due. One payable in one year, and the other two years from this date. It is also agreed that Hogle shall and may occupy the house in which he and his family now reside until the first day of April 1877 rent up to that date being included in this settlement. And if said Hogle longer occupies said house it shall be under agreement therefore made prior to April 1st, 1877.

And if no such agreement is concluded, Hogle is to remove himself from said house by said date.

Hogle is also to have all the furniture now in said house except such as he may admit belongs to King, and such as he, at his option, may leave in said house in case he removes therefrom.

In case Charles King and Sidney King, minor sons of said Charles King, live with said Hogle, or he incurs any expense on their account hereafter, it shall be deemed entirely voluntary on the part of said Hogle and said King shall not be liable or responsible therefor.

And, except as hereinbefore specified, the parties hereto acknowledge full payment of, and hereby release to each other, all claims, debts, liabilities, and demands whatever to date, Witness our hand and seals the day and year above written.

James Hogle (SEAL)
Charles King (SEAL)

Ida and the infant James Albert Hogle in 1876.

The April first deadline for renegotiating the rent was not met, and on May 29, 1877, Charles King gave a warranty deed to Louisa A. King, his second wife, for the property on Third South. The Hogles "removed" themselves from the property, and on May 23, 1879, the Kings sold it to a Herman Hill for the sum of $3,000. This building later became the site of Pembroke's, a prominent Salt Lake office supply store and stationer.

After their removal from "Louisa's" house, the Hogles rented a home on Fourth East, next door to the Wagener family. Henry Wagener had also made his way to Salt Lake via Virginia City, Helena, and Idaho. In 1870 he had built the California Brewery at the mouth of Emigration Canyon, soon one of the west's largest brewing and distilling concerns. The neighbors became the best of friends, and their association would continue into the next generation. The friendship between the Wageners and the Hogles would eventually result in a major contribution to the city.

The city directory shows that by 1882 James Hogle and his family had moved to a home at 16 South Fourth East. If relations between the Hogles and the elder Kings were strained, the same could not be said with regard to Ida's brothers, Charles and Sidney. The King brothers were very close to the Hogles, and James would, in the language of the agreement, voluntarily incur additional expenses on their account.

CHAPTER SEVEN

Mr. Clasbey's Partners, 1870–1880

JAMES T. CLASBEY WAS A SUCCESSFUL BUSINESSMAN. Like Hogle he was Irish. In Virginia City he had operated the Clasbey House, that community's first hotel. But by 1870 he had changed businesses and relocated in a place which was then known as Central City, Utah. There he operated Clasbey and Read's general store. As Fred Phillips, James Glendenning, and John David Wood had proven in Leesburg, and as James Hogle and Col. Shoup had discovered in both Denver and Alder Gulch, it was often as profitable to sell to the mine operators and their miners as it was to hit the motherlode. Premium prices could always be charged for bringing the goods to the more remote camps. Then as now the middleman got his due.

In 1870 the tiny mining town at the top of Little Cottonwood Canyon was not the easiest place in the world to get to. But the fabulous Emma Mine and the smaller operations which dotted the steep canyon walls employed more than 800 miners, and that many men had a variety of needs. James T. Clasbey and his partner set out to fill all of them.

The partnership with John Read was a natural. Read, who had briefly run tobacco shops in Virginia City and Helena, was an expert teamster and freighter. It was his job to bring the goods up the steep winding canyon from Salt Lake City. This was no small accomplishment, for the narrow road was often washed out or blocked by rock falls. In winter, the road up Little Cottonwood Canyon was under continuous reconstruction due to another canyon hazard, avalanche. Clasbey managed the business. It was he who put up most of the initial capital, selected and ordered the goods, kept the books, and hired the employees. The arrangement seemed workable.

But by the fall of 1871 it became painfully obvious to the residents of Central City that they had built their town in the wrong place. The more recent arrivals at the camp were settling in the wider and flatter section of the canyon, a good half mile below the original town site. The reason the canyon was wider and flatter there seems to have escaped everyone's notice. What they did notice was that the merchants there seemed to be doing a thriving business, while the original inhabitants noticed a sharp decline in customers. Half a mile farther up the steep canyon was half a mile too far, and so they moved the town.

Log by log, building by building, the old town of Central City was torn down and transported to the new location. The first building moved was the Alta Hotel, so the new town took its name from Central City's old hotel and the town of Alta, Utah, was born.

Clasbey and Read's was the second building moved. Photographs of the large two-story log structure taken in 1871 testify that this was no small feat. But it must have been worth the trouble, for by the fall of 1872 Clasbey and Read's was the most prominent mercantile business in Alta and employed more than twenty people. It also housed the town's post, telegraph, and stage line offices.

Clasbey and Read's was a mining camp's version of the modern department store and it handled a wide variety of merchandise, including groceries, hardware, steel, iron, lumber, explosives, china, glassware, tinware, boots, stoves, clothing, liquors, and provisions.

But no enterprise in the volatile mining camps was without some risk, and in Alta, Utah, the chance of being "wiped out" had a distinct and immediate reality beyond the calamity of mere financial loss. It happened during the winter of 1874–75: a sudden roar, a great billowing white cloud, a rolling wall of snow and rock, and it was gone — not just Clasbey and Read's, but half the town of Alta and a number of the residents as well. A fire started in the rubble, and much of what had been spared by the avalanche was quickly consumed in the flames. Alta would be rebuilt. James T. Clasbey, for the time being, had had enough.

And so it was that Mr. Clasbey moved to Salt Lake City, seek-

Clasbey and Read's store in Alta, Utah, destroyed by an avalanche in the winter of 1874–75. The owners are present but unidentified.

ing safer investment opportunities. He soon became partners with a man who held an exclusive distributorship for an obscure St. Louis Brewery called Anheuser & Co. By March of 1875 Clasbey and Hogle's Saloon was open to the public.

The Whisky Street Wars

In the 1870's Salt Lake City's main street was officially known as East Temple. While its name may have paid homage to the great L.D.S. edifice which was approaching completion at its northern terminus, the character of the street had never been "Saintly." As early as the 1850's it had been referred to by the unsavory tag "Whisky Street," and in 1875 it was still living up to its liquorous reputation.

In addition to Clasbey and Hogle's, the street was graced by twenty other saloons, two breweries, and a distillery. These thriving concerns, plus three other breweries and another twenty saloons in the valley made Salt Lake City the undisputed liquor capital of the intermountain west and was ample testimony to the rising influence of the Gentile population of Zion.

This did not mean that the Mormon church approved of or sanctioned the activities. Although the Mormons had yet to embrace the "Word of Wisdom" — the Mormon prohibition against alcohol and tobacco — and even made wine and sold wines and whiskies through the drugstore at Z.C.M.I., they were more concerned with controlling the growing Gentile saloon trade than with their own cottage industries.

In 1871 the city fathers attempted to rid the community of its bars, and perhaps its Gentiles as well, by imposing a $300 per month saloon tax. The measure was opposed and successfully thwarted through a coalition of mining and mercantile interests, headed by the Walker brothers, and the help of federally appointed officials including Governor Woods and Judge McKean. The coalition, which had many of the characteristics of a secret society, was called The Gentile League of Utah.

At the state constitutional convention of 1872, which was held at the City Hall on February 19, the "G.L.U." was thoroughly attacked in the keynote address given by Thomas Fitch. The address was delivered in support of the Mormons' continuing fight for statehood. In a backhanded way the speech complimented General Patrick Connor's anti-Mormon strategy and gave testimony to its partial success.

> The mineral deposits of Utah have attracted a large number of active, restless and adventurous men and with them have come many who are unscrupulous; who are reckless, the hereditary foes of law and order. This class, having found the courts and federal officers arrayed against the Mormons, have placed themselves on the side of courts and officers. Elements ordinarily discordant blend together in the same seething cauldron. There

is a nucleus of reformers, a mass of ruffians, a center of zealots and a circumference of plunderers. The dram shop interest hopes to escape the $300. tax on liquor by sustaining a Judge who would enjoin a collection of the tax. . . . Every interest of industry is affected by this unholy alliance; every right of the citizen is affected by this combination.

Your local magistrates are successfully defied, your local laws are disregarded, your municipal ordinances are trampled into the mire, theft and murder walk through your streets without detection, drunkards howl their orgies in the shadow of your altars, the glare and tumult of the drinking saloons, the glitter of the gambling halls and the painted flaunt of the bawd plying her trade now vex the repose of streets, which beforetime heard no sound to disturb the quiet, except the busy hum of industry, the clatter of trade and the musical tinkle of mountain streams.

There was, of course, another side to the argument. The Gentile miners and merchants saw the municipal authorities as agents of "Polygamic Theocracy." The attempt to impose an exorbitant sin tax on the saloons was but another example of Mormon oppression of the Gentile minority. Federal authority, in the person of Judge James B. McKean (chief justice of the Territorial court), was likely to view any ordinance drafted by the local government as subject to its review. If Gentile opposition were strong enough, Judge McKean would see to it that the law was found defective. These actions in turn infuriated the local officials, who saw Judge McKean's rulings as both federal usurpation of local authority and religious persecution. Both positions had their basis in fact. The last thing that the G.L.U. wanted in 1872 was statehood. Many members were openly advocating the imposition of martial law as being far preferable to what they believed was "theocratic" control.

A petition was gotten up against the admission of Utah to State sovereignty and forwarded to President Grant and Congress. It was signed by about five thousand names. For once the entire anti-Mormon force in the Territory was called into action. . . . It was at this time that President Grant declared to the effect that if Congress did not pass a bill potent enough to overthrow Mormon polygamic theocracy, he would put his troops into Salt Lake City and settle the matter by force.

The most radical element took Grant's threat at face value and set about to force federal intervention. The G.L.U. was a semi-military organization and more than willing to bring the dispute to the point of armed conflict. The eastern press generally assumed that Utah was on the eve of civil war, and Judge Hayden prophesied that "The streets of Salt Lake City would run with blood."

On July 26, 1872, *Salt Lake Tribune* reporter Joseph Salisbury covered a city council meeting with Brigham Young in attendance. The agenda for that evening is unknown, but the headline in the *Tribune* the following morning proclaimed "Brigham on the Warpath." Salisbury's reporting so enraged the city council that when he attended their next meeting on July 30 they demanded a public recantation on pain of expulsion. When the reporter refused to recant, he was banned from the meeting.

News of this "Attack on the freedom of the press" escalated the conflict to a dangerous level. G.L.U. leader "General" George R. Maxwell promised "One hundred armed men" to force the admission of the *Tribune*'s reporter to the next meeting. Maxwell said that, "If any hostile demonstration were made by the Mayor and Council, each of them would immediately be covered by a pair of pistols."

Less radical members of the Gentile opposition managed to dissuade Maxwell and his followers from carrying out this plan, but they could not entirely prevent the G.L.U. from making a show of arms.

On Saturday, August third, the Liberal Party held an outdoor mass meeting to ratify the nomination of George Maxwell, who was challenging Mormon leader George Q. Cannon as delegate to Congress. The street in front of the Salt Lake Hotel was crowded, but not with Liberal Party supporters. The events of the past few days had greatly disturbed the Mormon people.

The Liberal Party may well have believed it represented the legitimate political will of a certain portion of Utah's citizens, but the Mormons saw the party as a bigoted collection of hatemongers bent on religious warfare. "Speaker after speaker attempted in vain to address the indignant people," but all were interrupted with hisses and exclamations. The political meeting quickly degenerated into

an ugly cacophony of epithets and insults as speakers on the platform called the Mormons "Dupes," "Serfs," and "Geese." What
happened next could easily have become another Boston Massacre,
and the *Salt Lake Tribune* reported the affair accordingly:

> Now came business for the "G.L.U.'s" They sprang to the
> front. They were headed by ex-city Marshall Ore.
> "Follow me G.L.U.'s" he cried to his armed troops.
> They dashed after him, revolvers in hand, and formed a half
> circle in front of the stand. Flourishing their weapons, they
> awed back the people, each waiting eagerly for the command to
> fire into the crowd.
> For the anxious space of five minutes, it was almost certain
> that Judge Hayden's prophecy would be fulfilled that night and
> the streets of Salt Lake would run with blood.
> This writer saw their weapons brandished above the heads
> of their foremost men, gleaming in the flickering light of the
> lamps and heard the excited cries of the men eager for the word
> to fire.

It was a close thing, but the order never came, and gradually
the ugly confrontation was brought to a close. The "political"
meeting adjourned to the Liberal Institute.

On the Monday following, the *Tribune* headed an editorial with
the banner "Let us have troops today": "The conduct of the Police
on Saturday evening was such that not the slightest dependence can
be placed on either their willingness or ability to preserve the
peace."

On October 12 the Liberal Party held another "open air mass
meeting," this one in front of the Walker House. *Tribune* reporter
Joseph Salisbury covered the event:

> During the day it had been whispered around that an orga-
> nization had been effected and that prominent men of the
> City authorities would be watched by armed members of the
> G.L.U.'s. I subsequently learned that these were under the con-
> trol of the Chairman and that at his signal the body was to
> move en masse. I soon discovered that the program was well
> arranged, and saw men known to me as "G.L.U.'s" moving in
> the crowd in twos, with their hands upon their pistols, threaten-
> ing those who dared utter the slightest murmur at the wanton
> denunciations against the Mormon leaders.

I subsequently learned from conversations among the radicals, that had there been any counter demonstration, The G.L.U.'s at a given signal would have fallen back to the sidewalk, in front of the Walker House and that a volley from them and from others stationed in the windows above would have fulfilled the prophecy of U.S. Attorney Baskins uttered at the Liberal Institute in August "We shall have a hundred coffins at our next meeting."

Many of the men in the crowd both expected and invited bloodshed, but the chairman, Associate Justice Strickland, in the words of the reporter:

> . . . exposed the movement prematurely when at the first sound of an opposing voice he arose and proclaimed: "The first man who interrupts this meeting I will order shot." The radicals were extremely dissatisfied at the indiscretion of their chairman, who should have given the signal at the opportune moment, instead of an untimely warning.

The conflict between the Mormons and the Gentiles in the seventies and eighties was pervasive, continuous, and at times violent. That open warfare was averted in 1872 verges on the miraculous. The end result of this war of words was that for most of the next two decades Salt Lake City was "wide open." This was the state of affairs when Clasbey and Hogle acquired the lease to No. 90 South East Temple.

Clasbey and Hogle's Saloon

No. 90 South East Temple Street was originally a two-story wood frame structure. It was located on the west side of the street directly north and adjacent to the Walker Brothers' Bank. Walker Bank, a large brown stone building, had been a city landmark since its construction in 1857. No. 90 had most recently housed Alexander Toponce's Mammoth Boot & Leather Shop. True to its name, photographs taken in 1871 show the building sporting an enormous riding boot, perhaps ten feet tall. Directly north was a gunsmith and then a saddlery. The gunsmith mounted a sign which could have been fashioned by the same person who had created the boot, a giant flintlock rifle stretched more than twenty feet over the street.

When Clasbey and Hogle leased the property from Hugh Anderson, the first thing to go was Toponce's giant boot. Whether this action inspired their immediate neighbors can not be said with any certainty, but the giant rifle vanishes from photos about the same time. No giant bottles appeared over Clasbey and Hogle's Saloon. In the more than forty years of its operation as a saloon, not a single sign was ever erected on the building to advertise the establishment's function or character.

James Hogle brought to the partnership more than the Anheuser Beer franchise. In addition to years of experience in the liquor trade, he had some other assets: a number of Idaho mining stocks, a few silent partnerships with men he had grubstaked, and a good mind for business. In the coming months and years he was to turn these minor assets into moneymakers.

James had something else which was to prove crucial to the early success of Clasbey and Hogle's Saloon — a ready clientele. Many of the Leesburg miners had already made their way to Salt Lake, and as the Leesburg Stampede went slowly bust, many more would follow. Others who had known James in Helena and Virginia City were now located in the Mormon capital.

In addition, Salt Lake City was a major supply point for the entire intermountain mining industry. Hotels were always filled with mining men on business trips and, as Brigham Young discouraged his followers from mining, the men who worked the mines tended to be anything but abstemious. A saloon keeper with strong ties to the intermountain mining population had an edge over the competition.

To work behind the bar, Clasbey and Hogle hired an Irishman named John Patrick Quillen. Quillen had been in a gunfight down in Silver Reef, Utah, and was seeking more tranquil surroundings. He had been recommended by Enos A. Wall, so Hogle hired him on the spot. Quillen would retain his position as the bartender at the Main Street saloon for the next forty years.

James Hogle was well liked, particularly by the Irish miners, and his reputation as a generous and genial public man soon became well known throughout the Territory. To further this reputation of generosity and to assist in spreading the word of their resort, Clasbey and Hogle had minted a large number of saloon tokens. The face of the coins said simply: "Clasbey & Hogle, Salt Lake," and the reverse proclaimed their worth: "Good for A drink." The size of the "A" in the inscription clearly implied one to a customer.

The trade tokens, usually valued at twelve and a half cents each, were given as change for larger denominations of currency. The coinage was common tender in the nineteenth century and could be traded in at the bank for U.S. currency. The coins, one eighth of a dollar, were known as bits. Two bits, of course, was a quarter.

But Clasbey and Hogle used their coins in a unique way. Many were freely distributed in the surrounding mining camps of Bingham, Park City, Eureka, and Alta. Others were sent north to Idaho and Montana. The logic behind the giveaway was inescapable: the saloon where a miner began his drinking was very likely to be the saloon where he finished it, presumably spending in the interim some generous tokens of his own.

On the morning of November 11, 1876, the *Salt Lake Tribune* published an ad which displayed another coin, one given by the U.S. Centennial Commission at the World's Fair that was just ending in Philadelphia. In "City Notes," the *Tribune* added the following bit of advertising:

THE CELEBRATED ST. LOUIS BEER

We print this morning facsimiles
of the medals awarded to E.
Anheuser & Co. of Saint Louis
for the best beer exhibited at
the American Centennial. This beverage
now has a reputation extending from
the Atlantic to the Pacific and is
spoken of in the highest terms by
everybody. Messrs. Clasbey and
Hogle are agents in this territory.

Being sole agents for the beer that has just been named the best at the World's Fair was perhaps a bit of Irish luck, but the enterprising Clasbey and Hogle were to make the most of it. For the next three months the medallions were reproduced daily in the *Tribune*, often on the front page.

Messrs. Clasbey and Hogle may not have needed the giant liquor bottle over their door to attract customers. The "Best in the World" was a slogan that would make Anheuser the number-one American brewery for a century to come.

Business was good enough that the partners quickly added a chophouse and restaurant to the back of the building. This brick addition was built behind the original structure and met No. 90 at a right angle. The entrance was still on Main Street. An oak bar ran the length of the saloon until it met the open restaurant area to the rear. The result was a large L-shaped room.

However successful the retail operation may have been, the purpose of a distributorship was to distribute, and it was clearly in the wholesale liquor trade that the greatest profits were to be had. On February 13, 1877, a long article appeared in the *Salt Lake Tribune*, reprinted from the *St. Louis Republic*, which related that Anheuser & Co. had just contracted for the construction of: "Fifty refrigerator cars, built of rubber, and of superior design, for the purpose of supplying their customers throughout the United States. By means of these cars the celebrated beer is kept of uniform temperature and reaches its destination in as cool and fine condition as on the day it is taken from their great vaults."

The "article" went on to describe how Anheuser & Co. had grown in a few short years from a small brewery to one of the largest in the country: the enormous expansion of the St. Louis facility since the World's Fair, its modern machinery, and the "Special 40 car fast beer trains which rush the product across the country." The story closed with "This celebrated beer can always be had at Clasbey and Hogle's on main street. These gentlemen are agents for Salt Lake."

During the third week of March 1876, large ads appeared in the *Tribune* inviting the general public to attend a "Grand St. Patrick's Day Ball" at the Salt Lake Theatre. The program was billed as a benefit for Holy Cross Hospital. The "Committee on invitations" included both full-fledged and honorary Irishmen, J. T. Clasbey, James Hogle, S. S. Walker, R. C. Chambers, and Samuel Auerbach.

During 1876 and '77 Clasbey and Hogle's advertised frequently in the Gentile paper. On St. Patrick's Day 1877, yet another inducement appeared, directed not only at the customers of Clasbey and Hogle's but at the other saloon operators in the Valley as well:

Clasbey and Hogle's Saloon

The proprietors have determined to meet the times by making a reduction in the price of liquors, etc. by the drink to 12 cents! In doing this they guarantee to their customers the same choice quality of goods heretofore sold by them. The celebrated Anheuser beer delivered to any part of the city at $3.50 a dozen, $19.00 a barrel, or in lots of ten barrels at $18.50. The chop house will continue to run the same style of business with every attention paid to the requirements of guests. Hot lunch from 12:00 to 2:00.

An affordable and joyous St. Patrick's Day was, presumably, had by all.

How much attention was paid to the customers of the chop house is unknown. But the food itself, apparently, left something to be desired. The customers of Clasbey and Hogle's Saloon had to be content with "attention" until late 1879, when the proprietors worked out an arrangement with a new chef. The ads for the restaurant at Clasbey and Hogle's are suspiciously similar to ads for Guiraud and Lambrech's Star Restaurant in Denver and the Star Restaurant in Helena. Hogle had also had restaurants in connection with his establishments in Salmon and Leesburg.

On October 18, 1879, the *Tribune* printed the following:

This morning a new restaurant opened under the management of Mr. John Gallagher in the rear of Clasbey and Hogle's Saloon. Mr. Gallagher's cuisine is known in Zion as one of the best quality, and it is safe to say he will receive a liberal patronage. His accommodations are first class in every respect. Some very tasty private compartments are set off from the main room and everything has been arranged with faithful regard for convenience and comfort. Give him a call this noon.

What the "Private compartments" tasted like is unknown.

Gunplay on East Temple

Salt Lake City has a reputation as fairly quiet place. But latter-day residents would have a hard time recognizing the "Great Salt Lake City" of the mid-1870's. In addition to the more than sixty saloons and liquor stores, there were numerous gambling houses and other resorts of organized vice. Side arms were a common sight and often got used. The Salt Lake City police table for 1876 lists 197 arrests for "Drunken disorderly conduct," 46 arrests for prostitution, 106 arrests for criminal assault, and 2 arrests for murder.

Typical of the assaults was a gunfight which took place in front of Clasbey and Hogle's on the morning of October 17, 1877. The *Deseret News* reporter described the disturbance this way:

Pistols this Time — Something of a sensation was created on East Temple Street, about eleven o'clock today, by Major James H. Nounnan and Mr. Jeremiah M. Richardson, each trying to send the other to the world beyond by perforating each other with bullets.

Mr. Richardson was on the sidewalk in front of Siegal Brothers' clothing store, while Major Nounnan was in front of Clasbey and Hogle's saloon. Each party claims that the other fired first. From what we can learn from parties who were near the scene of the shooting, it appears that Mr. Richardson dodged behind Mr. Robert Dye Jr. (the barber) fired and then sprang into Siegel Brothers' doorway, while the Major fired and retreated toward the entrance of the saloon already named, where more shots were exchanged.

Major Nounnan was unhurt but Mr. Richardson received a painful flesh wound in the forearm. Mr. Dye, who was an entirely disinterested party, was slightly injured and narrowly escaped being dangerously, if not fatally wounded. One bullet struck his suspender buckle, made an indentation in it, glanced around and passed through his vest, without as much as inflicting a scratch on his body. Another ball struck his ear cutting it, and another the temple near the eye slightly injuring it. Both parties were arrested and taken to the City Jail and subsequently released on bail until an examination could be had.

We refrain from commenting on the affair of this morning, the facts not having yet been elucidated at a regular investigation.

Great Salt Lake City during the 1870's was still very much a frontier town, and while no one would claim that it rivaled places like Dodge City or Tombstone for lawlessness, it was not immune to the problems that beset other places on the frontier. The spires of the Mormon Temple were not yet in place in 1877. That familiar silhouette was growing daily, however, and its preeminence would eventually overshadow and obscure much of the flavor of nineteenth-century Salt Lake.

Newspaper advertisement for Clasbey and Hogle's establishment in Salt Lake City.

CHAPTER EIGHT

Expansion & Diversification

THE SUCCESS OF CLASBEY AND HOGLE'S SALOON in Salt Lake City was the result of clever marketing, sound business practice, and the fortuitous growth of the Anheuser Beer franchise. Other men might have been content to rest on the comfortable earnings of the saloon and the wholesale distributorship, but not James Hogle or his partner. What worked in Salt Lake could work elsewhere. If there was a profit to be had in operating one saloon, there could be a greater profit in operating two, or even three. Expansion of the infant saloon business was risky, but as any good gambler knows, those who play the game too safe are as likely to lose as those who play the long shots. The cards held by Clasbey and Hogle were good, and so in 1877, six years after he had left, James Hogle returned to the Idaho diggings.

RETURN TO THE DIGGINGS

By '77, the fabulous Leesburg Stampede was over. Most of the placer deposits had been washed from the sand bars and little bluffs along Napias and Panther creeks. The sluices, mine dredges, and high-powered hydraulic hoses which had followed the early gold panners had extracted an enormous quantity of gold from the creek beds and surrounding hillsides, but not without cost. The soil, stripped of its minerals, was incapable of growing anything; more than 400 miles of sluice ditches rutted the Leesburg Basin; much of the valley floor was a barren, bleached-out moonscape of eroded gullies and mounds of discarded tailings. Wells Fargo and other freighters had shipped out the gold: sixteen million dollars' worth between 1868 and 1877.

Fifty miles due south of Leesburg, however, a new town was being constructed in Round Valley near the junction of the Salmon River and a creek named for one of the Leesburg pioneers who had first worked it, Alvah P. Challis. This community was thriving on the recent discovery of rich veins of gold in the nearby Salmon and Lost River Mountains.

Challis, Idaho, was officially incorporated on August 29, 1877, but it already had several profitable businesses, including a freight office and several boarding houses. It was here that Clasbey and Hogle opened their second saloon.

Following the formula that had worked so well in Salt Lake City, saloon tokens "Good for A drink," bearing the inscription: "Clasbey & Hogle, Challis, Idaho," were minted and distributed in the surrounding camps. Newspaper stories touting the "Famous St. Louis Beer" produced by Anheuser and Co. were placed in the Salmon and Idaho City papers.

The customers were there too. Miners and merchants who had followed the gold trail from Pikes Peak to Alder Gulch, from Alder Gulch to Napias Creek, were on the move again. In addition to Alva P. Challis, Bat Doodey and Lorenzo Falls had pushed on to the new strikes, as had Eli Minert, who opened a freight line from Corinne, Utah. Mrs. Hagenbarth — who had saved James Hogle's life following the Loon Creek affair — now a widow, was in Challis with her son Frank. There were many others. If the Leesburg pioneers were interested in holding a convivial reunion, James Hogle and his partner were more than willing to host the party.

To operate the Challis saloon James hired two unlikely young men fresh from school in the east. They had come west the previous year hoping to make their fortunes scooping buckets of gold from the fabled creeks of the latest El Dorado; instead they found themselves mucking for a dollar-fifty a day. James would tutor these young students in successful gold panning, a lesson he had learned through years of experience and was more than willing to pass on to his two youngest brothers.

Patrick Albert Gilmore and Michael Henry Gilmore were twins. The youngest children of Patrick Gilmore and Ellen Tammary, they

had been only two years old when James left West Middleport, Illinois, to join the Pikes Peak gold rush.

While living in Idaho, Patrick Albert Gilmore was known as Albert Hogle and Michael Henry Gilmore became Henry Hogle. The new names were taken out of deference to their older brothers and also out of necessity as there was a very strong family resemblance. If they were going to work for brother Jim they had better forget the name of Gilmore, and for a time they did.

The Challis saloon, as anticipated, was a success. But some miles into the mountains a new town named Bonanza was booming on the profits of three major discoveries, the Badger Lode Mine, located by Lorenzo Falls, the Charles Dickens Mine, and the Custer Mine, named for the ill-fated general whose death at the Battle of the Little Big Horn was still a lively topic of debate in the papers.

George Hearst, father of William Randolph Hearst, had purchased the Custer Mine and was planning on opening a large mill to process the ore. But Bonanza was thirty-five miles over tortuous pack trail from Challis. A road would have to be constructed to bring mill machinery to the site.

Hearst hired Alexander Toponce to survey the trail from Challis to Bonanza. It was claimed that such a road would cost hundreds of thousands of dollars, but Toponce believed it could be done for a lot less. He approached James Hogle and two other Salt Lake businessmen, J. E. Dooley and Fred Myers, and asked them to help underwrite the construction. The other investors were Toponce himself and Hogle's old friend Fred Phillips of Salmon, Idaho. These five men received a charter from the Idaho Legislature to construct and operate the thirty-five-mile stretch as a private toll road. During the more than two years it took to build, James frequently journeyed to Challis to look after his investment.

The road was completed on the first of January 1880. Although the two communities were only thirty-five miles apart, the terrain

Twins Michael Henry Gilmore and Patrick Albert Gilmore in photos taken when they went west to prospect and later to work in the Hogle-owned saloons in Challis and Bonanza, Idaho. As with other members of the family, they assumed the name Hogle upon leaving Illinois in 1876.

was some of the most rugged in the Territory. The mountain passes
linking Challis with the new strikes on the Yankee Fork were well
over 9,000 feet, and freight wagons carrying supplies and equipment over the road required two to five spans of mules. The "short
haul" from Challis to Bonanza was usually a four-day ordeal. The
partners charged five dollars for each wagon and fifty cents for each
additional span of animals on a rig.

With James's brothers on hand to keep tabs on things, Clasbey
and Hogle decided to expand into the neighboring community.
Albert would stay in Challis and Henry would go to Bonanza.

On May 27, 1879, Clasbey and Hogle purchased from a David
Dorsey "All of a certain lot and buildings on main street in the City
of Bonanza, Idaho Territory." The price was one thousand dollars.
Shortly thereafter ads appeared in the *Yankee Fork Herald*, the
Bonanza newspaper, proclaiming triumphantly: "We are Here,
Clasbey and Hogle saloon." "Good for you" must have been the
reply, although the boom camp already had a number of saloons —
and one of them had a billiard table, an extravagant item for a place
as remote as Bonanza.

The holders of the "Celebrated St. Louis Beer" franchise were
not to be outdone by the competition, however, even if it meant
freighting a thousand-pound slab of Italian slate three hundred
miles across the wilderness. On October 18, 1879, the *Herald* could
report: "Clasbey and Hogle received a billiard table last week from
Salt Lake. There are now two tables in town and the balls of both
are kept flying day and night."

Challis and Bonanza flourished in 1879, and the Clasbey and
Hogle saloon chain shared in the general prosperity. More of the
old Leesburg acquaintances were showing up every day. On July
24, 1879, the *Herald* reported in "Challis briefs" that John David
Wood "will put up a fine new store adjoining Clasbey and Hogle's
Saloon. The lumber is already on the site."

John Wood, who had known James Hogle in Alder Gulch,
Helena, and Leesburg, would marry the Widow Hagenbarth in
1883. The partnership he would form with his stepson Frank would
eventually become one of the largest livestock baronies in the entire

west, with vast holdings from Montana to Mexico. But for the moment he was content to operate the Challis general store.

The presence of his young brothers did not relieve James Hogle of his managerial responsibilities in Idaho. Over the next ten years he would make frequent and extended business trips to the distant saloons. He also kept up his interest in mining by grubstaking prospectors and investing in mining stocks. On November 17, 1880, he and James Clasbey acquired from John Spalding an undivided ninth interest in the Beardsley Mine near Salmon. While not a major producer, the Beardsley was a good mine and returned a reasonable profit. The toll road had also paid for itself and was beginning to return dividends to the shareholders.

On September 21, 1881, James Hogle wrote Ida a short note from Challis. The letter is rich in phonetic spellings and colloquial expressions and gives a good feeling for the actual speech of the Irish-born immigrant whose only formal schooling had been from the French-speaking nuns in Quebec. The note reveals the author as a somewhat sentimental man with very practical concerns.

Challis, Idaho, Sept. 25th 1881

My dear wife

I ricived yours of the 22 and was very glad to huar from you but very sory that you was sick I told dock Young that I wanted him tu tak the calf too his pasture I want him too gird too the Bull that will hav tu drive the old cow with hur that is the only way too git hir that — I told him that hu could youse the wagon a round town it wont hurt it Times are very dull now I think times will be very good next month I am a gowing over too Beraugh too morro & try too colect sum money Try & get the house furnished As soon as posibille I will scent yers money in a few days My lov to all Kiss Jimmey for me/My lov to father I hop yer bitir It suams that every time I leav you must git sick I will tak you with me huarafter

I will close by saying good By

God Bless you all

Your Loving Hub, Jas. Hogle

Her "Loving Hub's" educational deficiencies must have been something of an embarrassment to Ida, because over the next twenty years she took it upon herself to correct them. But even in the rough phonetic letter there is much to admire as James's qualities come through clearly: affection, love, concern for the health and well-being of his family, generosity, respect for his father, and devotion to his son. Whatever grammatical deficiencies James Hogle may have had at the time, there is no question that he was a good man living a full life.

GROWING PAINS

Salt Lake City in the late 1870's and early 1880's was a town suffering from an "identity crisis." John D. Lee, the only man to be successfully tried and convicted for the Mountain Meadows Massacre, was executed on March 23, 1877, giving the Mormons another martyr and the Gentile authorities a dramatic, if shallow, victory. The death of Brigham Young on August 29, 1877, left a great void in the councils of church leadership. Judge McKean, the fiercely anti-Mormon leader of the Gentiles, died on January 15, 1879.

For a time the confrontation abated. But beneath the surface the warring tribes were as implacable as ever, and by 1880 sectarian tensions, as revealed in the pages of the Mormon *Deseret News* and the Gentile *Salt Lake Tribune*, were at an all-time high.

The entire political temper of the city was in a state of flux. The ever-growing Gentile population, the ongoing spectacle of polygamists' arrests, and the interference of federal courts with local jurisdiction continued to fuel the Mormons' resentment for all outsiders.

The Territory's unique social structure (Them and Us) made normal political activity impossible. The national Democratic and Republican parties were helpless and virtually inoperative as Utah voters opted for People's Party or Liberal Party candidates.

The city was going through a time of change, and no one knew where the changes were leading. Certainly it had already undergone changes which would not have been anticipated at its founding. Established as the Mormons' mountain stronghold against the outside world, Salt Lake City was now the mercantile capital of the intermountain west and, ironically, the Territory's principal connection with the rest of the nation.

Photographs from the early 1880's of Second South and Main streets, looking northwest. Courtesy Utah State Historical Society.

Even the names of the streets were changing. Within two years of Brigham's death, South Temple was known as "Brigham Street," and East Temple Street became Main Street. A new numbering system was also introduced. The saloon, which had been listed as No. 90 South East Temple, was now No. 174 South Main. Though this number would stick, many of the merchants struggled with a system that put numbers from 100 to 150 on the east side of the street and numbers from 151 to 199 on the west. This experiment was short-lived, but the city's sign painters, though shunned by Messrs. Clasbey and Hogle, could look forward to years of steady work.

Other more startling transformations were just around the corner. The electric light was first demonstrated to astounded Salt Lakers in 1880, and the first electric streetcars would spark and jingle down city streets by mid-decade. Change was in the air, and with it came anxiety, even fear. The city was, in fact, ripe for hysteria and anything might set it off. When it finally came, both Mr. Clasbey and Mr. Hogle were uniquely situated to witness some of the madness at first hand.

A PARTNERSHIP DISSOLVED

The partnership of James Clasbey and James Hogle lasted for eight years. From the beginning it had been a solid business relationship. James Clasbey entered the saloon trade because he saw an opportunity, and he left it for the same reason.

Throughout his career James Hogle stayed very close to the businesses he knew best, saloons, mining, and real estate. James Clasbey, on the other hand, went from venture to venture with little regard for consistency. He simply couldn't pass up a chance to try something else, and in the fall of 1881 he decided to become a druggist. The opportunity arrived in the person of A. C. Smith, Z.C.M.I.'s druggist and former Pikes Peaker, who was now interested in setting up his own shop. As with Mr. Read and James Hogle, Clasbey would provide much of the starting capital, and Smith would provide the expertise. The pending dissolution of the partnership did not mean that Clasbey was moving out. Rather, A. C. Smith was moving in.

The arrangement for the lease of the saloon property was between Messrs. Clasbey and Hogle and Hugh Anderson. If the partnership was breaking up, the lease with Mr. Anderson was still intact, and the building was to be shared, fifty-fifty.

In the late fall of 1881 Owen Hogle arrived in Salt Lake to take up permanent residence. He had done very well for himself in the years since the brothers had been together in Helena, and James naturally turned to him for help.

On January 3, 1882, James and Ida borrowed the sum of $5,190 from Owen. With this loan James bought out Clasbey's interest in the Main Street saloon, and the remodeling of the property to accommodate a new multi-purpose facility was started. The drugstore half was ready first. In February of 1882 the following ad appeared in the *Salt Lake Tribune*:

> A. C. Smith, for many years with Z.C.M.I., will be pleased to see his old friends at 179 So. Main, 1 door north of Walker Bros. Bank.
>
> Smith's Drugs
> Jas Clasbey Part.

It wasn't until May 9 that the *Tribune* could report on the remodeling of the saloon that "Jimmy Hogle will make more improvements in the way of a bar, where all the hungry and thirsty can get supplied as they now do at Clasbey and Hogle's."

The "improvements" to the bar must have been extensive. Photographs taken in 1883 show a two-story brick building where the old frame structure had stood. The new building had two doors instead of one; the northernmost (No. 174) had a hand railing, indicating that the saloon was now a walk-down.

Signs for Smith's Drug and Hugh Anderson Insurance are prominent on the building, but, in keeping with the previous establishment's policy, the saloon remained discreet. The era of Clasbey and Hogle was over. James Hogle was on his own.

A Tragic Eruption

If A. C. Smith wanted to have a quiet little drugstore, he should have stayed at Z.C.M.I. The corner at Second South was always a place of exciting goings-on, and never more so than on the afternoon of August 24, 1883.

It was one minute past one o'clock P.M. Smith and Clasbey were engaged in dispensing their medicines when a considerable commotion arose on the sidewalk in front of their establishment. Before they could determine the exact cause of the disturbance, a quick succession of gunshots rang out. Immediately following this, City Marshal Andrew Burt entered the drugstore. Officer Burt was a familiar figure, well liked by everyone on the street. No sooner had he entered than he dropped unconscious to the floor behind the prescription case. Mr. Smith tried to revive the officer and a doctor was sent for, but the marshal was beyond reviving.

Officer Burt's assassin, Sam J. Harvey, had been quickly subdued by city watermaster Charles H. Wilkins, who sustained in the fray an ugly flesh wound in his left arm near the elbow. He was assisted in disarming Harvey by Homer J. Stone and a Mr. Benjamin. Police officers arrived shortly afterward and took Mr. Harvey off to City Hall.

By this time rumors had reached City Hall that Marshal Burt was either dead or dying. The prisoner was searched, knocked down by Burt's fellow officers, beaten with billy clubs and brass knuckles, and "pummelled and kicked so that when he was lifted up some minutes afterwards, he presented a fearful sight."

Harvey's ordeal was far from over. The huge crowd which had gathered in front of Smith's drugstore and Hogle's saloon was getting uglier by the minute. When word finally reached the street that Officer Burt was dead, the mob went berserk. Rushing the two blocks to City Hall, they began shouting "Bring the prisoner out!" The prisoner was at this unfortunate moment being transferred to the city jail. The three officers in the transfer detail were immediately relieved of their charge. Harvey was again knocked to the ground, kicked, and savagely beaten. The *Salt Lake Tribune* recounted what happened next:

> Numerous straps were jerked from the harnesses of teams standing in front of City Hall so that there was no lack of instruments to hang him. The Call for "a Rope" was kept up and excited men were yelling and cursing while all the time the kicking and

beating was kept up. The efforts of the man to get away and the surging of the crowd were carrying him eastward in the jail lot, and he fell almost prostrated some fifty feet from the jail door. By this time a long rope had been brought to the spot and was placed around his neck. The rope was stretched out and taken by the excited crowd. The man was then dragged over 100 feet to the stable at the west end of the jail, and the rope being thrown over the beam, he was drawn up and hung until dead.

Some one who was careful as to look at his watch at the time of the shooting and again when the man was hoisted up found that only 25 minutes time was required to accomplish it all.

The violent death of Sam Harvey, a black man, was sparked by more than revenge for Officer Burt. The entire period of Reconstruction following the Civil War was marked by racism, hatred, bigotry, and fear. No section of the country was immune to the ugliness or spared its consequences.

Hideous as this incident was, it was not the only lynching in Utah that week. The following day another mob commandeered a train in Park City and took it to Coalville where they released one Black Jack Murphy, a white man charged with the murder of a popular Park City miner by the name of Brennan. Murphy was hanged from a telegraph pole before the train returned to the Park City yards.

The *Salt Lake Tribune* editorialized that this latter lynching was the more morally reprehensible because the stealing of a train implied "the existence of a matured plan rather than a sudden impulse and was less defensible than the sudden fury of the mob in this city on Saturday last." This did not mean that the *Tribune* condoned or sanctioned the lynching of Harvey, nor did the editorial staff of the Gentile daily pass up the opportunity to attack the municipal authorities for their role. Since the local government was controlled by the church, the editorial was a thinly veiled attempt to place the blame for the outrage at the door of the Mormons.

This, we must remember, was perpetrated in a community of perhaps 25,000, where all the courts are in full force, and it was accomplished with the direct assistance of the officers who are the sworn conservators of the peace. It was done under the noonday sun and in the shadow of the Temple of the Saints.

We do not believe that there has been a parallel to the case in American history where the policemen who had the prisoner in charge first beat the accused into insensibility and then turned him over to the mob.

This is not a question between Mormon and Gentile, it is one in which the good name of our City is at stake. Had the same thing happened in the office of the U.S. Marshal, we would demand the marshal's instant dismissal, and that of all of his deputies.

Now, in the name of the law, which yesterday was so cowardly insulted by officers sworn to uphold it, we call upon the city authorities to vindicate their claim, and the claim of their people, that they are a law abiding people and that they stand ready to punish unfaithfulness on the part of those in whom they repose official trusts.

Accusation and counter-accusation was the norm in the conflict between Mormon and Gentile in the 1880's, and the divisiveness of that conflict soured life in Salt Lake City for much of the decade.

James and Owen Hogle would each play a role in the reconciliation of the two communities. Without their efforts the "Whisky Street Wars" might have continued into the next century and the future of the city itself might have been jeopardized.

CHAPTER NINE

Hogle Brothers,' 1883–1890

OWEN HOGLE MUST HAVE ENJOYED HIS WORK. This is not to say that he led an easy life. His calling required considerable talent, years of study, continuous practice, hard work, and sometimes danger. If there was any truth to the folklore of his trade, he needed the insight of a psychiatrist, the mental prowess of a mathematician, a bookkeeper's capacity for detail, the integrity of a confessor, and the hands of a magician — for Owen Hogle was a professional gambler.

The occupation was steeped in tradition and regulated by the strictest of professional codes. The man who was anything less than scrupulously honest couldn't hope to succeed, for the stock in trade of gambling was the promise, and promises were based on mutual trust. The rewards for the dishonest gambler were established by tradition as well: two slugs from a pearl-handled, nickel-plated, .38 caliber derringer at point-blank range. Crooked gamblers tended to have short careers.

The professional gambler has to know a great deal about the mathematical sciences. Dice, roulette, keno, and slot machines are not so much "games of chance" as they are exercises in the laws of probability. Luck has little or nothing to do with it; the very laws of nature favor the house. While luck may be a nice thing to have, strength, skill, technique, and strategy are more consistent. So billiards, snooker, darts, even horseshoes, were often preferred in the nineteenth century to the games of chance. For all the attention given to the game of poker, the western gambler had to be skilled in card games like cribbage, gin, and bridge. In the mining camps of the intermountain west, a favorite game was a peculiar form of whist called "solo" or "slough" (sluff).

But more than all the games of skill he might play himself, the professional gambler was a cultivated and keen observer of the skills of others. He had to be able to assess the odds on any of a number of events, and this required accurate information, considerable research, and clear thinking. Then as now, the principal betting interests were in sporting events, horses, and politics. But people were likely to bet on anything — bicycle races, foot races, boxing matches, baseball and football games, elections, and weather, even the performance of mining stocks. The successful gambler had to be something of a wizard at accurately compiling and analyzing information.

From his father Patrick Gilmore, who had spent much of his life as a stagecoach driver and teamster, Owen had acquired a love of horses. He was an excellent judge of horseflesh, and it is little wonder that he spent much of his time around the many western race tracks. In his father's native Ireland, where horse racing remains one of the principal industries, the bookie is an honored and respected member of the community. It was much the same in the American west, and Owen Hogle was the consummate bookie. It was probably no small advantage that the best horses in the country were owned by a close friend of the Hogles, another Irishman, Marcus Daly. Daly's Anaconda Mine in Butte had made him one of the richest men in the country, and he put much of his fortune into breeding race horses and building race tracks. Owen was well known at tracks throughout the west.

It was the job of the bookie to act as an agent or broker between people wishing to make bets. For this service he charged either a nominal fee or commission to the winner or a viggorish, a fixed percentage of the winner's take. He did not ordinarily participate in the betting himself, although he usually established the odds or the line on the contest in question, which made him a "line broker." In order to put the individual bettors in touch with one another, a loose network of bookies was established based on a system of shared commissions. Because of their rabid interest in sporting events, members of this association were frequently referred to in the press of the day as "Members of the Sporting Fraternity" or simply "Sportsmen."

Original drawing by Jack Goodman (1988) of Hogle Brothers' saloon, as it appeared in the 1890's.

Into this great mix of skills and interests, Owen added those of the stock broker. The stock market of the 1880's was highly speculative, and trading in western mining stocks had much in common with the slough tables. There were no two ways about it, speculating was gambling, and the principles that applied to one often applied to the other. The bookie was effectively a broker, investments and venture capital another name for bets, mining stocks just one more game to be mastered. Owen Hogle's special talents, knowledge, and expertise had wide application and were useful in many areas of endeavor — business, investment management and, on at least one occasion, the law.

Owen was a dapper gentleman who might easily have been mistaken for a banker with his vested tweed suit, derby hat, gold watch chain and fob, and golden-handled cane, but there was another

item he always wore which hinted at his slightly gilt-edged tastes —
a large ruby stick pin he wore in his jacket lapel.

In an occupation where just breaking even is considered exceptional, Owen Hogle flourished. By any estimation his success was
nothing short of phenomenal. By the time he had moved permanently to Salt Lake City in 1881, he had already amassed a considerable fortune — enough to be able to lend James the money to
buy out Clasbey's interest in the Main Street saloon.

The Resort

Owen Hogle was a traveling man, and his decision to settle
in Salt Lake City did not affect his wanderlust; he simply needed
a base for his far-flung operations. He wasn't, in the normal sense,
"settling down," although he did take on at this time the added
responsibility of supporting a wife. Owen married Jessie L. (her
maiden name is unknown) in Oakland, California, on August 8,
1883. There would be no offspring from this seventeen-year union.

In the coming years Owen would travel a great deal, to Idaho,
Montana, San Francisco, and St. Louis — hub of the river boat
trade, Mecca for professional card players. Owen's business trips
were usually successful. Lena Wilson, who knew Owen late in the
century, remembered that he would frequently return to Salt Lake
with large amounts of money and jewelry. In the spring of 1883,
for the considerable sum of $15,426.35 in cash, Owen became
James's full partner in the saloon business. Clasbey's remaining
interest in the Idaho saloons and the cellar stock was purchased
and Hogle Brothers' was born.

Clasbey in turn now had some new working capital, and he put
it to good use by returning to the hardware business, this time in
partnership with a man named A. J. Lowe. This was the most successful and lasting of Mr. Clasbey's many business associations. The
Lowe and Clasbey Hardware Company would eventually become
The Salt Lake Hardware Company and James T. Clasbey would
be its president.

And so it went — the economy was being fueled and the city
gaining new industry from the earnings of the race track and slough

table. (This link in the economic life of the community was something which was certainly not anticipated by the city's founders.) With the addition of a gambling room, Hogle Brothers' quickly became "Salt Lake's most popular resort." Mr. Clasbey's younger brother "Juel" was hired as an assistant bartender for Mr. Quillen. (For a time Juel lived in the Wasatch Building, where Owen and Jessie were keeping house.)

In 1884 tobacconist M. C. Phillips installed a small shop in the front of the saloon and offered a wide variety of imported tobaccos and specialty blends. In the nineteenth century "tobacco" meant pipes and cigars. Pre-cut packaged cigarettes of the modern variety were not introduced in the United States until after the turn of the century and did not gain acceptance in the intermountain west until after the First World War. The specialty tobacco shop became known throughout the west, and mining magnates had their own private aromatic blends prepared and kept on file at Hogle Brothers.' The sweet aromas that floated from the open doorway onto Main Street in the summer of 1883 were the most alluring in town.

Shortly after the partnership was formed, Owen Hogle, former musician of the 25th Illinois Regimental Band, purchased for the new resort a Webber upright piano (serial number 303814). It may be assumed that the ragtime tinkle which enlivened the atmosphere of the establishment at 174 South Main Street was supplied by Owen himself.

Hogle Brothers' was not a run-of-the-mill western barroom. In fact and reputation, the establishment was without question Salt Lake City's finest saloon. In addition to the old whiskies, imported wines, sherries, brandies, aperitifs, liqueurs, and French Champagne featured in the bar, the restaurant in the rear of the building offered luncheon and dinner guests the finest in continental cuisine.

In the nineteenth century the word "saloon" was synonymous with gambling. As James Hogle's old friend Col. George Shoup pointed out in his memoirs, "Any reference to saloons also implies gambling houses, as gambling was the main diversion of the male population."

Owen Hogle kept his gambling room on the second floor above the saloon and restaurant. But it was not the typical western gambling hall or casino, filled with pinwheels, dice tables, and the like. The gambling room at Hogle Brothers' was a well-appointed card room with green felt tables and comfortable chairs, where influential mining men and Gentile merchants might invest in a quiet hand of slough, place a bet, or discuss with the proprietor his special area of expertise, horses.

Wide-open gambling of the "casino" variety was illegal in Salt Lake; playing cards was not. Though technically illegal, that 1890's wonder the mechanical slot machine was in wide use, but not in the typical western saloon. Blackjack and keno, though card games, were also considered illegal, but enforcement of the anti-gambling ordinance was haphazard. Few gambling raids were ever conducted by the Salt Lake City police department in the last century, and there were still fewer convictions. The idea of using an undercover policeman for the purpose of catching some sinner in the act of placing a private bet on a horse would have seemed absurd.

Profit figures for the Main Street saloon (liquor only) for the years 1883 to 1887 show that Owen's investment was a wise one. That first year the business returned a profit after expenses of $1,774.51; in 1885 $1,807.46; in 1886 $1,769.15; and in 1887 $1,930.

From 1883 to 1887 the Hogle brothers continued to lease from insurance broker Hugh Anderson. Confusion over the rental arrangement between Mr. Anderson, Hogle Brothers', and A. C. Smith's Drug Store resulted in a lawsuit in which the plaintiff, Owen Hogle, won a judgment in 3rd District Court on March 29, 1886. Then on September 2, 1887, James Hogle made a down payment of $6,666.66 toward the purchase of Hugh Anderson's half interest in the property and building, the other half remaining for a time in the name of Anderson and his wife Hannah until it was purchased for an additional $6,666.66 by Owen Hogle. The partnership was initially to be fifty-fifty all the way, even down to the ownership of the building. But on August 2, 1889, Owen and Jessie sold their interest in the actual property (but not the saloon business) to James for the sum of $7,500. At the same time Owen deeded to James a lot at No. 16 South Fourth East.

Hogle Brothers' saloon became an institution in Salt Lake City

Above, James Hogle had minted a number of tokens for each of his saloons. Clasbey and Hogle tokens are known to exist for the saloons in Challis and Bonanza, Idaho, as well as Salt Lake City. These are from the 1880's. Courtesy David L. Freed. *Below*, a rare Hogle Brothers' business card, circa 1890. From the author's collection.

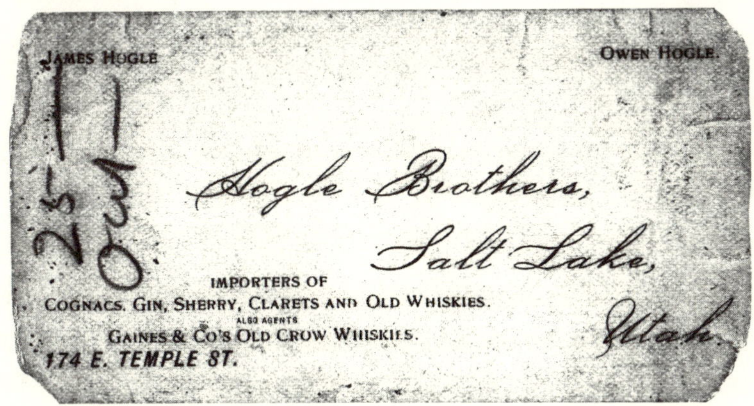

and for the next twenty years the most prominent establishment of its kind. Tab sheets and invoices show that the clientele included the richest and most prominent mining men in the west. Marcus Daly, R. C. Chambers, and Thomas Kearns appear on the sheets during the 1890's, as do the Walker brothers and James Glendenning.

Glendenning, who had worked in Fred Phillips' store in Leesburg, had married Col. Shoup's sister Margaret, and while living in Salmon, Idaho, he had been Shoup's full partner in the mercantile business. In the 1880's he moved to Salt Lake City and in 1893 he was elected the city's first Gentile mayor.

Hogle Brothers', with its fine restaurant, was the kind of place one might even take a visiting member of the clergy. During his years as a U.S. Senator, Thomas Kearns brought Park City's Marianist priest Father Guiraud to the establishment. (It is not known if James Hogle was already acquainted with the French Canadian.)

Nor was the reputation of Hogle Brothers' restricted to Salt Lake City — or even Utah. The saloon was well known throughout the west, and the *Salmon Idaho Recorder* would reminisce years after its closing that "The saloon, with a gambling room in connection, at 174 South Main Street was always considered one of the most popular resorts in Salt Lake City. The old timers of this country never thought of going to Salt Lake that they did not call on James Hogle."

CHAPTER TEN

A Member of the Jury

MUCH OF THE ANIMOSITY between the Gentile and Mormon communities in Utah stemmed from the invasion of Johnston's Army and the subsequent period of its occupation. Various incidents from that time were told and retold to illustrate either religious persecution or Mormon treason, depending on the persuasion of the teller. One long-standing Gentile vendetta was the unpunished murder of a Sergeant Ralph Pike, a member of the occupation forces, by Howard O. Spencer, which occurred on a Salt Lake City street back in 1859. Like the case of the untried and unpunished perpetrators of the Mountain Meadows Massacre, the killing of Pike was often cited as a clear case of murder and for more than thirty years it aroused passionate controversy. In 1889 Owen Hogle played a role in settling the controversy once and for all.

In the spring of 1859 Howard O. Spencer, then twenty, was working as a wrangler on his Uncle Daniel's ranch in Rush Valley, not far from the federal headquarters at Camp Floyd. The local population had grown resentful of the attitude and actions of Johnston's Army, and numerous confrontations resulted.

On the evening of March 22 a military squad led by Sergeant Pike arrived at Rush Valley to mow their next winter's hay. Spencer, who was feeding his stock in the valley, was ordered by Pike to vacate the land immediately and to drive off his cattle. What happened next is uncertain, and what was seen depended as much upon one's religious point of view as visual perspective.

A Mormon eyewitness was Elijah Seamons. He later testified that Spencer said it was too dark to move the cattle and that he would do it in the morning. Sergeant Pike became enraged. He

Owen Hogle, sportsman and professional gambler, in Sheldon, Illinois, about
1897.

raised his musket above his head and brought it down on the skull of the young Mormon, knocking him to the ground unconscious and producing a fearsome wound. Army companions of Sergeant Pike later claimed that it was Spencer who became enraged and tried to run the sergeant through with a pitchfork and that Pike had struck Spencer in self-defense. Both sides agreed that Howard O. Spencer's skull was fractured.

Agitation against Sergeant Pike by Spencer's relatives and friends finally resulted in assault charges being brought. Four and a half months after the incident in Rush Valley, Sergeant Pike was brought under military escort to Federal Court in Salt Lake City, arriving the morning of August 11, 1859.

It was shortly after noon and the streets were full of people. Cobbler Henry A. Cushing glanced out the back window of his shop on Main Street and saw several men examining pistols in his backyard. Thirty years later he would identify the men as Mr. Stringham, Mr. Hickman, Mr. Luce, and Howard O. Spencer. A short time later Mr. Cushing was in front of his shop drawing a bucket of water from the ditch when he became a principal witness to one of the boldest killings in the early history of the city.

Sergeant Pike and his escort had just left Townsend's Hotel and were walking down the sidewalk toward the Salt Lake House. It was here that a man came up from behind them and tapped Pike on the shoulder. Pike turned around. "Are you Pike?" the man asked. "Yeah, I'm Pike," came the reply.

Spencer raised his pistol, aimed it deliberately at the soldier, and squeezed off a single shot. The bullet struck the handle of a knife that Pike was wearing in his belt and fragments of the knife and the bullet pierced his side. Spencer turned slowly and walked casually into the street. The large crowd of onlookers was apparently too stunned to stop the gunman and Spencer then ran from the scene followed by a large body of men. According to some witnesses, the men leading the chase were Mr. Stringham, Mr. Hickman, and Mr. Luce. Despite his crowd of pursuers, the young gunman somehow managed to escape. Pike died at one o'clock the following morning.

After the escape, Spencer simply disappeared. Military authorities and the federal marshal periodically warned local leaders that a fugitive was being harbored in their midst and that anyone found guilty of aiding him would be punished to the full extent of the law. The threats, however, elevated Spencer to martyr status, and aided by a sympathetic population he was able to remain at large for much of the next three decades (most of that time in Salt Lake City's Fourth Ward).

In 1888, U.S. Attorney George S. Peters was told by an informant that Sergeant Pike's killer was employed under his own name at Liberty Park and was living at a certain rooming house in the city. Spencer was arrested and an indictment brought against him for first-degree murder on October 1, 1888, twenty-nine years, one month, and twenty days after the fatal shooting.

The decision to try Spencer was unpopular among the Mormons. It was said that a grand jury had been in session at the time of the shooting and "If nothing was done about it then why should the matter be brought up now?" It had been so long since the incident that an accurate reconstruction of the event was said to be impossible. A trial would accomplish nothing but dredging up old sectarian hatreds and further inflame the passions of the bitterly divided community. It was claimed that the witnesses were surely all deceased, and even if some were alive, who could trust their testimony after so many years? But Peters was determined to bring the matter to justice. The witnesses were found; the evidence was collected: there would be a trial. Assisting George Peters for the prosecution was Ogden Hiles. Attorneys for the defense were Arthur Brown and Legrand Young from the Salt Lake firm of Sheeks and Rawlins.

The well-publicized trial was understood by many Mormons to be the prelude to a new wave of federal harassment to complement the never-ending spectacle of the polygamy trials. It was an attempt to further embarrass the Mormon church, another example of religious persecution.

After numerous jurors had been examined, challenged, and dismissed, a jury of ten Gentiles and two Mormons was finally impaneled on the morning of May 7, 1889, before the fiercely anti-Mormon Judge Judd. Among those twelve good men and true was one unusually suited to sorting out facts, examining evidence, and judging character — a gambler named Owen Hogle.

The opening statement of the prosecuting attorney, Ogden Hiles, was clear and concise. Sergeant Pike had been shot, mortally wounded within the jurisdiction of the Court. Witnesses to the crime would testify that Howard O. Spencer had fired the fatal bullet and that he had been allowed to escape by friends and sympathizers. There had been a conspiracy, a conspiracy not only to protect and hide Spencer, but one to kill Sergeant Pike as well. The motive for the killing was revenge for an assault previously delivered by the deceased on the person of the defendant in Rush Valley. It was an obvious case of first-degree murder, clear and simple.

The opening arguments for the defense presented by Arthur Brown astounded everyone. While denying all the particulars of the prosecution's case, they were not going to pin their hopes on refuting the prosecution's witnesses. Instead, the defense intended to prove that at the time of the incident Howard O. Spencer was temporarily insane due to the blow on the head he had received from Sergeant Pike. Spencer, they claimed, was innocent by reason of insanity.

The testimony was difficult, much of it technical. There were enormous discrepancies in the accounts of various witnesses. Some of these contradictions could be accounted for by the three decades that had elapsed since the killing, others could not. The friends of Spencer testified to a completely different set of facts than the friends of Sergeant Pike.

The prosecution based its case on the many eyewitness accounts of the crime it had painstakingly gathered. The defense relied heavily upon expert medical witnesses who testified as to the probable mental state of Howard Spencer at the time of the killing. Dr. J. M. Benedict testified that as a result of the fractured skull he had earlier suffered at the hands of Sergeant Pike, "The defendant was of unsound mind and without the mental ability to control his actions." Dr. J. F. Hamilton agreed, saying, "I do not think that under such conditions he would be able to distinguish right from wrong or understand the nature of the act he was about to perpetrate." Dr. F. F. Bascome testified that "Insanity or the inability to control one's actions may be produced by injuries to the skull." More doctors were called until finally Judge Judd put an end to the discussion with the declaration that "We've heard quite enough of that kind of testimony."

The case went to the jury on May 10, 1889, and there was little doubt of the outcome. Judge Judd was avowedly anti-Mormon, and all but two of the jurors were Gentiles. The infrequently used insanity defense was seldom successful, and there was a general feeling that most murderers were somehow insane anyway. As the prosecution lightly dismissed it, "The insanity defense was no defense at all."

At exactly 9:30 P.M. the jury filed into the courtroom and took their places in the box. The court clerk rose and asked if they had agreed upon a verdict. The foreman of the jury stood and addressed the bench: "We have, Your Honor, and he handed the verdict to the clerk. Perfect silence followed and not a sound was to be heard from the large crowd. . . . The defendant moved uneasily in his chair but did not look up or manifest any other sign of interest." The clerk then read the verdict, "We the jury find the defendant, Howard O. Spencer, not guilty." There was a gasp in the courtroom, followed by a brief burst of applause. Judge Judd banged his gavel and brought the court to order. He then turned and addressed the jury.

> Gentlemen of the Jury, I want to say to you in reference to the verdict you have rendered that you have doubtless followed your oath according to your own conscience and you have doubtless done it honestly. But if this is not a case of murder, speaking from a practice of over 25 years, then I have never seen one in a court of Justice. . . . You may be discharged.

The jury filed silently from the courtroom.

Predictably, there were two schools of thought concerning the verdict. Some felt that divine providence had intervened on the side of justice, inspiring the wayward Gentiles to the paths of truth and righteousness — others that the jury had been shamefully bought. Under the headline "A Queer Jury," The *Tribune* reported: "The news that Spencer had been acquitted soon spread and at once became the principal topic of conversation. All, except the Mormons, denounced the verdict roundly."

In an editorial on May 12 the *Tribune* retried Spencer in its own court, from which there would be no appeal.

> The Spencer trial is over. It is proper now to review the main features of the case. The defense was insanity. The burden of

the evidence was to show that because of a blow received on the head, the mind of the man on trial was shaken from its level and that hence he was not responsible for the killing.

The facts of the case were that Spencer was an Old time Blood Atoner. He was in perfect accord with those other lambs, Hickman, Luce, Stringham, Taylor and the rest. The man whom he murdered had, in the strict line of his duty, ordered him away from a certain place. An altercation followed and Spencer, seizing a pitchfork, started to run the soldier through. The soldier to save his own life felled Spencer with his musket. Later, all the arrangements were made here and he deliberately killed the soldier. . . . Hickman, Luce, Stringham and the rest while pretending to arrest him, were really keeping the crowd back until the murderer should escape.

The whole business was as plain as the sunlight. . . . All the insanity in the brain of Spencer was there long before he received the blow on the head. . . . The murder was at a time when the whole Mormon people were wild under the teachings that the authorities of the United States were the enemies of the people, when the soldiers of the government were to Mormon eyes the materialization of what they hated . . . .

. . . .

The skulking, dodging and hiding of the man for thirty years were in effect a perpetual pleading of guilty to the crime. He is now cleared. A jury of his peers has decided that he is not guilty. He has no occasion any longer to dodge the officers of justice. But we opine that he does not feel entirely easy. We suspect that his thoughts are not all pleasant when the darkness will not keep out the spectres that haunt him. When nothing will relieve his brain from the visions that haunt him in his sleep.

The *Deseret News,* in a counter-editorial entitled "A Just Verdict," reflected the general feeling of the Mormon people:

. . . The approval of the verdict, so far as we have heard, is general. It would appear to be universal were it not for the remarks of Judge Judd after it was rendered. They were, to say the least, extraordinary. . . . The jury are to be commended for their impartiality and courage in finding such a verdict under the existing circumstances.

The trial of Howard Spencer was an important juncture in the history of Mormon–Gentile relations. It demonstrated to the be-

leaguered Saints that not all the non-Mormons were bent on eradi-
cating Mormonism and that some were capable of deliberate and
reasoned judgment. The war of words in the newspapers would
continue for many years to come, but something of the bitterness
which characterized the conflict in the early days was fading.

Following the Spencer trial, Owen Hogle took his young nephew
James A. on an extended fishing trip to Idaho. Not a few of the
regulars who frequented 174 South Main were displeased at the
verdict. Discretion was the better part of valor, and for a time the
gambler lay low.

Although the verdict was unpopular with a certain segment of
Hogle Brothers' clientele, it did not adversely affect business and
1889 was a record year for the saloon. Hogle Brothers' was not the
only game in town, however. The 1889–90 Salt Lake Business
Directory listed seventy other saloons and seven breweries in the city.

CHAPTER ELEVEN

Matters of Commerce, 1890–1896

THE FANATICS, BOTH GENTILE AND MORMON, had succeeded in polarizing the citizenry of Great Salt Lake City. They had brought their conflict to the point of open warfare and delayed Utah's admission to the Union for more than thirty years. But even at the height of the Whisky Street Wars there were peaceful and charitable men in both camps—men like Daniel S. Tuttle, whose sermons guided his flock toward Christian charity, tolerance, and forgiveness. But what finally turned the populace away from perpetual confrontation was not Christian charity but enlightened self-interest. Practical and farsighted men in both camps saw that a prolongation of the troubles would benefit no one.

In April of 1887 a small group of Gentile businessmen met in the federal court chambers in the Wasatch Building to form an organization which would promote the economic growth of the community.

General Patrick Edward Connor had once dreamed of establishing an organization which would attract eastern capital and investment to Utah. The plan was, of course, another scheme to increase the Gentile population and by so doing overthrow Mormon rule. The organization which was eventually formed would attract outside capital and investment, but the makeup and effect of this body was far from anything imagined by General Connor.

In 1887 the Mormon church was under enormous pressure from the federal government because of the ever-present issue of plural marriage. President Cleveland had insisted that the anti-polygamy laws be enforced, but he did not want the enforcement to in any way resemble religious persecution. The federal authorities were themselves divided on how to enforce the law. Some insisted that the Mormons be disenfranchised entirely, while others wanted a gentler and more reasoned approach. Local Gentiles, too, were divided on the question. In his *History of Utah*, Mormon historian Orson F. Whitney gives ample credit to a certain group of Salt Lake Gentiles for helping to defuse an ugly and potentially explosive situation.

> Thus was Gentile sentiment divided and to this division Utah owes more than perhaps will ever appear. Had there been no kind and generous spirits to hold in check the fiery fanatics, the history of things might have been vastly different. . . . All anti Mormons were not in the "rule or ruin" category. There were noble and generous spirits among them.
>
> One of the elements through which Providence worked at this critical period . . . was the Gentile business men of Salt Lake City. . . . They were weary of incessant agitation that strained to the utmost social and business relations, prostrating trade, frightening away capital and population and threatening to wreck the commonwealth.
>
> It was such feelings among such men that led to the formation of the Salt Lake Chamber of Commerce.

The Salt Lake Chamber of Commerce was the first organization in the history of the Territory that openly promoted Mormon–Gentile cooperation. Recognizing that such a coalition could only succeed if the divisive issues were left behind, the organization adopted as its motto: "No politics or Religion in the Chamber."

Chief organizer of the movement was Governor Caleb W. West. The first meeting of the Chamber of Commerce took place on April 2, 1887. Prominent Gentiles to sign the articles of incorporation included some men who would only be recognized as "gentiles" in Utah (even though as "peoples of the book" Muslims and Jews are technically not regarded as Gentiles under Mormon teaching). Leaders of the new organization included J. E. Bamberger, Sam Levy, the Walker brothers, Hugh Wallace, the merchants Henry Siegel, B. J. Raybould, Fred H. Auerbach, S. T. Teasdel, and James Glendenning, mining men J. C. Conklin and R. C. Chambers, hotel owner Matthew Cullen, insurance agent Hugh Anderson, brewers

Jacob Moritz and Emanuel Kahn, and saloon keeper James Hogle. Among the first Mormons to join the Chamber were Heber J. Grant, Henry Dinwoodey, and Elias Morris.

The organization of the Chamber was an important step toward normalizing relations between Salt Lake's two warring communities. It was in the words of Mr. Whitney "the inauguration of a better condition of things — the ushering in of an era in which old animosities would be forgotten, old political lines wiped out and new ones drawn not running parallel with former prejudices and predilections."

During the years directly following the founding of the Chamber, Salt Lake City went through a period of prosperity. But however successful the founders were at pursuing their cooperative goals, and however bright the future appeared in 1890, the community was not immune to the economic problems that beset the rest of the nation, and trouble was just around the corner.

A CREDIT TO THE COMMUNITY

The Panic and Crash of 1893 was similar to the 1859 event that had helped to create the Pikes Peak hysteria. But the crash of '59 was a short-lived phenomenon; the '93 crash would plunge the country into three years of depression, the worst it had known to that time. In 1894 more than 500 banks failed, more than 16,000 business firms collapsed, and unemployment soared to 20 per cent.

The causes of the disaster were hard to pinpoint, but there was no shortage of suspect policies and practices. Back in 1890 the United States Congress had passed the Sherman Silver Purchase Act under pressure of bimetallists and inflationists. The act required the government to buy 4.5 million ounces of silver each month and to pay for it with treasury notes redeemable in gold. This legislation was a windfall to mining camps like Park City which were rich in silver deposits. But it also resulted in a run on the country's gold reserves, which in three years fell from $190 million to just over $100 million.

In 1893 the only thing that was needed to start a bank run was a good rumor, and nothing fueled those rumors like the truth. The country's trade deficit was enormous, and gold was flowing out of the country at the very time it was most needed at home. In the early summer, British banking interests began liquidating American securities at an alarming rate. The subsequent fall in the market fueled a run on American banks and scores failed overnight.

President Grover Cleveland's second administration was three months old. To shut off the flow of gold, he persuaded Congress to repeal the Sherman Act, and silver mining in the west came to an abrupt halt. Cleveland then collaborated with banking giants like J. P. Morgan and "Arranged the sale of government bonds which allowed banking houses to manipulate the exchange rates in their own favor." In the view of many western mining interests and farmers, Cleveland had sold out to the moneylenders.

The issue boiled down to free silver versus the gold standard, currency restriction versus inflation. William Jennings Bryan became the spokesman for the Populist cause and stumped the country on behalf of Free Silver. His famous speech "You shall not press down upon the brow of labor this crown of thorns. You shall not crucify mankind upon a cross of gold" became the rallying cry for bankrupt farmers and unemployed miners and was delivered in both Park City and Salt Lake.

Although Walker Brothers' Bank, next door to the saloon, was in no danger of failing, other seemingly solvent Utah institutions had gone under, taking with them the hard-earned savings of many a poor miner.

The Irish miners in Park City, already stung by a banking-mandated devaluation in the price of silver, knew who to blame for their troubles: the British, the bankers, and President Cleveland. Given the politics of the situation, they were not about to trust their life savings to the vaults of their presumed oppressors. Why would any self-respecting Irishman want to put his money in a bank when James Hogle had such a big safe behind the bar in his saloon?

During the Panic of '93 and the depression that followed, it was commonly believed that there was more money in James Hogle's safe than there was in the bank on the corner. It was during this period that the genial saloon keeper became known as Honest Jim Hogle.

James did not give interest on his private accounts, but for the miner there were advantages that outweighed the fluctuating bank interest or the fickle performance of bonds. Much of the money James was holding was destined for his vault anyway, and what better place to keep it than where it was already bound. Then, too, it was always available in case of an emergency, a late-night sip, or an unexpected straight flush.

There was yet another advantage to banking at Hogle Brothers' saloon. The miners of the intermountain west were addicted to gambling in all its forms, and one of the biggest gambles of all was investing in mining stock. These miners often owned stock in the very mines they worked for. Their holdings were usually small, but they played the market with all the enthusiasm of dedicated capitalists.

The miners were uniquely situated to learn first-hand of any new development that affected the profits of a mine, whether it was the discovery of a rich new ore body or an unexpected encounter with water. They kept close tabs on the performance of mining stocks and measured that performance against their own informa-

Walker Brothers' Bank, about 1910. Courtesy Utah State Historical Society.

tion. In the 1890's, the market was driven by such "insider information," and trading the information was considered neither unethical
nor illegal. Sometimes a stock would go up in price for no better
reason than that somebody was buying it. The miners had an edge
in assessing the real value of a property.

Hogle Brothers' saloon was right around the corner from the
Salt Lake Mining and Stock Exchange, then located on Second
South. The saloon was one of the first subscribers to the infant telephone service with the easily remembered numbers 1-2-3. Mining
men from Park City, Bingham, and Eureka would often call James
Hogle to have him make stock purchases in their behalf. These
purchases were sometimes made with the very poke James was holding for them in his famous safe. James was more than happy to
provide the service, and as he was known to make occasional investments himself, all tidbits and tips were welcome. Hogle Brothers'
soon became a clearinghouse for mining information and a Mecca
for mining financiers and investors from throughout the west.

The Society of Women

In the society of men, James Hogle was prominent, prosperous,
and respected. In the local society of women, Ida Hogle had to
struggle with her designated role as "the wife of the saloon keeper."
It was not a title that she willingly accepted, and throughout her
life she struggled to elevate herself above that social station. Part of
her effort was focused on improving the educational and cultural
level of the man she married. During the 1880's, Ida ordered yearly
updates of the American Cyclopedia from D. Appleton and Co. in
Kansas City. She purchased dictionaries, self-improvement text-
books, and numerous literary and educational materials and subjected her husband to them.

Interestingly, James seems to have thrived under the tutelage of
his live-in teacher. By the mid-1890's his personal and business correspondence shows few of the phonetic spellings or haphazard punc-
tuations that marked his earlier letters. Ida was, evidently, a stern
task master, and James appears to have been a receptive, if, perhaps, not always willing pupil.

Mrs. Hogle's interests were culturally refined. In 1877 she became one of the first members of the Ladies' Literary Club and would serve in numerous offices in that organization over the next forty years. The programs of the society were broad in scope, the theme adult community education. Lectures were given on a wide variety of topics: Shakespeare, Milton, contemporary poetry, history, astronomy, geology, and current events. Each year the club would focus on a specific topic or geographic area. In 1893 the theme was "South America," and the weekly Friday meetings featured lectures on Argentine and Brazilian writers, the birds of Brazil, Inca pottery, the nitrate and silver mines of Chile, the war between Chile and Peru, life in Patagonia, and other subjects of topical interest. On April twenty-first of that year, Ida delivered a lecture on the cultivation of coffee and cocoa in Colombia.

The Ladies' Literary Club also sponsored theatrical performances, bank concerts, and art shows, and Ida spent much of her time helping to organize the events. The rest of her time she devoted to church work and the study of music.

From the very beginning of Bishop Tuttle's ministry in Utah, Ida had been a devoted and active member of the St. Mark's Cathedral. She was a close friend of Mrs. Tuttle and helped her with altar and vestment preparations for the services. She was also a member of the St. Mark's choir and worked diligently under the director, Mrs. Fidelia B. Hamilton, from whom she took instruction in both voice and piano. At the Easter service in 1888 she was featured as a "treble" in the choir. She helped to organize balls and fund-raisers for both St. Mark's and Holy Cross hospitals and also served as president of the St. Mark's Charity Association. In "Gentile Society," at least, Ida Hogle was as respected as her husband was in business circles.

Men of Property

It is said that a man will tell his bartender things he would never tell his wife, or his doctor. The men who frequented Hogle Brothers' were important men, and if they chose to talk, it was likely that they were well worth listening to. The records from that period show that the Hogle brothers learned a number of things worth knowing.

By the mid-1890's James and Owen were investing heavily in important properties. Their special area of expertise was western mining stocks, and their knack for finding good investments was altogether as good as their friend Marcus Daly's legendary "nose" for finding ore. Their portfolios reveal something of the brothers' personalities.

Owen's stock position was, as might be expected, speculative. He owned blocks of stock in the Boston Consolidated, Rover, Sunshine, Mammoth, Gold Dust, Raymond, Ajax, Lone Tree, Silver King, and Daly West mining companies — the last two being two of the principal Park City producers. He also owned stock in the Western Arms and Sporting Goods Company and served on its board of directors.

James's mining stock holdings were all solid investments. He had large blocks of the major Park City producers, the Silver King, Daly West, Daly Judge, and Ontario. He also had stock in the

Main Street and Second South, looking southwest, with Hogle Brothers' in the center. The patriotic parade could be a send-off for Spanish-American War troops in 1897 or 1898. **Courtesy Utah State Historical Society.**

Cardiff mine in Challis, Idaho, Scott Hardware Co., Utah Drug, Thistle Rock, Utah Savings and Trust, and Walker Brothers' Bank.

These investments grew substantially, and the brothers amassed large fortunes in the market during the 1890's. Owen re-invested most of his earnings — some, no doubt, on the ponies. James put the bulk of his earnings into the acquisition of local real estate.

James had acquired his first piece of Salt Lake property when he purchased the corner at Fourth East and Brigham Street, along with the saloon property, from Owen and his wife Jessie in August of 1889. On December 5, 1893, he purchased parcels of land and their buildings at First South and Second West and at Eleventh East and Third South for $4,600. On the same day he purchased a house at 675 Second Avenue for $2,649.90. These were rent-producing properties giving James a return on his investment.

On September 30, 1897, James purchased a large piece of land at the corner of First South and Second East for $10,000 and on

Corner of Second South and Main streets, looking northwest, around the turn of the century, showing the jumble of wires of competing utility companies overhead and the streetcar turnaround. Courtesy Utah State Historical Society.

October 6, 1899, another sizeable piece on West Fourth South for the same amount. Then on August 23, 1900, he purchased a large Brigham Street piece adjoining his Fourth East property, a parcel so large that it would eventually accommodate three separate homes at 364, 366, and 376 East Brigham Street.

In 1900 James would also buy property at Ninth East and Ninth South and at Third South near Fifth East, and in November of 1905 he purchased a house and lot at Sixth South and Fourth East for $3,015.

James's real estate investments were not restricted to residential lots. By 1900 he (with Owen) owned a controlling interest in the Boyd Park and Scott Hardware buildings. And so it went; in a series of purchases reminiscent of a Parker Brothers' "Monopoly" game, James Hogle was buying up much of the city.

CHAPTER TWELVE

Family, Friends, & Neighbors, 1896–1904

IT WAS EARLY IN THE SPRING OF 1859 that the family of Patrick Gilmore were all together for the last time. His eldest son, James, left home first to join the Pikes Peak gold rush. Then his wife Ellen died on March 31, 1860. Anna, the third child, married Mr. John Steele, a Middleport grocer, at a wedding held at Patrick's West Middleport home on April 2, 1861. Two months later his second son, Owen, went off to join the Union Army, and after the war went to Montana to find his older brother.

In 1869 Patrick Gilmore moved his family from West Middleport to Sheldon, Illinois, near the Indiana border. Here he built a large home which later became known as the Bonnett House. Three years later his second daughter, Mary, married Mr. Childs Mantor, the son of a prominent Middleport farmer, Aniz C. Mantor. At the time of their marriage, Childs Mantor was studying to become a doctor of medicine.

Patrick lived in Sheldon until his two youngest children, Albert and Henry, went west in 1877 to help their older brother James in the operation of the Challis and later Bonanza City saloons.

With his children all raised and moved away, Patrick Gilmore retired from the railroad. For a short time he lived alone in the home he had built for his family. Then he decided to move on and traveled some before coming to live with his eldest son in Salt Lake City in 1880. As with the other Gilmores who had come west, Patrick changed his name to Hogle upon his arrival in Salt Lake City. Patrick would live with his son's family for the next twelve years, assisting where he could around the house or at the saloon.

Mary came west with her husband in 1873. Dr. Childs Mantor

first practiced in the boom camp of Silver Reef, Utah, before moving to Park City in 1880. As one of two physicians, he would practice there for ten years. Dr. Mantor was respected and well liked, and owing to a confusion concerning his name, he came to have a large number of the town's pediatric cases. The city directory listed the good doctor as "Mantor, Childs physician." As the story went, mothers took his first name for his specialty, and he ended up with a thriving practice, not only among the miners' families in Park City but with the Mormon farmers in the outlying communities as well.

In the early 1890's, the Mantor family moved to Salt Lake. For a time the doctor had an office in the Scott Hardware Building. James owned stock in the business, and his brothers-in-law, Sidney and Charles King, had both worked in the hardware store for some time, Charles in the stove department and Sidney as a tinner. James Glendenning, soon to be elected Salt Lake City's mayor, was the firm's vice president.

The Mantor family lived in a home at 274 K Street. The 1892 city directory listed Mary's father Patrick as residing at the same address. Mary Mantor had been trained as a nurse by her husband, and Patrick Gilmore was getting old and needed nursing care.

One day in 1892 a man from the city directory arrived at the door of the house on K Street and Patrick obligingly gave his name. Whether from memory loss or out of a mischievous sense of humor, James Hogle's father listed himself in the directory as "Patrick Hogal, laborer." This error, or more likely joke, was short-lived, and later printings of the directory used the more conventional spelling, without the job description.

For the past three decades, the family of Patrick Gilmore had scattered far and wide seeking their fortunes. Now there was a definite sense that the clan was coming back together. With the families of James, Owen, and Mary all living in Salt Lake City, the last years of Patrick's life were spent surrounded by his family. They had grown up and moved on to live their own lives, but they had never forgotten him, or each other.

April 27, 1894, started out a beautiful, crisp day in Salt Lake City. When George Salisbury, the city's meteorologist, took his morning readings at 6 A.M., the temperature was 34 degrees under clear skies. The humidity was at 20 per cent, but the barometer stood at 25.28 inches of mercury and Salisbury knew the weather was changing for the worse. By noon the city was shrouded under low overcast skies, and in the early afternoon a cold drizzle began falling. The rain continued throughout the day, and by evening some of the higher mountains above the city had been covered with new snow.

At his weather station on the University of Utah campus, Salisbury received .13 of an inch of rain. At 6 P.M. the humidity was 94 per cent. It was an extraordinarily foggy and wet day, more typical of the mountains of Armagh where Patrick Gilmore was born than the arid desert climate of northwestern Utah.

It was the kind of day the Irish are likely to call "soft," a gentle turn of phrase for a genuinely miserable and soggy afternoon. It was also the kind of day that lends credence to myth, for on this day at the home of his daughter Mary, Patrick Gilmore passed away, and the heavens did seem to weep for him. Patrick died of causes incident to his eighty-four years.

The funeral of Patrick Gilmore was held at the Mantor home on Sunday, April 30, at two in the afternoon. The burial services at the Salt Lake Cemetery were conducted by the Rev. Brewster, from St. Mark's Cathedral. The Clan Mac Giolla Mhuire had gathered to pay their last respects to the teamster, frontiersman, stagecoach driver, deputy sheriff, and railroad man who was their father.

A Reunion on Brigham Street

In San Francisco it was Nob Hill, in Boise it was Warm Springs Avenue, and in Salt Lake City it was Brigham Street. These mansion-lined districts and thoroughfares were more than streets, they were monuments to the mining fortunes that built them. To walk down any one of them was to visit a mining men's hall of fame. Many of those who made their fortunes in the mining camps of Park City, Leesburg, and Virginia City eventually gravitated to larger communities, particularly the state capitals, where modern comforts and conveniences were readily available, and where the latest whims of fashions and novelty could be indulged in. These were places where the wealthy could live in style.

But there was more than wealth or extravagance involved in the building of these streets. There was a bond of friendship among these men which had more to do with their common histories than their wealth. Many of the men who built Brigham Street had known each other long before they made their fortunes. It was only natural that they would eventually build their homes in the same neighborhood as their relatives, friends, and business acquaintances.

At the turn of the century James was still living in the old house at the southwest corner of Brigham Street and Fourth East (No. 16). This home was adjacent to a new one he was building directly on Brigham Street, at No. 376. Just across the street on Fourth was the home of Henry Wagener, a former Helena brewer who now operated one of the city's largest brewing and distilling plants.

Col. Enos A. Wall had a home at 309 East South Temple, and in 1904 he built a huge mansion directly kitty-corner from the Hogles at No. 411. John David Wood, who, like Hogle, had followed the mining game from Virginia City to Salmon to Leesburg and Challis, was once again Hogle's neighbor and was building a new home for his wife (the former Mrs. Hagenbarth) across the street and down a half block at 305 East Brigham Street. His stepson and partner, Frank Hagenbarth, had a home half a block below this on the Hogle side at 260 East Brigham Street. Owen Hogle owned a home less than three blocks away, at No. 639 Brigham Street. James's brother-in-law, Sidney King, lived in a small home on a piece of property near the corner on G Street. James's old Salmon City friend and more recent customer, James Glendenning, had the home just east of this property, at 617 E. Brigham Street. Sister Mary and her husband Childs Mantor and their family lived four blocks away on K Street, but in 1906 they too would move to Brigham Street. Other acquaintances on Brigham Street included M. H. and J. R. Walker, and C. C. Goodwin. In 1902 it would have been difficult for James Hogle to go for a walk without running into either a relative or one of the old gang from Idaho or Montana.

The other mining contingent on Brigham Street was composed largely of men who had made their fortunes in Park City: David Keith at 529, John Daly at 319, Ezra Thompson at 576, and the John Judge family at 737.

In 1898 another Park City millionaire, now U.S. Senator, Thomas Kearns, was living one block south of James at 144 South Fourth East; but later that year he purchased the property adjacent to James Glendenning and adjoining Sidney King's residence. Work on the Kearns mansion would take more than two years, but it would be completed in time to host President Teddy Roosevelt during his visit to the city in May of 1903.

A Minor Order of Sainthood

The Hogle brothers had many mutual friends, but Owen had his own circle of acquaintances and his own special interests. His talents were not restricted to the practice of his trade, and he was additionally an avid outdoorsman, fly fisherman, hunter, and guide. He frequently organized fishing expeditions to Idaho and Montana for his friends, and these trips inevitably offered occasions to get in a few hands of cards.

There was a remarkable integration of Owen's professional and personal life which his many friends must have both admired and envied. It was no coincidence that he was on the board of directors of The Western Arms Company, a sporting goods firm that sold "Fly rods, fishing tackle, boxing gloves, baseball and football equipment, shot guns and fire arms."

Altogether typical of Owen Hogle was an elaborate fishing and poker expedition to Idaho that he organized in the early 1890's. In all, sixteen guests participated in the trip to the Wood-Hagenbarth Ranch at Spencer, Idaho. This huge spread was the headquarters of the Wood-Hagenbarth ranching empire, owned and operated by John David Wood and his stepson Frank Hagenbarth.

Among the participants in the party were the bankers J. R. and M. H. Walker and eight of their friends, E. R. Eldredge and S. J. Kenyon and four friends, Dr. Worthington, Dr. Pfouts, a Mr. Rogers, and a Mr. Pratt. In addition to the guests, the safari included two chefs and several wagon drivers, who doubled as porters. For anyone of less organizational ability it would have been a logistical nightmare, but Owen had planned and led many such adventures before.

For this particular trek into the wilderness the tents, bedrolls, cots, tables, tablecloths, chairs, and other necessary camp equipment were rented from Scott Hardware Company. This equipment plus meat, groceries, and a generous supply of liquid refreshments from the Kentucky Liquor Company (Hogle Brothers' wholesale suppliers), were shipped as far as Spencer by freight car on the Utah Oregon Short Line Railroad. Here freight wagons met the train. The drivers unloaded and repacked the supplies and de-

Owen Hogle, about 1900.

livered them to the secret fishing hole. Here camp was set up to await the arrival of the guests, who were brought in by passenger train and private stage.

How good the fishing was is unknown but the "Poker State-ment" for the three-day trip is extant. The big losers were Dr. Pfouts at $108.80, Dr. Worthington at $64.25, and Mr. Eldredge, who lost $42.80. The winner was S. J. Kenyon, who collected $83.45, and Owen won a respectable $52.35. All the men who participated in

James Hogle, about 1900.

the trip were wealthy, but the amount of money exchanged was relatively small, as this was a friendly game. The trip was a genial fraternal outing and not a gambler's scheme or guided expedition for profit.

For all his planning and work, Owen charged and expected nothing. The trip cost $429.65, and each gentleman in the party was assessed an incredibly cheap $26.85 to cover the expenses. Owen paid his fair share along with the others.

Owen Hogle was a man who enjoyed life and made others enjoy life as well. He was a good-hearted, joyous man who had legions of friends. In the Irish ecclesiastical pantheon, there is probably reserved for such a man a minor order of sainthood.

LETTERS FROM A GAMBLER

One of Owen's good friends and fellow sportsmen was Thomas W. Woodford, a gambler and bookie who traveled a good deal. From 1899 to 1902 he crisscrossed the country from San Francisco to New York, from Chicago to New Orleans, St. Louis, and Washington, D.C., making book on elections, horses, sporting events, and the stock market.

Sometime in 1900 Mr. Woodford became indebted to Owen Hogle, and between March of 1899 and December of 1901 the two men carried on a lengthy correspondence. Only a few of Mr. Woodford's letters remain, but these convey a sense of the relationship and the general comaraderie among members of the "sporting fraternity." The tone of the letters is chatty and informal — not at all like the usual correspondence between a debtor and his creditor.

Palace Hotel, San Francisco
March 15th, 1899

Mr. Hogle,

Beverley and Coleman both decided not to bet which is certainly all right. There was betting here on the same thing, Buows election, and money returned to both parties in case there is no election.

T. Woodford

A. A. Housman & Co, Brokers

20 Broad Street
New York, N.Y.

Sept 22, 1900

Dear Owen:

I wrote you a letter from Larchmont a few weeks ago I hope you received it OK. The betting on the election is Two and a half to one on McKinley. They will never be any better and McKinley, they say, is sure to win. Beverley is still in the same luck. Just about the same loser when you were here. Kate and Madge are going to write to you this week. We are in town now. Mrs Beverley wishes to be remembered to you.

Yours truly,

T. W. Woodford.

Chicago Ill.
August 1901

Dear Owen:

Wheelock went to Larchmont Wednesday. He's won $100,000.00 on the season. Beverley is here and is about even on the season. If I go to New Orleans and make any money, I will send you all I can. You will get it all sure before six months. Mrs. Beverley and Mrs. Stern send best regards. Kate and Madge say you must come here next spring. Gene wants to send his regards to you. Also he is going to send you some fine cigars for Christmas.

Your Friend,

Tom Woodford

Office of John W. Miller, Broker
16 West 25th St
New Orleans, La.

October 25th, 1901

Dear Owen:

Don't think I have forgotten you. I send you this $100.00 to let you know I will pay up soon as I can. I have been winning for Bennett and if I continue so I will send all to you this fall. Gene is in Europe and is much better. He sends his best regards to you. Don't sell your S.S. It is OK. Madge and Kate and Emma send best love to you. Mrs. Beverley sends her best regards. Also Mrs. Stern. Bill Beverley is loser on the season and Wheelock is a $70,000.00 winner. He bet $20,000.00 on Low yesterday. All the sports are on Low.

Write soon, your friend,

Thomas W. Woodford.

December 9, 1901

Dear Owen:

Gene is home and is just a little better. He says for you to keep your S.S. and you will get $90.00 for it this year. He has made up with his brother. I lost in Washington. I guess I will go to New Orleans and make book this winter. Bennett will give me a bank roll. Gene don't want me to go says for me to wait until the spring and I will have a better chance.

T. Woodford

Mr. Woodford and his associates were high rollers. They were characters like Damon Runyon's "Unser Fritz" in *All Horse Players Die Broke*, who lived at the Waldorf Astoria and thought nothing of blowing "A hundred and sixty thousand dollars on a hide called Sir Martin to win the Futurity" and who ever afterward was "as clean as a Jaybird."

DISSOLUTION

Owen Hogle had Bright's disease (Chronic Glonerulonephritis), which could progress slowly over many years or kill suddenly. The affliction destroyed the kidneys, and prior to modern methods of treatment and the invention of the artificial kidney was incurable. The debilitating effects of the disorder were progressive and becoming more pronounced with time.

As early as 1895 Owen must have known that the illness would eventually prove fatal, for on January sixteenth of that year he wrote the following note to Walker Brothers' Bankers: "In case of my death, you will pay over to James Hogle all money I may have on deposit, signed, Owen Hogle. Witness J. P. Quillen." Eight months earlier, when Mary Mantor had purchased the cemetery lot for the burial of their father, Owen had quietly purchased the adjoining gravesite and thereafter paid the assessments on both lots. By the summer of 1895 his illness had progressed to the point that he was no longer able to play the piano. It must have been hard for him to give up his music, but on July first he sold the instrument to a J. W. Maark for $150.

With the sale of the piano, Owen began the slow process of liquidating all his earthly possessions. The sales and divestitures over the next six years paralleled the slow and steady progress of his illness. A particularly sad point came in early January of 1899. Owen was in New York when he received the following letter from his wife Jessie:

Oakland, California
Dec. 31st, 1898

Dear Husband,

It is the last evening of this year, and as I have not heard from you for a long time I think I will write you and wish you a Happy New Year and many of them. Why do you not write? Are you coming home this winter and as I am your wife, why do you not call me your wife anymore when you do write? It is some months since I heard from you. Please write and tell me what is the matter. Good bye

Your Loving wife,

Jessie

Three months later Jessie filed suit for divorce in Third District Court in Salt Lake City. The action was uncontested, and on April 12, 1900, the final decree was granted. Jessie would receive $12,000 in full settlement of the action. Their seventeen-year marriage was over.

THE LAST BET

During the early summer of 1899 the Hogle brothers conducted a complete inventory of their saloon. The value of the business and stock jointly held was determined to be $82,023.96. On July 15, for a sum of $41,011.98, exactly half of the assessed value, Owen sold to James:

All of my interest in the stock of liquors, tobaccos and other goods now belonging and appertaining unto the business of Hogle Brothers on Main Street, Salt Lake City, Utah, including all stock in the saloon and cellar underneath the saloon and including the 50 barrels of whiskey in bond at Frankfort, Kentucky: also all my interest in the fixtures, furnishings and furniture and all personal property what-so-ever appertaining unto said business and situate at the saloon and building where said business has been and is conducted and all effects whatsoever belonging and appertaining thereto, including the good will of said business.

Brother James would continue to operate the saloon on his own and under the name "James Hogle, successor to Hogle Brothers,' dealer in fine wines and brandies."

Following his retirement from the saloon business, Owen returned to New York for a while, where the pursued his favorite pastime, horse racing. His condition continued to deteriorate, however, and by 1901 he was again in Salt Lake, living with the Mantor family, to whom he had previously agreed to give his house on Brigham Street. He made several trips east in 1901 and early 1902, primarily to purchase stock.

Mary Mantor and her husband cared for Owen as best they could. The ordeal must have been particularly hard on Mary, for she too suffered from the affliction. The *Salt Lake Tribune* faithfully reported the closing chapter on the morning of September 7, 1902, under the headline "Owen Hogle Dying":

> The sporting fraternity of this city heard with deep regret yesterday that Owen Hogle, of the firm of Hogle Brothers,' and one of the best known horsemen of the west, is lying at the point of death at the home of his sister, Mrs. Childs Mantor, on Brigham Street. He is afflicted with Bright's Disease of the kidneys and has practically been given up by the physicians.
>
> Mr. Hogle is one of the pioneers of the West. . . . For many years he was a successful and popular bookmaker on Western race tracks. For the past few years he has devoted most of his time to the Resort on Main Street owned by his brother, James Hogle and himself.
>
> He is also a director in The Western Arms Company and owner of stock in various mining corporations. He has been a sufferer of kidney trouble for a long time but has been able to look after his business affairs until about a week ago when he was obliged to go to bed.

By the time his many friends read the story in the *Tribune*, Owen Hogle was already dead. He died at six o'clock the very morning the story appeared in the paper. The funeral was held at the home of his brother at two o'clock on September 8, 1902, and he was buried next to his father in the Salt Lake City Cemetery. At the time of his death Owen was sixty years old.

Main Street, looking northwest, in 1901. Hogle Brothers' saloon is located under the first street-level awning. Courtesy Utah State Historical Society.

On the morning of September 10, 1902, James, in the presence of J. P. Quillen (Hogles' bartender) and L. H. Farnsworth, opened safe deposit box No. 514 in the vault of Walker Brothers' Bank. The box contained various stock certificates, deeds, abstracts of title, and personal papers. There were also found one diamond stud of about two carats, two gold watches, one gold square watch charm set with diamonds, two gold chains, and one gold match safe. The large ruby Owen had worn was not among the items in the box. The stone may have been given to Mary Mantor or to Jessie, but its final disposition is unknown.

CHAPTER THIRTEEN

Last of the Placer Boys, 1903–1908

THE HOGLES' TWIN BROTHERS Albert and Henry had left Idaho for Sheldon, Illinois, in 1883. In Sheldon they took the Gilmore name once more, and their old school friends were unaware of the other name the brothers had used in the west.

On Christmas Day, 1890, Albert married Nancy Clark, the eldest daughter of Mr. and Mrs. Archie Clark, members of a large and prominent Illinois family. Five children were born to this union, Archie Owen (named for his maternal grandfather and paternal uncle), born January 17, 1892, Anna (for her Aunt Anna Steele), born December 9, 1893, Mary (for Aunt Mary Mantor), born September 3, 1895, and James Henry (named for uncles James and Henry). James Henry died on November 30, 1900, at the age of seven months, seven days. The family names were very important to Albert, and he succeeded in honoring every member of the Gilmore family except for himself. But James had already honored Albert by naming his only son James Albert.

In 1893 Albert was appointed postmaster of Sheldon, a position he would hold for four years. He then opened a bookstore and newsstand which he ran successfully until his election as supervisor of the Sheldon Township in 1900. With a loan from James he went into partnership with a man named G. H. Gay and opened a general store in Sheldon which also thrived. Albert worked hard and usually made a success of whatever he attempted.

Henry Gilmore was a confirmed bachelor. Like his elder brother Owen, he liked to travel a good deal and like Owen he loved to play the ponies. Unlike Owen, however, he seldom backed the right horse. If Owen had the golden touch, Henry had something similar in a baser metal. He tried placer mining and prospecting in Idaho without success. When he first returned to Sheldon he tried farming but his crops failed. He then opened an insurance office and even a saloon, but eventually he went to work in Albert's store and worked local farms on the side. Henry's niece Mary ruefully noted years later that what Henry was particularly good at was attending Elks' conventions.

On October 6, 1902, less than a month after the death of Owen, James received a letter from Albert. Albert and Henry had a chance to buy a particularly good farm on the outskirts of Sheldon. It was 122 acres with two fine houses, two barns, granaries, outhouses and other buildings. The price was $110 an acre, buildings, houses, and stock included. Even at 1902 prices this was a steal and the twins knew it.

Henry had been working the land under a lease arrangement with the owner, a Mr. O'Brien. When the latter mentioned to Henry that he was putting the place up for sale, Henry and Albert immediately wrote their older brother James for the money to buy the property, Albert adding in a postscript, "Jimmie, I would like to hear from you at once. It will be picked up as soon as people know it is for sale." Nancy Gilmore, Albert's wife, also wrote to James about the dream farm. This was obviously a matter of some urgency.

James wrote back, informing his brothers that the settlement of Owen's estate would take some time. He was negotiating the sale of Owen's South Temple home to Senator Kearns for his contractor, Mr. Curley, but that deal was still in the works. Owen did have property in Denver, but the family had already agreed to deed it to Anna Steele. Owen had also owned a house on Third South that the family had agreed should go to Mary Mantor. He had also owned stocks, but it was not wise to sell his Saint Louis and South Western Railroad stock or his Silver King stock right away because the prices for both had recently fallen to new lows. These they would liquidate when the price was more advantageous to the estate.

James therefore made arrangements with a New York stock broker to hold the railroad stock until the price was sufficient to

The twins, Albert and Henry, in Sheldon, Illinois, about 1900.

cover the property purchase. He then got the draft through Mr. Howard at Walker Brothers' Bank with the aid of Owen's will, dated January 16, 1895, and the half interest in a note owned jointly by Owen and James for $16,500 from an A. W. McClure. Owen had already collected this note and it was with this money that he had purchased the railroad stock shortly before his death. James's interest in the stock was established to the satisfaction of the bankers, and a draft for $13,220 was sent to Albert's wife Nancy for the purchase of her dream farm.

In February of 1903 Henry and Albert again wrote James requesting more money from Owen's estate, this time to buy farm land near Lebanon, Indiana. To raise money for the purchase

James added his shares of Silver King stock to the shares in Owen's estate. This he sold, taking a one-fifth share of the proceeds along with the others.

But Henry needed more money. What about Owen's share of the saloon business? Wasn't that to be settled as well? James had the bill of sale from Owen relinquishing all rights to the saloon business partnership, and notices to that effect had even been published in the papers. But he evidently had not shown these documents to his relatives. If they felt they had an interest in the saloon because they were Owen's kin, he wasn't going to dispute it. No matter that he had built the business from scratch or that the family in Illinois had no legal claim to the business. James would buy out his siblings' claims to the saloon.

On March 9, 1903, James's brothers and sisters quit-claimed the real property of Owen over to James. The statement attached to the settlement read as follows:

Owen's Estate/Real Property

	Whole	Half
Saloon Stock business etc.	$25,257.92	$12,628.96
Lot and Building (saloon)	$30,000.00	$15,000.00
639 East So. Temple	$12,000.00	$ 6,000.00
TOTAL	$67,257.92	$33,628.96
EACH FIFTH	$ 6,725.79	

James Hogle had now purchased his brother Owen's half of the saloon business twice.

A Legacy in Dispute

About a year and a half later the price of the railroad stock was finally high enough to cover the loss James had sustained in sending Nancy Gilmore the money to purchase the first farm. It was sold by James's agent in New York for $13,820. James informed his brothers of the sale and asked them to sign a quit-claim deed to their interest in the stock so that the paperwork could be completed prior to the closing of Owen's estate.

The reaction of Henry and Albert was most unexpected. They did not write to James asking him to explain the request but instead wrote a provocative inquiry to the Importers and Traders National Bank, the New York firm that had handled the sale of the stock. In his correspondence with the bank Albert signed his name Hogle.

Gentlemen

Mr. Hogle of Salt Lake City, Utah has reported to me the sale of 400 shares of St. L. & S.W.R.R. stock. Will you be so kind as to let me know in whose name the stock was in and if this is the correct number of shares sold and prices etc. Thanking you in advance for your kindness in this matter,

I am yours truly,
Albert Hogle

The New York bank wrote to Walker Brothers' Bank, which had approved the transaction. Walker Brothers' in turn informed James of the inquiry that had been made and he told them to instruct the New York firm to send all the requested information along to Albert. On December 17, 1904, James received a letter from Albert stating that they would not give James a quit-claim deed to the stock and saying in part:

. . . the only way to get this and do it right is to have an administrator appointed. I do not understand how you can handle Owen's estate in any other way. I can not see how it comes that you have a half interest in Owen's property . . . This all seems very strange to me. . . . We don't want anything but a square deal but we want that. . . . You sold 400 shares of St. L & S W R R stock in October and we have found out that this stock was in Owen's name and that you were in no way connected with it and yet shortly after Owen's death you disposed of it without power of attorney from us.

James was understandably hurt and offended by the tone and accusations of Albert's letter. The whole transaction with the railroad stock had been undertaken so that Albert and Henry could have immediate money from the estate to buy their farm, and half of that money had been James's own. James was so furious with his ungrateful younger brothers that at first he refused even to answer the letter. His son James Albert could see that this would lead to nothing but further family quarrels, so he prepared a carefully documented reply which would clarify all the issues in contention.

James didn't feel that a long, detailed accounting was necessary, but on January 3, 1905, he finally took his son's advice and composed an answer to Albert.

Dear Brother

Your letter of December 17th was received. I was surprised at the way you wrote and it was only after realizing your mistake about the St. L & S W R R stock that I write to explain that matter to you. I have never claimed a half interest in all Owen's property. But $7,012.50 of the money with which Owen paid for the stock was mine. . . . You say that on October 10th I disposed of the stock without power of attorney from you. I have on file your letter asking me for $13,220.00 at once and telling me you and Henry had a chance to buy 122 acres of land and saying you had told Mr. O'Brien you would take the land. This was an urgent demand for you to make and for me to meet within one month of Owen's death but on October 11th I sent you on account $13,220.00 through Molly. . . . I did not dispose of the St. Louis and Southwestern Railroad stock in October of 1902 as you stated in your letter but on advice of the bank I had it transferred to the name of a bank employee in New York who could later dispose of the stock at the greatest advantage to us all. I had the bank make out a detailed report of the transaction with the New York bank and gave it to Molly and told her to send it along to you. The best thing for you to do is to come out here and go over these things for yourself.

Sincerely,
                         Your Brother

Albert and Henry were not satisfied. Perhaps James Albert's detailed explanation should have been sent, perhaps the long delay in answering the charges had further angered the brothers in Sheldon. After a suitable delay of their own, they wrote again on January 24:

Dear Brother Jimmie,

Your letter received and we note what you say. We do not want to be contrary in this matter but as we never had any state-

James Hogle with his niece Ella Mantor in Sheldon, Illinois, in 1905.

ment from you showing the amount of cash on hand at the time of Owen's death or the amount of life insurance or what property he owned independent of you we thought we were entitled to know all these things.

It would be useless for us to go out and examine all the books and records as we would not know how. We would have to employ an attorney. We thought of taking a man from here. This of course would be quite an expense and we would rather settle the matter without it.

We want you to say just what you will give us . . . . If it is or looks like a fair proposition we will write you at once . . . . We will quit claim everything. Now let us know at once what you will do. If you do not want to do this then we will send or bring our attorney and go over the things from start to finish and have an administrator appointed. That's what we ought to have done long ago.

All's well, your brother, Albert.

James had been planning a trip to Warm Springs, Arkansas, for some time. He made his travel arrangements so that he would change trains and have a one-day layover in Chicago. Here he could meet with Albert, Henry, and Nancy and, he hoped, resolve once and for all the squabble over Owen's estate. James wrote to his brothers and they agreed to the meeting.

The family met on February 16, 1905, in Chicago at the Grand Pacific Hotel. Here it was agreed that James would pay his brothers and sisters for Owen's St. L. & S.W.R.R. stock. As in the earlier saloon settlement, James bent over backward for his family. He had already made gifts of some of his own stock to his sisters Mary and Anna. If he could settle the dispute with Albert and Henry and at the same time unobtrusively help Anna, everyone would be happy.

James Hogle was a good-hearted and sentimental soul who, fortunately, could afford to be generous. The fact that some of his relatives were in need was sufficient reason to accede to unreasonable demands, even though some of these "needs" bordered on the luxurious. James's extensive real estate and mining holdings had made him a very rich man. The dispute over the railroad stock seemed unworthy of argument, and it would never be said of James Hogle that he didn't care for his own.

A Door Closes

In the spring of 1906 James Hogle's saloon, successor to Hogle Brothers,' was liquidated. The saloon stock, glasses, tables, chairs, fixtures, and movables were sold to John Mahan, who would continue to operate the establishment under a lease arrangement with Ida Hogle, to whom James had deeded the building.

John Mahan was yet another old acquaintance from the Montana days. In Virginia City he had operated a tobacco shop on Wallace Street with Arthur Griffith. Mahan later went into the wholesale liquor trade and had operated saloons in conjunction with that business. It was stipulated in the agreement with the Hogles that John P. Quillen would retain his position as bartender.

The Main Street saloon had borne witness to the growth and change of downtown Salt Lake City, from wooden sidewalks and dirt streets to paved walks and Harriman's Electric Street Railway. It had seen the introduction of gaslights, then electric lights, indoor plumbing, the telephone, and by 1900 the first automobiles. It had also witnessed some of the town's liveliest history: the Whisky Street Wars, the gunfight between Major Nounnan and Jeremiah Richardson, the killing of Officer Burt and the lynching of Harvey, the excitement during the polygamy trials, the controversial Howard Spencer case, the Panic of '93, the Statehood celebrations of 1896, and the patriotic parades during the Spanish–American War. The establishment at 174 South Main had enjoyed the patronage of the mining men who had helped to build the city, and the west — men like Marcus Daly, Senator Thomas Kearns, Mayor James Glendenning, and the Walker brothers. The place had operated under three names, Clasbey and Hogle's, Hogle Brothers,' and James Hogle's, but whatever title graced the stationery, there was one consistency — it was, while James Hogle operated it, Salt Lake City's finest saloon.

But those days were over. Already the clamorings of the anti-saloon movement were foreshadowing total prohibition. The writing was on the wall. It was a good time to get out of the saloon business, and for James Hogle it was time to retire.

The John Mahan Liquor Company would continue to run the saloon at 174 South Main until Mr. Mahan's death on July 1, 1912.

Charles R. Bates then took over the operation of the saloon and ran it until 1917. That year the Anti-Saloon League finally succeeded in getting open saloons banned in Salt Lake City. The doors which had first swung open back in 1875 were now shut forever. After forty years of service, John P. Quillen, who had been a bartender at the establishment from the beginning, had wiped his last glass and was hanging up the towel. It was over, but in 1917 when the bottle was finally corked, Utah had the distinction of being the last open-saloon state left in the country.

THE GENTRY GO TO EUROPE

Even after the sale of the saloon and the settlement of Owen's estate, James continued to make gifts of stock and money to his relatives, most particularly his sisters Anna and Mary. The sense of these obligations, about which James felt so strongly, he passed on to his son James Albert.

On March 1, 1907, James deeded all his stock holdings over to his son with the proviso that James A. would continue to make contributions of support to his aunts, $250 a month each, for life. James A. accepted the responsibility, but he quickly learned that the task would not be an easy one.

As a matter of information only, he sent Aunt Anna an accounting of the money already given. This left her with the mistaken impression that James wanted the money paid back. Anna wrote back a sharp letter of protest to her nephew which led James to think that she was questioning his math rather than his intent. After several notes of clarification, which resulted in more misunderstandings, he finally caught Anna's drift.

> Dear Aunt Anna:
>
> Enclosed you will find a draft for $185.20. If I misunderstood your letter, you certainly did mine more. I had no intention that you should have taken it the way you did, for it was simply a statement of the stocks held for you, and the money sent you. I had no intention of conveying the idea that the monies sent you . . . at any time, were anything other than presents to you. I am very sorry and I wish to correct it at once.
>
> I did not mean to convey to you the idea that you were ever expected to repay them . . . .

Damaged photograph of Anna Gilmore, James Hogle's sister, taken about 1905.

We leave tomorrow for the east. How long we shall be away I do not know. Father came back from California feeling splendidly and he is glad to be able to take this trip. We sail March 9th. Father and mother send their love to you all. I hope your cold is better.

Your Affectionate Nephew,

Jim

The sailing that James Albert mentioned in his letter was a trip that Ida had been planning for many months. The past few years had been hard on James Hogle. The death of Owen and the squabble over the estate had taken their toll. A photograph of him with his two Mantor nieces at the time of his visit to Sheldon in 1905 revealed the strain. His face was drawn and there was a sorrow in the eyes that betrayed his weariness. Ida knew he needed a rest.

After his retirement, James and Ida took several trips to the coast — the most recent a tuna-fishing trip off the coast of Santa Barbara. This vacation, however, was something special. Reservations had been made back in January. The voyage as planned would last five months and take the family to eight countries. In the parlance of the day this was the Grand Tour.

For one-time immigrants and first-generation Americans the pilgrimage back to the "old country" was already a tradition. This was the heyday of the great luxury liners, when a long sea voyage was a status symbol and a mark of achievement, when the finest hotels were at sea and the best chefs in the world were on the Atlantic.

For those who had fled European wars, religious persecution, or the potato famine, the Grand Tour was also a kind of triumphal march through Europe. The planned itinerary for the Hogle family's trip in 1907 was nothing if not triumphal.

April 8	Gibraltar	May 25–27	Paris
April 22–27	Naples	June 4–7	London
April 29	Rome	June 10	Dublin
May 3	Venice	June 12	Cork
May 7	Budapest	June 14	Killarney
May 13	Dresden	July 13	Return New York.
May 20	Berlin		

It is significant that the family had reserved the most time for exploring James's native Ireland. There would be plenty of time to return to Armagh, time to find the church in Lurgan where Patrick was married and the little cottage in Armagh where James was born, time to look up relatives, if any were still alive, time to explore the ancient Irish castles, Georgian manor houses, the rocky abandoned farms, time to scratch around the crumbling Celtic crosses in the churchyards and the ancestral homelands of Castelreagh, but James made it only as far as Killarney.

The Cook's tour of the Killarney Lakes and Glengarriff Bay was to have included day trips to Innisfallen Island, Ross Castle, Muckross Abbey, Kenmare House, and the rugged Gap of Dunloe.

But sometime after their arrival in Killarney, James suffered a debilitating stroke. From the very first the prognosis was grim. The family returned home immediately, well ahead of schedule. By July 13, the day James was supposed to embark from Ireland for New York, he was already at his home in Salt Lake City.

THE UNEXPECTED ENDING

During the month of August James's condition seemed to be improving, but the family's hopes for a full recovery were dampened when the news arrived that his brother Albert had died on September ninth from the effects of a similar stroke.

After the sale of the saloon and the settlement of Owen's estate, Albert had retired from business and moved with his family to Lebanon, Indiana, where he built a large home, and where, it seemed, he had every prospect for a long and happy life. But such was not to be the case, and in October of 1906, while attending a family picnic on the farm near Lebanon, he was stricken with paralysis. For a brief time he recovered and was even able to assist his brother Henry with the farm work, but a full recovery didn't develop and gradually his condition deteriorated. As 1907 wore on, Ab became weaker and weaker until August, when he was admitted

Ida and James Hogle (at right) on a fishing trip to Catalina Island, California, in 1903.

to a sanitarium at Martinsville, Indiana. But receiving no benefit from his treatments there, he returned to his home in Lebanon and took to bed. Albert was in great pain and suffered intensely until death ended his ordeal. He had celebrated his fiftieth birthday on August 11 and was eighteen years and ten months younger than his similarly afflicted brother.

Reports of the decline and death of Albert were particularly hard on the family in Salt Lake City, for James now appeared to be on the same fated course. At first there was a generous amount of optimism and there was also a sustained period when he seemed on the road to recovery. During the Christmas season of 1907 he was able to get out and around on his own and was reported to be feeling much better. But at the end of January 1908 he suffered another stroke, this one leaving him paralyzed and bedridden.

During the whole ordeal James Albert faithfully attended his father, and with the help of his Aunt Mary, nursed him and made him as comfortable as possible. It could not have been easy on the young man. The stroke had not only immobilized his father but had so stunned his mother that James had to care for the elder Hogle's every need.

Yet for all the hardship, there was a great reward that went with the task. As the months wore on, James A. grew closer to his father than he had ever been before. He had always respected his father for his accomplishments, but now he felt a special bond of love for the man who had given him so much and was now so helpless.

On February 24 it became necessary for James A. to hire a full-time live-in nurse to assist with his father's care. Dr. McDowell made several house calls at the end of February and gave James a complete examination on March 4. The doctor noted how much worse the patient was since his last visit and told James A. that there was little hope of recovery. The end could come at any time.

The week of March 8–14, 1908, was beautiful and clear. Though neighboring states suffered from late winter storms, northern Utah was spared. It had been a hard winter and the good weather was the general topic of conversation. It had also been a good week on Wall Street. Mining and manufacturing stocks made substantial gains in the closing sessions and optimism was in the air. That week the *Salt Lake Tribune* reported on a variety of ventures that reflected the general optimism of the time. A Mr. Langford, the manager of Saltair Beach Resort, announced plans to build a large steamer for excursions on the Great Salt Lake. The steel framework for two new skyscrapers, the twin Boston and Newhouse buildings, had been completed, and the *Tribune* printed impressive photographs of their skeletal superstructures on the front page of the March 14 business section.

It was a good week for the owner of the structures, "Gentile" financier Samuel Newhouse, who was declared by the *Tribune*'s sports editor to be the favorite in the annual automobile race from Fort Douglas to Ensign Peak. It was a particularly good week for another sportsman, "Cyclone" Thompson, who had KO'd Jonney Murray in the eighth round of a scheduled twenty-round bout in San Francisco.

It was also a good week for the Salt Lake Theatre, which had enjoyed a booming season and was touting a new musical, *Forty-five Minutes from Broadway*. Ads for another musical event also appeared in the pages of the *Tribune*. St. Ann's Orphanage was selling tickets to the annual St. Patrick's Day fund-raiser. Touching photographs of the costumed orphan children to be featured in "A Night of Irish Melodies" were printed in several editions.

The orphanage's principal benefactor, Senator Thomas Kearns, would not be in attendance, however. Sunday's society page had reported that the Senator and his family were still in Europe. In fact, on St. Patrick's Day they would be sailing from Ireland for New York on the new White Star Liner *Adriatic*. They were not expected to return to Salt Lake until April first. Also expected in Salt Lake the first week of April were Mr. and Mrs. John David Wood, who had spent the winter in Ocean Park, California. It had been thirty-eight years since Mrs. Wood had saved James Hogle's life following the Loon Creek incident.

Friday the thirteenth of March was clear, except for a few scattered white clouds in a sea of blue. It had been just a little chilly in the early morning, 47 degrees, and the 26 per cent humidity had left a heavy dew on the windowpanes. But by mid-afternoon the

Ida and James Hogle at their South Temple home, about 1906.

temperature had risen to 63 degrees, and boaters at Calder Park on the city's southern outskirts were in shirtsleeves. On this day James Hogle entered his final sleep. He would die at one o'clock the following morning, March 14, 1908, at the age of sixty-nine.

Ida Hogle and her son were grief-stricken at the death of the man who as faithful husband and loving father had provided for their every need. Though warned by Doctor McDowell not to expect any miracles, both had quietly harbored the hope that James would recover. All their hopes had now been dashed. He was gone.

For the past eight months all of James Albert's energies had been focused on caring for his stricken father. Now that the battle was over, he was left drained and exhausted. Never had he felt so tired, but the strain, agony, and grief of that long day had so mastered him that he found it impossible to lie down. In the "little hours" before dawn James Albert sat alone in the room where his father had died. As he kept his weary vigil over the remains, he thought that the spirit of his dead father appeared to him. "It's all right, Jimmy," he said. "Everything will be all right." James Albert Hogle had finally fallen asleep.

A Startling Revelation

The death of James Hogle was a loss deeply felt in Salt Lake's Gentile community. The morning of his death the *Salt Lake Tribune* reported the following:

> A familiar figure, one known for many years in this City, will be seen no more, for James Hogle died at 1:00 a.m. today, age 69 at his residence at 376 Brigham Street from paralysis due to imperfect circulation. He leaves a widow and one son, James A. Hogle, a graduate of Yale. The deceased first came to Salt Lake in 1864 so he was an old timer and in 1871 he opened the Main Street Saloon which he conducted with his brother Owen, since dead. Mr. Hogle was friend of the late Marcus Daly and of many prominent people. He will be much missed.

The *Salt Lake Herald* announced the death under the banner "Passing of James Hogle, A Western Character, Friend of Marcus Daly."

> The announcement of Mr. Hogle's death yesterday morning was a cause of wide spread sorrow among his numerous friends in Salt Lake and the surrounding country.
>
> Mr. Hogle was widely known in the Intermountain region and up to his retirement four years ago, his place at 174 Main Street was a gathering point for all the men of note passing through the city. There were hundreds of successful mining men, financiers and commercial travelers who would not have thought a visit to Salt Lake complete without a chat with James Hogle.

The story then outlined the life of James Hogle: his birth in Armagh, his immigration to Quebec, his family's migration to Illinois, the Pikes Peak, Alder Gulch, and Loon Creek gold strikes, and his professional career in Salt Lake City. But the thrust of the story was his friendship with Marcus Daly.

> Late in the 80's Marcus Daly, the Montana millionaire, urged Mr. Hogle to move to Butte, offering to back him in business enterprises there. Mr. Hogle refused to leave Salt Lake.
>
> Daly and Hogle were warm friends. They were acquainted before fortune had smiled upon either of them. When Daly lived in Salt Lake he was employed by Walker Brothers and was sent by them to Montana where he made his millions. Whenever he came to Salt Lake he remembered his old friends of less prosperous days and would not go away until he had exchanged reminiscences with Hogle. He also had Hogle visit him at his home in Montana.
>
> But while fortune was pouring millions into Daly's lap, Hogle was not being neglected. Through his mining interests and his business here he amassed a substantial estate.

The death of James Hogle was also noted with sorrow on the editorial pages, the *Salt Lake Telegram* commenting:

> With the death of James Hogle a worthy citizen has gone to the beyond. He was a resident here for a generation: He was an honorable and honest man, a good citizen, the best of neighbors; in his home the perfect husband, brother, and father and we do not believe one reproach follows him to the grave.
>
> He was a man of clear judgment; if careful and cautious always, he was always absolutely reliable. He made his money here and invested here — this was his home in every sense of the word. He will be missed most by those who knew him best. In his home the sorrow will be profound, for that home was all in all to him, and he cared more for the comfort and happiness of those who leaned upon him than for himself. May the Great Comforter comfort them.

The *Tribune* also editorialized on the passing of the Gentile pioneer, saying, in part:

> The late James Hogle was one of Utah's most prominent citizens and was honored and respected by all who had the good fortune to have his friendship and acquaintance. Mr. Hogle was widely known in the inter-mountain states and counted as his friends the best element of citizenship in that section of the country. . . . At the time of his demise Mr. Hogle was sixty-nine

years old. He is sincerely mourned by all who knew him for his lovable disposition, charitable nature and extreme generosity.

The funeral was held on Monday afternoon, March 16, 1908. Dean Benjamin Brewster of St. Mark's Cathedral conducted the services, which were held at the Hogle residence on Brigham Street. A large crowd of mourners accompanied the family to the City Cemetery. Among the out-of-state visitors who attended the funeral were Mr. and Mrs. Frank Guiraud of Denver, Colorado.

In the days that followed, the news of James Hogle's death spread through the surrounding states. The article in the *Salt Lake Herald* was reprinted in a number of western newspapers, including the Salmon City, Idaho, *Recorder*. In Challis, Idaho, this story was read by James Horton, the former Loon Creek livery stable operator, a man intimately familiar with the career of the late James Hogle. He and a reporter for the *Challis Silver Messenger* got to talking about the old days, and Horton told the reporter of an incident involving James that had occurred some thirty-seven years earlier. The following week the tale appeared in the Challis paper under the headline "Late James Hogle had great history. Was badly wounded by a desperate man near Leesburg, Idaho. His assailant was shot by friends of Hogle and fatally wounded." The article described in some detail the killing of George Moyer and closed by saying:

> . . . James Hogle was made out of the material to make his way on the frontier, where often a difference of opinion was settled at the mouth of a gun and the one who was the most accomplished in this line of argument was the one who usually came out ahead in the controversy. He was one of those free hearted, honest men, whose word was considered as good as any man's bond, but had the nerve to fight his own battles, which was necessary when Alder Gulch, Leesburg and Loon Creek were furnishing such fabulous sums of yellow metal.

James Horton's memory was faulty, however, and his recounting of the incident contained factual errors. He confused the names of some of the principles, had the incident set in Leesburg rather than Oro Grande, and spelled Hogle's former name Gereaux rather

than Guiraud. But these were small matters, and thirty-seven years
is a long time. The tale was essentially correct.

Someone in Idaho who read the account clipped the story and
sent it along to James Albert, for whom it was a scandalous revelation. His father had told him about his family's name actually
being Gilmore, and he had, of course, been well acquainted with his
grandfather, Patrick Gilmore. He had even heard how his father
had gone under the name "Guiraud" for a time, but he had never
thought it appropriate to press his father to reveal the reason behind
the adoption of the new name. Suddenly it all seemed painfully
clear. His father had adopted the name to hide his role in the killing of George Moyer!

Two weeks after the funeral, James Albert took a trip to Challis
and Salmon, Idaho, perhaps to further investigate the mysterious
tale of the killing on the William's Lake Trail, and perhaps to interview James Horton himself. Whatever he learned, it wasn't enough,
and during the next few years he continued to look for answers.
James Hogle's surviving siblings, Mary, Anna, and Henry, knew
very little about the name change. Whatever had happened had
occurred when they were very young. Nor was his mother any help,
since by the time she met James A.'s father he was already known as
Hogle. Eighteen months after the death of James Hogle, his son
was still looking for answers.

In December of 1909 a former Montana resident came through
Salt Lake and inquired after James. It was Nathan Thompson, the
one-time owner of the Exchange Saloons, who had employed and
known James Albert's father more than forty years earlier. James
A. spoke to Thompson at length and in detail about his father's
activities and movements during his days in Virginia City and
Helena. The information he supplied was so important to James
Albert that he asked him to take a sworn deposition in the presence
of himself and a Mr. W. M. Bradley. The deposition was as follows:

Salt Lake City, Utah
Dec 9th, 1909
Statement of Nathan Thompson to James A. Hogle.

I went to Virginia City, Montana in July of 1863. Your
father arrived in the fall of 1863. Several men, who knew your

father in Denver, recommended him to me. They called him "Jimmy Guiraud." I employed your father as long as I stayed in Virginia City. In the fall of 1864 I went to Walla Walla. I spent the winter of 1864–65 in San Francisco. From there I went to Idaho, but returned to Walla Walla in the summer of 1865 and in August of 1865 my brother died there.

In the middle of September I started for Montana and arrived in Helena in October of 1865. Your father was in Helena when I arrived and your Uncle was in Helena that fall. Your uncle was known as Owen Hogle.

I bought into business in November of 1865 and your uncle Owen Hogle went to work for us, and worked for us continually as Owen Hogle until I left there in 1868. He continued to work there until after I left.

After I arrived in Helena in 1865 some Colorado people still called your father, Jimmy Guiraud, but he explained to me how he got that name by living with that French family in Colorado. But after your uncle went to work for us in 1865, your father was known as Jimmy Hogle. From Montana your father went to Idaho, either in the winter of 1866 or the spring of 1867. He came back to Montana to visit two or three years after that. In 1872 I went to Salt Lake City and found your father living there and known as Jimmy Hogle.

Nathan Thompson

Signed in presence of
W. M. Bradley

James A. took the signed deposition and placed it with the article from the Challis paper in a safe deposit box in Walker Brothers' Bank, and there it would remain for forty-five years.

LAST OF THE PLACER BOYS

There is little wonder that the history and folklore of the nineteenth-century American west dominates every period of popular American literature. Each subsequent generation has produced authors who have found powerful themes to be explored in the epic story of the American frontier: Mark Twain, Bret Harte, Ambrose Bierce, Zane Grey, Louis L'Amour, to name only a few, were some of the most popular writers of their respective periods.

Nor is it surprising that so many American films are about the Wild West. The westerner, in all his various poses — pioneer, cowboy, prospector, gambler, lawman, and outlaw — is the archetypal American. The western is our literature. No other genre speaks so directly to the individualistic temperament of the American character.

But all fictional representations aside, nineteenth-century westerners were remarkable people. Somehow they seem to us a different breed of men and women — their deeds more daring, their characters stronger, their lives somehow more heroic. Through the veil of history they loom as giants, bolder and wilder than their twentieth-century counterparts, accustomed to, even comfortable with, the harsh realities of their times and the inevitability of death.

But life in the nineteenth century was physically more demanding. Hard manual labor still accomplished most of the work. Travel was arduous and the need for physical exertion was unquestioned. Given the times, strength was a prerequisite of survival, and survival in those times built physical strength.

If they appear to us now as somewhat hardened toward life and cavalier about death, it was probably because death was all around them. Medicine was primitive and haphazard. Yellow fever, smallpox, diphtheria, measles, and pneumonia — diseases which seldom worry modern Americans — were common and fatal. The men who accompanied James Gilmore across the plains, the men who worked the gold camps of Alder Gulch, Last Chance, Leesburg and Loon Creek, the great figures who really built the west and made so much history were themselves products of the history they were making. The times in which they lived molded their lives as they molded their times. History is a reciprocal arrangement.

When James Hogle died in 1908, many of the "B'hoys" were already gone. The Vigilante leaders, X Beidler, Nathan Langford, and Col. Sanders had joined their less pure fellows at the last roundup. Helena acquaintances G. Julius Germain, Billy Mather, Sam and Charlie Greer, Dan Flurry, and B. F. Crocker were gone, as were Leesburg pioneers Alva P. Challis and Bat Doody, the latter of a stroke upon returning to his native Ireland.

Marcus Daly, the millionaire Irish prospector and founder of Anaconda Copper, had died on November 1, 1900. James Hogle's multi-faceted partner James T. Clasbey had died during the Christmas season of 1904, and former Salt Lake mayor James Glendenning died shortly after moving to Washington in 1905.

Some of those left would not linger long. A little over a year after his death, Hogle's old friend John David Wood was tragically crushed under the wheels of a train on a Salt Lake City street. Nathan Thompson would die in Portland, Oregon, in 1914, Enos A. Wall in Salt Lake in 1920, Luke Voorhees in Cheyenne in 1922, and Bishop Daniel S. Tuttle that same year in Saint Louis.

Their ranks were definitely thinning, but there were still old-timers around. In the years to come James A. would receive from time to time letters intended for his father: a short note from an A. P. Curtin in Helena asking the whereabouts of Nate Thompson, a Christmas card from an old Leesburg acquaintance. These communications from the past were precious treasures to James Albert, threads of memories which linked him to the life of his departed father, and he put them in the safe deposit box with Nate Thompson's deposition and James Horton's account of the Loon Creek incident.

One particularly haunting letter arrived at the Hogle home in June 1909, a year and three months after the death of James. That summer James A. had taken his mother to Europe, and the communication went unopened until their return.

Saint Mary's Hospital
6/9/1909
Tucson, Arizona

My Old time Friend, Jimmy Hogle,

I dreamed about you a few nights ago and I thought we were back in Helena, Montana as we were in 1866 and 67. I have no doubt that you have forgotten me, but when I mention my name and that of G. Julius Germain and The Old International Hotel when you boarded there, when Owen, your brother was tending bar for Dan Flurrey in the Exchange Saloon, when I was the chief steward to Germain in the Hotel, and afterward when I tended bar for Billy Mather and Crocker at the Billard Hall. . . . My name is Edward Rafferty. . . . No doubt you will recollect me now, as you and I had so much fun together about Germain as you was the only man who gambled who could borrow money from him. So I think you know me now.

Well Jimmy, to be brief about it, I have been sick for three years and got broke and I am compelled to go to Saint Mary's Hospital on the County. I am entirely out of money and about half out of tobacco. I wish you would send me a few dollars. I am 72 years old and can't do much on this earth but we might meet in the next world.

I heard you are well fixed up and I'm glad of it. Now Jimmy, I shall never forget you if, without straining yourself, you could favor me with a few dollars. I don't want much, just what you can spare. All the old timers are about gone to the next world and I expect to go over the divide at any time.

There is another old timer there, I forget his last name, only Andy. He was steward for Sullivan in the St. Louis Hotel. Give him my best regards. Hoping you will get this letter, I still remain your old friend,

Edward Rafferty, Adios

Tucson, Pima County, Arizona Territory
Care of St. Mary's Hospital,
for me.

James A. read and reread the letter that Ed Rafferty had intended for his departed father. He struggled with his emotions as he composed a letter informing the old friend of his father's death. He purchased a tin of M. Stachelberg and Company's Leland Stanford Havana Cigars, packaged it up with a little money, and sent it on to Tucson. Eight days later the package was returned unopened with a short note of explanation from the attending physician. Edward Rafferty had died at St. Mary's the previous week.

Part II

JAMES ALBERT HOGLE

CHAPTER FOURTEEN

A Childhood in Zion, 1876–1892

JAMES ALBERT HOGLE was born to James and Ida E. Hogle on October 12, 1876. His birth took place in Mrs. King's old rooming house on Third South, which Charles King had started building for Ida's mother Elizabeth back in 1854. James A. was born in the same room that his mother had been born in twenty-one years earlier.

James A. Hogle was baptized into the Episcopal church at St. Mark's Cathedral on December 31, 1876. Bishop Tuttle was out of town at the time, so the services were conducted by the Rev. R. M. Kirby. The child's godparents were June K. Daggett and the old friend who had also served as best man at James Hogle's wedding three years previously, Luke Voorhees.

For all the tradition of the old boarding house, the baby's parents and his maternal grandfather were not on the best of terms at the time, and so in March the family moved from the Third South home to a small cottage on Main Street. Here they resided for a little over a year. After a short stay at the home of a Mrs. Barnum, they rented a home on Fourth East, next door to the Wagener family. (Henry Wagener owned and operated the California Brewery, one of the west's largest brewing and distilling companies.) The neighbors became best of friends and their association would continue into the next generation. The Hogles lived in the rented home on Fourth East for three years and five months.

As a baby, James Albert strongly favored his mother. Photos of the infant with Ida reveal a marked resemblance, particularly about the mouth, nose, and brow-line. He shared his mother's high cheekbones and faintly wry smile. It would not be until some years later that his father's strong features came into prominence — broad forehead and slightly rounded jaw — but as with all family resemblances, there were times when certain expressions or glances might suddenly bring to light other, less dominant familial characteristics. At different times, various relatives saw in him features or mannerisms of his Uncle Owen Hogle or Uncle Charlie King or, most often, his grandfather, Patrick Gilmore.

When James A. was five years old, the family moved into their own new home at the corner of Fourth East and Brigham Street, No. 16. Moving day was October 29, 1881, Grandfather Charles

Little Jimmy Hogle and the family dog in a C. R. Savage portrait, taken around the time of his misadventure with the rain barrel. The inscription on the back, in his uncle Sidney King's childish hand, reads: "Man's Best Friend the Dog Spot who led me tu save Jimmy's Life Who fall in a rain barrel. Unkel Taggy."

King's sixty-fifth birthday. The Hogles would reside at No. 16 for the next twenty years, and this is the residence that James A. would always remember as the old family home.

THE RAIN BARREL INCIDENT

When James A. was just a toddler an unusual accident occurred which very nearly cost him his life. The story of this incident is only partially known. Certain facts are clear and others are the product of fable, conjecture, or faulty memory, and some details are in dispute.

It was sometime in the early spring, and snow still covered the higher foothills surrounding the city. James A. was playing alone behind the house where there were various objects to climb on and over, among them a huge wooden rain barrel. Somehow or other the inquisitive tot managed to climb up the boxes and crates until he reached the top of the large water tank. Whether he stood or crawled onto the top is uncertain; what is known is that the top of the rain barrel gave way and the child was plunged into the frigid water.

The family dog, a Dalmation named Spot, saw the child fall into the tank and started barking and howling. Sidney King, the child's uncle, heard the commotion and came running. The dog led Sidney to the rain barrel and he pulled the drowning tot from the water. The Rin Tin Tin–fashion rescue was successful, and James A. Hogle owed a debt of gratitude to the animal kingdom.

There is no direct evidence that the rain barrel incident had any consequence beyond the terror of the moment and the cold that he caught because of his freezing bath. But James A. did suffer a number of illnesses in his early years, one of which had a lasting effect upon his life.

Some of the most crucial turning points in history are little things which go entirely unnoticed at the time, or if noticed are thought to be unimportant or trivial. A certain man gets up one morning and puts on a pair of felt boots instead of the rubber ones directly beside them. He goes duck hunting, his feet get wet, he catches pneumonia, and the subsequent history of a nation is forever altered. From the vantage point of hindsight it is clear that if Leon Trotsky had been well enough to attend the Politburo meetings following the death of Lenin, Stalin might never have come to power. The boot decision had consequences in disproportion to its seeming importance at the time. If the rain barrel incident was to blame for James Albert's later illness, then it, more than any other single factor, may have influenced his subsequent career, and by extension the history of the intermountain west as well.

James possessed many of the same qualities his father and Uncle Owen had had in abundance: boundless energy, a strong sense of duty, keen insight, determination, and a drive to succeed. But his father and uncles were outgoing, with scores of close friends and hundreds of personal acquaintances. As little Jim grew older it would be noted that he was quieter and more reserved than any of his immediate relatives. The friends he acquired were themselves more reserved and conservative than the friends of his father. There were no James Hayden or Ed Rafferty types among them, no gamblers like Thomas Woodford or adversaries like X Beidler.

James Senior was a colorful character whose actions reflected his outgoing and, at times, volatile personality. Young James had always seemed cut from a slightly different mold, yet there was a simpler explanation for what became a profound divergence in personality.

In his early years, James Albert suffered from a number of serious ear infections and abcesses which resulted in a loss of hearing that through the years became progressively worse. As a result of his increasing deafness, James Albert became an introvert. The kind of energy that his father might have used to break up a saloon brawl, haul a slab of pool table slate 300 miles into the mountains, or build a toll road, James A. would use in concentrated study. The shivering child Ida frantically dried that cold spring day in the late 1870's would eventually become a scholar. His capacity for study, precise observation, and reasoned judgment were in part responsible for his later success. In education, in business, and particularly in the development of Salt Lake City and the west, James Albert Hogle's accomplishments would far outstrip those of his father.

An Old Man and a Cow

James Albert's earliest memories were of the old home on Fourth East and of his mother. The Ida Hogle he remembered from those earliest days was a strict woman who was known to use the stick. Though not un-loving, she demanded from her son proper behavior at all times, and correctness was strictly enforced around her. Ida was also the boy's first teacher. Before he was six he could read simple sentences, write his own name, and add. Ida wanted her son to be a success, and she drove him with the same carrot and stick approach that her own mother, Ida King, had used. In the nineteenth century there was one accepted maxim for bringing up children: "Spare the rod and spoil the child." James Albert Hogle was an only child; he was wealthy; he had his own pony and a devoted coterie of loving relatives; but he was in no danger of being spoiled.

Living with the Hogles at this time was the boy's paternal grandfather, Patrick Gilmore, an easygoing and gentle old man who was a playful foil to his mother's serious intentions. Though separated in age by more than seven decades, James Albert and Patrick were fast friends.

Jimmy's other recollections from childhood were of Salt Lake City. From the very earliest days, the city had been touted as a good place to raise children, and it wasn't just the wholesome influence of the L.D.S. church that made this so. The physical and geographical plan of the city contributed to its beautiful appearance and reputation.

The Mormon pioneers of 1847 had laid out Salt Lake City on a giant, orderly grid system. As a city planner, Brigham Young was an unquestioned genius, with few equals in the nineteenth century. The large eastern cities of the day were object lessons in bad planning. They were traffic-clogged mazes and congested fire traps with narrow streets, tiny blocks, meandering roads, and little open space. Much like the western mining camps that grew up haphazardly from the bottoms of mountain gulches, most eastern cities were not so much laid out as extended across whatever terrain and roads were already there. Brigham Young was determined that his capital would not mimic the mistakes of the past.

The streets were wide, 132 feet from gutter to gutter. Sidewalks, too, were ample, twenty feet from building front to street. Nothing inhibited or obstructed the free movement of people and commerce through the city. The grid was uniform — mountain streams, hills, ditches, and other obstacles notwithstanding; all the streets ran north–south or east–west without variation. Irrigation ditches and gutters were also laid out in an orderly fashion.

All of this demanded meticulous surveying, extensive site preparation, thorough land clearing, ditch digging, draining, and land filling on a grand scale. It was a job that could only be accomplished by an army of talented and well-organized workers. None of it would have been possible if it hadn't been for the autocratic power of Brigham Young and the dedicated obedience of the faithful.

Brigham Young's original plan had another innovation, over-sized city blocks. Salt Lake's so called "super blocks" had their origins in the Mormons' early commitment to cooperative labor and communal experiments and their passion for community projects and farming. Earlier Mormon communities had benefited from open spaces, and the city's original plan provided that large sections within the city would remain vacant of cluttering buildings.

Great Salt Lake City's first residential areas were to consist of 135 ten-acre blocks. Houses were to be built on the outside of the blocks only, the interiors to be used for orchards, gardens, or common grazing. The center of each block was an open space, and though farming was primarily conducted outside the city, mini-farms dotted the heart of the metropolis. More even than the wide streets or the uniformity of the grid, these interior open spaces gave nineteenth-century Salt Lake City its distinctively expansive and uncrowded character.

It was in the interior of the block behind their home at the corner of Fourth East and Brigham Street that the Hogles kept their family cow. In the early mornings, after milking, Patrick Gilmore would take his little grandson out with him to drive the cow to pasture. She was a particularly ill-tempered beast whose stubborn disposition and frequent bolting tried the patience of the old man, to the delight of his grandson. One of Jimmy's earliest

C. R. Savage portrait of Jimmy Hogle at three years and nine months.

memories was of the two of them chasing the old cow about the field. It was the kind of memory that might have been expected from a boy who grew up on a farm, not the son of a saloon keeper living four blocks from the center of a city with a population well over 30,000.

In those early days, the old man and his grandson were constant companions. The two were so often seen "toddling off" together that James Albert soon acquired the nickname "Little Pat," which he would keep through his early school years. While he lived with the Hogles, "Old Pat" contributed to the household by performing many of the chores: milking the cow, feeding the chickens, working in the garden, and doing light work about the house. But the old man's first love was horses, and it was in feeding and grooming the horses, hitching up the carriage, and training his grandson's pony that Patrick was most happy. This love and expertise he had passed on to his son Owen, and Little Pat would also learn from the ancient horseman something about the animals. It ran in the family.

EARLY EDUCATION

The first St. Mark's School was opened in an old bowling alley on East Temple in 1868. In 1869 it was moved to Independence Hall, and in 1870 to Groesbeck's old store. In 1872 the school was moved again, this time to a building specifically designed as a school, located directly across from City Hall on First South (now the site of the city's main fire station). St. Mark's would operate out of this facility until the late 1890's.

St. Mark's School or Girls was conducted in the basement of St. Mark's Cathedral. Young children, boys and girls, attended kindergarten and received religious instruction in the basement of the church, and it was here that Little Pat began his formal education in the fall of 1881.

In 1882 he entered St. Mark's School for Boys. He would spend the next eight years there and the training he received would do much to mold his thinking. Though the church-run school offered a good dose of religious instruction, the majority of the classes were practical and down-to-earth. The three R's were at the core of the curriculum, and study and hard work were the principal lessons taught.

By 1884 James's writing skill had developed sufficiently for him to begin corresponding with his aunts, uncles, and cousins. In these early letters school was his favorite topic, as in this note to his Aunt Anna Steele:

Salt Lake City, Sept. 24th, 1884

Dear Aunt Anna,

I thought I would like to write to you and send it in Mama's note. Tell Cousin Jim to write to me. I have commenced school and have five lessons to get every day. I also go to dancing school. I have been head scholar for a week.

I am getting tired and will stop now.

Good buy from

Jimmie

Two years later he detailed his scholastic progress to his cousin Jimmie Steele. His style was factual, direct, and to the point; his abrupt closing was becoming habitual:

Salt Lake City,
October 6th, 1886

Dear Cousin,

I will write about Salt Lake City and school. I am in the fourth reader in "Swinton's Word Speller," in Appleton's Standard Geography, in Ray's New Elementary Arithmetic of Long Measure, and in English Grammar.

Now about Salt Lake City; There was a circus here two weeks ago.

I will be ten years old next week. All send love. I hope you are all well. You must write soon.

I am getting tired now and so I will stop.

Jimmie

His brief epistles had a factual air about them, and his school essays were exemplars of brevity. In 1886 Jimmy Hogle, then a fourth grader, composed the following fact-laden essay for Miss Hayden, his teacher at St Mark's.

WOOD

There are a great many different kinds of wood in America. Walnut, mahogany and rosewood are used for making furniture. The hickory is the hardest wood there is and is the most valuable. It is used for making buggies and wagons. The Japanese are famous for their wood carving and are much admired. Wood is one of the most useful things that grows.

Jimmy Hogle, Nov. 18th, 1886.

It would later be said of James Albert Hogle that he had a special talent for reducing difficult problems to their simplest elements.

The winter of 1886–87 had been long and hard. The students had been cooped up inside their classroom for most of the previous three months and the strain was telling. Spring was anxiously awaited and in March the weather broke. The Pacific westerlies blew the smoke from the valley, the air was again clean and fresh, and for one student, at least, the sudden thaw was too much to bear.

In March of 1887 James was eleven years old, and try as he might it was hard for him to keep his mind on his work. He wrote a letter to Miss Hayden which expressed his thoughts succinctly, if rather transparently.

March 28th, 1887

Dear Miss Hayden,

Spring has come and we will soon have our Easter vacation. I think these pleasant days make us feel as though we would rather be out of doors than in the schoolroom. If this weather continues the trees will be in blossom and our City will be very pretty. We are looking forward to the time when school will close. Bishop Tuttle will be with us then, and I for one will be very glad to see him.

I am your loving pupil,

Jimmy Hogle.

James A. Hogle, age eight.

Summer in Salt Lake City meant more than the return of Bishop Tuttle, although even Miss Hayden must be looking forward to that event. Surrounding the Salt Lake Valley were the Wasatch Mountains, and from the earliest days the scenic canyons were places of refuge from the summer heat. The recreational value of the canyons was exploited early, and by 1887 several tiny railroads operated excursions into the mountains.

A summer Sunday picnic in the canyon was already a tradition, and in Big and Little Cottonwood canyons, Millcreek, East, and Emigration canyons, buggies wound their way up the narrow roads to the favorite spots. A day in the cool canyons of the Wasatch might be spent hiking, horseback riding, or fishing for native cutthroat trout on one of the many mountain streams.

In the city itself there was boating on the little lakes in Calder (now Nibley) Park and Liberty Park. There were the famous hot springs just north of the city, which from the first decade of settlement were touted for their "healthful properties," and on Brewery Hill, named for the two large breweries which dominated the hillside, there was Fuller's Pleasure Gardens.

Fuller's Pleasure Gardens was an amusement park that featured giant rope swings, slides, and a polished obsidian camera obscura housed in an octagonal room at the top of an observation tower. From here "pleasure seekers" could discreetly view their "unsuspecting fellow citizens at work or play." Through carefully arranged slits and mirrors in the sides of the camera, images were projected on the round obsidian screen in the floor of the tower. The projection mirrors ranged not only down on the city, but also on well-placed secluded benches in the park directly below.

But during the summer months of the 1880's, Great Salt Lake City's most popular attraction was the lake itself. Through the decade a variety of recreational activities were offered by competing resorts at Lakeside, Black Rock, and Garfield beaches. The lake was a favorite site for bathing, picnicking, sightseeing, and boating. Several excursion steamers plied the salty waters, including the *Susie Ritter*, the *Whirlwind*, and the *General Garfield*. In 1886 more than 100,000 visitors thronged the resorts. The lake business was in its heyday, and not before or since have conditions at the water's edge been as conducive to recreation. Two frequent visitors to the lake were James Albert and his uncle Owen.

It was a hot August day in 1887, and the *General Garfield* was returning to the dock after an excursion to Lakeside. As Little Pat and his Uncle Owen waited on the pier a man, who later proved to be drunk, suddenly slipped from the deck of the steamer and fell into the water near the dock. The floundering man screamed for help and Owen quickly came to the rescue, diving from the dock, swimming the short distance, and pulling the man to shore.

There are many things that can be done on the Great Salt Lake, but diving and swimming are not among them. The heavy brine, full of dissolved minerals as well as salts, is normally hard enough to knock a man out if his "dive" is from any height. The salt water stings the eyes like knife blades, and the brine shrimp and brine fly larvae make the water taste like insect soup. Swimming in the lake is a memorable experience, and the sight of the gasping, coughing tourist and his rescuer made a lasting impression. Owen Hogle's heroics were duly noted in the papers the following day and must have raised knowing grimaces from properly initiated readers.

Owen, always an avid outdoorsman, instilled in his young nephew an appreciation for the "great outdoors" and its wildlife. As James would later recall in a letter to his cousin Archie Owen Gilmore, "Fishing reminds me of my boyhood days, and you may be interested to know that Uncle Owen was a great fisherman. He took me on many of his trips for years, probably because I was the only nephew available. . . . Owen had a great influence on my life."

In August of 1889, Owen took his nephew on one of their many fishing trips to Idaho, and on the eleventh James wrote to his parents from Geyser Hot Springs:

Dear Mama and Papa,

I thought I would write you and tell you I'm all right. The reason I write so badly is because I cut my finger. Uncle Owen and I have hired a team. We are going fishing tomorrow.

I have caught the biggest fish that has been caught up here. Perhaps we will send you some fish.

I hope the cow is all right.

I am your loving son,

Jim

Uncle Owen taught his young nephew more than how to set duck decoys or tie flies. There were special skills that Owen possessed which might be useful in young Jim's later life, skills that had to do with careful planning, probability, and assessing odds.

Bishop Tuttle Takes a Hand

At St. Mark's School James A.'s grades were always excellent and he made rapid progress. His summers were spent working around the house with his grandfather, fishing with his uncle, and taking weekend excursions into the canyons with his parents. In 1891, following his graduation from St. Mark's, he enrolled at the College Preparatory Department of the University of Utah. He would attend the "U" through the spring of 1892.

Throughout his first year of secondary education, Jim was encouraged by his teachers, who all seemed to praise his abilities and intelligence. His mother, however, was not entirely pleased with the marks he was receiving and was even less enthusiastic about his course of study at the University. She grew impatient with her son, who seemed to her to be sliding and not applying himself to the fullest. James Albert could not understand his mother's dissatisfaction, and the relationship between them became increasingly strained.

The University of Utah, founded in 1850, was the oldest state university west of the Missouri River. It had a long and distinguished history, and its preparatory department was certainly adequate for preparing students for college. That is, the subjects offered were the ones required by most of the colleges in the country. But Ida sensed that there was something missing. What she wanted for her son was more than simply adequate preparation for college; she wanted little Jim to be prepared for life. The Preparatory Department at the "U" may have been very good, but its reputation was distinctly provincial. Jim had already demonstrated that he was an exceptional student; if some day he wished to attend one of the better schools in the country, it might be wiser if he attended a preparatory school with a proven reputation. The Hogles turned for advice to their old family friend and confidant, Bishop Tuttle.

For the past few years he had been living in the east, and perhaps he could recommend a school for Little Pat.

Bishop Tuttle's reply was prompt. There was only one school suitable for James Albert Hogle. It was on the other side of the continent and admission requirements were strict, but Bishop Tuttle was an old friend of the school's headmaster and rector, Henry Augustus Coit. He would personally write to Coit and recommend the young Hogle for admission. It was all quickly done and settled. James was enrolled at St. Paul's in New Hampshire and would leave for the east in August.

A New York Vacation

Through the summer of 1892 the knowledge that James Albert was leaving in the fall not only cooled the feud between mother and son, but brought them closer together. Now that he was leaving, both avoided any confrontation which might result in a renewal of argument. James Albert was particularly dutiful. Ida was at times uncharacteristically tearful. The thought of her son growing up and leaving home was more than hard to accept, it was almost unbearable. Her husband wisely counseled that it was time to cut the apron strings, and she knew he was right. But the rightness didn't make it any easier. Ida didn't want to suffocate her son, but she also found it difficult to let him go. Her short temper had in part been a product of her inability to reconcile her feelings. Her outbursts had been more the result of her own frustration than anger. Sometime during the summer it was decided that the family would accompany Little Pat on his trip back east. Ida could then satisfy herself that St. Paul's School was indeed the place for her son, and the family would have a vacation together before the school term started.

James, Ida, and Little Pat boarded an eastbound train the morning of August 26, 1892. After switching trains at Union Station in Chicago two days later, they proceeded to New York City, arriving there on Monday morning, August 29. They checked into the Oriental, a seven-story, 400-room hotel which stood on Broadway and 39th Street. Here they stayed for the next twelve days while they took in the sights of the city. One of those sights was directly across the street, the Metropolitan Opera House. But the day before the Hogles arrived, the building had been gutted by a huge and deadly fire that had started in the scenery shop and then spread to the stage and auditorium. Though the fire was confined to the Opera building, the smell of smoke was heavy on Broadway and lingered about the hotel through the duration of their stay. Years later, the acrid smell of "wet smoke" from a doused fire would conjure up for Jim memories of the old Oriental Hotel.

As far as the Hogles were concerned, New York City was the most exciting place on earth, and during their stay they absorbed as much of its sights and culture as possible. They went to the music halls and the theater, taking in a performance of *Around the World in Eighty Days* at Niblo's Garden. They went shopping and sightseeing, visited the museums, and saw a tennis match in Central Park.

One afternoon the family visited the Statue of Liberty, which had been completed just six years earlier. It was a windy day and the ferry pitched in the heavy swells. The cold wind-driven spray soon forced the parents inside, but Jim remained at the rail of the boat to peer at the sights of the world's busiest harbor. Little green and red tug boats were everywhere, scurrying about the great ships and easing the large steamers into their berths. Though steam had long since replaced sail for the bulk of the Atlantic passenger trade, there were still many sailing ships in service as fishing and cargo vessels, and the boy gazed in wonder at the tangle of tall masts, huge sails, and the clutter of rigging. It was on just such vessels that his grandfather, and later his father, had made their way from Ireland to Quebec a half century ago.

James Albert Hogle was a first-generation American, and the Statue of Liberty and the old sailing ships had special and personal meaning for him. But the highlight of the family's trip to New York was the day his father and his father's old friend Marcus Daly took him to see the races at the Sheepshead Bay race track on Coney Island.

A Day at the Races

Marcus Daly was one of the richest men in America. Since leaving Utah in 1876 he had worked hard at developing his Anaconda Copper Mines in Butte, and the effort had paid off in riches beyond imagination. There were no income taxes, no severance taxes, and no luxury taxes. Marcus Daly's personal income was, in its entirety, disposable.

Daly, an Irish immigrant from County Cavan, had received his American citizenship in a Salt Lake City courtroom in 1874. He retained, however, his Irish nationalism as well as an Irishman's love of horses and racing, and he indulged in this pastime with complete abandon, paying unheard-of prices for the finest thoroughbreds in the world. He once turned away disgusted from one of his agents who had failed to bid high enough to purchase the great Hungarian horse Ormonde. The agent told Daly that he had "Bid as long as I dared." "I told you to buy him," was Daly's angry reply. The price had reached $140,000.

James and Owen Hogle had often visited Marcus Daly at his home, the Bitter Root Stock Farm, a fabulous estate nestled in the Bitter Root Valley of western Montana. The towering peaks of the northern Rockies were background to the ranch where Daly had constructed artificial lakes and stocked them with trout. The extravagant flagstone ranch house, with its swimming pool, private laundry, greenhouse, and gardens, was overshadowed by the ranch's luxurious stables. Outside of the courts of Europe there was nothing to rival them. Daly had spared no expense in their building. He was said to have paid out $200,000 for the construction of one irrigation ditch alone. The pastures were verdant; the stables and barns were all heated and kept improbably spotless. There were exercise tracks and training tracks and a covered five-eighths of a mile track, with its own heating plant, for winter use.

But even more impressive than the facilities were the horses who stabled there: China Silk, the champion trotter; Scottish Chieftain and Colin, winners of the Belmont Stakes; Ogden, Hamburg, Hamburg Bell, and Artful, winners of the Belmont Futurity; Sysonby, winner of the Saratoga Stakes; Montana, winner of the Suburban Stakes; and Tammany, winner of the Lorillard Stakes at Monmouth, the Tidal Stakes at Sheepshead Bay, the Lawrence Realization and the Withers Stakes at Belmont Park. Tammany was the most famous of Daly's thoroughbreds. His barn was so lavish it was known as Tammany's Castle.

On the morning of August 30, 1892, James Hogle and his son had breakfast with Daly at the Hoffman House. They then climbed into Daly's private carriage, drawn by four beautiful Hambletonians, and proceeded to Sheepshead Bay Race Track for the fourth day of the fall racing season. It had drizzled two days earlier, and again today the skies threatened rain. Daly had horses in every heat, not one of them a proven mudder. The owners had their own special boxes. Daly's was decorated with colored bunting which matched his silks, Irish green and copper.

The big race of the day was the third. Daly's high-strung and powerful stallion Montana was the odds-on favorite. But Pierre Lorillard's Lamplighter was also entered. Lorillard and Daly had been racing rivals for years. The *Times* described Lamplighter as "The colt of the year," and betting interest was heavy in this, the first match-up between the two horses. The two best jockeys at the track were on top, E. H. (Snapper) Garrison on Montana and Hamilton on Lamplighter. The track was fast, damp but not muddy.

Both Montana and Lamplighter were slow out of the gate, and at the first pole Pretorious and Recon were in the lead. Gradually Lamplighter took over, and at the halfway mark it looked like Lamplighter in a runaway. Garrison had been holding Montana back, however, and by the three-quarter mark he had pulled ahead of Lamplighter by a nose. The spurt was momentary, however. Hamilton showed Lamplighter the whip and he soon overhauled the Bitter Root Stable entry. As Montana faded, Lonataka squeezed into second. In the green and copper-festooned box there was an appalled silence. The *New York Times* commented the following day: "One thing for certain, Mr. Lorillard has got a very good, and very cheap horse in Lamplighter. . . . He only paid $35,000 for him. . . . He's the very best of the three years olds this year. The best we have seen, not excepting Tammany."

For Marcus Daly it was a bitter disappointment. His revenge would come the following year when Tammany, with Garrison up, would defeat Lamplighter by four lengths at the Guttenberg race track in a match race which was billed at the time as "The greatest race in American turf history."

Montana lost that gray day in late August of 1892 when James Hogle and his son went to the races with Marcus Daly. But nonetheless it was all very exciting. For Jimmy, the day at Sheepshead Bay was one that he would remember for the rest of his life, and it wasn't just because of the events on the track.

During the day James Albert told Marcus Daly about his past education, about the school he was heading for in New Hampshire, and his hope of eventually going to Yale. Daly listened with interest to the boy's plans for the future. (He would eventually enroll his own son at St. Paul's.) He then promised Jimmy that when he graduated from college Daly would give him his first job, working at the Anaconda Mine in Butte, Montana. The two shook hands on the arrangement.

CHAPTER FIFTEEN

St. Paul's, 1892

ST. PAUL'S SCHOOL IN CONCORD, New Hampshire, had opened in 1856 and was the most prestigious of New England's boarding schools. Its founder, George Shattuck, was a prosperous Boston physician and an accomplished scholar. A convert to the Episcopal church, he had a great love of both the humanities and nature. Dr. Shattuck had accompanied Audubon to Newfoundland and Labrador and had a keen scientific mind. The mixture in him of religious reverence with independent thinking made him appear something of an eccentric. When the time came to educate his own sons, he found that no school then in existence quite suited his pious and yet fiercely inquisitive temperament. St. Paul's was to be a school based on his ideas and, though he would never teach at the school, his educational notions would guide St. Paul's through its first five decades.

Dr. Shattuck set out to "Establish a school exempt from the moral temptations of towns and villages," where example, discipline, persuasion, and nature were to be the principal tools of teaching. He once wrote that "Green fields, trees, streams, ponds and beautiful scenery are great educators." St. Paul's was set in the wooded hills west of Concord. There were meadows, lakes, streams, ponds and, in the 1850's, an abundance of wildlife.

But it wasn't just the wonders of nature that inspired Dr. Shattuck, it was also those things unseen, the truths beyond and behind the purpose of nature that moved him. St. Paul's was not going to be just another academy, but rather a place where students would live their lessons. The fact that it was to be a boarding school was central to Dr. Shattuck's whole philosophy. Day students would not be allowed because St. Paul's was to be a full-time educational experience. The school was dedicated to the education of the whole being, mind, body, and soul.

In the nineteenth century the accepted method of teaching the soul was through the purgation of the body. This notion, whose roots can be found in both ascetic tradition and monasticism, was deeply ingrained in both American and European educational tradition. It was understood that spiritual discipline was not something that was acquired without pain. If the soul were to profit, the body, at times, had to suffer.

This did not mean that Dr. Shattuck advocated or condoned physical punishment for its own sake. If anything, his views were enlightened: Discipline was a stratagem for self-improvement; transgression would be punished; accomplishment would be rewarded. It was a system perfectly suited to the purposes and the philosophy of James Albert's mother, Ida Elizabeth Hogle.

Henry Augustus Coit, Bishop Tuttle's old friend, was the man charged with carrying out Dr. Shattuck's plans. As the first headmaster and rector of St. Paul's, it was Coit who saw to the actual hiring of teachers and the administration of the school. In the earliest years, Coit himself was the only teacher. More even than the notions of the good Dr. Shattuck, it was Henry Coit who would mold St. Paul's into one of the finest college preparatory schools in the country.

Though practical, competent, and demanding, Coit was at heart a poet and dreamer. Greatly influenced by the English Romantic movement, the first rector set the tone for St. Paul's on a lofty, idealized plane. More than facts, St. Paul's would teach values: honesty, duty, courage, generosity, and respect. Dr. Coit firmly believed that education was not just for this lifetime, but for eternity.

HOMESICKNESS

On the morning of September tenth, the Hogles left New York, arriving in Boston late that evening. They stayed in Boston a day and a half before setting off for Concord and St. Paul's. Their first glimpse of the school was on the evening of the twelfth. At dusk, the darkened battlements of St. Paul's "Big Study Hall" brooded at them as their carriage passed slowly down Dumbarton Road. On that night they stayed as guests in the home of Dr. Coit. Jim was delighted and relieved to learn that three other Salt Lakers were to attend the school that term: George and Dean Lyman and Malcolm Glendenning, the son of James Glendenning, another of his father's old friends. Malcolm had attended St. Mark's and the U. of U. Prep Department with Jim and had also been recommended to Dr. Coit by Bishop Tuttle.

On September 13 the Hogles were given a tour of the school and shown about the grounds. St. Paul's did not then so much resemble a campus as a rural village. Each building was well set off from the others, each surrounded by lawn and each separately fenced, as houses might be on a tree-lined street. The terrain surrounding the school, hills, woods, streams, and lakes, contributed to its arcadian atmosphere. But what impressed the Hogles most was the sense of purpose and the feeling of community. St. Paul's School was much more than a little town; it was a special place, set off from the rest of the world and dedicated to its own pursuits. After the tour, they were introduced to members of the faculty. Then Dr. Coit had a long talk with Mr. and Mrs. Hogle while James Albert was taken by "master" Lampson, who was in charge of the third form, to get settled in and introduced to his roommates.

On the afternoon of September 14, 1892, at the railroad station in Concord, James Albert shook hands with his father. It was a good strong handshake and said more than words might easily have expressed. He then kissed his tearful mother goodbye. He would not see them again until June.

That evening James and Ida had dinner in Boston. They departed for New York at midnight and arrived there the next morning, once again checking into the Oriental Hotel.

Back at St. Paul's, Little Pat was still moved by the parting scene at the railroad station, but he was also confused as to its meaning. His mother's tears sparked in him pangs of remorse, as if he had been somehow guilty of some undefined transgression; as if he, personally, rather than their parting, had been the cause of her sorrow. He resolved, then and there, that he would never again, even unwittingly, be the cause of his mother's tears. On the morning of the sixteenth the Hogles received in New York a brief penciled note from their son:

Concord N.H.
Sept. 15th, 1892

Dear Mother and Father,

I am in the schoolroom and am waiting for a class to begin. As I am not busy I have time to scribble this note. I have no ink here or I would write this with it. George and Dean Lyman came yesterday and Malcolm Glendenning came late last night. I slept all right and I like the school very much.

I was sure last night that I would have to go in the second form but I think now I am in the third.

Mamma, please don't be lonesome as I will write often.

Hoping you are both well, I remain as ever

Your affectionate son,

Jim

The first day at a new school always has its awkward moments. That afternoon as Jim peered out the window of his dorm room, he saw a number of boys playing ball on the great field across the road. They were wearing, or so it appeared, slacks and white knit underwear tops.

Jim remembered that his mother had packed him just such an article. He hurriedly changed into the peculiar garb and rushed to join the other boys outside. When he reached the field, his error made him the object of curiosity and laughter. The other boys weren't wearing underwear tops at all. They were wearing cardigan sweaters, something Jimmy had never seen before. His first social gaffe at the new school mortified him. But the other boys invited him to play ball and the embarrassment of the moment was soon forgotten in the exhilaration of the game.

He was already homesick. He was already missing the familiar faces and sights, already longing for the comforts of home and eager for any news from Salt Lake. Before his parents' train had reached

Chicago he had worked out a remedy and sent them a request by special post:

Concord
Sept 14th, 1892

Dear Parents,

I just received your letter about five minutes ago while I was at dinner. Dr. Coit says I can take the paper if it only comes once a week. So please send me the *Weekly Tribune*. Subscribe for it until June 1st.

I hope you will receive this in Chicago. I will have a long letter for you when you get home. I must stop now as I want this to go with the afternoon post.

Hoping you are both well I remain your affectionate son,

Jim

Oral reading after dinner was a long-established tradition at St. Paul's. It was said to have been started in the very first weeks of the school by Mrs. Coit to help young boys get over their home-sickness. But by the 1890's oral reading was more formalized and prescribed. When Jim's turn came to read he would often amuse his fellow students with stories of the wild west from his weekly issue of the newspaper sent him from home. The vaguely derisive nick-name given to students from Utah was "Brig." But because of his frequent recitations from the pages of the *Salt Lake Tribune*, Jim was quickly given the new nickname "Salt Lake." It was appropriate that his schoolmates at St. Paul's should re-christen him. He was on his own now and growing up. Little Pat was gone forever.

The Bell Tolls

Back in 1858 Dr. Shattuck had purchased a bell for the school which had once hung in the belfry of a Spanish convent and had later announced trains in a Boston railway station. As with all things, Dr. Shattuck saw in the contradictions of its past use an eternal harmony which transcended its temporal function. Upon the bell he had had inscribed in Latin five separate mottoes:

Tempus fugit	Time Flies
Ars Cogit	Art Spurs Us On
Dulce Ludendum	We Must Play Sweetly
Vita Decresit	Life Ebbs
Futura Instant	Future Events Press Upon Us

For the students at St. Paul's, the bell was an encompassing symbol, for the regimen of the school was a healthy cross between life in a railway station and life in a monastery. The original school bell had been lost in a fire in 1878, so when James A. attended St. Paul's it was the chapel bell which, with somber urgency, pressed upon the lives of the students. The mottoes which had been inscribed on the original bell were now permanent fixtures in the school's lexicon of tradition and were engraved on matter more indelible than iron.

At five A.M. the bell sounded the morning reveille and the students tumbled from their beds to wash and dress for the day ahead. Student dress was strictly prescribed: high stiff collar and tie, pointed leather shoes (meticulously polished), jacket, and hat. Not only was the hat required, but its use was specified: "To be tipped respectfully to masters, superiors and visitors when encountered on the grounds." At 5:45 the students assembled for morning prayers. Breakfast was at 6:00. At 7:00 the bell tolled again to mark the beginning of morning classes and the doom of students still scurrying down the halls, inexcusably late for roll call. Classes, which seemed to last forever, were in fact but an hour long and continued in an uninterrupted procession of lecture, drill, and recitation until 12:00, when the bell was tolled again, this time to call the students to chapel, where they would hear announcements and frequently the sermons of Henry Augustus Coit. At 1:30 the students assembled in the school's dining hall for dinner. The afternoons (from 2:30 until 6:00) were the students' own. It was at this time that the students took care of their personal needs, studied their lessons, worked on their assignments in the library, wrote letters home, or participated in the many organized athletic activities.

At 6:00 the bell rang again, calling the students to evening prayers. "Tea," the evening meal, was at 6:30. The forever-hungry, growing boys had anxiously awaited this final repast through the long afternoon. They were seldom disappointed. Henry Coit knew the importance of good nutrition and saw to it that the school had an excellent kitchen. St. Paul's had a reputation for its food which was unrivaled in American boarding schools of the day. There was plenty of meat, usually beef but sometimes pork, poultry, or lamb. There were always mounds of buttered potatoes and tureens of rich gravy. There was fresh milk from the school's own diary, freshly baked breads and pastries from the kitchen, and fresh vegetables of the season. St. Paul's was good for the soul but perhaps even better for the stomach.

From 7:30 until 8:30 was a time reserved for "Conversation and Reading." This was not as it may sound, a private activity, but a rigidly prescribed period under the direction and tutelage of the form masters. During this hour students were called upon to read aloud or share their insights on selected topics with their fellow students. At 9:00 the bell was sounded for the last time; the long day was finally over. It was lights out, and every student was expected to be in bed. At 5:00 A.M. the bell would toll again and the routine would begin anew.

Curriculum and Discipline

The curriculum at St. Paul's reflected the personality and prejudices of Henry Coit. It was designed to give the student "An advanced liberal education." Though broad in scope and application, the courses were deeply rooted in the classics. Students were required to learn Latin and have a knowledge of Classical Greek. There were heavy doses of Virgil and Horace, as well as Shakespeare and the Bible. There were also the standard prep courses: history and mathematics, modern languages (French or German), English composition, and literature.

Jim Hogle was one of only three third-form students who had not had Latin before, and through the year the headmaster personally tutored them in the mysteries of Latin grammar: "I got to know Dr. Henry Coit very well because he took three of us in my first year who had never had latin and gave us our lessons, a personal value which I have always appreciated."

This special attention endeared the aging rector to Jim. By spring he was more than able to make it on his own, but he continued to attend the sessions anyway. As with his association with his grandfather, age was no barrier to friendship and a special bond developed between the young student and the headmaster.

Jim was enrolled in the "scientific" course at St. Paul's, but it was the literature courses that he most enjoyed, and he would later write, "I think I got more good out of my English Lit. courses at St. Paul's than any other classes I took, there or at Yale. I learned to read the best kind of books there, which I have retained all my life, much to my benefit and pleasure."

In a letter he wrote over fifty years later he confided, "I got nothing out of English in College but in Boarding school there was one teacher who really got us started right and the satisfaction I have gotten out of reading alone has been worth all my other educational efforts combined."

As with everything else at St. Paul's the English literature courses reflected the personal tastes of Dr. Coit, particularly his keen appreciation and understanding of Shakespeare and his passion for the English Romantic poets. These loves were passed on to many of St. Paul's students, including James Albert Hogle: "At school I liked and understood Goldsmith, Coleridge, Scott and Byron and, of course, Shakespeare. . . . When I was in school I began to appreciate Byron. I have always thought that the Fourth Canto of 'Childe Harold' would give the average man a better education than most colleges do."

For all its formalities of dress and conduct, St. Paul's was not a draconian institution. There was a purpose behind the regimen and isolation which belied its severity. The urgencies of the outside world were excluded so that students had the time to grow up on their own; so that an individual boy could advance at his own pace without the pressures that usually accompany scholastic achievement.

At St. Paul's, students were never rushed from form to form. There was plenty of time for them to learn, not just about their studies but about themselves. There was always time to explore, time to walk in the woods, time to think, time to set goals, time to plan, time to read and time to dream. During his first year at St. Paul's Jim Hogle found the time to read three romantic adventure novels, *Ivanhoe*, *The Prisoner of Zenda*, and *Amos Judd*.

Though discipline was strict, there was a surprising amount of freedom in the school, more freedom than was generally considered proper at the time. The freedom never became license, however, and there was behind the system the certain knowledge that any breach of this trust would result in immediate punishment. Each student knew what was expected of him. As a classmate later joked, "You could do anything you wanted to at St. Paul's, as long as you got a permission slip."

There was no nonsense allowed at St. Paul's School in 1892. Matters of discipline and punishment were taken care of publicly. Each Saturday afternoon, just before supper, the marks of every student in the school were read aloud in the chapel. Assignments for tardiness, extra work for missed assignments or "lack of application," and kitchen duty for transgressions in deportment were given out without favor. Student by student, subject by subject, the rolls of honor and disgrace were opened for everyone to see. More than any physical abuse, it was the fear of being humiliated in front of the entire student body that kept the boys in line. There was never any vindictiveness in the process. Swift justice was expected and bitterness over disciplinary measures was the exception.

THE SERMONS OF HENRY COIT

The chapel at St. Paul's had been designed by the English architect Henry Vaughan. It was High Anglican, old English gothic, huge enough to accommodate the entire student body and faculty. It was a somber and impressive edifice with high vaulted ceilings and ornately carved oak choir stalls facing each other across the long aisle which led to the altar. So arranged, it was reminiscent of a medieval English monastery. A carved oak screen of elaborate filigree separated the ante-chapel from the nave. The place was austere in dark wood and white plaster. The high, arching gothic windows, which soared above the top tier of the choir stalls, were lightly frosted to allow the light from the outside to penetrate the vast hall. There was not, at that time, a single cut of stained glass to color or darken the crystalline air.

The chapel services were tortuous ordeals for many of the young boys. The benches were uncomfortable, the kneelers hard, the sermons, at times, inordinately long. But these things, too, were part of spiritual training, part of the discipline which Henry Coit imposed upon the wayward flesh for the benefit of the immortal soul. It was not easy for a boy of sixteen to sit quietly without moving for a protracted period of time. But fidgeters were well advised to beware! No single act was more severely reprimanded than "causing a disturbance in chapel." So the boys sat frozen to their seats while Dr. Coit burned into their consciousness the lessons of salvation.

Henry Coit would move from his stall to the altar, where he would kneel for a moment in silent prayer before taking his place at the lectern. It was a ritual which brought the youthful congregation to a state of excruciatingly reverential silence. Then Dr. Coit would solemnly unfold his written notes, adjust his glasses, and begin.

The sermons, though often rambling, had themes running through them of epigrammatic clarity. Many of these themes they would hear over and over again in slightly different versions. Henry Coit would often tell the students that "Steady work and perseverance were more important than talent or genius. . . . As fire tempers metal so too does hard work temper the soul. . . . God sends adversity that we might learn by it. . . . The worth of a man," he said, "was tempered by his struggles. . . . Work is Holy. . . . Once we surrender to the Will of God a higher truth enfolds us. . . . When we give our wills to God, a Higher Law will compensate us."

For Henry Coit, the central message of Christianity was Charity. "Giving to gain, losing to find, sowing to reap." Personal sacrifice was the one true path to salvation. For Dr. Coit it was the divine law of cause and effect. In all the sermons there were common underlying themes: That death was inevitable, that divine truth was the highest good, that man must have unquestioned faith in divine guidance, and that accomplishment in life was the fulfillment of God's will. There was also a fierce spirituality which Dr. Coit tried to instill in his students. It was his principal weapon against the growing skepticism of an increasingly materialistic age. In James Albert's private papers there was a fragment of verse which could well have been recited by Henry Coit as a testament of faith:

> Man is not dust — Man is not dust, I say.
> A lightning substance through his being runs;
> A Flame he knows not of illuminates his clay,
> The Cosmic Fires that feed the swarming suns,

> Hold in their center still the Parent Flame;
> So Man within that undiscovered place,
> His Center — Stores the light from which he came.

There was a certain Calvinistic strain in some of Dr. Coit's sermons which might not have been fully appreciated by his Episcopalian superiors. Since God guided our lives, it followed that "The blessings of God would fall on the righteous."

The blessings of God certainly fell on the young Hogle's fellow students at St. Paul's. The school's reputation had attracted the sons of the nation's richest families, the Mellons, the Morgans, and the Vanderbilts. Cornelius Vanderbilt, one of Jim's classmates, must have been particularly righteous, as he arrived at St. Paul's in his own private train car.

The Lessons of the Playing Field

One of Dr. Shattuck's major contributions to the school was his insistence on organized athletics. There was nothing in the country to match the fervor of athletic competition among the students of New England's boarding schools. This was the legendary era of the dime-novel hero, the heyday of fictional all-Americans like Frank Merriwell, who was scrimmaging, rowing, and batting away for the greater honor and glory of "Faredale Academy" and, later, Yale. Merriwell was a superathletic hero who fought arrogance and sham with his unhittable "Double shot curve ball," a man of infinite talent and moral scruples to match, who dispatched villains with athletic prowess and brazen honesty. One oft-quoted line is " 'You are a cheap cad,' Frank Merriwell told the overdressed Harvard bully."

This was the time when men were said to be "molded by the rigors of the playing field." It was a time when the prep school and collegiate athlete represented all that was good and holy in America, an innocent time when winning really wasn't everything and athletic competition was understood to be as much a test of character as strength, as much a contest of spirit as skill. Dr. Shattuck would have endorsed these notions wholeheartedly. As the school paper, the *Horae Scholasticae*, noted in 1895: "If gentlemanly football is played anywhere, it is played at St. Paul's."

By the time Jim Hogle came to St. Paul's, three athletic clubs were competing for sports supremacy of the school: the Isthmians, the Old Hundred, and the Delphians. Hogle was an enthusiastic Delphian. The clubs were primarily organized for intramural team sports, specifically hockey, cricket, and football. But individual sports, track and field, and swimming were also popular, as were squash, tennis, lawn bowling, and golf. In the early years boxing was a favorite, but injuries had prompted Dr. Coit to outlaw the sport prior to Jim's arrival.

Baseball was also played at St. Paul's, but America's national pastime was regarded by Henry Coit as being "unworthy of gentlemen." He even attempted to ban the game altogether. This, of course, proved impossible, so he conspired to elevate the English version by hiring an English cricket coach, who also doubled as a groundskeeper. James A. was induced by Henry Coit to join the Delphian cricket team. He liked the ancient cricketer, Mr. John Morley, but the game itself left him cold. As with most of the boys, James A. preferred football.

The St. Paul's athletic association also sponsored track and field meets in the fall and spring. On October 4, 1893, Hogle competed in "putting the 16 lb shot and in the 12 lb hammer throw." These events would become his specialty.

For the boys who belonged to the athletic clubs at St. Paul's, the seasons were marked not by changes in the weather but by the trading in of footballs for hockey sticks, hockey sticks for oars, and oars for bats, wickets, and rackets. Each season had its own special memories. The smell of wet leaves and grass dominated the fall. It was a rich, fragrant odor made all the more pungent by the fact that a good footballer's nose was usually very close to, if not actually in, the turf.

The Delphian Club had three teams in the fall of 1892. They were ranked by size and talent, and though Hogle was only a third-former, his natural athletic ability earned him a substitute position on the Delphian's first team, a squad made up primarily of fourth- and fifth-form athletes. In 1894 and '95 James made the first squad of the Delphian First football team and, with his fifth-form roommate, Chris Oglebay, served as team co-captain.

In addition to the intramural squads, St. Paul's fielded a school team made up of the best players from the various clubs and trained by a full-time "professional" football coach. Hogle made the school team his fifth- and sixth-form years. The school league was a tough one. The squad not only played against other neighboring prep schools like Groton and St. Mark's, but also against Frank Merriwell's heroic Yale and the dastardly villains from Harvard.

By 1895 the Harvard game was a regular on St. Paul's schedule. That year the much larger Harvard team came to Concord and defeated St. Paul's by a narrow margin in a game played on a rain-swept field. Football was already a major spectator sport, and more than 500 people braved the storm to cheer on the out-manned St. Paul's squad. James A. later wrote that he got "a lot out of playing football" and believed that the sport taught him invaluable lessons, namely: "dedication, perseverance, and courage."

In the winter, skating was the regular afternoon pastime and not only for the boys but for the masters and faculty as well. Jim had learned to skate early. His Uncle Albert had been a champion skater back in Illinois, so the skill ran in the family. Sledding and tobogganing on Fiske Hill was always popular, though Dr. Coit himself often lectured the students on its dangers.

Organized hockey games had been initiated so early at the school that students came to feel they had invented the game. Indeed the version played at St. Paul's was unique, featuring eleven boys on a side and with rules that were, for the most part, improvised.

The ice hockey season was memorable for the stinging cold of the wind off the lakes, the frantic chase of the free-for-all, the sizzling sound of the skates on the ice. The strange experience of a hand stuck to a freezing skate blade was no worse than the inevitable cases of frostbite that went unnoticed at the time because the game was so close or nerves were too numb to respond. Then later, back in the dorm, came the agony and burning pain of the tingling nerves stabbing back to life as the victims thawed out their frozen feet in the purloined heater water. Hockey, too, inspired strong rivalry, and the annual games against Yale and Harvard were always fiercely contested, as was the annual contest against the alumni played in the St. Nicholas Rink in New York. This battle royal was initiated the year Jim was a sixth-form student.

Spring was a time which many boys at St. Paul's would remember for tennis, lawn bowling, golf, and squash. Jim played squash for the Delphians and enjoyed it thoroughly. Spring was also a time he remembered for painful blisters on his hands. St. Paul's was surrounded by water, so it was only natural that rowing was popular. There were two rival boat clubs, The Halcyon and The Shattuck. The latter had been named for the school's late founder and was Jim's choice when he took up the sport his sixth-form year. The two clubs had competed since the early 1870's, and by the 1890's, race day was the spring event, with each club launching a number of crews.

The boys who stroked for the rival St. Paul's crews were the product of strict discipline and meticulous training. The sport required a degree of mental concentration and timing which had a special appeal to James. The instructions of his rowing coach made such an impression on him that he was able to recall them with perfect clarity in a letter to his grandsons more than fifty years later: "Learn to use your wrists and hands in holding the oars. Most beginners try to do too much with their bodies. The skill rests with the hands and the wrists. If I were you I would ask the coach to show you exactly what the wrist and hand action is. . . . I only wish I had begun rowing my fourth form instead of my sixth."

The rich athletic traditions at St. Paul's taught James A. other memorable lessons, among them the value of preparation, the importance of setting goals, and the necessity of perseverance to achieve them. But "Salt Lake" took something else away with him from the playing fields, ice rinks, and rowing courses of St. Paul's — an indispensable tool called teamwork. It was something he would take with him from St. Paul's to Frank Merriwell's beloved Yale and from there to his professional life. Teamwork would one day prove to be a crucial element in his success.

Memories of the Third Form

Communicable diseases were the bane of any boarding school. Measles, mumps, diphtheria, scarlet fever, and chicken pox swept periodically through St. Paul's during its early history. Twice the school was closed due to epidemics, and the all-too-real tragedies of the early years added to the folklore and fanciful tales which the older students whispered to the wide-eyed horror of the first-formers. The old lower dormitory was said to be haunted by the ghost of a student who had died one Christmas long ago. As might be expected, the infirmary was another object of student lore, as was Fiske Hill, where a student had been killed in a sledding accident. The oral history of St. Paul's was rich in anecdote, and each new class added its own incidents to the ever-evolving matrix of school tradition.

Epidemic was always a threat, and the masters were always on the lookout for any telltale signs of contagion. In October Hogle came down with a rash and a fever, and he was quickly isolated in the infirmary. Dr. Dix, a Concord physician, was sent to examine the boy. Jim remembered the doctor as a gentle old man with a long dark beard. The doctor determined that the rash was probably due to a food allergy rather than the dreaded measles, but to be safe the patient was kept in the infirmary for a week.

As with any boarding school, there were traditions and customs at St. Paul's which no rector had any part in originating, secret clubs, candle-lit initiation ceremonies, midnight "tutorials," and hazings. That first autumn at St. Paul's, James A. had a tiny alcove room on the third floor of the Old Lower Dormitory. This dorm was under the supervision of a former student, William Scutter, who had just returned to St. Paul's as a master following his graduation from Trinity College. Master Scutter was new to the role of disciplinarian and he may have still mistakenly identified himself with the students. For whatever reason, dormitory discipline in the Old Lower during Scutter's first few years at the school was lax. The students had their way with him and there were predictable, and at times unfortunate, results. In the room next to James A. was a younger boy, Henry Staunton. Staunton was unsure of himself, shy, distant and, to some of the students, odd. Through his third- and fourth-form years, Staunton was the continuous victim of cruel jokes and "terrible hazings" by the older students.

Jim neither understood nor approved of the treatment afforded his younger neighbor. He had learned from the good Bishop Tuttle long before attending St. Paul's that Christian charity was not just a matter for the collection plate. He knew what was right and proceeded accordingly. Though he risked becoming a target of harassment himself, he befriended Staunton and did what he could to lessen the boy's plight. Staunton would never forget the kindness.

Master Scutter's indulgent temperament also made possible certain "creature comforts" that the Form Master, Edward "Birdie" Lampson, would never have approved. Jim Hogle and another third-floor resident, Elton "Reddy" Littell, succeeded in tapping into the hot water line which fed the dormitory radiators. With the steaming water they collected, the boys made "brew" on cold winter mornings before setting off for chapel. Littell would remember the liquid as "a bitter, foul tasting decoction, full of rust and mineral deposits." Its appeal was chiefly in the secretive nature of its manufacture and the fact that it was hot. Many years later Littell, who became a doctor, would marvel that they both survived the repeated poisonings.

The operation of the school's weather station was an honor reserved for upper-school students enrolled in the scientific course. It was tedious work, but it was also a matter of personal duty and school pride. The temperature, barometric pressure, wind direction, humidity, and other measurements were taken daily with meticulous accuracy. By any measurement, the New England winter of 1892–93 was cold. The temperature sometimes dropped well below zero, and water often froze in the pipes and the students' water jugs. The many lakes and ponds near and about the campus, Big Turkey, Little Turkey, Turee Pond, and the School Pond were all frozen over by mid-November.

In mid-December came Christmas vacation. For three weeks the students would return to their homes. Dr. Coit's notice of the recess cautioned that, "It is most earnestly requested that boys should be guarded from exposure to contagious disease during their stay at home, and if exposed should be delayed in returning to school. The Rector expects an immediate notice if for any reason a boy is not to resume his place here after the recess."

It was assumed by the rector, and naturally so, that Jim Hogle would be going home for the holidays. But for most of the other boys the trip home was at most a one-day excursion. In 1892 the train trip from Concord to Salt Lake City took four days and three nights. The long round-trip journey must not have seemed worth the effort, and so it was decided that James Albert would spend the holidays where he was and the rector was notified accordingly.

All but a handful of upper school students and a master or two had gone away for Christmas. Malcolm Glendenning and the Lyman brothers had been invited to the homes of relatives and friends back east. Hogle was the only third-form student left on campus. He was alone in a quiet world that only the day before had been filled with the cacophonous chatter of youthful voices and the bedlam that always accompanied the breaking up for vacation.

Abandoned by his fellows and driven by boredom, Jim wandered the empty campus and studied the details of his surroundings: the well-worn corridors and stairs in the Old Lower Dormitory, the hauntingly empty rows of desks in the Big Study, the windblown drifts of snow on the unshoveled steps of the infirmary, and the somber vacancies of the playing field, the gymnasium, and the frozen skating ponds. But the campus, emptied of its students, had voices of its own — sounds that had been there all along but had been masked by the general din of student life, or had gone unnoticed by the boy because of his partial deafness, now made their presence known with ringing clarity: the unbelievably loud clanking of the steam radiators; the sudden, inexplicable, creaking of the stairwells; the scraping of a windblown tree limb against a window pane; the strange hollow echoes of his footsteps against the vaulted ceiling of the darkened chapel, and the ticking of the great clock in the foyer of the study hall. He had never noticed these incidental background noises before, but now, he fancied, they were making themselves heard just for him. The musty smell of the empty buildings added to the somber new mysteries of the place, as did the genuinely doomed feeling of being left behind. Without any other students, the Old Lower Dorm was uncomfortably cold. This Christmas vacation was one that he would long remember.

Joseph Howland Coit was the rector's younger brother. He had taught at St. James School in Maryland and was now serving as vice-rector at St. Paul's. Joseph Coit played a somewhat different role in the scheme of things than his brother Henry. While the rector preached discipline, Joseph pleaded for understanding and sympathy. He wanted to become a father to the boys and sought a personal relationship with the students on a one-to-one basis. This was a practical impossibility, but for a student left behind at Christmastime, the genuine sentiment of Joseph Coit's approach was welcome and appreciated.

Dr. Joseph Coit usually spent the Christmas season in Newport, but that year he had decided that the needs of the few remaining students were greater than his own and moved into the alcove next to Hogle's in the Old Lower Dorm. Here he would stay through the Christmas vacation and keep the young man company. The two took their meals together, and Coit gave Hogle some books to read. Once a week he took James with him into Concord shopping, and each evening the two had long conversations before turning in. They were soon fast friends.

School reopened on Thursday, January 12, 1893. The rector had written to all the parents, warning them again that "No boy who has been exposed to infection should be allowed to return to school without communication with the Rector. It is earnestly requested that no supply of eatables be brought back by any boy to the school."

Jim was now in the unique position of being personal friends with both Coits, and when school resumed after the holidays he quickly discovered that his personal prestige had increased substantially, not just among the students but with the masters as well. This was in part due to the fact that he had spent the entirety of his Christmas vacation getting ahead in his studies. In the winter and spring of 1893 Hogle was first in his form, getting high marks in Latin, Greek, math, sacred studies, English, and history.

Henry Coit was most pleased with Hogle's work and gave him perfect marks in punctuality, industry, and decorum. On the back of the report card Coit wrote a short note to James's father: "His work is excellent in all respects, thoroughly good and honorable. James deserves the greatest credit for his steady, faithful effort. The boy has my esteem and confidence."

The young Hogle had a noticeable rapport with the powers that

The roommates, St. Paul's School, 1893, with Jim Hogle in the center. The others include Holkins Palmer, "Stuffy" Welch, James Gray, and Elton Littell, but they have not been individually identified here.

be. Throughout his career at St. Paul's he retained his standing as a top scholar and while never found below second in his form in academic rank, he was usually first.

On March 22, 1893, Dr. Shattuck, the school's founder and principal benefactor, died. Most of the middle and all of the upper school attended the funeral in Boston. Jim remembered marching with his classmates from the railroad station to the church where the services were held. The death of Dr. Shattuck was sad, but those who knew the aged physician and naturalist took solace from the success of the school he founded. He was gone, but his work went triumphantly forward.

In addition to his old friend Malcolm Glendenning, young Hogle's closest acquaintances during his third-form year were the students with whom he shared the third floor: Staunton and Littell, Dick Stoddard, Parker Straw, "Stuffy" Welch, Dick Stewart, James Gray, and Holkins Palmer.

James would later recall that throughout his third-form year, Dick Stoddard had the choir stall next to him in chapel and Dick Stewart had the desk next to him in the Big Study. But Holkins

Palmer was the closest of the new friends he made that first year. Palmer was a happy-go-lucky and outgoing young man who made friends easily. He truly liked people and was concerned for their well-being. When Holkins heard that "Salt Lake" had spent the Christmas holidays at St. Paul's, he wrote to his parents about it and arranged for Hogle to spend Easter vacation with him in Summit, New Jersey. Palmer's parents made the young Hogle feel like one of the family. They were, as Jim described them, "The salt of the earth. I shall never forget their kindness and hospitality to me." He met Holkins's best friend, Earnest Truslow. He met the grandparents, aunts and uncles, cousins, neighbors, and old schoolmates, even the girl Holkins would one day marry. That Easter Jim was more than two thousand miles from Salt Lake, but he felt very much at home. His two vacations that first year at St. Paul's were stark contrasts — the warmth of friends at Easter versus the cold loneliness of Christmas.

The Spring term of 1893 was spent in taking examinations and studying for the Sacrament of Confirmation. Both Henry and Joseph Coit taught sacred studies, and both shared in the task of preparing the boys for the Bishop's inevitable questions. The Bishop had been known to turn down whole classes before, so the boys were drilled over and over again on the Articles of Faith, the Confirmation prayers, and the renewal of baptismal vows. On May 11, Ascension Day 1893, in the Chapel of Saints Peter and Paul in Concord, James Albert Hogle received the Holy Sacrament of Confirmation from William W. Niles, Bishop of the Diocese of New Hampshire. The long first year was drawing to a close.

VACATION

In the summer of 1893, "Salt Lake" returned to the place which had given him his nickname. His parents, Uncle Owen, Old Pat, and the Mantors (Aunt Molly, Elsie, and Ella) met him at the railway station. It was a reunion which had been long anticipated, and everyone remarked on how good he looked. Jim searched the faces of his closest relatives. Everyone was there and yet he felt that someone was missing. Salt Lake City had changed little in the nine months of his absence, but in the days to come he found that the friends and relatives he had left behind had.

It was hard to put a finger on, but something was different. In a perceptible but indefinable way he felt that they had changed. He puzzled over the problem but could not pinpoint the cause of his uneasiness. True, his grandfather Pat looked more stooped and weaker than he had the previous fall, but everyone else appeared and acted as he remembered them. Their mannerisms were instantly familiar; their voices were exactly as they had been the year before. He noted that his feeling of strangeness was general and that he felt it toward all his old acquaintances equally. It was then that he realized that they had not changed, he had.

The year at St. Paul's had indeed had an influence on Jim, and it wasn't just the class lessons or the sermons of Dr. Coit that made this so. The whole boarding school experience was something that his family and friends in Salt Lake would never know. It separated him from them, and no telling of it could ever make up for the experience itself. Henry Coit wrote to his young scholar frequently that summer to remind him of just what he had learned. On July 10, he wrote:

My Dear James,

I am glad to hear of your safe arrival. You must do all that you can to show them at home that there has been some real and substantial result from your years absence.

I wish you would read over and weigh the private letters enclosed. You want to be a faithful Christian and that is hard work. It means all the time a struggle, resistance to evil and the evil around us, by good deeds and works, by reverence for sacred things and use of all the helps the church affords.

God's blessing upon you this summer and a hearty welcome for you in September.

I am always your faithful friend,

Henry A. Coit.

That summer was a good one. He took several fishing trips with his Uncle Owen, and his relationship with his parents, particularly his mother, had never been better. But as the vacation wore on he began to anticipate his return to school, and he longed to see his friends and teachers. He knew then who had been missing at the railway station back in June. They were the family he had left in Concord, the masters and fellow form students at St. Paul's.

CHAPTER SIXTEEN

The Upperclassman, 1893–1896

WHEN JIM HOGLE RETURNED TO SCHOOL in the fall of 1893 he found that there were changes afoot. The "haunted" Old Lower, where he had lived the previous year and had suffered the deprivations of that first Christmas, was to be demolished and a New Lower was already under construction. James was now a resident of Middle House, a large white frame building behind the chapel on the hill. Hogle soon discovered that fourth-form students had privileges that were not allowed the younger boys. Chief among these was the liberty of actually leaving the campus on certain long weekends. St. Paul's students took advantage of the mini-holidays by taking frequent excursions to Boston and New York.

Jim would visit Boston several times during his fourth-form year. One of his new friends, a fellow resident of Middle House, was James Cunningham Gray. "Jimmy" Gray came from a prominent Massachusetts family, old-line, blue-blood, and moneyed. One fall weekend James A. was the guest of the Grays at their home in Dorchester. Jimmy Gray was an expert sailor, and he delighted in showing his young western friend the ropes on Boston Bay.

Jimmy Gray invited James A. to spend Christmas vacation with the Gray family in Dorchester, and so he spent his second Christmas in New England visiting and attending holiday parties of Gray's Boston friends and distinguished relatives. On Christmas Day the Grays gathered at the home of Jimmy's older sister on Beacon Street. It was a large, traditional family Christmas party and James Hogle was made to feel a part of it.

When the boys returned to school after Christmas vacation, they found that an owl had moved into the bell tower of the chapel. This

[228]

was considered by the ever-superstitious students to be a bad sign and, as luck would have it, the omen would prove grimly prophetic.

The first week of February 1895 was one of the coldest on record. During the early morning hours of February fifth the temperature had dropped to 16 degrees below zero.

That morning the shivering boys were unexpectedly called to early morning chapel and it was announced that Henry Augustus Coit, the man who had served as rector of the school from its beginning, the preacher whose sermons on Christian Charity had inspired the young students in chapel, the gentle tutor who had drilled young James on his Latin and had written to him through the summer, had died of influenza during the night. It was a great shock. A numbness settled over the student body that had nothing to do with the frigid temperature. The school was accustomed to Henry Coit's watchful presence. In a very real sense Henry Coit *was* St. Paul's. It was hard to imagine the place without him.

A wicked blizzard struck New Hampshire the morning of the Coit funeral, and many of the students were unable to attend the services of their departed headmaster. The heavy snow was piled in deep drifts by a biting Arctic wind. The storm was said to have been unrivaled in the annals of St. Paul's, and the students who did attend the service in the chapel were advised that there would be no school procession to the cemetery. It was simply too windy and too cold to attempt. Despite the warning, Jim and several other students fought their way through the storm to attend the hasty service in the tiny windswept cemetery. By late afternoon the front had passed over and the campus was strangely still.

There is a silence that follows a heavy snow in New England that blankets the very air, muffling the traffic on the cobblestones and filling the landscape with a profound quiet, as still as a Currier and Ives print. That cold winter afternoon in 1894 there was such a silence at St. Paul's.

That spring, Jim was invited again to spend Easter vacation with Holkins Palmer and his relatives in New Jersey. He accepted the invitation and was very pleased to find that Holkins' friends and relatives seemed as glad to see him as they were Holkins.

When the boys returned to school, Hogle found that a Night

Wire, as ominous as the Christmas owl, had been awaiting his return. His grandfather, Patrick Gilmore, the little old man who taught him to care for his pony, the playful foil of his boyhood days, whose nickname he had carried, was dead. This was the hardest time to be away from home and Joseph Coit, no stranger to grief himself, comforted him. The lives of the boys growing up in boarding school were filled with distant sorrows.

TRADITION AND REBELLION

If James A. Hogle's early years at St. Paul's were models of conformity and discipline, his final years were marked by controversy and turmoil. Joseph Coit succeeded his brother as rector in June of 1894, and with the changing of the guard there were inevitable losses as well as gains. Discipline was now tempered by a tolerance for self-expression, and students were given liberties unheard of in the days of Henry Coit. But unfortunately, Joseph's temperament and his gentle methods were mistaken by the students as signs of weakness, and where the inch was given the students thought it their right and duty to take the mile.

The strictness of the school's disciplinary code was increasingly challenged and successfully thwarted by the students during the tenure of Joseph Coit. In part this was less the fault of the rector than the times. The "gay nineties" were known for experimentation and invention. The old ways of doing things were being challenged by men like Edison, Ford, Marconi, and Bell. A new age was dawning, and in 1895 it was hard to sort out just what of the old was to survive through the turn of the century. The boys at St. Paul's had always been encouraged to think for themselves. But now they were thinking things on their own which shocked their teachers, men still firmly entrenched in the Victorian past.

During his fifth-form year, Hogle lived in a large dorm room on the top floor of the Old Upper with fellow students Sanford Stoddard, Jimmy Gray, Holkins Palmer, Parker Straw, and Chris Oglebay. Another fifth-form student, Malcolm K. Gordon, had the room directly across the hall. He would remember Hogle and his roommates vividly, particularly for the tobacco smoke that sometimes was seen escaping through the transom above their locked door. The pungent smell of the tobacco would linger in the hall, and Gordon feared what would happen if the form master happened to visit the floor when Hogle and his roommates were sampling a particularly aromatic blend. He need not have worried. The general laxity which had set in since the installation of the new rector was pervasive.

Though Hogle and his roommates were content to indulge in the evils of tobacco, August Heckscher, in his book *St. Paul's*, noted that some students in 1895 smuggled liquor into their rooms. If discovered, this, of course, would have been cause for immediate expulsion.

Although the school's general discipline was fast eroding, the quality of the teaching remained high during the years of James A. Hogle's attendance. The faculty was dedicated and that dedication was repaid by the loyalty and devotion of the students. In addition to his literature teachers, Jim was most influenced by Dr. Milner, who was in charge of the scientific course. But Hogle honored the memory of all his teachers at St. Paul's and would write to a former classmate half a century later, "I remember my schoolday happenings better than any period of my life. I can recall the names of 31 teachers and instructors at St. Paul's including Lester Dole, and Old John Morley, the english cricket coach, and Bishop Niles at Concord and John Wilcox . . . and Freddy Kinsman and Tibbits."

Hogle's roommate Sanford Stoddard wrote back to him that he too remembered their teachers, and to prove the point added, "We could sit in the same two seats we had right in front of Patty Laubertsen . . . sit in the stall in Chapel and have a great time turning back the pages of the calendar."

James A. Hogle graduated from St. Paul's (as was then the practice) in 1895 at the end of his fifth-form year. That spring following the close of school he went again with his friend Jimmy Gray to Dorchester. Here the two schoolmates plotted their futures while they took in the sights of Boston. One day they attended a prize fight at the Massachusetts Yacht Club on Rose Wharf, but most of the time they spent sailing on Boston Bay.

Though he had graduated, he was not yet finished with St. Paul's. James A. and five other students (Chris Oglebay, Richard

Graff, J. B. Johnson, Phillip Dashiel, and one other named Parks) would return for an extra year of study, a sixth form, which was then called the "extra remove." This special course was for students wishing to receive additional training in science and engineering before going on to college.

Jim wanted to attend the Sheffield Scientific and Engineering School at Yale, and at the end of his fifth year he wasn't sure if he was up to the task. Then too, he didn't want to take the chance that he wouldn't be accepted. The extra year at St. Paul's would eliminate any risk of rejection.

When school opened on September 19, there were 331 boys enrolled for the 1895–96 term. Jim's course load was specialized, and he found that he had more time on his hands than during his previous years. This time was quickly filled as he indulged himself in the many extracurricular activities available.

On October 1, Hogle was elected Secretary of the St. Paul's Scientific Association, a club that sponsored monthly guest lectures by noted scientists. Many of these were professors from Harvard, Yale, Princeton, and M.I.T. who were some of the foremost scientists in the country. He also belonged to the Missionary Society and played in the school's Mandolin String orchestra, which was under the direction of Mr. Osgood. The orchestra performed at many of the school's social events and also at performances of the plays given by the drama club. Jim was coincidentally a member of the school's entertainment committee, and he and his roommate Chris Oglebay were members of the Athletic Association's executive committee, the body responsible for scheduling and arranging the school's many athletic contests. Lighter classload notwithstanding, it was going to be a full year.

Regular football practice began on September 30. James was a prominent member of the Delphian's first squad. He did all of the team's kicking and doubled as a running back. Chris Oglebay was the signal caller and captain. The first game for the Delphians on October 6 was something of a disaster as the Old Hundred Club

The Fifth Form at St. Paul's School in 1895. James A. Hogle is seated second from the right in the first row.

managed to defeat Hogle's squad for the first time in several years. Worse, the team suffered a number of injuries which would cripple them for the entire season. As the *Horae Scholasticae*, the school paper, reported,

> The Old Hundred have broken the spell and won a first 11 match. The Delphians were very unfortunate in losing three of their best players on account of injuries, including the captain, and although they played a plucky uphill game, they were unable to overcome the handicap. . . .
>
> . . . Among the Delphians Oglebay and Hogle deserve special notice. The former was injured early in the game but pluckily continued until forced to stop. Hogle was in splendid form and made some fine plays. N. Biddle put up a good game and Graff ran well.

It was later determined that Oglebay's collarbone was broken. Following the injury to his roommate, Hogle assumed the captaincy of the Delphian squad. It would prove to be a very long season for the club as injuries continued to sideline key players. The *Horae* also recounted in detail another losing effort for the Delphians, this time to the Isthmians, commenting that: "The Delphians were compelled to play with an eleven badly crippled on account of injuries. . . . They did their best to repair the loss. Hogle put up a wonderful game at half back, being the life of the whole team."

In the fall of 1895, the *Horae* repeatedly mentioned the athletic feats of James A. Hogle, usually in a losing cause. But there was no question that he was regarded as one of the best players in the school. "Hogle and Graff held first honors for the Delphians" was a much-repeated line in the paper. Hogle had little trouble making the school eleven.

On November 7 the athletic clubs met to elect the captain of the football team. James and his roommate were both nominated for the position, which Oglebay won in a close election. The team had but eight days to practice together before the big game against Harvard. During a practice session Jim sprained his ankle badly, and the school's premier halfback was sidelined for the biggest game of the year. It was a bitter disappointment.

The big game was played on a muddy rain-swept field, and the Harvard team, bullies to the end, defeated the much younger and smaller St. Paul's squad 10 to 4. The *Horae Scholasticae* commented on the game and what might have been:

> The Game of the School 11, vs. Harvard was in no way, as some of the players seem to think, a disgrace to our team. On the contrary it was practically a victory for St. Paul's. When you take into consideration the weather which was the worst in which we have ever seen a game played and which rendering any trick plays impossible, gave every advantage to weight. We were beaten by a score of 10 to 4 with everything pointing to a victory for us in clear weather. Further than this Harvard expected to win easily and did not for a moment look for a touchdown from St. Paul's. A very great deal of praise is due the captain as well as the coaches. . . .
>
> . . . This year we had a misfortune which probably outweighed [all else] and this was that four of the most promising players were laid off by injuries. Had Hogle, Nickerson, Glidden and Schwartz been able to play, our chances on such a wet day would have been much brighter.

Nevertheless, the St. Paul's team won more games than they lost that year, and their reputation as a prep football powerhouse soared. The graduates of St. Paul's went on to play for their bigger neighbors and sometime opponents. In 1895 the school had seven alumni on Yale's first team, four on Princeton's, and three on Harvard's. St. Paul's was the recruiting ground of the Ivy League.

Following the football season, James began training for the "Indoor Games" in the school's gymnasium. The winter of 1895–96 was very cold, with temperatures frequently dropping below zero and once hitting 30 below. The heated gymnasium was a favored location that winter, and Hogle decided to forgo the questionable pleasures of ice skating and hockey. There wasn't enough snow on Fiske Hill for sledding that year, but a unique ice-lined toboggan run was constructed and was said to have been exceptionally fast.

On December 5 the entire sixth form went to the orphans' home just off campus. The orphanage had been established by Dr. Coit back in 1866 and was supported in part by contributions from the students at St. Paul's. The *Horae* reported that James Hogle led the delegation.

On February 26, 1896, the indoor games began. They lasted for over a week and pitted students against each other in a variety of track and field contests, tugs of war, wrestling matches, and other events. Jim won the rope-climbing competition, his time ten seconds flat. After the indoor games, the events of the school year telescoped into one another in a flurry of activities, and Jim's final months at St. Paul's were a blur.

In March, the Halcyon and Shattuck clubs began training for the annual boat races. The ponds were still frozen, so training was restricted to exercising in the gymnasium and running on campus. The Mandolin Club held its annual recital on the nineteenth, with Hogle and several other boys performing Irish fiddle tunes, airs, and jigs, and on the twenty-third, the Scientific Association heard a lecture on the principles behind the telephone by M.I.T. professor C. R. Cross.

On April 18 the temperature was 28 degrees below zero, the coldest reading recorded for that month in the history of the school. On April 29, Professor Kelly from Haverhill, Massachusetts, brought his large telescope to the school at the invitation of the Scientific Association, and the fascinated students saw, for the first time, the moons of Jupiter and the rings of Saturn.

As the school year drew to a close, Dr. Joseph Coit entertained the members of the entertainment committee at his home. The Scientific Association had their last meeting of the year on Thursday evening, June 11, 1896, and the *Horae* reported that, "Dr. Hoyt lectured on Roentgen rays and made interesting experiments with the fluoroscope. He had with him a very powerful tesla coil. . . . James A. Hogle, secretary of the club, made his final report for the year."

The following week the *Horae* went to press for the last time that year and printed, as always, the names of the two top students for each course and form. The honors list for the scientific course was headed by the names Dashiell and Hogle. The paper also reported the results of Race Day. The program of the day listed the crews and gave the particulars and statistics which mean so much

to the fans of any sport. Leading the second Shattuck crew was
Captain James A. Hogle. He was listed as 5 ft. 9 in. tall, weighing
175 lbs. at 19 years 7 months of age.

On the morning of June 18, Long Pond was once more the
scene of the Halcyon and Shattuck boat races. . . . The day
dawned clear and bright no wind to speak of, the conditions
perfect for rowing the great races.
It was announced at chapel that the crews would follow the
precedent established last year and row in the morning. Regular
recitations were held for the first two hours and the school was
dismissed at 9:50. The crews left the Upper at 9:15 and went
directly to the pond. Here they were rubbed down and put in
the best possible condition for the coming contest, while the
floats were put out, and the pair oars and press boat were rowed
down the pond. There was not a ripple on the smooth surface
of the lake and many predicted that old records would suffer.
The crews were roundly cheered as they pulled away from
the dock and all started out with the best possible determination. . . . Now the waving of the white flag far down the pond
announced the preparations for the start and a few minutes later
the signal was given. All that could be seen of the rival crews
was the flashing of the oars in the sun a mile away. Soon they
appeared plainer and it was evident to all that the blue was in
the lead. [Hogle's crew lost.]

There had been many changes at Saint Paul's in the last two
years. During the summer of 1895 Saddle Rock, an old landmark,
had to be blasted out to widen the road from Concord. Then, the
school's own dynamo, which had supplied St. Paul's with all its
electricity, was abandoned and the campus was connected by overland line to the main power station in Concord.
When Jim Hogle first came to St. Paul's, the ivory tower con-
cept was still very much intact and was even revered. The petty
concerns of commerce and trade were kept at a safe distance and
political expression of any kind was discouraged. But during Hogle's
fifth- and sixth-form years the invisible wall barring the outside
world had been irrevocably breached, blasted away with Saddle
Rock and the other symbols of the school's isolation. At the 1894
Anniversary Service, the speaker told the students that they must
fight the encroachments of "Foreign Socialism" before it destroyed

the American Republic. If the speech was symptomatic of the enormous changes that were taking place at the school, as in society, perhaps the power line from Concord was symbolic. The outside world and its problems had finally broken through. The ivory tower was crumbling.

In the struggle between the new ideas and time-honored tradition there was no question where James A. Hogle stood. Although he was very aware of recent scientific and technological breakthroughs, he was firmly committed to the values and traditions of the past. He hadn't forgotten the sermons of Henry Coit, the lessons of sacred studies or the chapel.

Some things at St. Paul's had not changed in the four years since he had first set eyes on the Big Study Hall. Some traditions were inviolable. As it had in the past, the chapel bell tolled five times each weekday and twice on Sunday, marking out the steady procession of time. From its reveille call before dawn to the final stroke of curfew, the chapel bell tolled not only for the boys then enrolled at St. Paul's, but for the hundreds of students who had gone before and the thousands who would follow.

An upper school student was selected by the headmaster for the honor of ringing the chapel bell. In the hours before dawn, while the rest of the campus was still asleep, the dutiful servant of the bell had to rise, dress, and traverse the quiet campus to the chapel. He would then climb the darkened, winding stairs from the antechapel to the place in the bell tower where the bell rope hung. At the stroke of five, with a mighty pull on the rope, he would bring the campus to life. For the entire year that student had been James Albert Hogle.

CHAPTER SEVENTEEN

The Young Engineer

James A. Hogle was accepted at Yale and entered the Sheffield Scientific School in the fall of 1896. Richard Graff, Phillip T. Dashiell, Holkins Palmer, and Sanford Stoddard also enrolled at Yale. Malcolm Glendenning, who had attended St. Mark's, the U. of U., and St. Paul's with Hogle, was already at Yale, having started there a year earlier. The large contingent of former St. Paul's students became one of the ruling cliques at New Haven. There were only forty-five men in the senior honor societies at Yale that year, and of these, eleven were graduates of St. Paul's.

At Yale Hogle, Dashiell, Stoddard, and Graff resumed their athletic careers. Hogle made the freshman football team and played in two games before re-injuring his ankle, which effectively ended his football career. He also made the school's freshman rowing crew and was elected Coxswain, an honor he would always cherish. Stoddard made the ice hockey squad and Hogle, Dashiell, and Graff were on the track and field team. Graff ran the hundred yard dash in ten seconds flat and Hogle became an expert at the hammer throw.

Jim's roommate at New Haven was Seth Thomas III, the great-grandson of the Seth Thomas who had founded the famous clock company. Hogle and Thomas became good friends, and during school breaks and holiday weekends Hogle visited Thomas and his family at their home in New York City. During this juncture James cultivated an interest in the New York stage. His favorite actors were the comedians Nat Goodwin, Sol Smith Russell, and Louis Mann. His trips to New York were so frequent that he became concerned that he was taking advantage of the Thomases' hospi-

tality, but Seth joked that his family regarded their New York residence as: "The clearing house for all my friends west of the
Hudson."

At Yale Jim became a member of the St. Elmo Society, a social
fraternity to which Malcolm Glendenning had introduced him. The
friends he made in St. Elmo included Paul N. Dann, John C. Green-

James A. Hogle at Yale in 1897.

leaf, and Edward Skinner. The warm fraternal camaraderie of the St. Elmo Society was very important to the young Hogle. In the socially conscious east, westerners were sometimes regarded as beneath contempt. Though by no means the equivalent of a listing in the Social Register, membership in a fraternity was an indication of acceptance.

Although his social life and athletic career at Yale were matters of great personal satisfaction, Jim was not terribly impressed with his educational experience at New Haven. The Sheffield Science and Engineering School was staffed by the most eminent of scholars, but eminence was no guarantee of teaching competence, and Hogle found many of them too old and pitifully behind the times. He admitted to his former St. Paul's classmate Elton Littell that "I got more out of St. Paul's than I did College, and I certainly enjoyed it more too . . . . I got little out of Yale."

An indication of his attitude toward his classes at Yale is found in a revealing story he told many years later. It was the night before his final examinations and he was supposed to be studying, but Hogle was distracted: "I happened to run into a fine volume of *The Three Musketeers*. I did not stop reading until daylight the following morning. It's the only time I have ever done that in my entire life . . . . I was absorbed."

Dumas' romantic adventure tale is absorbing, but to choose to read it on the night before finals was no compliment to the scientific course offered at Yale in 1898. (About that time he was also interested in Marian Crawford's romantic books, "the best of which," he remembered, "were Roman and Italian adventure stories.")

His three years at Yale were all the more disappointing to James because he had spent so much time preparing to get there, including the "extra remove" at St. Paul's. But his mother's insistence that he get into a good school was based on more than the quality of the education. Ida knew the ways of the world better than her young son, and an engineering degree from Yale was certain to open doors.

However disappointing his engineering course may have been, he never forgot that he was a Yale man to the core. In the west, a Yale degree was both rare and highly esteemed.

During the week of June 25–30, 1899, the *New York Times* gave Yale's graduation extensive coverage. The class procession was headed by the Second Regimental Band. The exercises were held in an amphitheater specifically constructed for the occasion; inside, each graduate was smoking the customary long pipe; humorous class histories were read; and the program ended with the ceremonial planting of ivy at Vanderbilt Hall. After the exercises, the class in caps and gowns paraded through the streets, cheering the professors at their homes.

Hogle and Dashiell were not the only former St. Paul's students graduating from "Shef" that spring. Both men were surprised when Cornelius Vanderbilt showed up to collect his engineering degree from the college, a feat he had accomplished by attending one lecture a week, with the added help of "private tutors at home." The *Times* noted that "most of his work consisted of drawings." But Vanderbilt Hall has already been mentioned, and it was not the only facility on campus that profited by the Vanderbilt family endowments. "Cornie," as his former St. Paul's classmates called him, no doubt deserved, at the very least, an honorary degree.

Hogle received a Ph.B. degree in civil and metallurgical engineering. The metallurgy classes he had taken with one thought in mind, employment at Marcus Daly's Anaconda mines. His schooling, he thought, was now at an end. It was time to begin his career.

In late June of 1899 Jim returned briefly to Salt Lake City, where his mother proudly feted him to a series of parties to celebrate his graduation from Yale. He then set off for Anaconda, Montana, to collect on the promise made by Daly at the Sheepshead Bay race track seven years earlier. True to his word, Daly immediately put Hogle on the payroll of the Amalgamated Copper Company. His first position was in the assaying laboratory.

For seven years James had lived the life of the pampered student. He had excelled in his studies and was confident that he was well prepared to go out and conquer the world. But New Haven and Concord were a long way from Montana, and the distance was more than physical. The real world had bitter lessons to teach a young man fresh out of school, and James A. Hogle quickly discovered that he really didn't know everything after all.

The rude awakening came his very first week on the job. Assuming that the bright young Yale graduate had been brought to Anaconda by Daly to introduce the latest laboratory techniques, the staff gave him a crucial position. As he later wrote, "Never was I more embarrassed or more disappointed in my life, the techniques I had learned in school were completely impractical . . . and the mistakes I made were ridiculous." Although all young collegians eventually undergo some such revelation, for the young Hogle the discovery of his inadequacies was a particularly bitter experience, and like the "underwear" mistake his first week at St. Paul's, he would remember it for the rest of his life.

After a mercifully brief career at the assaying laboratory, Jim was moved to the refinery office for several months and then to the ore sampling station at the new mill and smelter. Daly's next assignment for young Hogle was more to his liking, a position with Anaconda's engineering department in Butte. Here he worked for some time, helping to design and install the pumping station at the 1,200-foot level of the Leonard mine.

In this job too Hogle was technically out of his element. His degree was in civil, not mining engineering. But although challenging, this job was not beyond his capabilities, and it gave him his first taste of success as an engineer. That satisfaction had seemed long in coming.

James A.'s successes and failures working for Marcus Daly gave him a unique glimpse of Anaconda's entire mining operation, from ore sampling and assaying to office management and engineering. It seemed as if he were being groomed for something special. He later joked that "if only" he had stayed with Anaconda he would certainly have ended up a vice-president of the company, for all his colleagues there had later achieved that position.

In 1899 Marcus Daly was very ill. He went to Europe for a time in an effort to regain his health, but died upon his return to New York City on November 12, 1900. Hogle was grateful to Daly for both the experience and the practical lessons he had learned about mining, but perhaps more grateful for what he had learned about himself. At Anaconda, James had learned that his education was not over, and Daly's death freed him from any obligation to remain there. Hogle was going back to school, and this time his emphasis was going to be on mining engineering and geology.

Continuing Education

In June of 1901, Jim took an indefinite leave of absence from Anaconda. When George H. Robinson, chief engineer of the Montana Ore Purchasing Company in Butte, learned that Hogle would be spending the summer in Salt Lake City, he asked if the young man would consider a temporary position as assayer at the Yampa mine in Bingham Canyon, outside of Salt Lake.

The Yampa mine was just being opened by the Tintic Mining Company, and the position of assayer would put the young Hogle on the scene of any new discoveries. The position was also important because it bridged the gap between prospect geology and mine development.

The first few months of any mine are the most crucial. Being in at the beginning of such a job taught Hogle valuable lessons in mining engineering that could be learned in no other way. He was also pleased to be offered such a position in spite of his early mistakes in the laboratory of Amalgamated Copper. He had, evidently, learned his lessons well.

The superintendent of the Yampa mine was Billie Craig, a well-known mining engineer who had worked at some of the richest mines in the west. The shift boss at the Yampa was another old hand, Fred Turner. Under the tutelage of these two hard-rock mentors, young Hogle would gain invaluable experience.

In September of 1901, Hogle went east again to resume his education. The mining men he had known over the past two years had convinced him that the finest school of mining engineering in the country was an institution in New York City noted for its pure science, Columbia University.

James would remember his classes at Columbia for both their difficulty and their practicality. His classes at Yale had been all theory, at Columbia they were all application. Hogle also took a number of geology courses, four of which were taught by the renowned geologist James F. Kemp.

James A. Hogle at Columbia University in 1903, where he took a master's degree in mining engineering.

Kemp's lectures on the geologic history of the Great Basin, in particular, fascinated Hogle, and he quickly became one of Kemp's favorite students. The other students, who naturally had had no first-hand experience with the geologic formations of the Basin, were at a distinct disadvantage. Seeking to remedy the problem, Hogle and Kemp worked together on a unique project. The idea was to bring the students face-to-face with the geology they were studying.

Hogle approached the management of the United States Smelting Company with the proposition that they should host Columbia geology students for a special summer course of classroom and field work studies at Bingham Canyon. The course would be taught by Professor Kemp, and any increased knowledge of the area produced by the field work was certain to benefit the company.

U.S. Smelting was impressed with the proposal and agreed to house the students at the company's old Jordan Boarding House. Hogle also arranged, with the help of Senator Kearns, for an extensive tour of the Park City mines.

In the summer of 1902 Professor Kemp and his students trudged over the Oquirrh Mountains southwest of Salt Lake City, collecting rock samples, studying formations, and assaying ores. A fellow student who became Jim's close friend was Charles T. Van Winkle, who would work with him on many ventures in the years to come.

Professor Kemp was surprised at what they found that summer, and at one point he remarked to his class, "This copper deposit is probably the largest of its kind in the world, but it has no economic value."

The professor's assumption was based on the low-grade nature of the deposit and the enormous expense that would be required to extract the metal from the ore. Seldom has anyone been so quickly proven so wrong as Professor Kemp!

The Wall Properties

The man who first recognized the potential of the vast low-grade copper deposit in Bingham was an old family friend of the Hogles, Col. Enos A. Wall, who first visited the district in 1887 and was struck by the dark green stains on the canyon wall at a spring near Carr Fork. Wall took many ore samples in the area and discovered that the rock contained 2.4 per cent copper. Many of the early claims in the Bingham Canyon area were from the earlier period of gold and silver mining. These claims had been abandoned and were subject to relocation. Wall acquired several of these properties and over the next ten years quietly began buying up additional claims. By 1900 Wall was vigorously promoting his large holding and openly seeking investors in the project. His belief in the value of the deposit was met with skepticism, and locally his claims were often derided by the tag "Wall Rock."

In the fall of 1902 Col. Wall approached the junior Hogle and asked him to help finance the venture. Hogle was offered one-eighth interest in Utah Copper for $75,000. With this money Wall promised "to build a mill which would show the world that this worthless ore could be handled successfully." Wall had hired Charles T. Van Winkle to develop an extraction process for the ore.

Hogle was convinced that Wall was right about the property's potential and was in the process of putting the money together for the deal when Daniel C. Jackling and Charles M. MacNeill arrived on the scene and bought the controlling interest in Utah Copper from Wall for $385,000.

Daniel Jackling was a brilliant metallurgical engineer. For his work in developing the process for extracting the metal from the ore, he would receive the lion's share of the credit for opening "The richest hole on earth." Van Winkle, however, did much of the preliminary work on the process. Jackling and his associates were also able to attract the outside capital that had eluded Col. Wall. The Guggenheims assisted Utah Copper in constructing a huge concentrating mill at Magna, Utah, and a smelter at Garfield. By 1906 Utah Copper had the largest such facilities in the world.

For young Hogle, the whole experience was a monumental disappointment. He had narrowly missed being in on the greatest mining venture of all time. But while disappointed, he was far from being bitter, and, characteristically, viewed the episode philosophically. There was, it seemed, as much to learn about mine financing as about geology or assaying.

While Jackling was developing Utah Copper, Hogle was employed by the Starless mine, which adjoined the Utah Copper properties. The Starless was owned by the Oquirrh, Bingham Mining Company. Working as an agent for the owners, Hogle negotiated the sale of the Starless to Col. Wall. Many years later Wall would sell the Starless to Utah Copper at a substantial profit. Hogle soon gained a reputation for being not only a fine mining engineer but also a skilled negotiator and honest middleman. In the mining business, these were highly esteemed attributes.

The Independent Mining Engineer

Following the sale of the Starless mine, Hogle began a career as an independent mining engineer. For the next seven years he inspected properties for prospective buyers and investors. His reputation grew, and he was frequently brought in by companies to verify or reject the opinions of their own engineers and assayers. Hogle's expertise would have pleased his old patron Marcus Daly, whose own early career had followed similar lines.

In the spring of 1904, one of Hogle's former Anaconda associates engaged him to accompany a small party of mining men who were interested in a silver mine thirty miles east of the small village of Tonichi in the state of Sonora, Mexico. The area was primitive. The road to the mine was no more than a pack trail, and Hogle and his companions had to ford the Yaqui River to reach their destination. In 1904 the territory beyond the Yaqui was considered bandit country.

Hogle and his party, which included Mr. Van Winkle, reached the mine without incident, but soon after their arrival, disturbing news was brought to their camp. The Yaqui Indians had gone on the warpath, and the isolated stage stations through which their party had passed had been burned to the ground; it was reported that travelers had been robbed and murdered. They could not risk returning to Sonora the way they had come.

To avoid encountering the Indians, Hogle and his companions had to take a long, tortuous route around several rugged mountain drainages. They were not properly supplied for such a long journey and quickly ran out of food. After two and a half weeks on the trail, the party arrived at Sonora. They had not encountered any Indians, but they were on the verge of starvation. It was the kind of prospecting adventure that his father might have relished; James A. hated the entire experience. He was determined that he would never suffer from hunger again.

Other Responsibilities

The senior Hogle had been, for a time, a silent partner in the Scott Hardware Company. In 1904 James A. served for his father on the board of directors of that firm as secretary-treasurer. Late that same year the elder Hogle sold large blocks of Silver King and Daly West mining stock and purchased the Scott-Stravel Building, where the hardware company was located. This building, at 168 South Main, was two doors north of James Hogle's saloon.

James A.'s uncles, Charles and Sidney King, his mother's younger brothers, had worked for Scott Hardware for many years — Charles in the stove department and Sidney as a tinner. With the acquisition of the Scott Building, the firm was reorganized as the King Hardware Company with James A.'s uncles managing the business.

The Scott Building was a remarkable structure. Photographs from the late 1870's to 1904 show that when the owners needed more space they simply added another story to the existing structure. By 1904 the building had soared to six stories, each of stone and each of a different architectural style. Hogle's mining engineering office was perched on the top floor in room 600. James's uncle, Childs Mantor, also had his office in the building.

James Hogle knew that his health was failing, and during 1906 and 1907, he began turning the management of his business affairs over to his son, as well as deeding to him his personal property and stock certificates. In February of 1907 he deeded to the younger Hogle the Scott-Stravel Building and the Boyd Park Building which adjoined it.

James A.'s increased business and family responsibilities did not prevent him from continuing his career as a mining engineer. In early 1907 he spent some time examining mining property at Galena, south of Battle Mountain, Nevada, owned by W. H. Clark of the Nevada Hills Mining Company and Utah's Dern family. James A. was eventually put in charge of the development of this property, and he would work off and on at Battle Mountain for many years.

The death of his father in March of 1908 placed other burdens on James Albert. He not only had to care for the business interests of his mother, but he had inherited the responsibility for his father's extensive family as well. It was more his education than his wealth that made James Albert the titular head of the clan. For the next half century he would give his aunts, uncles, nieces, nephews, and cousins both financial assistance and sage advice.

The year 1908 was important in the life of James Albert for yet another reason. That year he became acquainted with an exceptionally beautiful young graduate of the University of Kansas who was teaching French at Rowland Hall School, Mary C. Copley.

CHAPTER EIGHTEEN

A Time Recaptured, 1909–1910

Late spring in Salt Lake City can be spectacularly beautiful. Though snows still cover the high peaks, the lower foothills are seas of mountain wild flowers. The spring of 1909 was particularly mild, and the *Deseret News* commented on the pleasant weather and beauties of the season. The nightly breezes were fragrant with scents from the blooming buds of the Mormons' many fruit orchards, and it was on one of these lovely evenings that James A. Hogle took Mary C. Copley on an evening hike to a place called Ensign Peak, a rocky, bulb-like protuberance at the west end of the city's North Bench. Though not high when compared to the towering mountains to the east, it was a favorite point for viewing the lights of the city. An observation tower had been built on the nob, and from there telescopes ranged down Main Street.

On this particular evening, as the couple climbed up the face of the hill, there was, as might be expected, a full moon, for the young man had a diamond engagement ring in his pocket. James A. had not forgotten the tutelage of Uncle Owen; he was leaving nothing to chance. His planning and execution were flawless, and the answer was "yes."

"Polite Society" in Salt Lake City in 1909 was Victorian in attitude, custom, and, particularly, courtship ritual. The engagement was to be proper and long, sixteen months. During this lengthy socially prescribed period Jim would take several business trips and a long sea voyage which would take him half way around the world.

Adventures Abroad

There are certain episodes in the lives of men that stand out as the highlights, important incidents which later are told to children

Mary C. Copley, the young French teacher, in Salt Lake City, about 1908.

and grandchildren as vivid memories of distant places, of times and events long past, and of people long dead. Such an episode in the life of James A. Hogle was the journey he made in 1910.

In January of that year Hogle learned that Mr. W. R. Van Liew had been sent to the Caucasus Mountains in Russia to open up a copper mine. Anaconda's Frank Kleptko asked James if he would like to go to Russia to inspect the property and report on the progress that was being made, and the young man jumped at the opportunity.

In late February, James headed east by train, stopping to visit with his relatives — the Steeles in Denver and the Gilmores in Sheldon — to clear up several details of his father's estate. This done, he proceeded to Pittsburgh to meet, for the first time, the eastern relatives of his betrothed.

Mary Copley Thaw was his fiancée's paternal aunt. Mrs. Thaw was the widow of Pennsylvania industrialist William Thaw and was the recognized matriarch of the Copley-Thaw families. Hogle's intended had been named for her, and Mrs. Thaw had taken a keen interest in her niece from an early age. It was important that young Hogle make a good impression.

It was not, however, a particularly good time to be meeting Mary's aunt. The Thaw family was deeply embroiled in a scandal so notorious it was considered at the time the sensation of the decade. On June 25, 1906, Mary Copley's first cousin, Harry K. Thaw, had shot to death the noted New York architect Stanford White in full view of a large crowd at a Madison Square Garden musical performance. Thaw had accused White of alienating the affections of his wife Evelyn Nesbit, a former chorus girl. Mrs. Thaw had hired a team of lawyers to defend her son and was closely involved in the trial. Harry's defense was insanity.

The first trial was long and unseemly, replete with scandalous accusations of Evelyn's infidelity, and ending with the jury unable to deliver a verdict. Harry's second trial resulted in his acquittal on the murder charge, but he was committed to the state hospital for the criminally insane. Harry escaped from the hospital but was recaptured and returned to captivity, this time under tight security. Since that time, Mrs. Thaw had spent herself in a tireless effort to get her son released. The numerous appeals and motions filed by Mrs. Thaw's attorneys dragged on in the courts for years, to the great delight of the gossip-mongering press.

Mrs. Thaw was so burdened and preoccupied with the legal and mental problems of her son that during his visit James never actually broached the subject of the upcoming marriage.

He stayed with Mrs. Thaw for several days and then accompanied her to New York, where the Supreme Court was hearing arguments in yet another plea for Harry's release. During his short stay in New York, James took a room in the Holland House Hotel.

On Saturday morning, March 12, Mrs. Thaw drove James to the boat dock to see him off on his voyage. The North German Lloyd steamer *Berlin* sailed at eleven o'clock for Gibraltar, Naples, and Genoa. That afternoon James wrote to his fiancée:

My Dear Mary,

You could not have timed your special delivery letter better. After I wrote you this afternoon I wandered around the boat like a lost child. I finally discovered the Gymnasium. It is the first I have ever seen on shipboard and its strange apparatus rather moved me to scorn.

I watched several novices try the numerous appliances and like the little girl who was watching, I too wanted to laugh at the antics of the performers.

Finally, all left but one and I, still doubting, mounted the english saddle on the automatic steed. The horse may be artificial but the motion is the real thing. I rode the trot, posted, and rode the trot again. I did not leave the saddle for half an hour.

It is remarkable how they are able to impart so natural a movement to such an inane looking object. The spirit of the thing having taken hold, I tried the vibrators. One was so restful that I fell asleep.

. . . After lunch a telegram was handed to me from your aunt. She sent her best wishes and asked me to telegraph her my European addresses. . . . She is so lonely after all her sorrow. But she has kept herself cheerful and sweet and is so thoughtful of others. I don't wonder that you are so proud of your aunt. You did not praise her half enough.

The first few nights out were bitterly cold, but as the steamer headed south into warmer currents the temperature rose and the voyage became more enjoyable. The *Berlin* made the crossing to Gibraltar in ten days. During the passage James made the acquaintance of Marian Crawford, the author of the romantic adventure novels he had so enjoyed at Yale. He also became friends with a young man whose mother was Russian and whose father was American. He had graduated from the University of Odessa and had just completed a year of study at Cornell. The young man was an unlikely companion for James, who wrote Mary about him after the *Berlin* docked in Naples:

> My Russian friend got into a card game three nights before we landed and lost all his money. He is off trying to telegraph his father for help. Until he hears news I will try to take care of him.
> I can see you smile, but if he never paid me back I would still be repaid, for he is the funniest, best company imaginable and its not much fun in a foreign city if you are alone. He is about the most irresponsible young fellow I have ever met.

The *Berlin* made the port of Naples on March 25, which happened to be Holy Thursday. The crossing, including a one-day stopover in Gibraltar, had taken two weeks.

James checked into the Excelsior Napoli Hotel and then went off to see the sights of the city. He described Naples as being "Lively, dirty and noisy but oh so beautiful. . . . [T]he peach trees are all in bloom and everything is green and fresh." On the afternoon of the twenty-sixth he joined some American tourists in an auto tour around the Bay of Naples. They drove along the shore and through "Posolipo" and stopped at one point to see the tomb of Virgil.

At Naples James had to make arrangements to continue his journey. On Holy Saturday morning he went to the North German Lloyd office and learned that the S.S. *Skutari* was sailing for Odessa on the following Monday. From Odessa he could take a Russian steamer to the port of Batumi and from there continue his journey by land. The mine he was to inspect was near the Kurd village of Elizabetpol in the Caucasus Mountains, more than 100 miles east of Tiflis.

Naples was picturesque, but James decided to chance a quick visit to Rome rather than spending another day and a half waiting in the port. He was on a tight schedule, but the chance to spend Easter in the Eternal City was worth the rush. He arrived in Rome late Holy Saturday night. He was awakened early the following morning by the chiming of hundreds of church bells proclaiming the Resurrection. On Easter morning St. Peter's Square was thronged with the faithful who had come to hear the Easter message and receive the blessing of Pope Pius X. Hogle was unable to get anywhere near St. Peter's, but Easter in Rome has its own special magic, and he wrote to his fiancée that "I was fully repaid for the hurried trip."

Coincidence has its own laws of probability. The experienced traveler is constantly reminded that everyone knows someone, somewhere, and the hackneyed expression "It's a small world" didn't become hackneyed by disuse. On Monday morning when James returned to the steamer office in Naples to secure his berth accommodations, two ladies were talking to the same clerk who had waited on him. When one of them asked, "Will there be any Americans on board?" the clerk turned to James and said, "This is an American who has reservations." Hogle introduced himself. There must have been something familiar in his western manner or his speech, for the lady immediately asked where he was from. When James said "Salt Lake City, Utah," the woman looked surprised and exclaimed, "Why that's where I live! I am the wife of Professor Cummings, head of the English Department at the University of Utah." Hogle stared at the unfamiliar and disbelieving face in front of him. He had known Professor Cummings for some time and had recently had lunch with him at the University Club in Salt Lake. The travelers laughed at the startling coincidence and James pondered the odds of the chance meeting. The other woman was the mother of the Standard Oil representative in Romania, and Mrs. Cummings was accompanying her to Bucharest to visit her son.

The liner sailed on the evening tide. In the ship's dining salon that night, as James Hogle waited to be seated, a strikingly beautiful woman entered the salon. Her bearing and the deference with which she was treated by the steward made it obvious that this was someone of importance. James thought to himself that she must be a princess.

According to the printed schedule, the first stop on this voyage was to have been Messina the following morning. But the great earthquake of 1908, which had leveled the town and killed more than 60,000 residents, had destroyed the dock facilities. A year and a half later they had yet to be rebuilt, so the *Skutari* landed instead at the port of Catania farther down the coast and the passengers disembarked for the afternoon.

As the ship approached the coast, James could see a towering plume of smoke rising from the top of a mountain behind the Sicilian city. The purser explained the phenomenon: "Mount Etna is in eruption. From Catania you can drive right up to the flowing lava."

Before landing, James told Mrs. Cummings that he was planning on driving to the lava flow and asked if she would like to accompany him. Mrs. Cummings agreed and suggested that they also invite a certain Russian lady she had met the previous evening. Mrs. Cummings said that the Russian woman had been seated at dinner next to a German engineer and his wife who she grew to dislike so much that in the middle of the dinner she moved her place to Mrs. Cummings' table, commenting that she preferred the company of Americans to that of Germans.

Mrs. Cummings went off to find her Russian friend. When the ship landed at Catania that morning, James met the ladies at the gangway and was surprised to find that Mrs. Cummings' Russian friend was the "princess" he had seen the night before. Though she was not a princess, James had been correct in assessing her aristocratic bearing. She was the Baroness Maindorf.

The three travelers spent the morning together. They hired a car and drove to the foot of Mount Etna, where they observed lava flowing very near the statue of a local sainted priest who, it was said, had stopped a previous eruption through prayer just before the molten rock could engulf his church. The proximity of the current flow to the base of the shrine was disconcerting.

In the afternoon they attended an open-air concert in Catania. The fifty-piece orchestra had been founded by Rossini and was very fine. In the evening, as the S.S. *Skutari* sailed out of Catania's harbor, the erupting volcano lit up the entire sky. Bright streams of fluorescent red lava could be seen flowing down the lower slopes very near the city. James stood at the ship's rail and peered back at the receding mountains of Sicily. He continued to watch until the distant red glow had completely faded from sight.

On the passage from Catania to Greece James became acquainted with four other ladies: Mrs. McCullough, Miss Stone, Miss Leckley, and Miss Baker. Mrs. McCullough was an elderly American who was traveling with Miss Leckley, a very plump Scottish lady James described as having "little mischievous eyes and a red face." Miss Stone was dark-haired and mysterious. Hogle thought she might be a spiritualist. She was in fact a professor of antiquities at the American College at Athens. Miss Baker was an English tour guide who was taking the trip in connection with her employment.

The *Skutari* docked at the Greek port of Piraeus a little before seven on the morning of April 2, 1910. The port was just a few miles from Athens, and the strange translucence of the Aegean Sea illuminated the Acropolis and the Parthenon which overlooked the city.

James encountered the Baroness on the gangway. She was in a hurry and was carrying a grapefruit wrapped in a lace handkerchief which she said she was delivering to a friend in the city. Hogle accompanied her to the Russian consulate, where her acquaintances were living. But it was still too early in the morning and her friends had not yet awakened, so the Baroness and James took a short drive about the city before going to meet Miss Stone and the other ladies at the Acropolis. Before the others arrived, James left the company of the Baroness and wandered alone among the ruins of the Parthenon for several hours.

That afternoon Miss Stone gave a fascinating and authoritative lecture on the ruins. James wrote that "She did not seem like the same person who was on the boat. She was in her element, and near what she knew best. Her personality seemed to change and for two hours she gave out the best she knew how. She had an interested and appreciative audience." Miss Stone was remaining in Athens. The other travelers re-boarded the *Skutari* to continue their journey.

At Surynna [Smyrna?] the representative of the American Tobacco Company came on board and asked to see any Americans. The gentleman took James and the American women to lunch and then took them on a short motor tour of the city.

When the ship reached Constantinople on April 4, James's bevy of female companions disappeared. The American women went to find passage to Constanzia, from where they would travel by train to Bucharest. Miss Leckley went in search of her brother, who was to meet her at the Pera Palace Hotel. The Baroness again went off seeking old friends.

Hogle was expecting mail at Constantinople and went in search of the Cook's Travel office where his mail was being forwarded. But in the crowded streets he very quickly became lost. No one spoke English; the jumble of Turkish signs meant nothing; not a taxi was in sight, and the babel of foreign tongues brought James to a state of momentary panic. Finally, on a busy corner he noticed two men whose dress appeared English. He approached them and asked if they knew the location of the Cook's Travel office. They replied that they were going to the hotel directly across the street from Cook's and would be happy to take him there in their carriage. James was much relieved at their prompt and generous offer.

In the carriage he learned that one of the gentlemen was Mr. Leckley, the brother of the plump Scottish lady. He was on his way to the Pera Palace Hotel to meet her. Again Hogle puzzled at the odds of coincidence.

After picking up his mail he went to the Pera Palace to read it over. There were letters from his mother, from Mrs. Thaw, from Mr. Van Liew, and a large packet of mail from Mary. Hogle was suddenly homesick and wrote Mary a short note on the hotel stationery:

Mary My Dearest,

Your good letters were here this morning. . . . I don't wonder that you were blue. I tore up some pages I wrote on the *Berlin* about the same time you did. I am more lonesome and home-sick than I admitted.

It hurts anytime I go any place not to have you with me. This might have been not only an interesting trip but the best in all the world, if only you were with me. . . .

I am glad to hear all your "proper east" liked me but if you are pleased that's all I care about. If your aunt comes out when we are married that would mean a lot of responsibility for you, a formal wedding and all that sort of thing.

My Dear, let's get quietly married with as little fuss and trouble to all our dear relatives as is possible. I don't see how I can wait until the fall anyway.

Some day I shall carry you off as I should have for this trip. No duty will be in the way to hold us back next time.

I love you better every day

Jim

At the Pera Palace James was reunited with his traveling companions, and they spent the day together touring the city. It just so happened that on that particular day both the Sultan and the King of Serbia were in town, and the whole city was brightly decorated with Turkish and Serbian flags. Military bands marched through the streets and the sailors and soldiers were in their dress uniforms. It was all like being part of a gigantic costume ball. There was, as James described it, "Life and action every minute and dogs, dogs, dogs everywhere, every kind and size and color, but mostly yellow and such strange people!"

When the travelers arrived at the famous drawbridge across the Golden Horn, they found that it had been raised to allow the Sultan's yacht to pass. In order to cross, the party hired a large rowboat with two oarsmen. The water was alive with boats and men and women stood in them as if waiting for something. As James and his party were making the crossing, the Sultan's large steam yacht pulled into view. They were half way across when the yacht passed close by them, and from the tumult of the cheering crowds on the shore and in the other boats, it was obvious that the Sultan was on board.

They spent much of the morning at the huge covered bazaar at Stamboul. There were thousands of booths, each presided over by a single vendor. The variety of exotic items being peddled was unbelievable, as was the shouting confusion of the hawkers' foreign cries. James contented himself with the purchase of two items, a pair of long wooden-handled inlaid scissors and an antique silver inkstand.

From the bazaar, the party went to the Armenian restaurant in the Catlian Hotel that Miss Baker, the English tour guide, recommended. Miss Baker spoke Turkish and did all the ordering for the party. The food was strange and James did not know what was in the dish that he was eating. "It was," he wrote, "queer, but good." The food was washed down with strong Turkish coffee.

Following their meal, the travelers set off to see Constantinople's most famous attraction, Santa Sophia, the "Mother of Churches," built by the emperor Justinian and completed in 537. Since the victory of the Sultan Muhammad in 1453, it had been a mosque. To James, the architecture was reminiscent of St. Paul's in Venice, but the lavish designs which adorned the stone work were unlike anything he had seen before. At the corners of the huge stone building were four towering minarets from where the muezzin called the faithful to prayer.

At the door of the mosque, Turks were taking off their shoes and just inside, washing their hands, faces, and feet before beginning their worship. Hogle donned large slippers to cover his shoes before entering. The huge gilded dome, the high graceful columns supporting it, the oriental decorations on the walls, and the prayer rugs covering the entire floor seemed to him a strange combination. But the whole effect of it was, to his mind, only surpassed by St. Peter's in Rome. James described the Muslims' devotions in another letter to his fiancée.

> It is something to behold. After bowing toward the altar, toward which all the prayer rugs are laid pointing the direction to Mecca he drops to his knees bows his head between his hands and three times touches the floor with his forehead before proceeding with his worship. Some were alone, some in twos and threes and one group mass assembled before, what appeared to be, a priest in something like one of our pulpits.

After leaving Santa Sophia the travelers went to the museum nearby and saw many of the relics of Babylon and the ancient Trojan and Persian cities. The best relic was the supposed sarcophagus of Alexander. Whether it truly was or not, James thought the sarcophagus "a great work of art."

As they left the museum they passed Santa Sophia. The muezzin was again calling the Muslims to prayer. James marveled at the voice of the singer and wrote to Mary Copley, "Such a weird but strong beautiful voice he had, it was haunting and chilling at the same time."

James said goodbye to the American women in Constantinople. They would leave the *Skutari* and make other travel arrangements while James and the Baroness Maindorf would continue to Odessa.

James had dinner at a Turkish restaurant that evening. This meal was heavily spiced and followed by a course of rich Turkish sweets. That evening, as the *Skutari* rocked quietly at anchor, he paid dearly for his dietary indiscretion by becoming "disastrously sea sick." He wrote to Mary that he "had never been so sick in all his life." He remained in his cabin the following morning and missed the ship's passage through the Bosporus.

James A. Hogle on shipboard during his long journey to Russia in 1910.

While crossing the Black Sea James got better acquainted with the Baroness Maindorf. At dinner she told him about her family and her life. The Maindorfs had originally come to Russia from one of the Baltic provinces of Germany. Her father, a military man of some note, had risen to the rank of major general in the tsar's imperial army. Her mother's family were nobility.

The general had been killed seven years earlier during the Russo-Japanese War. She herself had served as a nurse during the conflict. Through her work in the army she had become very influential in her own right, and since the war she had saved the lives of four men who had been condemned to death during the 1906 Revolu-

James and a companion during the young engineer's Russian trip in 1910.

tion. She had personally pleaded with the tsar's sister for the retrial which eventually resulted in the men's release.

The loss of her father, the rigors of wartime service, and the turmoil of the revolt had impaired her health, and for the previous two years she had been under treatment for an undisclosed disorder. That spring she was returning home from a sanitarium in Austria where she had spent the winter. She now felt completely recovered.

Hogle also learned why she had left the table of the German engineer and his wife on the *Berlin*. She admitted openly that she hated Germans and that many former Teutons felt the same way after living in Russia. The remark which prompted her to leave the table was a comment by the engineer that Germany would eventually "absorb weaker Russia."

Though James Hogle was not a novice traveler, the Baroness, who traveled a good deal, spent some time volunteering advice on hotels in Odessa, passports, customs inspections, and other matters relating to traveling.

When the *Skutari* docked at Odessa on April 6, James and the Baroness said goodbye. She was met at the dock by a car and he did not expect to see her again. He went to the Hotel d'Europe, which his Russian friend had recommended. That afternoon he began looking for passage to Batumi. A Russian luxury liner was leaving in three days, but the exclusive vessel was completely booked and he was unable to get a berth.

The following morning, the hotel porter came to his room and told him there was a lady downstairs who wanted to see him. In the lobby James met the Baroness. "It's Annunciation Day," she said, "A great festival in the Russian Orthodox Church. You must come with me to the Cathedral."

The Russian Orthodox cathedral in Odessa was richly ornamented with statuary and lavishly decorated with frescoes and stained-glass windows depicting various scenes from the life of Christ. Hogle later described the service as "The most colorful and impressive one could imagine." The mass was preceded by an elaborate procession of bishops and priests. They carried various religious articles, golden crosses, elaborate icons, and clanking incense burners. The air inside the cathedral was permeated with the heavy sweet smoke from the thuribles. The male choir impressed Hogle the most. "The singing," he wrote, "was magnificent."

As the Baroness and James were riding back to the hotel following the service, she said, "I have talked to my cousin, and you are invited to dinner tomorrow evening at the palace." The word "palace" startled Hogle and the Baroness added by way of explanation, "My cousin is the wife of the prince."

Hogle was flattered by the invitation but wondered if he had the appropriate attire for such an occasion; he had brought a dinner jacket with him but not "tails." The Baroness told him not to worry and that "There would only be relatives there."

The next day Hogle, the Baroness, and one of her cousins drove to the Princess's dacha on the Black Sea. This was not the palace that was used for formal receptions. The prince, as it turned out, was in St. Petersburg, and dinner with James Hogle was not considered a "state occasion." The dacha had been used several times recently to entertain Americans, including an editor of the *New York Sun*, a Mr. Dana, and the daughter of the president of the American Steamship Line. They were so taken with the latter that they had become fond of "everything American," and that included James Hogle.

The women were in evening clothes, but the two other male guests, also relatives, wore dark business suits. Hogle wrote that "The Baroness evidently did not know that my Tuxedo was an informal dinner jacket and told them not to dress."

Neither of the men spoke English, but the women spoke English as well as French and German. French, it seemed, was the language they preferred in conversation. James did not catch the Russian name of his hostess, but he did not want to seem overly inquisitive about the family either. He listened politely through the meal and learned what he could. "Her husband was the first cousin of the Tsar and was also an accomplished sculptor."

James Hogle was struck by the similarity between this evening and formal gatherings of high society back in the States. Were it not for the language differences, it could well have been a dinner party at the Grays', the Thomases', or the Vanderbilts'. The only thing he noted as being different was that the two butlers who served the dinner wore undressed white kid gloves.

Much of the dinner conversation concerned the family's experiences during the Revolution of 1904. That brief and prophetic rebellion had been caused in part by the disastrous defeat of Russia in the Russo-Japanese War. In Odessa the rebellion was particularly violent. The mutiny aboard battleships in Sebastopol and the shelling of the palace itself by the Black Sea Fleet were recalled with horror. Sometime during the dinner James mentioned that he was unable to get reservations to continue his journey to Batumi. His Russian friends told him not to worry, that he would be taken care of.

The following afternoon James again went to the Russian steamer office. His berth accommodation and ticket were already waiting for him. That evening when he boarded the ship he was taken to an exclusive stateroom that was the largest he had ever seen. As James was unpacking his suitcase, "a heavy set, and rather tall man with a pointed beard" entered and seemed most surprised and put out by Hogle's presence. The man asked James something abrupt in Russian, but he replied that he spoke no Russian. The man then asked in English, "Are you the American?" When Hogle replied "Yes" the man smiled and seemed to relax.

James was seated next to the gentleman at dinner that evening. The man did not talk about himself and the conversation was casual. The man impressed James as being "perhaps, a successful manufacturer." After he had gone to bed that evening, the man entered James's room, where his steamer trunks had been stored, and removed from one of them a pair of bright red pajamas. A short time later the man returned to the trunk, now garbed in the fireman red pajamas. James was amused at the sight of that large, distinguished gentleman dressed in clothing that looked for all the world "like the red flannel underwear I wore when I was a boy. It was certainly something to remember." The comical apparition was vividly etched in his memory.

The next morning the steamer docked at Sebastopol, where it would take on cargo all day. James rose early and had breakfast, but when he left the ship he found that his "roommate" had already been in the port and was returning to the ship just as James was coming down the gangplank. The man said he had been for a walk and that if Hogle would care to join him he would take him to see the Greek Orthodox Cathedral, which was something of an architectural curiosity.

James and his Russian guide went to the cathedral and then to the fish market near the anchorage of the Black Sea squadron of the Imperial Russian Navy. Here there were several Russian battleships and James's companion suggested that they hire a boatman and row out to the closest of the great vessels.

As the two men approached the massive floating armory, James could not help but recall that these were the same vessels that had shelled the summer palace in Odessa a few short years before. His Russian companion commented that his father had been in the siege, but since that incident there had been a major shakeup in the Russian navy and imperial officers were once again in firm control.

When they drew alongside the battleship, the Russian called up to a sailor guarding the rail and an officer came to the ladder. The officer informed them that they did not allow visitors on board, but James's friend interrupted him and after a brief exchange the officer went off to get the captain.

James later wrote of the incident, "My companion must have told him who he was for when the officer left, my Russian friend said to me: 'My family's name is well known in Russia, the Captain will let us on board.' "

His family's name was known indeed throughout the world. He was Count Lyof N. Tolstoy, the son of the famous Russian novelist and second cousin of the tsar. Tolstoy himself was still alive. He would die on November seventh of that same year at the age of eighty-two. His passing came just before the end of the Romanov dynasty, which had ruled Russia for two and a half centuries.

Tolstoy had depicted Russia's nobility with uncompromising honesty. He saw, as few of his class had seen, the shallowness and ineptitude of the ruling elite and the extravagant excesses that would eventually lead to its downfall. Seven short years later the Romanovs would be gone forever and with them the pampered court life that James Hogle had glimpsed, if ever so fleetingly, that spring of 1910.

The brief encounter with Count Tolstoy was the high point of James A. Hogle's trip to Russia. The unlikely friendship between the two men continued for many years afterward and the count's brother, Illya Tolstoy, would later visit the Hogle family in Salt Lake City.

James spent most of April inspecting the mines in the Caucasus. There was great potential in the property, and the assay reports had all been good; but there were difficulties in securing clear title to the mineral deposits. Imperial Russian bureaucracy moved very slowly, and not even James's high-placed friends seemed able to make it move any faster. It was very frustrating, particularly for Mr. Van Liew, who had spent the better part of a year on the project.

James returned to Constantinople on April 28 and sailed for Cairo on May 2; there he was to meet his mother, who had been touring the Continent with some of her friends. On the short passage, he compiled his notes on his Russian experience for a lecture at the Ladies' Literary Club that he would deliver upon his return. There were many contradictions, and he tried to analyze his mixed feelings. James checked into the Shepheard's Hotel in Cairo and typed up his notes. The Cairo papers reveal keen insight and accurate prophecy:

> I was only in Russia twenty days and spent the whole of that time in the southern part along the shores of the Black Sea and in the caucasus and trans-caucasus. In so short a time one can form only a vague idea of a country composed of races so complex.
>
> Twenty seven languages are spoken in the Caucasus; More Asiatic and European races represented than any place I know — Turks, Native Georgians and Russians, Tartars, Kurds, Kossacks, Armenians. One day while driving from Elizabetpol, a Tartar City east of Tiflis, we entered a large village made up almost entirely of Germans whose ancestors came from the Vaterland in the 18th Century. They have the best vineyards in the country and have grown rich from their wine, for the Georgians are great wine drinkers.
>
> . . . The Russians are polite and generous to a fault. When a Russian says a thing he means it, and his politeness is not the suave superficiality of the French. They differ greatly from the English; they are not staid, reserved, or unchangeable. They

Ida Hogle in Egypt in 1910. Ida is mounted on a donkey at the far right.

have a keen sense of humor. . . . The Russian character is not the free lighthearted irresponsible one of the Italians, but is thoughtful and introspective. In many ways the Russians resemble us, in fact, they are more like us than any race on earth.

Under our liberal form of government, we are apt to criticize the restrictions and oppression of the Russian Government, but conditions have changed in the past few years, and it is an actual fact that the working man is looked after more carefully by their Government, than are ours.

From serfdom they have been used to little, and living in somewhat the same environment, seem still willing to exist on little. It will be slower for them to progress than if they emigrated, but as they do progress, and fit themselves to more constitutional government, just so fast will it come to them. It is principally because the mass of the people are not ready for them, that the reforms secured have accomplished so little.

I believe today that there are better opportunities to exploit the natural wealth of the country, around and adjacent to the Black Sea, than any place on earth.

Mary C. Copley in 1910, at about the time of her marriage.

The Russians still have the upper hand in Persia, but the English in the South and the Germans in the North have strong interests. For many years it was England's dread that Russia might control the Persian Gulf. . . . It is only a few days from there to India and many weeks from India to England. The Persians themselves will tell you that they have not the men fit to rule. The Shah, deposed last year, now lives in Odessa under restraint. If Russia joins Persia on the South, they could rule the country with less disturbance and give better protection than any country at a distance.

Russia already has railways to the border and good roads into the interior. Russia must have an open seaport. A country, so vast and wealthy, which has grown from a small inland state, not much larger than Ohio, to the powerful country she has become, shows that she is not to be held back. Russia can assimilate the various races the same way we do, and partly on account of the mixture of races, and principally on account of the resources, Russia and the United States are destined to become the great nations of the earth.

Cairo, May 4th, 1910.

Ida Hogle joined her son in Cairo. It was an interesting place to shop, but James wrote to Mary that, "It's been too raked over by the tourists." He purchased for Mary's mother an Egyptian shawl, "black net covered with gilt spangles. I think when the *Cleveland* reaches port every family in America will have one of those wraps. They cleaned Cairo out."

The Hogles had their photos taken on camelback in front of the Pyramids, and on May 11 set sail from Port Said for Naples aboard the S.S. *Cleveland*, a first-class packet steamer of the Aller-Bremen Line.

They toured Italy together, visiting Milan, Genoa, and Rome, before proceeding to Lausanne, Switzerland. That May Halley's Comet was making its return to the inner solar system, repeating its seventy-six-year cycle. James got his first glimpse of the spectacular comet from an observatory in Italy.

He would remain in Lausanne from June 7 through 25 while his mother rejoined her friends for two weeks in France. In Switzerland James stayed at the Hotel Cecil on Lake Geneva. In Lausanne he underwent treatments for his hearing loss at a clinic operated by a Dr. Mermod. He also took brief classes in German from the Berlitz school in the city.

On June 27 he visited Munich; on July 6 he arrived in Paris, and on July 9 rejoined his mother in London. He had been away now for more than five months and was tired of traveling. Back in Salt Lake a certain French teacher was waiting, and James A. Hogle was ready to settle down. As he sat in his room in the St. Petersburg Hotel on North Audley Street, Grosvenor Square, London, he composed an artful piece of romantic poetry to express his feelings. He dedicated the work to Mary C. Copley. It was entitled, "An Island in Arcady."

> There is an isle, within a crystal stream,
> Whose loving waters hold in fond embrace.
> It lies there throned in perfect peace,
> Kissed only by the rain upon its face.
>
> Nor foot now desecrates this sacred place
> Which God has consecrated with haughty glance.
> Hence only from the further hills I gazed
> Across its gentle, graceful shores so grand.
>
> Mirrored in beauty, the peaks up-raised,
> Like sentry spirits sent to guard this scene,
> I loved forever more this Isle serene,
> Praised by man, and yet unseen.
>
> And so, in truth, one day I found thee dear,
> Your life touched by currents of a dream.
> Moved to laugh, then cry, then shed a tear,
> So little had life's action been thy scene.
>
> To stir thy nature from its cast serene,
> And reach thy heart, that love it might contain,
> Fate gave to me, thank god, the sight to see
> What lay unseen, behind that pure and pale face.

James sailed for New York on July 12. Over the years he would write forty versions of the poem.

Part III
MARY CECILIA COPLEY

CHAPTER NINETEEN

The Copley Line

THERE ARE MANY COMMON CHARACTER TRAITS among the ancestors of Mary Cecilia Copley, most notably their strong religious faith and their love of education. Without exception, Mary Cecilia's ancestors of record were educated people. In the eighteenth and nineteenth centuries this was rare in all but the richest of families. Notable too are the careers pursued by her forebears. They were doctors, ministers, educators, writers, editors, inventors, social reformers, and revolutionary leaders. The Copleys were people of strong convictions. They were also visionaries.

The Copley name is of Norman French origin, but the family has been in England since the time of William the Conqueror. The Copleys originally settled in Yorkshire, but by the fourteenth century the name could be found in Dorchester and London as well. In Yorkshire, very near the city of Leeds, in a village once called Bailey, stands a small medieval devotional shrine called Copley Chapel. This chapel is associated with the Copley family burial plot, and the headstones record Copley burials there from 1300 through 1700. This Yorkshire branch are the direct ancestors of Mary Cecilia Copley.

Copley Chapel houses an elaborate oak screen upon which are carved the Copley coat of arms and the coats of arms of the families the Copleys were associated with through marriage. These included the Sevilles of Normandy and the Howards, the family name of the Dukes of Norfolk. The Copleys were a most distinguished and honored family of noble lineage. Among the Christian names recorded at Copley Chapel are five that would appear again and again: Robert, Edward, John, William, and Josiah.

One particular eighteenth-century William Copley was a manufacturer of woolen goods in Leeds. William was a brilliant man of inventive genius, and his elaborate mills were precursors of the technology that created the Industrial Revolution. His revolutionary ideas were not confined to the textile industry, however, and he was also a social and political reformer. Though a member of the established church, he fought for religious tolerance. William's political convictions eventually led to his vocal support of the Colonies during the American Revolution, a most unpopular stance in his native Leeds.

William had four sons, all of whom emigrated to America as young men. The two eldest, John and Samuel, arrived in Boston in 1792 and for a time were partners in a business there before moving to Pennsylvania. John and Samuel too engaged in the manufacture of textiles. Their mill was located in the Cumberland Valley near the small town of Shippensburg, Pennsylvania.

In 1801 Samuel, the second son, married Jane Sibbet. Their children included William and Josiah; the latter, born September 20, 1803, was Mary Cecilia Copley's paternal grandfather.

The Sibbets

The Sibbets were originally Scottish Presbyterians who had emigrated to Ireland with the plantation of Ulster in the early seventeenth century. The history of the family closely parallels the history of that plantation.

Initially, these lowland Scots were strong supporters of the English crown, but circumstances would eventually force many of them, the Sibbets included, to join the Irish cause.

Following the defeat of Catholic James II (1691) and the flight of the "Wild Geese" which followed, the English government enacted the infamous series of penal laws directed against the Catholic population of Ireland. But the laws also discriminated against anyone who was not a member of the Established Anglican Church of Ireland. As a result, Protestant dissenters, particularly Presbyterians, found themselves brutally victimized by many of the anti-Catholic laws. The "penal times," as they are known, lasted through most of the eighteenth century.

Many thousands of Scotch-Irish emigrated to America during this period to escape the religious persecution. They would provide both manpower and leadership for the American Revolution. This Scotch-Irish line would eventually give America a host of generals, statesmen, industrialists, and ten presidents.

The Protestant dissenters who remained in Ireland became increasingly allied with the native Irish. This Scotch-Irish Protestant class would provide the leadership for Irish revolutionary movements through the next two centuries. The Sibbet family was very active in these movements.

In 1798 the Irish, inspired by the success of the American Revolution and aided by the sympathetic French Republic, mounted an ill-fated rising under Theobald Wolf Tone, Henry Joy Mc-Cracken, and Lord Edward Fitzgerald. Their organization, the Society of United Irishmen, was mostly Protestant, but they believed strongly in Catholic emancipation and Irish independence. A prominent leader of the United Irishmen was Samuel Sibbet, Jane Sibbet Copley's oldest brother.

The rebel organization was riddled with government spies and informers, including Leonard McNally, one of the group's founders. The British military knew in detail the plans for the rebellion and the date that hostilities were scheduled to begin, May 23, 1798. There were more than 2,000 separate groups of men enlisted for the rising, but the British had systematically hunted down and arrested most of the leaders before May 23 arrived.

Although the Irish knew they had been betrayed, they proceeded with the Rising anyway. It was a fiasco. Disorganized and leaderless mobs of men ambushed British troops, officials, and landlords. What began as a heroic rebellion for Irish freedom quickly degenerated into a series of ugly sectarian massacres and bloody reprisals.

A small force under Henry Joy McCracken briefly held the city of Antrim on June 7, but after a counterattack he was captured, brought to Belfast, and promptly hanged. On August 22 a French army under General Humbert landed in County Mayo but was quickly surrounded and forced to surrender. Another French army landed in Donegal but returned to France after learning of General Humbert's fate. Wolf Tone was captured on October 12 after his small fleet was destroyed by the British navy off Donegal. It was over.

Samuel Sibbet avoided capture, but he was known to the British authorities and a price of fifty guineas was on his head. Sibbet would remain in Ireland for the next year and a half, living for the most part in hiding. During this period he worked in close association with a young Trinity College student and fellow United Irishman, Robert Emmet.

Early in 1800 Sibbet was warned that the British were closing in on him. His friends managed to smuggle him aboard a ship bound for America. He arrived secretly in Baltimore, Maryland, in the spring of 1800.

In 1803 another futile "Rebellion" was attempted, this one led by Samuel Sibbet's friend, the twenty-four-year-old Robert Emmet. His attack on Dublin Castle, the seat of British government in Ireland, resulted in the deaths of the Lord Chief Justice and his nephew.

Robert Emmet was captured, tried, convicted, hanged, disemboweled, quartered, and beheaded, but his heroic "speech from the dock" made Emmet one of Ireland's most revered martyrs. In the next generation four Sibbet children would be named for Robert Emmet.

Some months after Samuel Sibbet's escape, his wife Alice (Lowry), and their three children, James, Thomas, and Robert, followed Samuel into exile. Also fleeing Ireland were his brothers and sisters, John, James, Robert, Eliza, and Jane. The reunited family then moved to a Scotch-Irish settlement at the head of Big Spring in the Cumberland Valley, and it was here that Jane Sibbet and Samuel Copley were married.

From the beginning of the marriage Samuel and Jane were plagued by financial problems. Shortly after the birth of their son Josiah (Mary Cecilia's grandfather), Samuel moved his family to Blairsville, Pennsylvania, where he operated another textile mill. The family struggled at making a living from the mill for the next eight years, but however great their effort, the mill seemed doomed to failure.

Jane Sibbet Copley

Throughout history, the appearance of comets has been believed to portend disaster. The Comet of 1811 would lend powerful credence to the myth because wars, rumors of wars, pestilence, and natural disaster did follow within a year of its arrival. First there was the Great Missouri Earthquake of December 16, 1811, vividly remembered by the young Josiah Copley, then the War of 1812, the Napoleonic Wars, and the subsequent disruption of the economy. Some saw the series of disasters as fulfillment of the comet's prophecy. For the Copley family, the heavenly apparition seemed particularly prophetic, and the young Josiah Copley always believed it a terrible omen sent from God.

The War of 1812 had widespread economic effects, one of which was the collapse of the woolen trade. Coincident with that collapse, Samuel Copley's textile business failed and then his health. He never recovered and died during the winter of 1813. His widow, now nearly destitute, was left to care for her two young children. At the time of his father's death, Josiah was nine years old. He later wrote of those dark times: "It was a time of stern necessity, yet my memory of it is sweet; for there was more light than darkness, more joy than sorrow; and it was during this trying period, that my sainted mother was made perfect through suffering."

Jane Sibbet Copley was a gifted teacher, and she taught young Josiah how to read, write, sing, and pray. He vividly remembered her reading to him accounts of the burning of Moscow during its occupation by the French and other news items from the journals of the day.

But Jane Sibbet Copley's reading was not confined to the news. Josiah wrote of her:

> She was a woman of strong and original mind; gentle but firm; sensitive yet patient. She was the pleasantest and most impressive reader I ever knew; and the keys of knowledge, the first germs of thought, I gained from hearing her read, especially the Scriptures. She read admirably . . . no one I ever knew surpassed her in reading or reciting poetry, or in singing Scotch ballads, with which her memory was well stored.

Josiah Copley emulated his mother and from her acquired strong religious convictions. Throughout his life he would remain a faithful Presbyterian, but his convictions, like his mother's, were tempered by tolerance. Bigotry of any kind was foreign to his nature. He believed that "denominational differences were divisions of one grand army." Like his mother and his Uncle Samuel Sibbet, Josiah had a passionate love of freedom and liberty. Like his mother, Josiah was strong-willed and independent. These traits were crucial, for before he reached his fourteenth year his mother too had passed away.

Josiah was then sent to live for a time with the Sibbet family before being apprenticed to James McCahan, printer and publisher of *The American*, a weekly newspaper in Indiana, Pennsylvania. It seems probable that the McCahans were relatives, as one of Samuel Sibbet's sisters is recorded in the family Bible as "Mrs. McCahan."

Josiah Copley

Josiah would live with the McCahans from 1818 to 1825. He wrote that while he lived in their household he was always treated as a member of the family and "enjoyed all the social and domestic privileges of a son." But Mr. McCahan was also a stern taskmaster who continued the training and education begun by Josiah's mother. He was continuously drilled in the formidable skills of the printers of that day. Spelling, writing, reading, and editing were the essence of his apprenticeship, and from the very beginning Josiah was destined to become a man of letters.

In addition to operating *The American*, James McCahan held the mail contract between Kittanning and Indiana, Pennsylvania. Part of Josiah's work was delivering the mail. His route took him through country that had few roads or bridges. In winter he often traveled through unbroken snow, and in spring high water made the route particularly dangerous, but "no inclemency of weather was ever considered sufficient excuse for not setting out." His route took three straight days to complete.

When Josiah's apprenticeship was completed in 1825, he went into partnership with a man named John Croll and founded a newspaper of his own, *The Kittanning Gazette*. That same year, while he was visiting his Uncle John Sibbet in Philadelphia, he became acquainted with his uncle's stepdaughter Margaret.

Margaret Chadwick Haas was the widow of a Philadelphia physician who had died of cholera while treating victims of an epidemic in that city in 1824. After her husband's death, she returned to the house of her stepfather, John Sibbet. Margaret Haas and Josiah Copley were married in Philadelphia in 1826. Their long life together would span fifty-nine years. Nine children were born to the couple, six sons and three daughters. From both parents these children would acquire something of the Sibbet family's fiery hatred of injustice. Among those children were Mary Sibbet Copley, Henry Weldon Copley, and Josiah Copley, Jr., father of Mary Cecilia.

The professional career of Josiah Copley was long and distinguished. *The Gazette* later merged with *The Columbian* and became the *Democratic Press* and then *The Union Free Press*. Josiah served as managing editor of all three papers before joining the editorial staff of *The Pittsburgh Gazette*. In addition to his work as a journalist, Josiah Copley was a botanist, an essayist, a religious philosopher, and a writer of political tracts. His political essays were written in support of the growing Abolitionist movement and later the Republican Party.

Josiah Copley served on the platform committee of the first Republican Convention in Pennsylvania and helped to draft the anti-slavery resolutions of that body. He was a regular contributor to *The Presbyterian Banner* and *The United Presbyterian*. A number of his essays and articles were collected and published in 1877 as *Gatherings in Beulah*. Another volume, *Gathering Sheaves*, was published posthumously by his daughter, Mary Sibbet Copley Thaw, in 1886.

In the early 1840's the Copley family moved to Appleby Manor Township, Armstrong County, Pennsylvania. Here Josiah and his brother William operated a factory for the manufacture of firebrick. The business was located on property owned by his Aunt Eliza Sibbet, yet another sister of the Irish rebel. It was here also that John Sibbet and Josiah Copley built adjacent homes overlooking

Josiah Copley, Sr., 1803–1884.

the valley of the Allegheny River. In the mid-nineteenth century
this was an unspoiled pastoral land with farms and fields on the
valley floor and dense woodlands on the rolling hills above. Members of the Copley-Sibbet family would reside in Appleby Manor
Township into the next century. Another prominent resident of
Appleby Manor was a man named William Thaw.

William Thaw also came from Scotch-Irish stock and also had close association with the Sibbet family through business dealings with Emmet and John Sibbet, Josiah Copley's nephews. William Thaw was a brilliant industrialist who served as director of the Pennsylvania Railroad, vice-president of the Pennsylvania Company, and vice-president of the Pittsburgh, Cincinnati and St. Louis Railroad. He also served on the board of directors of the American Steamship Company. After the death of his first wife, William Thaw married Mary Sibbet Copley, daughter of Josiah Copley and Jane Sibbet.

The Copley-Thaw families were very close and continued their association throughout the century. They jointly contributed to a number of community and charitable projects in Armstrong County, most notably in the founding and construction of Appleby Manor Memorial Presbyterian Church.

THE TRIAL OF CIVIL WAR

Shortly before Bull Run, the first great battle of the Civil War, a comet appeared in the sky. It seemed to have two separate tails, and Josiah Copley had no doubt as to the meaning of the "fearful heavenly messenger." He had worked tirelessly for the abolition of slavery and knew that the issue would not be resolved without bloodshed. When the war finally came in April of 1860, Josiah was certain that it was part of the inevitable consequence of injustice and the Will of the Almighty. To Josiah, the appearance of the comet verified this belief.

Until the publication of the Emancipation Proclamation late in the war, many northern politicians expressed uncertainty as to the goals of the conflict. Josiah Copley knew from the beginning that the war was not really about Southern secession but about slavery, and throughout the war he continued to write in support of the Union cause. His editorials and essays contained no uncertainty about the goals of the Union. "The abomination of slavery," he wrote, ". . . would be purged from the land with fire and blood." His support was in more than words. Four of Josiah Copley's sons served in the Union armies, and their tragic stories are at the center of the Copley family legacy.

Before the war, John Sibbet Copley, Josiah's eldest son, was a clerk in an iron foundry. A few days after the firing on Fort Sumter, he enlisted in the Pittsburgh Rifles. After a six-month tour of duty, he re-enlisted for three years of service. The Rifles were soon merged into the Ninth Pennsylvania Infantry. John participated in two campaigns and numerous battles with Company A of that regiment.

In September of 1862, General Lee's Army of Northern Virginia was invading the north for the first time. His objective was the railroad junction of Harrisburg, Pennsylvania. General McClellan, the Union commander, learned of Lee's plans and attempted to block his line of march. On September 14, at South Mountain, Maryland, at passes called Crampton's and Turner's gaps, the Ninth Pennsylvania engaged Confederate units under Generals Longstreet and D. H. Hill. The Battle of South Mountain was fierce but was only the opening round in the great Battle of Antietam two days later. John Sibbet Copley was struck down by a Minieball and killed when his regiment stormed the Confederate positions at Turner's Gap.

Before the war, Albert Copley managed his father's farm and flour mill in Armstrong County. In the spring of 1862 he enlisted in the Seventy-eighth Pennsylvania Volunteers. In December of 1862 that unit was under the command of General Negley and part of General Rosecrans's Army of the Cumberland, then encamped near Nashville, Tennessee.

In late December, in miserable weather of mixed snow and rain, the Seventy-eighth was sent toward the Confederate army of General Bragg, then wintering at Murfreesboro. The Battle of Stones River (December 31–January 3) was confusing and bloody. In the fog-shrouded woods and thickets, units became separated from each other, and an attack by Confederate General Polk succeeded in breaking the Union line. As Union generals Thomas and Sheridan struggled to form new positions, forward units were surrounded and overrun. Albert Copley was wounded by a Confederate cannon shell and was being treated at a field hospital when it was captured by the Confederates. Though tactically meaningless, the Battle of

Stones River was one of the costliest fought in the west. The Federals had lost more than 13,000 men, the Confederates more than 10,000.

Albert Copley and his fellow prisoners were put on a train bound for a prison camp in Florida. Before it reached there, however, Union forces had severed the rail line and the train was re-routed to Richmond and then to a prison hospital in Knoxville, Tennessee. Albert's wounds were not thought to be serious, but the 1,200 miles of continuous travel had so weakened him that he died of erysipelas two months after the battle was fought.

The death of his two eldest sons within six months of each other was a devastating blow to Josiah Copley. But a curious incident in a Pittsburgh aid station restored his faith in the Providence of God.

Late one evening Josiah Copley decided to go into Pittsburgh to see the wounded soldiers who passed through an aid station run by the Pittsburgh Subsistence Committee:

> When I entered the hall I found them sitting around long tables, ten or twelve hundred in all. I walked among them but spoke to no one until I noticed a good looking young man standing all alone. I went to him and entered into conversation. He told me he was a member of an Ohio regiment in the Army of the Cumberland. "Did you ever meet any men of the 78th Pennsylvania?" I asked. "Yes" he replied; "We lay for some time along side that regiment." "Did you ever know a man named Albert Copley?" He startled at the question and then exclaimed, "Albert Copley! why I was lying beside him in the hospital when he died." He then told me that they were captured at the same time — that they traveled around in the same car — that he dressed Albert's wounds daily — that they were both put in the same hospital in Knoxville. He said that Albert was in a fair way of recovery until erysipelas set in, which soon terminated in death. He told me that Albert had given a nurse what little he had in return for her "unwearing kindness."
>
> Now what shall we say to all this? If you ask me why I went over there at all at that unseasonable hour, I can not tell you. And when I got there, was it chance that led me to the only man among ten or twelve hundred who was able to give me the information for which I so earnestly yearned?

The incident at the aid station in Pittsburgh would become a powerful exemplum to the Copley family and a story often repeated to the children of the next generation. But it was the experience of Josiah Copley, Jr., during the Civil War that would become the central theme of the family's history and lore. That experience would put their faith to the test as no other. It would radically alter Josiah Copley, Jr.'s, career and would influence the philosophy of Mary C. Copley, his daughter.

CHAPTER TWENTY

The Ordeal of Josiah Copley, Jr.

BEFORE THE CIVIL WAR, Mary Cecilia's father, Josiah Copley, Jr., third eldest of the Copley boys, was following closely in his father's footsteps. He had attended Western University and Amherst and frequently contributed to the *Pittsburgh Gazette*. He was teaching school in Danville, Illinois, when the war began. Like his older brothers, Josiah was strongly for the Union and so, full of patriotic fervor, he quit his job and enlisted in the 21st Illinois Volunteers. His commanding officer was Colonel Ulysses S. Grant.

Shortly after he joined the Union Army, Josiah wrote a letter to his sister, Mary Sibbet Copley, describing his first six weeks as a soldier. The war was still an adventure for young Josiah — all drill and muster, flags and marching. The grim reality would come later. In these early days he thought more of his company's First Lieutenant than of the man who would eventually become the commander of all Lincoln's armies.

Camp Yeats,
Springfield, Illinois
June 30, 1861

Dear Mary,

No doubt you were surprised at my sudden enlistment, but then I had a chance to go with a lot of good fellows who were not strangers.

We are having a good time and I am well liked from the captain on down and have already gone through the hardest part of camp service without flinching, as for instance, during the last 24 hours I stood sentinel at the camp gate four times for two hour shifts besides one on extra patrol. It was raining all the time.

Today we have only a dress parade, as they call it for form sake, as we have no uniforms yet. I feel no worse for last nights ordeal. Indeed, I never felt better in health and spirits and have a splendid appetite and plenty of good rations to supply it with. We have baked bread, fresh beef, bacon, beans, potatoes, rice, crackers, tea and coffee. We get good meals when our time comes.

Our Capt. and Col. [Grant] are well thought of but I think our 1st Lieutenant is the best officer in the Regiment. He is a West Point graduate and drills us to perfection.

Our regiment stands high but not first among the trust of this state. But our Company is certainly the crack of the regiment, both in officers and men, and we have by far the finest flag. It is very large, of silk and beautifully fringed, but, as yet, without a motto.

Our regiment numbers about 1,000 men besides the field artillery company connected with it, which has a brass field piece of twelve pounds calibre. The gun came yesterday, all ready for action. They have not fired it yet. . . . Besides the gun I spoke of, the company has more of larger calibre in town which I expect will be here tomorrow. Our large number and these guns will make us a formidable regiment.

> Your brother,
> Josiah Copley

Within four months of Josiah's enlistment, the 21st Illinois was in action. That summer Grant had been promoted to General and the 21st Illinois was moved with Grant's division to Cairo, Illinois, soon marching on to Paducah, Kentucky, for its first campaign. The regiment's baptism by fire came at the Battle of Belmont, Missouri, and it was here that the 21st suffered its first casualties.

In December of 1862 the 21st Illinois was attached to General Rosecrans's Army of the Cumberland and fought in the confusing Battle of Stones River (Murfreesboro). Josiah did not know that his older brother was also engaged in this battle, or that he had been wounded and captured. The 21st Illinois was overrun by the Confederates, and Josiah too was captured and sent to Libby Prison in Richmond, Virginia.

In the first year of the war prisoner exchanges were frequently arranged between the warring armies. After two months of imprisonment, Josiah Copley was part of an exchange, and by June of 1863 he was back with his unit, once again part of General Rosecrans's Army of the Cumberland.

In the fall of that year Rosecrans was again facing Confederate General Braxton Bragg, now greatly reinforced by General Longstreet's division from the Army of Northern Virginia. On September 19 the two armies clashed on the banks of a small creek called by the Cherokee Indians Chickamauga, a word which literally meant "river of death." The stream was well named. The Battle of Chickamauga was one of the bloodiest of the war, with casualties exceeding 34,000. It was also an unqualified disaster for the Union.

The root of the debacle was a mixup in orders on the second day of the engagement which caused a Union unit to pull out of

Josiah Copley, Jr., as a private in Ulysses S. Grant's 21st Illinois in 1861.

the battle line just as General Longstreet's crack division attacked. The entire right wing of Rosecrans's army was swept from the field, Rosecrans and most of his division commanders included.

The 21st Illinois was part of a division commanded by a Union general with the unlikely name of Jefferson Davis. Josiah Copley was in the thick of the battle and witnessed at first hand the turning point of the engagement. At the battle's end he found that he was once again a prisoner of war. He wrote a letter to his father from Libby Prison in Richmond, the same prison he had been released from six months earlier, which gives a remarkably detailed account of the fighting.

Richmond, Va., Oct. 4, 1863.

Dear Father,

I last wrote to you from Sand Ridge, about Sept. 1. I had written again, but could not mail the letter before the battle occurred. The first half of the month we were continually marching and manoeuvreing. On the 17th we crossed Lookout Mountains for the third time, just west of Lafayette. At this time Gen Rosecrans was drawing in his far extended wings, mostly by night-marching, to avoid observation. On the morning of the 19th we were ten miles south of the battle field. Negley was attacked about 9 A.M. and we [Davis's Division] marched rapidly up, passing through Negley's division to a point four miles beyond, where a threatening attack was made at 10 or 11 A.M. We hurried at double quick into the fight, without halting, and found our troops being driven back. Our division charged the rebels and drove them a short distance to where they had a strong force of infantry and artillery in a good position, and were driven back in our turn. For some time we had varying success, losing heavily, but were finally routed and driven across a farm, where we reformed and repulsed their charge at 100 yards distance.

This occurred while our division was in utter disorder hundreds of yards away, and hundreds of other troops were now fighting with us. In the rush of troops, guns and ammunition-wagons, our division had been broken up, and most of the men fought "on their own hook." I fought with a line of stragglers, without any commander. We did first rate, repulsing their part of the rebel line at a hundred yards. General Carlin then came up and led us and a fragment of another regiment forward. The men, not thinking the rebels beaten back, would not go at first.

I started on and shouted back a few words which started them, and then kept on ahead to a good place, where I opened fire, until half our regiment, with the colors, under Capt. Blackburn, came up. I joined on to its left and we moved on. It soon halted, and I went a few yards ahead to a stump, along with another man. We fired several times while the rebels were again charging in force. Our regiment fell back before I noticed it, and I and my comrade lay flat, there being no chance of escape other wise. He had nearly all the stump, I the level ground in an open field. We lay close, so that each should be partly sheltered by the body of the other. The rebs soon passed us on our left and right, but did not quite reach us in that part of the line, until checked by a new line of our men. For over ten minutes they fought across us at close range. My comrade was shot in the body. The balls cut the ground on both sides several times, knocking dirt into our faces. I calmly awaited my turn, but at length our men gained ground. I raised the butt of my rifle as a signal for them not to fire there, then rose, was fired at by several of our men in mistake, and ran nearly back to our line, calling to them to come on, for they had completely routed the rebels. This was impractical, however, for the rebels were still in the woods on both our flanks. The sun was nearly down, and we fought on at long range in our part of the field until almost dark. Of thirty-four men in our company, we had lost five killed and wounded and three prisoners. That night our division, reduced to a little over half its number, lay a little to the rear. I expected a decided victory next day, and slept soundly, knowing nothing of Bragg's reinforcements.

At 3 A.M. we moved two miles to the left still drawing in our lines — took a good position in reserve — whence we moved at eleven to the front line on our right — lay behind a slight breast-work of rails and sticks, with orders to hold it to the last. At this time the rebels were making a general charge for as far as I could see, or distinguish by the sounds, in triple lines. In half an hour I noticed that our line to the left of us was being forced back before the enemy broke upon us. It was the most regularly conducted battle I had ever seen, and the finest one. The firing was heavy enough to cause a cloud of smoke, high over head, to reach a mile from the fight.

In front of us the rebels broke out from a thick wood two hundred yards off, driving in our skirmishers. As soon as the skirmishers had run back we opened fire, throwing their first line into confusion and checking them, until reinforced by the second line, they moved steadily up under our fire, taking the breast-work by storm. We had not time to fix bayonets, or we might have held them for a few moments; but our line on the left was already forced, and they had got in our rear to the right. Seeing this, many of our men fled contrary to orders, leaving gaps in our line at the very moment of assault. Just as I was ramming my last lead, a ball struck my ram rod, bending it over. I tried to get another, but I could not in time, and the two lines of rebels poured over the breastwork. I saw some of our men club guns and strike; but they were shot or knocked down. While most of the regiment, with the Lieutenant Colonel and some of the other officers surrendered, I sprang through the rebel lines, and met an officer who cut at me with his sword, which I dodged before he could repeat the stroke. I shouted, in a tone of simulated offense, "I'm all right," which took him a little aback, when I ran and dropped behind a log, where I played possum about fifteen minutes, until the coast was clear, got off to the woods, went over half a mile, nearly to the Chickamauga, where I could have hid till night — but was at last taken.

Ten days' ride through Atlanta, Augusta, Columbia, Charlotte, Raleigh and Weldon, brought us here, where we are quartered in a tobacco warehouse, faring somewhat better than last time. Most of the 21st are here, and I know not how many others. But I am out of paper.

Thankful to God for my preservation through many peculiar dangers, I am your son,

Josiah

Josiah's letter describing the Battle of Chickamauga was the first of a series he would write during his seventeen months of incarceration. This time there would be no prisoner exchange. Excerpts from these letters show the deterioration of prison conditions and the extremity of suffering inflicted on the prisoners:

Richmond Virginia
Dec 6, 1863

Dear Father,

I wrote you soon after coming to Richmond relating our part in the battle, the capture, almost in body of the survivors of our Regiment including our officers and our after treatment. Soon after arriving our rations were cut down very small and we suffered much for nearly two months from hunger as well as from cold, our blankets having been taken away at Atlanta.

We had also to give up our money here, excepting some who secreted theirs. I gave up what I had left, $32.00. . . . A few days ago we began to receive provisions from the Soldiers Aid Society, and afterward, clothing and blankets. . . . There is no prospect of an early release, but my health is good. . . . We were removed last month to this tobacco warehouse which makes pretty good quarters.

The time has come when you may send me a box by express . . . directing to Josiah Copley, 21st Ill. 3rd Floor prison #4, Scott Tobacco factory. Send a bible and one or two small volumes, if no others my Shakespeare . . . two quires of paper . . . needles . . . yarn & thread . . . a lb of candles and ointment for killing lice. Write me precisely regarding private affairs as long letters are apt to be supressed, saying nothing of public matters.

During my long imprisonment my time has not passed wearily. . . . Before we got our blankets I suffered much from toothache produced by cold but that is over now. I have much reason to be thankful to God.

Josiah

Danville Virginia,
February 12th 1864

Dear Father,

We came here in December. I have not written for want of paper. When I last wrote I sent for a box of things I needed. But most of those who sent, myself included, did not get them. Do not send anything now, it is too uncertain. . . . There has been much sickness among us and about an eighth of us have died. I have not been unwell since I left home . . . my constant good spirits is one reason for this. . . . There seems no prospect for an exchange. . . . Trust in God's favoring care.

Josiah

Danville, Va.
March 9th 1864

Dear Father,

I wrote to you about three weeks ago. Since then I have received your letters of Dec. 22nd and 29th and the Greek testament. . . . Although these letters were old they were a great satisfaction to me. . . . Some prisoners have escaped, I had hopes of being able to do so but more effective measures have been taken to prevent it and I see no way to accomplish it.

We are crowded and closely confined. Our food is mainly baked corn bread. . . . Our quarters are cold during the winter, we having no fires. We keep lice pretty well thinned out by daily searches. I have been able to employ most of my time without wasting it. . . . We play chess. . . . I am well and cheerful and let nothing trouble me. . . . My Philosophy will bear me through this, not to mention higher support.

Josiah

Shortly after writing this letter, Josiah was suddenly transferred with an entire trainload of prisoners to Andersonville Prison in Georgia. There he would remain through the next thirteen months of the war. The name of Andersonville became synonymous with "hell on earth," and the northern press frequently referred to the prison as a "Death Camp." Few of Josiah's letters got through during his open-air imprisonment in the Andersonville stockade, but the following uncensored one gives a vivid description of the camp:

Andersonville, Georgia
July 18th, 1864

Dear father,

Letters have been stopped so I have not written since May 8th. I have been well the whole time and have been doing as well as any of the men. . . . There are over 28,000 prisoners now here. The open ground occupied has nearly doubled but we are closely crowded. It is very hot but three Southern summers have inured me to the heat. The health of the men is worse, though the percentage of deaths is less, about 80 daily die . . . some, the day before yesterday by our men for robbery. . . . It was necessary to lynch them.

We are having preaching and prayer meetings every evening. A mass religious feeling is prevalent among the soldiers, yet not such as would be called a revival.

For myself I hold fast to my faith and the precepts of Christ and rely more than ever before on the worth of religion and though I have little hope of release this year, I am not disheartened . . . .

Luck be with you and all our friends. Affectionately,

Your son, J. C.

Josiah somewhat underestimated both the number of prisoners in the camp and the death rate. In the summer of 1864, Andersonville held more than 32,000 Union prisoners, and the death rate was about 3,000 a month.

Understandably, Josiah was not entirely honest about his own condition. He was suffering from malnutrition, swamp fever, scurvy, and dysentery. These diseases plus exposure and starvation were the principal causes of death at Andersonville, but as he noted there were other causes as well. During Josiah's long ordeal at Andersonville, he witnessed scenes of incredible desperation. He vividly recalled men fighting to the death over clumps of grass thrown over the stockade fence and others driven mad by drinking fetid water from the muddy sewer ditch that ran through the camp.

Reports like Josiah's filtering out of Andersonville horrified the North. Josiah Copley senior and other parents of the prisoners at the camp repeatedly petitioned the War Department to reinstitute negotiations for prisoner exchange. But many in the department felt that to parole Rebel soldiers might prolong the war and thus the suffering. Josiah senior helped to draft a number of petitions critical of conditions in Union prison camps which the prisoners' families believed aggravated the plight of the Union soldiers held by the South. The following letter to President Lincoln, which failed to produce an exchange, was written in the fall of 1864.

To the President of the United States:

Honored Sir: The undersigned fathers, mothers, wives, brothers, sisters, friends and fellow citizens of our suffering soldiers now confined as prisoners of war at Andersonville and other places in the Rebel States, beg leave to appeal to you in their behalf.

All these noble men are volunteers who went, at your call, to the defense of our country, leaving the pleasures, profits, and endearments of domestic life to battle for it. Long and heroically they fought until the fortunes of war threw them into the hands of their enemies. Thousands of them have been in captivity for many months, and thousands have perished under the cruel and barbarous treatment to which they have been subjected. . . .

It's idle to utter invectives against the barbarity of their captors and keepers. These things we leave to the historian and to God to judge. We do not desire that the principal of retaliation should be resorted to — that the rebel prisoners in your power should be subjected to like treatment. It would be small consolation to the father and mother of a starving and tortured son to know that for his sake, another poor wretch was enduring similar tortures. . . .

. . . More than 30 thousand of our self sacrificing heroes are at this moment shut up, like a vast herd of swine, in a confined, foul, shelterless enclosure, almost naked, with inadequate supply of coarse and revolting food, and exposed to the scorching rays of the sun, the chills and damps of the night, and the peltings of storms, without any shelter whatever, it is more than humanity can bear.

. . . Now, Honored Sir, with all deference to your exalted station . . . we beseech you to use all your wisdom and power for the speedy deliverance of those suffering dying men.

Josiah Copley

When Josiah Copley, Jr., was finally released from Andersonville near the end of the war, he was little more than a skeleton, but he was alive. The horror of his experience and his physical condition had lasting effects. He did not return to his former occupation as a teacher. Nor did he pursue his once-promising literary career. Andersonville did not break his spirit or shake his faith in God, but Josiah's pre-war idealism was gone, as were his ambition and health.

Josiah recuperated on a farm in Kansas, the green pastures and quiet groves seeming like heaven after the hell of Andersonville. As the months went by, his health slowly returned, but not his strength, and for the first few years following the war he was physically incapable of employment.

General Palmer, a family acquaintance, was informed of Josiah's condition and offered the young man a surveying job with the Kansas Pacific Railway. Josiah worked for the line for several years as he fought to regain the pre-war physical strength that never fully returned.

In 1870 Josiah went to work as a surveyor for the Union Pacific Railroad before accepting a position as agent for the railroad in Junction City, Kansas. He would work there in that capacity for many years.

While working as a surveyor Josiah was stationed for a time in Fort Hays, Kansas. It was there that he met Anna Maria Woodward, the daughter of George Henry Woodward and Mary Caroline

Hollister. Anna was a compassionate woman who shared Josiah's strong religious convictions. They were married at the home of M. L. Treat in Fort Hays on November 10, 1872. Five children came of this union, George Hollister, born 1875; Edward, born 1879; Benjamin, born 1887; and Josiah Copley III, born 1889. The lone girl was Mary Cecilia, born December 5, 1881, in Junction City, Kansas.

THE WOODWARD FAMILY

Mary Cecilia Copley's maternal forebears were prominent on both sides of the Atlantic. The Woodwards hailed from London, where for many generations they engaged in the trades and professions. One, Dr. Samuel Woodward, Mary Cecilia's maternal great-grandfather, was a distinguished physician.

Mary's father, Josiah Copley, Jr., in Junction City, Kansas, about 1878.

Mary Cecilia Copley in Junction City, Kansas, about 1886.

Medical practice in the early nineteenth century was haphazard, and the accepted methods of the profession included bleeding patients and treating disease with deadly toxins. Samuel's practical experience gradually convinced him that prayer, faith, and belief were more effective than the conventional treatments. His vocal expression of these observations brought him into disfavor with the medical establishment of the day, and so he closed his London practice and emigrated to America.

Samuel's strong religious convictions were passed on to his son, George Henry, born in Hector, New York, May 12, 1827. George H. Woodward became a fiery Methodist minister. His granddaughter Mary Cecilia later described his method of spreading the Gospel: "The rafters of the old church shook with the power of his preaching. Those who heard him realized that his purpose was a simple one — merely to fortify the feebleness of human resolutions — and his examples of hellfire and brimstone were so skillfully presented that the members of his congregation quaked in their shoes as well as in their pews."

In his early years, George was a missionary preacher, and he spent much of his time traveling to spread the Gospel. It was while preaching in Wisconsin that he met his future wife, Mary Caroline Hollister. They were married in the small town of Beloit, Wisconsin, on October 9, 1850.

THE HOLLISTER FAMILY

Mary Cecilia Copley's mother's maternal line is associated with the place name Hollister in Gloucestershire and Somersetshire, England. The name is said to have meant "land of the holly tree" and is found in very ancient English records with a wide variety of spellings. Families of this name were found in Gloucester, Somerset, Hants, Wilts, Monmouth, Middlesex, and London. From early days they were landed gentry and yeomanry of England.

The Hollisters first came to America in 1642. That year a John Hollister settled in Weymouth, Massachusetts, later removing to Wethersfield, Connecticut. Over the next 130 years the name spread to every colony. A number of Hollisters served in Washington's Continental Army and in the American Navy during the Revolutionary War, including Captain Jesse Hollister and Lazarus Hollister of Massachusetts, and Lieutenant Thomas Hollister, Ensign Jonathan Hollister, and Gideon Hollister of Connecticut.

Gideon Hollister was Mary Caroline Hollister's grandfather. He married Sarah Davis, daughter of John and Sarah Davis, in 1780. Ten children came of this union including Cornelius, their fifth child, born June 28, 1790, in Fairfield, Connecticut. Cornelius Hollister married Sarah Maria Hayden, daughter of Lewis and Naimo Hayden, on June 22, 1815, in Glastonbury, Connecticut. Mary Caroline, their fifth child, born August 7, 1826, would become Mary Cecilia Copley's grandmother.

When James A. Hogle exchanged vows with Mary Cecilia Copley, he was well aware that he was marrying into a family rich in

The Copley family in front of 800 L Street, Lawrence, Kansas, in 1897. *Left to right*, George H. Woodward, George Hollister Copley, Anna Woodward Copley, Josiah Copley, Jr., Mary Cecilia Copley, Aunt Jennie Copley, and Josiah Copley III.

heritage and achievement. He was also aware of the troubles the family had endured, most recently the Harry K. Thaw scandal. But the tragedies and hardships the family had suffered had served to strengthen their profound religious beliefs. The men of Mary's ancestral line were not afraid to take on the world, and although the tasks were sometimes beyond their capabilities, there was an endurance in their makeup which sustained them through failure, defeat, suffering, and tragedy. The women of the line were strong-willed yet sensitive and artistic. Going back as far as Jane Sibbet, they were all educated in literature and poetry as well as the Bible. All appear to have loved music and all were imbued with a profound love of nature.

These qualities and traits were passed on from generation to generation, and in Mary Cecilia Copley could be found all the elements of her heritage.

CHAPTER TWENTY-ONE

Mary Cecilia Copley

Mary Cecilia Copley was born and raised in Kansas. Her upbringing, though perhaps typical of that place and period, was as much a product of family tradition as of the midwestern ethic. She came from a long line of strong, self-sufficient, and devoutly religious people, "Doers" as she described them, and the family history was as much a part of her makeup as the Kansas landscape.

Late in her life she attempted to describe the important things she learned from her family in a short collection of autobiographical essays collectively entitled "Say 'No' to Fate." The work was fragmentary in nature and never completed. Its theme, as implied in the title, is that our lives are our own and our destiny is in our own hands. It is a uniquely American sentiment, full of hope, promise, and vitality. It was also the philosophy of the nineteenth-century American frontier. Excerpts from the essays (rearranged from the original) reveal a great deal about Mary Cecilia Copley and the influences that molded her character.

"Say 'No' to Fate"

I was born in Kansas in Junction City, so named because the Republican and Smoky Hill rivers — two muddy streams — unite here to form the broad, devastating Kansas river . . . . Junction City was a town with homes built of native stone, almost buried in a forest of green trees, where the sluggish waters of the two streams melt into one, a town between two rivers, in a shallow valley.

My environment was typically mid-western, shady lanes — quiet streets — lumber wagons loaded with sacks of wheat and other grains — busy and outwardly happy people. My earliest

Mary C., about 1887.

recollections are of my mother driving Barney, our trusted bay, hitched to the surrey, to the homes of neighbors and friends, carrying with her a quiet smile and a basket of freshly baked whole wheat bread. An indelible impression must have been left on my mind, for today I find myself driving here and there, not with a basket of bread or old Barney, but with other things and in much the same way.

I know of people who have no feeling for their parents, but I have the warmest and closest feeling both for my father and my mother; my father influenced my mind, and the warm affection in me belongs to my mother and her influence.

My mother was nineteen when she married my father. She had beautiful blue gray eyes and hair of burnished gold piled high on her head. She was quiet and poised. She had an air of resignation about her or perhaps pride. My mother's voice always arrested my attention, especially when she would read to us. She read with sympathy and understanding and she had a certain gift for story telling.

I can not remember when I first longed to treasure up and recount all her tales. Her singing was sweet and it came from the depths of a calm contented soul. She was a beauty, a wit, and was kind and generous of nature.

The Copley home in Junction City, Kansas, where all the children of Josiah, Jr., and Anna W. Copley were born.

Every child should have a bit of heaven about him in his infancy. I was no exception, but today much of the heaven seems lost in the mist. In my youth, my days were filled with work and pleasure. The idea never dawned on me that there was anything wearisome about work. I helped with the household duties, I took my weekly music lesson, and too often reached out to the boundlessness of the great outdoors. We took so much for granted in those days. I sensed I was going to live forever in the big white house, under the shady trees, scraping

Slightly damaged photograph of Josiah Copley, Jr., about 1900.

food off a tin plate for the chickens, the cat or the dog. They were days of enchantment.

Dolls I had, of course, in those very early little girl days. I am sure I did not differ from the other little girls in the neighborhood unless, perhaps, I was less of a lady and more of a tomboy due to that fact that I was constantly up to my ears in the mischief my four brothers loved to make. My interest in my brothers was never casual or trivial. I was never punished for anything in my life but how well I remember begging my father not to punish my brother for some boyish prank he had played.

It is said that the pearl is born in pain; that sometimes a grain of sand manages to lodge itself in the shell of the oyster and after years of suffering, when the oyster's life is over, the pearl is found. In my youth I was conscious of the grain of sand. Providence had woven sorrow deeply into the elements of my character, though it was my father who experienced the actual suffering.

My father had taught school in Danville, Illinois, until the call came for him to join the fight to preserve the Union. The complete reversal of his life — the overthrowing of all his dreams — his capture with his regiment — his incarceration in Libby Prison — his transfer to the hell of Andersonville — his stay there of seventeen months — the days of torture from hunger and scurvy — were memories which ran through his shadowy past, like a shroud that Time had thrown over his youthful hopes.

I think often of my father's thwarted plans — no different, I am sure, from those of other boys called out to the battle field from the school room. When a man has experienced such horror as my father, he is apt to be patient, if the pain he has endured has not broken the shell that encloses his understanding. Troubles are the tools by which God fashions us for better things. My father was so fashioned by Andersonville.

Kansas seemed another name for Opportunity to many warworn men soon after the horrors of the Civil War. Surely my father thought so, for when he crawled from Andersonville Prison into the heaven of its green pastures and quiet groves, he believed that Divine Providence had guided him there to show him again how beautiful the earth is. He was nursed to recovery by an unknown woman. As the days went by, his health, the soul that animates all the enjoyments of life, came back to him. For my father and myself, health became both a means and a goal.

Mary C., about 1895.

One impression will remain with me forever — it has influenced my estimates and opinions — and that was the fact that the food given those boys in blue did not contain the substances essential to life. Much of my life has been spent searching for those essentials.

There were three ranches near our home owned by well known families, the Hendersons, the Savages and the Murphys. Seven Springs was the home of Charles Murphy. It was the largest ranch in the area and had the largest outlay of buildings. Charles Murphy had left his home in Detroit, Michigan, to preside over this fruitful valley, where long before I can remember Mr. Murphy held me in his arms and carried me about the ranch.

Practical jokes and a joyous heart were as much a part of this handsome man as were his ruddy cheeks and his expressive eyes. His hearty laughter exploded in the right places, and showed that his soul was in healthy condition. I sat at Mr. Murphy's feet often in my hours of play, content in the love of this great friend. As I grew older, I sat at his feet and asked all manner of questions.

Later it was my delight to ride riotously over Mr. Murphy's ranch on a cow pony, then breathlessly stop to rest by the stream that seemed to flow from the spring house. I remember the pony nosing around the watercress until it found a spot most suited to his drinking. It was here in the roofless, stone-walled spring house, that I began my first study of biology.

The deep pool of water, made amethystine by the sunlight which streamed in from above, fascinated me. From the clear, crystal depth of the water, ugly little crawfish would emerge from under the rocks on the smooth sandy floor and then retreat into the shadows.

When I was in school, I was prone to sit in class, clam-like, until something interested me. Then I'd brighten up, make mental notes, then easily lapse back into the listlessness which came from lack of interest.

At the University of Kansas, however, there were several brilliant teachers who always held my interest. Mlle. Gallou, was the professor of French. She was possessed of every virtue found in the French and Irish natures, for that was her heritage. She had a keen sense of balance and discernment, rare wit, and a determination that I should excel in her native tongue. It was she who taught me to always discern the false from the true.

It was her inspiring interpretation of Molière that made the greatest impression on my mind. She taught us his wholesome hatred of affectation and insincerity and his passion for truth and honesty. These overcame, what appeared to my young mind, a shocking lack of spirituality.

Kansas University showed its vision in the selection of another teacher, Dr. Ida E. Hyde, the first woman to graduate from Heidelberg Medical School. She was a very remarkable person. I remember particularly the morning she showed us the change in the cells of the esophagus of a frog when one of the boys, at her direction, blew cigarette smoke into the hollow slide. The normal action of the cells stopped at once, such was the powerful poisonous effect of the nicotine.

I know that the truth-loving souls who were beside me in those first days would want me to give a sincere and honest story of the many things that shaped my life and the lives of those about me. It was they who taught me that we should measure life according to the needs of this world, rather than sit idly waiting for the rewards that we might reap in the hereafter.

Some may think that life is something that should be covered up — something not to understand — something to blindly accept, until old age leaves them nothing else to do but chatter. I was not taught by their likes.

In 1905 I graduated from the University of Kansas and had applied to continue my studies in biology at the University of Columbia, when a summons came from my aunt Mary Thaw, for whom I was named, to join her on a trip abroad.

I very much wanted to get started at Columbia, but it was her desire that I should leave the study of biology and finish, what she called, my "education." It was her right to command. Not a right transmitted by relationship, exactly, but a right conferred because she had ever reigned over me with affection. I had been forever a child in my submission to her love. I knew I had to go.

My aunt, my father's sister Mary Sibbet Copley Thaw, was the widow of William Thaw, the director of the Pennsylvania Railroad. If it had not been for the benevolence of my aunt, Helen Keller might still be in her native darkness, for it was she who hired Miss Sullivan to be her constant companion and teacher.

Mary C. at Charles Murphy's Seven Springs Ranch, which she recalled with affection in her autobiography.

Mary Copley Thaw, Mary Cecilia's favorite aunt, in Cresson, Pennsylvania, at the age of eighty.

My aunt chose to sail on the *Minneapolis*, a slow boat taking over ten days to make the crossing to England. I asked her why we were taking the *Minneapolis*. There was an unexpected weariness in her answer: "Ten days will give us time to rest" she said, "the rest one craves occasionally."

That was quite like her. She believed the hours were for necessities, not delights. The time spent resting would repair nature for greater trials. As things turned out, she needed those hours of repose badly.

The *Minneapolis* was the favored ship of Sir Henry Irving, the distinguished English actor and manager. We had been assigned to Henry Irving's suite. The staterooms were large but simple. This was my first trip abroad. Me and my Kansas world were suddenly cut apart — by the great broad Atlantic. To a young woman brought up on the Kansas prairie and who warred with the wind when the weather was rough, the trip was most thrilling. Probably no girl ever had a more exciting or emotional trip across the blue waters than I. It was as if the world I had been accustomed to had been thrown into the ash heap and a new one created.

All my dreams were rudely broken one morning as I paused to read the ship's bulletin board. Picked up by wireless the night before was a brief account of the tragedy which had befallen the family. My first thoughts were for my aunt. I had to protect her from the knowledge that her son, Harry K. Thaw, had shot and killed Stanford White.

In my mind I saw her only as my beloved aunt, standing in her accustomed pew in her own Presbyterian church, singing as did the Puritans of old: "A Mighty Fortress Is Our God." Mary Thaw represented to me the very invulnerability of a mighty fortress.

It was during this trying time that I began to appreciate my aunt Mary's character. I also began to see the difference between character and reputation. Here was a woman whose reputation might be destroyed by slander, but her character remained steadfast and true. She was like the Rock of Gibraltar and established an impregnable kingdom within herself.

The truth could not be kept from her. The Captain and all on board were most considerate and when we arrived at Tilbury docks, her son-in-law, the Earl of Yarmouth, who had taken a tugboat down the Thames to meet us, hurried us down the gangplank toward a private car waiting nearby.

Then the scramble began! A dozen reporters lifted their hats, eagerly but softly saying: "Mrs. Thaw! Mrs. Thaw! Mrs. Thaw!"

Knowing well that her voice would give her son courage — and believing to the depths of her staunch Presbyterian soul that her son had a right to live — Aunt Mary Thaw took the next boat back to New York to fight for his life.

When my aunt left me that morning in England, I turned helplessly to the comforting presence of my host and hostess, Mr. and Mrs. Montrose Cloete, whose palatial home in Berkeley Square became a home to me.

It was a source of constant wonder to me that many of these homes had been built before America was discovered. Great halls with stained glass windows, emblazoned with colored coats of arms, the antiques, all intoxicated me with their bygone glories.

Slightly damaged photograph of Mary C. rowing at Vevey, Switzerland, on August 12, 1906.

Those were the days when women were beautifully gowned. I remember so well the afternoon I saw Mrs. Cloete in her red flowered organdie, amid the tea service, the crumpets, the muffins, marmalade, and pound cake. I spent many unforgettable hours with that charming family.

For all the bewildering excitement of life, I still treasure the ecstasy of my first ride in the Cloete's Victoria with a coachman and a footman in livery. It was in Hyde Park and my girlish fancy wandered often to the duels, the deer hunts, and the horse races that had been so much a part of that Garden of the Crown.

At the time of my visit, the trees were in full leaf, the lilacs were in blossom and the tulips and daffodils were pushing their heads out of the earth in hidden corners of the park.

One other remembered beauty in England was the Wallace Art Collection. I saw in it all of man's delight in that particular form of expression — the talking of one soul to another. Young as I was, I had been given an appreciation of the beautiful. All too soon I left for Paris, under the protection of proper chaperonage which was the custom. I went at once to the apartment of two young women who lived on Boulevard Montparnasse,

Mary C. at the Thaw home in Pittsburgh in 1907.

where I was to be a visitor for a time before going on to the scene of my further "education."

It has always been my opinion that travelers should be insatiable devourers of time, and fit enough to go continuously. But the weeks of inactivity living at my aunt's house in Pittsburgh, followed by the recent incidents aboard ship, left me exhausted. I gladly accepted an invitation to join the two women, Alvina and Alice Wilhelmi, on a trip to the mountain province of Haute Savoie.

Haute Savoie borders on Switzerland and Italy, and just to the north is Lake Geneva. We spent several delightful days here making occasional trips to the nearby towns of Lausanne, Vevey, Montreux and Evian-les-Bains.

We were the guests of a family at a Villa on Lake Annecy. Our conversations were pleasant, mirthful, jocular, enlivened by the advent among us of French soldiers stationed at the Artillery Post nearby. They taught us the most entrancing dances. These young men seemed to have borrowed dance forms from every civilized country. I thought the dances most divinely interpreted, especially the passepied and the minuet.

The change in diet from my American bill of fare caused my brain to screw itself up in little question marks which have never been untangled. I was expected to partake of goat's milk and black bread for breakfast; cheese and diluted wine for lunch; and chicken — cooked with its head still on — for dinner. There was also the invariable crème à chocolat.

Every day a new food was demonstrated to me. One day we saw on a truck in a railway baggage room a huge loaf of bread made in the shape of an automobile tire, unwrapped but nevertheless, carefully checked and tagged as we might check a trunk in America.

My classes at the Sorbonne in Paris were taught in a cold, poorly ventilated classroom. If ignorance is a painless evil, as far as cleanliness is concerned, then I must accept the notion that dirt isn't dirt — it's only something in the wrong place. The students had an intense disregard for cleanliness. . . . It is good that young girls are made of uncrushable material . . . .

Mary Cecilia Copley's autobiographical memoir was never completed. Nor did she complete her studies of French literature at the Sorbonne. After several months in Paris she returned to America.

The ordeal of her Aunt Mary through the sensational trials of her cousin Harry K. was painfully tragic to the Copley–Thaw families. Mary Cecilia was deeply moved by her long-suffering aunt's fight to save Harry's life. She was determined that Mrs. Thaw would not shoulder that burden alone, and it was, in part, for this reason that she returned home. It was a long and exceedingly painful struggle, much of it fought out under the glaring eyes of the press, but Mrs. Thaw would one day win her battle for Harry's life, and within the decade she would see him released.

Perseverance and family loyalty were traits that ran deep. Mary Cecilia had her Aunt Mary in mind when she wrote the following:

> There are three kinds of people in the world — the wills, the won'ts, and the can'ts. The first are the doers, the second are the againsters, and the third are the failures. Almost every family enjoys the distinction of all three, but as I scan the roster of those who made life what it is for me, I am convinced that my forbears, almost without exception, realized that time is the chrysalis of eternity; for though there was a prodigal son now and then, for the most part they spent their time in nothing which they knew must be repented of; in nothing which they might not safely and properly be found doing if death should surprise them in the act.
>
> Some things will never be lost. The substantial people who gave me life and the right to stand out from the rest of the world, are like threads of scarlet — that long roll of my father's and mother's people, men and women of keen business sense, clear reasoning power, executive ability, and the courage to meet life and life's challenge.

CHAPTER TWENTY-TWO

Another Generation

After Mary Copley returned to the United States, she took a job as a French teacher at Rowland Hall School for Girls in Salt Lake City. In 1905 her father's family had moved to Salt Lake, and he was working for the Union Pacific Railroad. Josiah Copley was enjoying a turn-of-the-century form of railroad retirement. On days that were too hot to work he came home and sat in a bathtub of cool water and read — a practice he had also followed in Kansas. His daughter was now supplying the family with a good portion of its income. Mary C. would teach French at the school for four years. Rowland Hall was associated with St. Mark's Episcopal Church, and it was through mutual friends at St. Mark's that Mary C. became acquainted with James A. Hogle.

Before he met Mary, James had had no serious romantic involvements. He was an excellent dancer, however, and attended many social events at school in the east and later in Butte and Salt Lake City. For a time he had dated a neighbor girl, Louise Hagenbarth, the daughter of the woman who had once saved his father's life. But Mary Copley's arrival on the scene would put an end to his days as a bachelor. The beautiful young French teacher with the large expressive eyes won Hogle over completely.

Much of their courtship was carried out in letters while James was on his business trips and his long journey to Russia. But his return to Salt Lake City in late July ended the wait. James A. Hogle and Mary C. Copley were married less than two months later, on September 7, 1910. The ceremony was at St. Mark's, the Rt. Rev. Samuel R. Colloday officiating. The witnesses were George D. Keyser and Cyril C. Sanders. It was a traditional family affair attended by Mary's parents, her three brothers, James A.'s mother, and his aunts and cousins.

The honeymoon began with a train trip to San Francisco, where they stayed briefly at the home of Cyril Sanders. They selected and purchased silverware and plate which they shipped back to Salt Lake. Other close friends, Francis and Katharine Crosby, gave a

Mary Copley Hogle and baby Katharine in 1911.

Mary C. and Katharine in 1912.

dinner and reception for the couple at the Mark Hopkins Hotel. (Mary and Katharine had grown up together in Kansas.) The Hogles then took the train to Los Angeles. They spent the remainder of their honeymoon at the St. Catherine Hotel on Catalina Island.

A Marriage of Contrasts

James A. felt very lucky to have married such a beautiful and intelligent woman, but he was plagued by jealousy. His uneasiness was as much the product of his own insecurity as of his wife's attractiveness. Perhaps he recalled John Donne's admonition, "And swear, No where, Lives a woman true and fair." Mary attracted attention wherever they went, particularly from men.

In sharp contrast to the somewhat introverted James, Mary was vivacious, outgoing, and friendly. It didn't take them long to discover that there were other differences, in temperament, taste, philosophy, and the handling of money. If there was a continuing task in their long life together, it was the accommodation necessary between these two very opposite personalities.

Sometime during the honeymoon, Mary Cecilia smiled at a friendly vendor selling her a bag of roasted peanuts. James A. suddenly found himself consumed with jealousy. He need not have worried because Mary adored her husband and felt blessed to have made such a perfect union. Years later James would recall the encounter with the friendly peanut vendor with mixed amusement and anguish.

During their first year of marriage the couple lived in the Hollywood and then in the Caithness Apartments in Salt Lake. Nine months after their marriage, on June 5, 1911, Mary Hogle gave birth to a daughter, Mary Katharine (spelled with a "C" on the baptismal records). The rooms at the Caithness Apartments were small, so the birth took place at the home of a friend of the family, Irene Dixon Schilder. Two more children followed, James Edward, born September 16, 1912, and George Hollister, born April 10, 1915.

Childhood Memories

The early memories of childhood are stamped as much by surroundings as personalities. The Hogle family moved a number of times over the next nine years, and these shifts of lodging and neighborhood fixed in the memories of the growing children the episodes and incidents of their maturation. The children's recollections are windows on the early married life of their parents.

Shortly after the birth of Mary Katharine, the young family moved to 1021 East South Temple, then in 1912 into Ida Hogle's home at 376 East South Temple. That same year Ida moved permanently into a suite of rooms at the recently completed Hotel Utah. In 1914 the family moved into a home at 503 First Avenue and in 1920 to 548 East South Temple.

Ida Hogle with her grandson James Edward.

Ida Hogle occupied rooms 910 and 911 in the famous luxury hotel. When she felt particularly affluent, she would sometimes expand into room 909 or 912 as well. Almost from Mary Katharine's infancy, she and her grandmother were very close, and Katharine's earliest memories are of her and of the Hotel Utah.

Particularly significant is Katharine's recollection of watching a parade with her grandmother from the balcony window of the Hotel. The parade was a large Suffragists' march held in the late summer of 1914. There in the first rank of marchers, garbed in white dress and straw bonnet — the uniform of those most activist of women — was Mary C. Hogle. Katharine was terrified and began to howl with fright when she saw her mother. At the age of three she knew it was dangerous to walk in the street.

Although Ida was fond of all three of her grandchildren, Katharine remained her favorite. Jim and George would have lunch with Ida, but Katharine had breakfast with her grandmother at the Hotel every Sunday morning. Ida also had her dinner with the family every evening. She would take the trolley car up to the Hogle home and be driven back to the Hotel afterward by her son.

Katharine remembered the seed pearl brooch that her grandmother wore, her high-collared dress, and her proper manner. Ida sometimes took the little girl for short drives in her own car, a black Baker Electric, which Katharine noted for its big square windshield and the additional oddity that it was steered with a tiller.

The Hogles lived at 503 East First Avenue for six years. Katharine remembered the front parlor where her mother held club meetings and entertained her friends. She remembered at a very early age reaching up to the big round table in the parlor to pilfer grapefruit sections prepared for her mother's guests. During the First World War, her mother tutored officers from nearby Fort Douglas. They were bound for the trenches of France, and Mary volunteered to help them learn the language. The furniture in the parlor was Chinese and very delicate. Mary was so afraid that the husky soldiers might accidentally break the parlor table that Katharine and her mother sat through the lessons with their arms under the table to hold it steady.

She remembered, too, the library where her father would retire most evenings to read or work and the kitchen where she had spent many hours helping Elsie Seifert shell black walnuts. Elsie was the family's cook, maid, housekeeper, nanny, and general factotum. She had been hired to help Mary with the children, and she stayed on with the family through their adolescence. Her older brother Martin was employed by the Hogles as a caretaker and gardener.

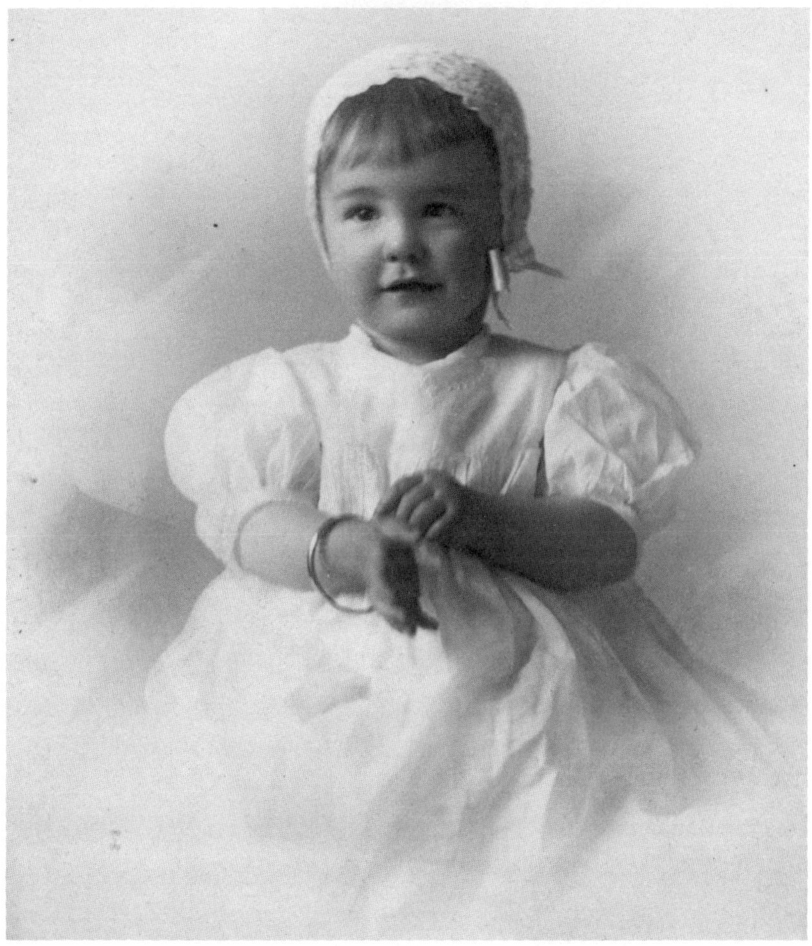

Katharine Hogle at the age of three.

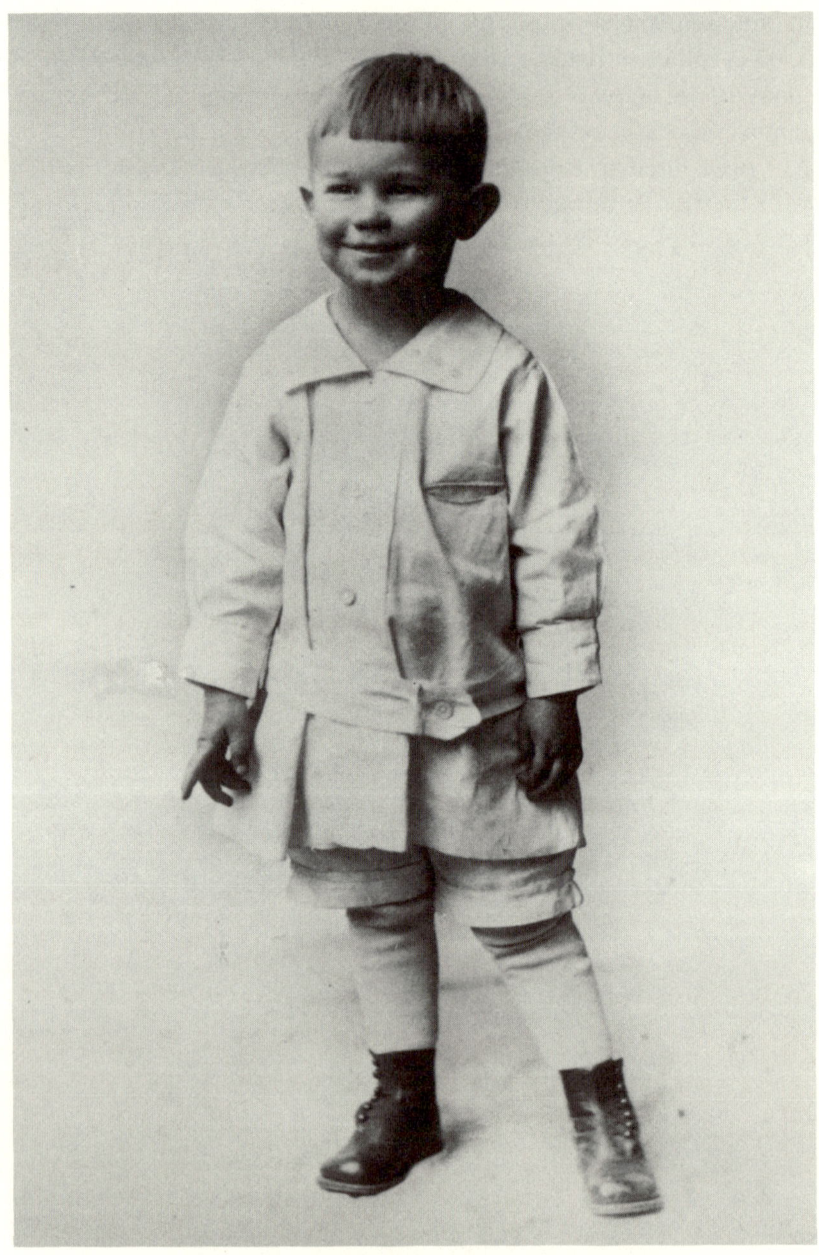

James Edward Hogle at the age of four.

Katharine recalled an early incident at 503 when some neighborhood boys had done something that greatly angered her father. She remembered "Pa," as she always called him, chasing one of the culprits down the street and onto the porch of a neighbor's house, where Pa was promptly attacked by a protective mother wielding a broom. The little girl was never told the specific cause of this minor neighborhood skirmish.

At an early age Katharine accompanied her father on a fishing trip to the Flat Rock Club on the Snake River, near Mack's Inn, Idaho, south of West Yellowstone. One evening she encountered a moose at the stream's edge, its eyes glowing in the moonlight. They stayed at Mack's Inn, a favorite haunt of Owen Hogle and a frequent retreat for James A. Another time Pa went on an extended hunting trip and returned to 503 with a black bear he had shot. Katharine remembered the animal slung over the back of her father's horse, Ginger, and recalled it later as a rug with staring glass eyes and fierce teeth in its open mouth.

One of James Edward's earliest memories was also of the home at 503 and the funeral of his grandfather, Josiah Copley, Jr., which was held there on February 16, 1916. Since his retirement from the railroad, Josiah and his wife Anna had been living in Long Beach, California. On Thanksgiving Day 1913 he suffered a stroke, and he was an invalid for two and a half years, until death mercifully ended his ordeal. The veteran of General Grant's 21st Illinois, survivor of the battles of Stones River and Chickamauga, of Libby Prison and Andersonville, was brought to Salt Lake City by train for burial. James Edward remembered the large number of people who came to the house that day, and he recalled being taken to the coffin and lifted up by his father to see his grandfather's remains. The little boy was three years, five months old on the day of the funeral.

George's earliest memory of that home was of a dinner party he successfully crashed as a toddler and the amused admiration of the guests for his cute answers to his mother's questions. Jim recalled that the children would sometimes sneak out of their beds at night and huddle together behind the upstairs bannister to listen to the conversations of the guests below. George's room was above his father's library, and sometimes at night he could hear his father talking to guests or friends directly below. The muffled sounds of the unintelligible voices sounded to George like the growling starter motors of stubborn car engines.

George also remembered being sent to Murdock's Grocery store on F Street for a loaf of bread and being scolded on his return for having eaten the inside of the loaf, returning home with only the hollowed-out crust.

A vivid incident occurred on G Street by the house, where the driver of an ice wagon was beating his horse to get the heavy load up the hill. George recalled that his sister ran into the road and grabbed the whip away from the man, yelling at him for his cruelty. Katharine too remembered the incident, but in her mind the heroine who accosted the villainous iceman was her mother.

All three Hogle children remembered a trip to the swimming pool at Beck's Hot Springs, a sulfur bath resort just north of the city. George remembered the drive to the springs in the family's red Thomas Flyer touring car. Little Jimmy Hogle was in a mischievous mood that day, and on the way he spat out the side of the vehicle. The car was immediately stopped, everyone got out, and the blemished fender was cleaned on the spot.

The children had not yet learned to swim and spent most of their time wading in the shallow end of the pool. Mary was due at a social function later that afternoon and was sitting in a chair at the poolside, wearing her fox stole and a broad-brimmed straw hat. Jimmy was crouching beside the deep end of the pool, gently rocking back and forth and staring at the water. Suddenly he toppled over into the water. His mother charged across the deck and jumped headlong into the pool, furs, hat, and all, almost on top of Jimmy. Both were rescued by the men present. For the children this was the high point of the summer.

The tale of the rescue spread, and during dinner that evening one of Mary's brothers called on the phone to inform her that he was circulating a petition to have Mary made the captain of a women's lifesaving brigade. Mary hung up on him. Nevertheless, one of the first courses offered by the YWCA, which Mary Hogle helped to found, was in lifesaving.

Taking Grandma to the train. Baby George, Mary C., her mother Anna Copley, Katharine behind Jimmy, and James A. at the Union Pacific depot in Salt Lake City, 1916.

From her earliest days, Katharine recalled accompanying her mother on visits to the homes of elderly widows and spinsters. Mary believed that concern for the elderly was a duty that went beyond the immediate family. She brought the ladies bouquets of freshly cut flowers or sometimes loaves of bread. During the summer months, Mary would take them for drives along the benches to see the sunset or the lights of the city, or sometimes out along Highland Drive for the cool canyon breezes.

The Hogle children in front of Murdoch's store on F Street in Salt Lake City, about 1919. George is having his turn as the driver.

Katharine remembered in particular the spinster Woodward sisters and her mother's comment about one of them, "She doesn't have any wrinkles because she never smiles." George's favorite was Mrs. Boggs, an aristocratic lady from Virginia who would occasionally have dinner at the Hogle home. She was an entertaining conversationalist and a good storyteller. George particularly remembered her holding her nose and entertaining the children with hilarious bagpipe imitations.

On one occasion when his mother was driving a group of ladies to a meeting in Provo, George, not wanting to be left behind, secretly climbed into the spare wheel on the back of Mary's Lincoln sedan. They traveled all the way to 21st South and were very near the state prison before a passing motorist managed to inform Mrs. Hogle of the small boy riding in the wheel at the rear of the car. With much clucking and moaning by the women, George got taken along.

The Hogles were a major part of St. Mark's Church, and St. Mark's was a major part of their lives. They were very close to

Bishop Arthur W. Moulton and Dean William Fleetwood, and Jim remembered the Dean and his wife as frequent dinner guests at his parents' home. Mary, in particular, was very involved in church activities. She was a member of the altar guild and for a time also taught Sunday School. She headed several development campaigns at St. Mark's as well as charity drives conducted under the auspices of the parish.

The children recalled that their father seldom attended Sunday morning services at St. Mark's. His deafness made it almost impossible to hear the sermons anyway — but their mother and grandmother Ida were devoted members of the parish, and every Sunday the rest of the family would make the little pilgrimage to the church. Ida Hogle had long been active in St. Mark's choir, and though Mary confined her singing to the church proper, her children recalled the beauty of her voice as she sang the hymns during the Sunday services. But Mary's activism was not confined to church work. She was a tireless community worker and volunteer as well. Over the years she would assist in the founding and support of many organizations, including the Humane Society, the YWCA in Salt Lake City, the Alliance Française, the American Association of University Women, the Art Barn, the NAACP, the Soroptimist Club, the National Recreation Society, the League of Women Voters, and an organization she founded with Jane Addams, the Women's International League for Peace and Freedom.

Katharine accompanied her mother to a number of meetings. One in particular that she remembered was a session of the WILPF held at the Beehive House, Brigham Young's old home, which was sometimes used for small gatherings. Utah's Senator Smoot was addressing the group on the subject of tariffs. Mary C. Hogle was a woman who held strong opinions, and seldom were these opinions in agreement with the man Ogden Nash once dubbed "The Republican Ute." At the end of his lecture, Mary stood up and told the Senator that he shouldn't be back in Washington, and in a firm though pleasant voice, said, "We need you back here at home, Mr. Smoot." The remark, though gentle, was understood by all. The Senator would remember it for years to come.

George, Jim, and Katharine Hogle.

Whether Mary knew it or not, she was part of the Progressive movement that swept the country during the second decade of the century. The many organizations that she founded, worked for, or contributed to were all expressions of a fierce desire to improve the lot of humanity, to move away from political corruption, poverty, injustice, ignorance, cruelty, and discrimination. The progressives believed that through hard work, education, and concerted group action even the worst social ills could be cured.

Though not politically active in the Progressive Party, Mary was a vigorous advocate of their philosophy. She was also a motivator and a doer in the active tradition of her family. She believed that it was necessary "to take arms against a sea of troubles," and there was scarcely an aspect of society that was not touched by her efforts.

But there was a price to pay for her activism. During the weekdays Mary was continuously attending meetings, organizing charity drives, or working on any of a number of pet projects, and was seldom at home with the children. At one point in the early 1920's she was the president of five organizations simultaneously. During the week, the Hogle children were left to the care of Elsie Seifert, who would fix their breakfasts and lunches, bandage their scraped knees, greet them upon their return from school and, frequently, put them to bed when their parents were attending dinner parties or other functions.

The Hogle children were well aware of their mother's priorities and obligations. From their earliest days, they were made a part of her multi-dimensional crusade, albeit involuntarily. Improving the lot of humanity was a monumental task demanding sacrifices by the entire family, and the growing children begrudged Mary's absence; but when serious sickness or accident struck, she would drop all her outside activities and devote herself entirely to their care. She nursed George through rheumatic fever and Jim through a very serious bout of bronchial pneumonia and, later, scarlet fever.

In 1920 the family purchased the Cosgriff mansion at 548 East South Temple. The home had a huge backyard with fields and outbuildings in the interior of the block. Shortly after the move, George, then five, was riding his tricycle in front of the Bamberger home next door. He heard a noise above him, ran out in the street to see his first airplane flying above South Temple, and was run down by a Pierce Arrow Roadster driven by young Ezra Thompson. George was knocked out by the impact. As he was carried into the house, his mother, fearing the worst, was hysterical. Katharine recalled that her mother was so upset that she wrapped her face in a beige bath towel to catch the flood of tears. But George's only injuries were a cut lip and a broken toe. He was delighted to find that the heavy cast Dr. Allison placed on his foot was just the thing he needed to best his older brother at kicking a football.

Katharine too contracted rheumatic fever, and her recurrent bouts with the illness were so serious that she was hospitalized several times with the affliction, on one occasion at St. Mark's Hospital. Katharine remembered her mother's presence at the hospital during the illness and recalled a fragment of conversation between her mother and a nurse: "I know she's had a nap because her cheek is pink where she's been sleeping on it." The day her fever broke, Katharine remembered getting two ice cream cones from her mother in celebration, one pineapple sherbet and one chocolate.

The Cosgriff–Hogle home at 548 East South Temple.

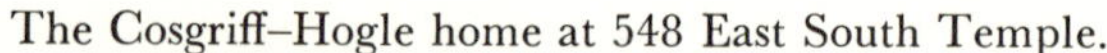

On another occasion she remembered waking up in the middle of the night with a bad cough to find her mother there bringing buckets of steaming water into the room for her to breathe. In the morning her cough was gone. The quick cure convinced Katharine that her mother was some kind of angel.

Once Katharine was injured when she and a neighbor, David Hempstead, were sleigh riding down Second Avenue below Virginia Street and her knee struck the rusty fender of a parked car. Dr. Allison called her parents, who rushed home from the dinner party they were attending. They put her in the downstairs guest room so that Mary C. could be closer to her. Katharine had always loved this room with its two huge mahogany beds, their silk sheets and pillow cases, and the matching silk draperies over the windows. Though her feelings were hurt by the scolding she received for her carelessness, she was also aware of the special attention she was being given.

The parents' weekdays may have belonged to society at large, but the weekends were reserved for the family. The Hogles would all pile into the bright red Thomas Flyer and go off together on frequent outings and picnics, sometimes on the open train to Saltair Resort at the Great Salt Lake, sometimes to Brighton in Big Cottonwood Canyon, but usually to the family's farm, which overlooked the Salt Lake Valley from the mouth of Emigration Canyon. The old dirt road to the farm passed through Fort Douglas at the mouth of Red Butte Canyon. To get to the farm they had to ford the shallow waters of Red Butte and Emigration creeks. Katharine in particular remembered the weekly passage through the streams in the open touring car. Her father would rev up the engine and they would roar through the shallow water, their wheels splashing a cool spray on the excited children. It was the anticipated highlight of these trips to the farm.

Animals were a large part of the Hogle family's lifetime interest. In addition to the animals at the farm, they kept chickens, rabbits, pigeons, and a prize rooster at the home at 548. Also residing there were Jim's pony, George's German shepherd Cerro, several parrots, and five or six cats. The menagerie was frequently augmented by strays that Mary C. would bring home. Katharine remembered the time that her father slammed on his brakes, bringing his car to a dead stop in the street, enraged that someone had turned four huge dray horses loose in the alfalfa field behind the house. That someone turned out to be his wife, who had rescued the beasts from a teamster's whip.

The alfalfa field behind 548 was the scene of another vivid and revealing memory. On summer evenings, James A. liked to go out back and look at the stars. At St. Paul's he had been the secretary of the science club, and the stars had always held a particular fascination for him. One evening, he and Katharine were out in the alfalfa field looking at the night sky and her father suddenly stopped, frozen in his tracks. Katharine asked him what the matter was and he replied, "That's the first time in years that I've heard the crickets. Listen! Can you hear them?" James A. was overjoyed at the experience, but to Katharine the crickets were almost deafening. She was startled to realize the profoundness of his hearing loss.

Although his deafness was severe, the children all recalled how much their father loved music. Katharine and George were both given piano lessons at an early age by Mrs. Jack, who lived in the house next door, but George managed to escape the ordeal by hiding his music. His parents never pushed him; the lessons were dropped.

James A.'s special musical love was opera. He had heard his first opera in the fall of 1893, and from that year on it was one of his most cherished pleasures. His favorite works were Puccini's *Madame Butterfly*, *La Bohème*, and *Tosca*. He would listen to the opera with his left ear against the loudspeaker of the radio. Katharine remembered how she and her father once attended an unusual performance of *Siegfried*. The action and staging were on silent film, the music and singing supplied by a live orchestra and performers in the pit. James A. and his daughter sat as close to the performers as they could get. The result was a stirring artistic success, and afterward Katharine and her father walked all the way home together from the theater, enraptured by the power of the experience.

Katharine recalled how during Prohibition her father once tried to make wine in the basement. She remembered the burp, burp of the water seal valves on the casks and the heady smell of yeast on the back porch. She cannot remember her father ever drinking or serving the wine and believed that the experiment was more a test of his personal invulnerability than a serious attempt at oenology.

George remembered the other families in the neighborhood: the Thompsons, the Browns, the Tyngs, the Golpes, the Bambergers, the Jacks, the Keiths, the Whittakers, and especially the Kearns family. Jack Gallivan, who was a frequent guest at the Kearns home, was George's contemporary. Gallivan recalled that the two boys would sometimes amuse themselves by placing small blasting caps on the streetcar tracks on South Temple.

Entertainment

As the children grew older, they were invited to attend some of their parents' garden and dinner parties, for which Mary C. was renowned. These were exquisite and beautiful social affairs, frequently reported on the society pages of the papers. The backyard directly behind the house at 548 was a large grass area surrounded with a hedge and shaded by lofty trees. Mary had enough card tables, chairs, linen, china, silver, and crystal to serve more than a hundred people. At ladies' teas and luncheons given for Mary's various club memberships or church groups, it was Katharine's duty to help serve the tea and coffee and then the large silver platters of hors d'oeuvres and elegant canapes.

The tables were always brightly arrayed with fresh-cut flowers, carefully selected and arranged for color. A typical arrangement might be pink gladioli, golden marigolds, and yellow roses. Katharine remembered that a close friend and neighbor, Daisy Raybould, would assist Mary in planning and hosting the tea parties. Other friends who helped with the larger events were Mrs. Roger Strobel, Mrs. Dean Brayton, Mrs. Daniel Alexander, Mrs. Percival Perkins, and Sarah Boggs, George's bagpipe lady.

Sometimes there were large dinner parties, usually to honor a visiting celebrity, artist, or house guest. House guests were always special, and the week before their arrival was a hectic time for the children, who were put to work helping to clean the house or polish the silver. By the time the guest arrived everything was expected to be spotless. The Hogles lodged and entertained many prominent visitors to the city. The children remembered the visits of Ethel Barrymore, Selena Royle, John Collier, Karl Conway, Seth Thomas, Martin Pretorious, and Illya Tolstoy.

Mary C. Hogle in the fox stole and hat her children remembered her wearing when she dived into the pool at Wasatch Plunge to rescue Jimmy.

James Hogle had stayed in touch with Illya's brother, Count Lyof N. Tolstoy, since first meeting him in 1910. Katharine recalled that during Tolstoy's stay she succeeded in getting him to autograph her book, but the ink was so faint that she attempted to go over it with her own pen and ruined it. But all the guests at the Hogle home signed the green leatherbound guest register in the parlor.

Emil Coué was another prominent house guest. Coué was the founder of the French School of Auto-Suggestion, a believer in the power of positive thinking, whose advice "Every day, in every way, I'm getting better and better" became a stock phrase in the Hogle household. Jim remembered too that on at least two occasions the family played host to Stanford White's killer, their mother's cousin Harry K. Thaw — a somewhat intimidating event for the children.

James A. always did the carving at the dinner table. On one occasion he was carving a hen and the knife slipped; the drumstick flew high into the air across the room and landed directly on the plate of the honored guest at the far end of the table. The group fell awkwardly silent until the guest commented that he had never seen such an astounding feat of precision carving, and the room erupted in laughter. It was a special moment and the story was often retold with pleasure.

Though James A. apparently enjoyed these social occasions and displayed his pleasure with a broad smile, his deafness was a marked disadvantage. Katharine recalled how at dinner parties her father would cup his hand over his ear and lean to the lady inevitably seated on his right in order to engage in conversation. He tended to sense, more than actually hear, the drift of the dialogue. It was a skill he had acquired through many years of practice. Katharine joked that there was only one woman who her father ever actually heard at a dinner party, Mary McCaskell, an attractive and vibrant woman who was a particular favorite of his and who had a huge, booming voice.

CROSS PURPOSES

Not all of the Hogle children's memories were of beautiful parties and domestic bliss. In household financial matters, particularly, there were frequent squabbles. Their father was a firm believer in the philosophy that if you took care of the pennies, the dollars would take care of themselves. The more minuscule the waste, the more apt he was to be angered by it. His personal preoccupation with thrift was more than a cultivated neurosis, it was a stratagem for justifying his investments. The more money he saved, the more he felt he could put at risk — though few of his investments proved especially risky. James Hogle was not a penny pincher in the miserly sense. He didn't mind spending money. What bothered him were avoidable expenditures.

For James A. Hogle, electricity was an invention which had been designed for the sole purpose of burning up his money. The Hogle children recalled that their father was frequently angered if a light was left on in an unoccupied room or if too many lights were burning unnecessarily.

Another cultivated pet peeve was the waste of soap that was left to melt away in the basin or the bathtub. Huge losses on the stock market were to be expected; contributions to charity were volitional; dinner party or recreational expenses were thrown off without much notice; but to let good soap go down the drain through careless neglect or to waste a penny on the lights were sins of such enormous proportion that they threatened the very foundation of his financial empire — or so it seemed to the children.

Mary C. had none of her husband's peevish concerns about spending money. In fact, she had no problem at all spending money. It was as much her nature to be generous and expansive as it was his to be cautious and protective, and therein lay the cause of occasional disruptions in the domestic tranquility of the Hogle household. A frequent subject of discussion was the bimonthly bill from Makoff's, usually for shoes. Why someone who had only two feet needed a hundred pairs of shoes was beyond James Hogle's comprehension. In fact there was a reasonable explanation. Mary suffered from an edema which caused her feet to swell. For all her shoes, it was a difficult task on any one day to find a pair that both fit and matched her clothing. And she also spent money on her clothing. She even employed a seamstress, Mrs. McCartney, who worked at 548 most of the time doing nothing but working on Mary's dresses.

Mary also liked to buy new cars. Katharine recalled that at one point the family had five automobiles: a Packard, and an Auburn, two Lincolns, and an Essex. By this time the red Thomas Flyer had been sold, appropriately enough, to the fire department. Katharine recalled the time that a visitor seeing all the cars in the driveway asked her, "Just how many cars do you Hogles have?" Katharine was embarrassed by the question and sheepishly replied, "I don't know." She realized instantly that her answer was infinitely worse than the truth.

James A. tolerated Mary's free-spending ways, but only up to a point, and periodically he insisted on putting his foot down. These efforts to rein in household spending were more for the sake of form than effect, and he once joked: "My function here is to make money so that she can spend it."

Following one argument George came into his father's study and attempted to help cool him off. He had picked a bag full of seed pods from the box elder in the yard and asked if he could sell them to people. His father gave him a dime and seemed touched by his young son's attempts to soothe him.

The years 1917 through 1924 were personally trying for the Hogles. Aunt Molly Mantor died February 5, 1917, in Long Beach, California, and her husband Childs in the same city in 1921. The obligation that James had undertaken at his father's request to look after his aunts he now assumed for his cousins Elsie Mantor and Edna Weed as well. Elsie and Edna were frequent visitors at the Hogle home, as were Ed and Maud Copley.

The children remembered that Elsie was a very pleasant and friendly woman, always cheerful and kind. Edna's disposition was sour, and they remembered her chiefly for her snippy manner. George chipped the white keys of her piano beating on them with his toy popgun. The anguish on Edna's face was etched in his memory. James A. rather enjoyed the open, if sometimes caustic, frankness of his opinionated cousin, and he carried on a long correspondence with her throughout his life. During the early years of their marriage James and Mary both put considerable effort into developing much-needed tolerance for each other's relatives.

Family concerns were very much on James A. Hogle's mind during those years. His mother suffered from heart disease, and by early 1924 it was apparent to everyone that her health was declining. Ida died at her rooms in the Hotel Utah on March 30, 1924. The funeral was at the Hogle home, the Rev. William Fleetwood from St. Mark's officiating. It was a very sad occasion and James A. took it hard. Katharine remembered that she and her brothers stood silently in the corner of the room and were later criticized by their mother for abandoning their father; but the children had sensed that the devoted son wished to be alone with his sorrow.

Katharine had been especially close to her grandmother, and through the years she would frequently think back on their breakfasts and luncheons together at the Hotel Utah, sitting between her father and grandmother at the dinner table, and the rides in the old Baker Electric. Ida Elizabeth Hogle remembered Katharine in her will, leaving her the old saloon property on Main Street, which had stood empty since the beginning of Prohibition.

Ida was buried at Mount Olivet Cemetery in Salt Lake City. Her son purchased a large lot for the family and quietly arranged to have his father reinterred there as well.

During the early twenties, the Hogle family took several vacations together. Sometimes they went to Long Beach, California, to visit Grandmother Copley, sometimes to Nevada, Montana, or Idaho. In the years before his elder son, James Edward, was old enough to be sent to St. Paul's, James A. began to teach him how to fish and hunt, skills he had learned from his Uncle Owen. He belonged to a number of sportsmen's clubs, including the New State Gun Club and the Flat Rock Club, and he took his son fly-fishing and duck hunting. His favorite fishing holes were on the North Fork of the Snake River, an area that his father and uncle had explored, prospected, and fished more than half a century earlier.

In 1924, James A. Hogle's Yale class of 1899 celebrated their twenty-fifth reunion. The entire family took the trip together back to New Haven to attend the festivities. The extended vacation was one that would be long remembered. They took the train east and picked up a new car in Detroit, a seven-passenger Lincoln. Then they boarded a Great Lakes steamer bound for Buffalo. Katharine remembered that on the voyage across Lake Erie they saw one of the last of the great clipper ships, a magnificent vessel with towering masts and full sails. She also remembered that the family, after arriving in Buffalo, visited Niagara Falls and then drove across the border into Canada. Her father purchased beer there and smuggled some bottles back across the border, which Katharine viewed as yet another test of his invulnerability to the law. But it was also a prankish challenge to his wife who, at the time, generally favored Prohibition.

For the next two weeks the Hogles toured New England, stopping for several days at Concord, New Hampshire, to visit St. Paul's. James A. took great delight in showing his sons about the grounds and buildings and regaling them with stories from his school days. Soon James E. would be enrolled at St. Paul's and George shortly thereafter. The trip to Concord later became a family tradition. St. Paul's School would have Hogles in its student body for generations to come.

After leaving Concord, the family took in the Yale–Harvard crew races at New London and rode the open-air train that followed the race events along the river.

The trip east was the longest of the Hogle family vacations and they all fondly remembered the old New England hotels and the lush countryside. For the children, the trip was especially memorable because the family was all together for an extended period of time. Soon the children would be away at school and Mary would be involved in her numerous projects, but for the moment they were all together and felt very close. It was one of the happiest episodes of the Hogle children's early years.

CHAPTER TWENTY-THREE

Of Hospitals, Schools, Zoos, & Carrot Juice

As JAMES A. HOGLE WENT HAPPILY ABOUT HIS BUSINESS of building capital, Mary C. Hogle went happily about hers — distributing the same, not only to car dealers and shoe salesmen, but to charities as well. This is not to say that there was a family conflict over the need for charitable giving. James believed that he owed the community where he made his money a very real debt. Contributions toward improving the quality of life in Salt Lake City improved his lot as well. His philanthropy was as generous as his wife's, although he couldn't devote all his time to it as she could. James's special area of charitable interest was education. Throughout his life he contributed to St. Paul's School, Yale, Columbia, the University of Utah, and Westminster College in Salt Lake City. For thirty-three years Hogle served on the Westminster College Board of Trustees. During those years, he quietly made up many a shortfall in the College's budget.

Mary devoted both her time and her money to many diverse social and educational causes. Her philanthropy was distributed among a number of projects and private charities. She was a patron of the arts, of children's recreational programs, of health and social services, of humanitarian and peace movements. These were not random donations, but well-targeted contributions to specific groups to achieve specific ends. Moreover, her charity reflected her personality, inclinations, and upbringing.

Mary's interest in the Women's International League for Peace and Freedom sprang from an abhorrence of war whose origin can be traced to her father's ordeal at Andersonville. Five members of that organization would eventually receive the Nobel Peace Prize, including Mary's friend Jane Addams, who was awarded the prize in 1931 for her efforts in helping establish social work as a profession.

Mary Hogle's patronage of organizations such as the Art Barn, the Ladies' Literary Club, and the Alliance Française was an expression of her love of music, the arts, and literature — a love she had inherited from her forebears and cultivated while studying in France.

Her support of the National Recreation Society and the YWCA sprang from her personal belief in physical as well as mental education, and her support of the Humane Society came from her own deep-seated hatred of cruelty to animals.

Mary also supported Rowland Hall School, St. Mark's Church, and the American Association of University Women. There was a consistency to all her charitable efforts, and the organizations she funded were extensions of her philosophy. The family's best-known philanthropy was the donation to the city of Hogle Zoological Gardens. The story of Hogle Zoo is typical of how Mary directed her philanthropic efforts, and it must be understood in the context of her philosophy.

Hogle Zoo

Man has always been a hunter and a meat eater. From the dawn of time his survival has depended upon the skins and flesh of animals. Man's relationship to the animal kingdom is expressed in the creation myths of many cultures. Central to Western myths is the belief that animals are creatures whose sole function is the sustenance of man. In Genesis we read that man was given "Dominion over the fish of the sea and the fowl of the air and over every living thing that moveth upon the earth." Since animals were regarded as God's gift to man, he exploited the resource to its fullest.

Although Mary had a strictly traditional religious upbringing, she did not believe that man had absolute dominion over the animals. She did not think that a drayman had a God-given right to whip his horse. She did not believe that man's purpose on the earth was the eradication of the animal kingdom. She believed, in fact, that to treat animals cruelly was sinful.

Mary frequently took her campaign to the schools, and Katharine remembered that her mother once broke into tears when describing some act of animal cruelty to an assembly at Rowland Hall School. Her beliefs were deeply felt, but this did not mean that her campaign was based on sentimentality. She had a practical side to her makeup that understood, most clearly, the ways of the world. She believed strongly in sterilization and euthanasia for dogs and cats to control overpopulation and also recognized the value of game management and hunting to control populations of animals in the wild. What appalled Mary Hogle was mindless cruelty to animals and the wanton destruction of the animal kingdom, both of which, she believed, were primarily caused by ignorance.

From the 1890's Salt Lake City had a small zoological exhibit at Liberty Park. Wild animals would sometimes visit the city from the nearby mountains. These were captured and brought to the park. The menagerie was a haphazard affair — more an open pound for wild animals than a zoo — and was located in the old barnyard of the Chase–Young farm where the park was located.

It wasn't until 1911 that the city attempted to actually run a zoo. It was in fact the man who served as best man at James Hogle's wedding, Salt Lake Commissioner George D. Keyser, who first proposed that the city build a facility for exhibiting animals at Liberty Park. Over the next few years the new zoo grew rapidly, and by 1916 it held black bears, brown bears, deer, elk, wild cats, porcupines, coyotes, cougars, monkeys, and a large number of birds. That year too, the zoo acquired an Indian elephant, "Princess Alice," from the Sells Floto Circus. Princess Alice was donated to the zoo by Salt Lake City school children who had contributed nickels and dimes for her purchase.

The addition of the pachyderm to the barnyard menagerie was a big step — too big a step for the Salt Lake City Parks Department of 1916. During the next ten years the zoo continued to grow on the donations of animals to the collection. Unfortunately the city's budget for the zoo was not increased proportionately, and by 1926 the conditions at the park were horrendous.

About this time a City Zoological Board was formed and included in its membership the Hogles' neighbors Julian Bamberger, Mrs. Edmund Kearns, Gus P. Backman, and Mrs. E. F. Dryfous. The group was headed by Dr. George A. Allen and Mr. Russell L.

Tracy, two distinguished naturalists who led the fight for improved zoo facilities.

The Zoological Board examined conditions at the zoo and submitted a scathing report which was subsequently published in the city's Municipal Record:

> There is an old ramshackle building out at Liberty Park which in its confines houses a regular Noah's Ark. . . . The animals are closely crowded together and there is our elephant (shackled to the floor for seven months of the year) her kind eyes look down at her neighbors in confinement, two lions, one lioness, two hyenas, two leopards, two Japanese deer, two reindeer, an alligator and, screeching loudly, seven parrots.
>
> Very little sunlight penetrates this building through its two south windows. The air is foul, and it is a place we hope strangers visiting our city in the winter months will not see. There is only one solitary, permanent structure; only broken down sheds for these magnificent animals. . . . Most of the fences of the present zoo are broken down.
>
> The present zoo occupies slightly more than two acres including the ponds. . . . There is no silly sentimentality about all this. Despite the fact that humanity prompts us to see that the animals are properly housed — good business prompts us to give thought to the question of whether we should close this "Wonderful attraction" or have the animals in proper buildings year round. To accomplish the latter requires that the zoo be removed from Liberty Park.
>
> The present crowded condition of the animals is disgraceful from a humane standpoint, but with the present facilities nothing better can be done.

Mary was horrified by the report and went to Liberty Park to see for herself. It was all true and she was particularly disgusted by the sight of Princess Alice chained to the floor of the tiny compound. She resolved then and there to do something about it. There were no easy solutions. The animals could hardly be shipped back to their homes in the far corners of the earth. Even if they could, there was some question whether former circus animals could survive in the wild. Nor was it simply a matter of selling the animals off to some other city, thereby passing the responsibility on to someone else. Mary Hogle had come from a line of doers who took responsibility for things. It would have been completely against her nature to turn the care of the animals over to some unknown entity simply to be rid of the problem. But the prospect of an Asian elephant quietly grazing in her husband's alfalfa field behind 548 didn't seem very likely either.

The Zoological Board campaigned during the mid-twenties to have the zoo relocated on the site of the state's prison farm above the State Penitentiary on 21st South, but this initiative failed to win the necessary support of the state legislature.

Mary approached her husband with the problem and the two agreed on a course of action. They would donate their family farm at the mouth of Emigration Canyon to Salt Lake City Corporation for use as a zoo. The land had been purchased from the Wageners — old family friends and neighbors when James was growing up — who had operated the California Brewery on the site.

The Emigration Canyon farm was one of the most valuable tracts of land the Hogles owned, but it was also the only piece suitable for use as a zoo. Emigration Canyon Creek ran through the property; there was plenty of water and trees for shade. But the Hogles knew that it would take more than land to make Princess Alice and the other animals comfortable; it would take care and commitment from the city as well. The Hogles needed a guarantee that the animals would not be mistreated as a result of their charity.

If the city accepted the gift, it also accepted the duty to honor the intent of the gift with continuing support for the proper care of the animals and maintenance of the facility. So the gift was offered to Salt Lake City with strings attached. If the zoo was not properly operated and maintained, the land would revert to the Hogles. Over the years that provision has been used by the family to insure that Hogle Zoo would be properly run. The clause has been invoked several times when the city allowed conditions at the zoo to deteriorate, and in 1942 James A. actually demanded the return of the property unless the zoo grounds were cleaned up, the buildings repaired, and the zoo budget increased.

The land was first offered to the city in 1926. As other options disappeared, and as city officials came under increased community pressure to do something about the problem, the city turned to the

Hogles and accepted their offer. During 1930 and 1931, the farm was gradually transformed into the zoological gardens. The dedication of the zoo took place on July 31, 1931. Mary C. Hogle, Dr. George Allen, Julian Bamberger, and Commissioner Harry Finch spoke at the ceremonies. Cutting the official ribbon, Mary dedicated the zoo for the enjoyment of children. She told the crowd of 3,000 spectators that the family had planned to use the property as a goat farm, but that it would now "be put to public benefit as a park where children might learn to love both the outdoors and wild animals."

The zoo's primary function was to be educational. The magnificent animals in the ever-increasing collection brought millions of children to a greater appreciation of the animal kingdom, a greater awareness of man's place in nature, a greater understanding of animal habitat and ecology, and, every spring, practical lessons in biology.

The Salt Lake Zoological Society reported back to the city on the move from Liberty Park to Hogle Gardens:

> The long planned removal of the Salt Lake Zoological collection from Liberty Park to Hogle Gardens has become a reality.
>
> Over forty thousand people have visited the new zoo following its opening about three weeks ago. The new zoo is located at the mouth of Emigration Canyon on a forty acre tract of land ideally suited for the purpose.
>
> The canyon which runs directly through the property has been developed with trails declared by those who have seen them to be the finest in the state. As one walks along these trails and turns corners, suddenly appear animals native to our country.
>
> Instead of pacing back and forth in a small board cage, for instance, the wolves are found among a grove of trees. Since their removal to the new zoo the wolves have grown sleek.
>
> Near the entrance to the zoo is monkey island 55 ft. long by 35 ft. wide with trees and artificial amusement devices for the primates. Instead of looking at a monkey family through the bars of a cage, children have the pleasure of seeing monkeys as they would in their native land.
>
> . . . Instead of looking at deer, elk and buffalo through cage bars or a mesh, the visitor to the new zoo follows a path which brings him above the ranges. From the path he looks down on

the animals and sees them in their natural state, his view uninterrupted by enclosure.

The value of the new zoo to the city can not be estimated.
It will become our greatest civic attraction . . . . The new buildings enclosing the tropical animals will be heated and open to
the public year round.

The Utah Traction Company conducted an experiment to
ascertain if it would be possible to successfully run busses to the
zoo. In the first day it was discovered that 14,000 people went
out to the zoo. It is believed that this service will be a regular
Sunday feature.

The Hogle family's interest in the zoo did not stop with the donation of land, and during the next fifty years they would take an
active and concerned interest in the project.

An Odyssey of Health

Mary Hogle once described herself as "an acolyte in the temple
of health." Her interest in nutrition and health sciences was first
kindled while she was attending the University of Kansas. Later,
illness and circumstance would lead her on a long and dangerous
course before a strange encounter with a door-to-door peanut brittle
salesman resulted in an abrupt restructuring of her life and a world-
wide crusade on behalf of the carrot.

Mary's health had been generally good until 1916, when she
suffered an attack of appendicitis and had her appendix removed.
By 1921 she had begun to experience a number of complaints which
marked the beginning of a ten-year bout with illness. Her complaints included stomach, intestinal, and eating disorders, and through
"kind friends" and acquaintances she eventually placed herself
under the care of a Dr. Tilden. Dr. Tilden's treatment primarily
consisted of a regimen of strict fasting, and during the twenties she
subjected herself to a number of prolonged fasts at his clinic in
Denver.

Twice in 1922 she fasted for periods of fourteen days each, living
on little but water. She lost weight and began suffering neuritis
in her arms and shoulders. Aunt Mary Copley took Mary to Pittsburgh, where she was placed under the care of another "hunger

artist." In 1924 she was again treated, this time by a homeopathic doctor in Chicago, and again the prescription was fasting — thirty days this time on nothing but water. Her weight dropped to 100 pounds. Her suffering during this time was not only physical, and she went through periods of extreme depression.

During the next six years Mary went through alternating periods of eating and fasting with increasingly disastrous results. Her last fast in the summer of 1929 lasted thirty-nine days, one day short of the fast of Jesus. That fast she broke by leaving the clinic and ordering a bowl of tomato soup at a small Denver cafe. The acid of the tomato soup hitting her empty stomach after the long starvation made her violently ill. Somehow she managed to catch the train back to Salt Lake City. From there she went to the home of friends, the Crosbys, in Burlingame, California, to recover.

James did not know what to do about his wife's condition, but he was certain that the "specialists" she had been seeing had come close to killing her. He retained Dr. L. G. Visscher in Los Angeles to examine Mary thoroughly and report his findings. Dr. Visscher described Mrs. Hogle as "an extremely emaciated, very introspective patient, of pale complexion who was still in a fasting state . . . exceedingly nervous, full of fears and misgivings." Dr. Visscher induced Mary to take nourishment of rice and melba toast and admitted her to St. Vincent's Hospital for further testing and observation.

In the weeks that followed, Dr. Visscher conducted exhaustive tests but could find nothing physically wrong with Mary that could not be attributed to her state of near-starvation. Dr. Visscher agreed with James that "her fasting and starvation were most unfortunate to her interest." He warned Hogle to keep his wife away from "Theories and *Doctors!*"

Shortly after her return to Salt Lake in early 1930, Mary rose from her sickbed to answer the bell and there stood a door-to-door salesman who was peddling peanut brittle, sewing machine oil, and magazine subscriptions — a Mr. Holderness. Mary was impressed with the man's healthy appearance. His looks were unquestionably striking; he was tall, erect, almost totally bald, with a light fringe of gray hair. He had sharp features, a straight nose, and high cheekbones. He was hatless and his bald head was darkly tanned. His shirt was open at the front and he wore blue-and-white-striped dairyman's overalls. He also had a heavy Australian accent, but what impressed Mary most was his complexion. Mr. Holderness's skin was a deep golden color — not a tan, exactly; he seemed to glow from within. Mary described what happened next:

> During the ensuing conversation he told me of his own previous affliction and remarkable restoration to health by drinking carrot juice. His symptoms had been so similar to mine that I was glad to listen to him and, of course, I was more or less receptive to the idea because of articles by Dr. Kellogg and others which I had previously read.
>
> Carrot Juice! . . . Drink your vegetables. It was worth trying. Anything is worth trying when you are desperate. . . . Within a few days after commencing to take the carrot juice, I was convinced that my body was actually [recovering] . . . . I noted with great satisfaction that my erratic, wobbly, fluttering heart was picking up strength and vigor. Within a period of several months, all the distressing symptoms, however long withstanding, had disappeared. My recovery is so complete that the present years find me enjoying the best health of my entire adult life.

Mary Hogle's condition improved so dramatically that she had no doubt what had caused the miraculous cure. For many years to come, the "carrot juice man," Mr. Holderness, would be employed by the Hogles as a gardener and caretaker at their home, but his primary responsibility was manufacturing the golden elixir that had restored Mary to health.

The apparatus that Holderness employed for extracting the carrot juice consisted of a hand grater, a number of clean flour sacks, and a cider press. The carrots were grated by hand; the shavings were put in the flour sacks and then squeezed under the large wooden screw-type press. The juice ran out the sides of the press and dripped onto a grooved board which collected the drippings and directed them into a wide-mouthed funnel inserted in a bottle. It was an arduous procedure and no doubt part of the benefit of drinking the juice was the exercise one got in going through the collecting process.

Mary began to deliver quarts of carrot juice to sick friends and relatives. What had worked for her could work for them. She then went into the carrot juice manufacturing business by converting the basement of 548 into the kind of factory that Bugs Bunny might have operated, but with Mr. Holderness at the controls.

> As soon as I was convinced of the remarkable healing action of carrot juice, I wanted other people who were suffering to have it. I had especially constructed electrical machinery; I set up and subsidized the manufacture of it on a rather large scale, ten gallons daily — sending much of it to sick and ailing individuals. I discovered that it rapidly corrected acid conditions, and found it valuable in the treatment of all infective disorders. It appeared to be the specific treatment for blood disorders, blood poisoning, anemia and other bad blood conditions. It had the effect of improving the quality and texture of teeth. People afflicted with serious wasting disease could, by taking enough of it, become strong, active and robust. . . . A most gratifying revelation was that several who were afflicted with cancer were helped by it.

Her gratifying revelation that carrot juice helped people afflicted with cancer was a claim that would eventually get her in some difficulty with the authorities, but the golden juice did seem to help the people she gave it to, and whether miracle food, sensible vegetable product, or placebo, Mary had no trouble gathering countless testimonials to the curative powers of the liquid. Not all of the users were satisfied customers, however. Dick Andrew, one of James A.'s employees, told the story of how he was taken ill in 1931 and how Mrs. Hogle brought him a quart of carrot juice every day before lunch for about a month. One morning he looked in the mirror and found that he was "starting to turn yellow. . . . I remember that I didn't drink it all that day and she asked me what the trouble was. I told her I thought I was having too much of it. I'm sure it was healthy but carrot juice will do that to you."

Mary Hogle was not frivolous in her investigation of nutrition. She began exhaustive research on the properties of carrot juice and consulted with nutritionists, chemists, and doctors to support and corroborate her theories. In 1933 she established the Mary C. Hogle Foundation, which sought not only to promote carrot juice, but health and nutrition research and education generally. Mary operated her foundation from her husband's old office on the fifth floor of the Scott Building. Ames Bagley was hired as her personal secretary, and Mary and Ames worked together on a pamphlet which would elucidate her ideas.

The product of their efforts was entitled "Building up with Foods That Alkalinize and Heal, by Mary C. Hogle." This remarkable pamphlet was a concise explanation of Mary's nutritional and dietary discoveries. It was a farsighted little text and contained valuable information on health and nutrition. The pamphlet praised the value of fresh fruits and vegetables, particularly carrots, for their vitamin content. It cautioned against the use of tobacco, alcohol, and coffee as being cancer-causing agents. The book stressed the importance of a balanced diet and warned against the excessive use of sugar, salt, fatty meats, and butter. The pamphlet praised exercise and stated in part:

> No dissertation on health would be complete without a reference to the value of exercise. Whatever manner of exercise we employ we should remember this rule: exercise below the point of fatigue. Do the simplest exercises first and as you become stronger the nature of your exercise should be altered to conform to your improved condition.

The booklet spoke of the importance of roughage, it outlined the importance of vitamins, particularly A, B, C, D, and E, and identified the foods that contained them. It described the taste properties and nutritional value of various fruit and vegetable juices and gave a number of carrot juice recipes. It stated flatly that a number of cancers were caused by the ingestion of chemical compounds found in certain foods (carcinogens) and stressed the relationship between diet and health.

All of this was perfectly acceptable, but the booklet also contained a number of testimonials which claimed, among other things, that carrot juice had cured the testifiers' malignancies. Mary also claimed that vitamin A, found in carrot juice, helped to prevent malignancy, and although it was not stated directly, the clear implication was that carrot juice prevented cancer. The pamphlet did not advocate that carrot juice replace "orthodox methods of cancer treatment, surgery, X-ray and radium." Nevertheless, the strong claims made on behalf of carrot juice would eventually bring the Mary C. Hogle Foundation under the scrutiny of the AMA and the Federal Trade Commission.

The pamphlet was first published in 1934 and was an instant success. From that year through 1941, eight separate editions, each revised and updated, were published. Two hundred thousand copies were printed in the United States alone. It was also published in England, Scotland, and New Zealand, and several pirated foreign-language editions were known to exist. In the arena of nutrition and health, Mary C. Hogle's fame was world-wide. She was frequently invited to lecture on health and nutrition and traveled widely, disseminating her ideas and distributing her pamphlets.

In addition to Mr. Bagley, the Foundation office in the Scott Building was staffed by Lillian Taylor, the file clerk and correspondence secretary, and a Mrs. Robb, who assisted Mary with scheduling and appointments. A man named Herbert Selfrige now helped Mr. Holderness make the juice, and two boys helped deliver the juice locally to the sick. The juice was also sold at local pharmacies and stores and was sold over the counter at the old Main Street saloon location, now operated by Mary and Holice Joy as a health food store and cafe. This short-lived enterprise, which never did attract many customers, was known as White House Catering. Some of Mary's husband's employees felt obliged to eat there.

A visitor to the Foundation office in the early thirties would certainly have had a hard time pinning down what it was that the Foundation did. It would have been obvious that the office in the Scott Building was more than a business address for pamphlet and carrot juice sales. In one large room there was a library with a large center table filled with books and magazines, surrounded by chairs and benches. The library consisted mostly of texts on nutrition and health, but there were also pamphlets on the world peace movement, the YWCA, the Humane Society, and other subjects of interest to Mary Hogle, including music and art. Seated about the room the visitor might have seen artists, writers, musicians, and students.

The Mary C. Hogle Foundation was conceived and organized to coordinate Mary's many charitable and social interests, but in the thirties it was also a distribution center for countless acts of private, unseen, and discreet charity to individuals needing help. So it was really a front, a cover for Mary Hogle's private guerrilla war on poverty, ignorance, and disease.

Part IV

J. A. HOGLE & CO.

CHAPTER TWENTY-FOUR

The Brokerage House

FROM 1910 THROUGH 1915, James A. Hogle continued his freelance consulting work as a mining engineer and prospected in the Oquirrh Mountains. He also continued to oversee the development of the Dern properties near Battle Mountain, Nevada, and to invest heavily in mining properties. Among his principal investments during this period were blocks of stock in Utah Copper, Amalgamated Copper, Bethlehem Steel, Newhouse Mining, Silver King, Daly Mining, Anaconda Copper, Boston Consolidated, and Nevada Consolidated. It was also during this time that he began to expand his real estate holdings. He purchased several unoccupied tracts of land on the outskirts of Salt Lake City, among them the Emigration Canyon farm that would become the Hogle Zoological Gardens.

On February 6, 1911, James purchased a seat on the Salt Lake Stock Exchange. He had intended originally only to reduce his own commissions but found that his time was increasingly taken up with handling investments — his own and those of others, particularly the investments of his extended family.

On May 29, 1915, James sent a letter to his aunts Anna and Molly, his uncle Henry, and his Weed, Steele, and Mantor cousins. The letter was written on stationery he had had printed up the previous week, and in it he outlined a new family enterprise. At the top of the sheet was the straightforward heading "J. A. Hogle & Company Stocks-Bonds-Grain." He wrote, "You will see by this paper that I have gone into the brokerage business. There has been a great opportunity here for some time in that line of work, but I could not get the right kind of man to help out until lately with the exchange work, which on account of my deafness I would not attempt myself."

James Albert Hogle, mining engineer, at the Irma Hotel in Cody, Wyoming, about 1913.

Before the start of World War I, the mining industry had been in a slump, but the increased demand for strategic metals had brought about a surge in prices and a minor boom. James A. reasoned that a brokerage house specializing in the metals industry would be in great demand. He began with only two employees, Charles T. Van Winkle, to handle the exchange work, and a secretary. His new company was located in rooms 500 and 501 of the Scott Building, a convenient location one floor below the office where he continued to act as president of the Scott Hardware Company. Since he owned the building his overhead was small — but not small enough. His first month's commissions came to a grand total of $20.65, and he wondered if he hadn't overestimated the market.

But James was not discouraged. In the fall of 1915 he opened a second office at 2409 Hudson Avenue in Ogden, Utah, and became the correspondent of Logan and Bryan, who handled the firm's transactions on the eastern grain, curb, and stock exchanges. Logan and Bryan had their own direct private wires to Chicago, New York,

The Scott Building at 168 South Main Street in Salt Lake City, about 1900.

New Orleans, Boston, Los Angeles, and San Francisco which were reputed to be much faster than any of the commercial lines then in operation; so when Logan and Bryan offered to sell Hogle their Salt Lake office in 1917, he immediately took them up on the offer.

Edwin G. Woolley was the manager of the Salt Lake Logan and Bryan office. His brother Paul was a broker with the company, and part of the deal was that Paul would come into the Hogle firm. John Clifford Johnson, bookkeeper and office manager, also came at this time. As Hogle commented several times to his son Jim, "Your success will depend upon the men you have around you." This was a great compliment to the men that he first hired to work for the brokerage firm.

The early acquisition of Johnson and Woolley, two highly competent and professional men, proved a crucial step in the early success of J. A. Hogle & Co. It also set a pattern for Hogle takeovers in the years to come, when key personnel were brought into the company from acquired firms.

When Hogle acquired Logan and Bryan he moved his business to a street-level office in the Herald Building at 169 South Main Street, directly above Browne's Billiard Hall and across the street from his father's old saloon. Hal Browne was the Utah state billiard champion, and his establishment was a favorite haunt of aficionados of the game.

In 1917 there was something devilishly appropriate about a brokerage house operating above a billiard room. Both activities required great skill, and in the minds of many Salt Lakers they enjoyed an equal reputation for crookedness and gambling. In the lexicon of the day, the shady brokerage houses were known as "bucket shops," and in general repute they stood with the pool rooms as singular attractions for unsavory characters.

Although there were indeed several questionable brokerage houses in Salt Lake, J. A. Hogle & Co. was not among them, and no one would ever have accused Hogle of running a "bucket shop." Hogle, Woolley, and Johnson were scrupulously honest, hard-working, and dedicated, setting an example for the many others who would join the firm later. An oft-quoted Hogle aphorism was: "In the brokerage business your success depends upon the success

Slightly damaged photograph of the Herald Building, original offices of J. A. Hogle & Co., at 169 South Main. In 1988 Lamb's Restaurant was a long-term tenant.

of your customers." At J. A. Hogle & Co. that philosophy became both motto and watchword.

Nevertheless, a physical description of J. A. Hogle & Co. offices in the early years might bring to mind something more akin to a billiard hall than a modern brokerage house. Zitelle McClellan, who went to work for the firm in 1920 as a switchboard operator, and later as James A.'s personal secretary, remembered that No. 169 was dark and dingy. The office had once been the printing room of the *Salt Lake Herald* and later the ticket office for the San Pedro, Los Angeles and Salt Lake Railroad. The area was divided by wooden partitions along one side and across the back that separated the board room from the cashier's cage, order room, back office, and bookkeeping areas. The board room, managed by Paul Woolley, was usually crowded with men sitting on wooden slat chairs watching the board markers post quotations. On rainy days there were always many more men in the place than on sunny days, only a portion of whom were actual customers. Like the pool room below, Hogle's was a place of refuge for people who just wanted to get in out of the weather.

Three expert telegraph operators, R. L. Scott, W. F. Rice, and A. K. Arpin, chalked up the quotations on the board simultaneously. Each had replaced the base of his telegraph key with a Prince Albert Tobacco tin which amplified the quotations keyed from the east in Morse code. Each tin was bent slightly differently for a different tone so that the cacophony of coded quotations could be distinguished by the individual operators.

The tinny ping of the telegraphs combined with the clackity sound of the ticker tapes and the voices of the messengers, local mining brokers, and customers created a din that would never have been tolerated in a pool room.

The private wires often contained flashes of news items from the east, and reporters from the *Salt Lake Tribune* were usually on the scene to pick up the latest and fastest-breaking stories. During the twenties the *Tribune* kept a special display of late items in the front window of the paper. Below the display was a sign which read: "Courtesy of J. A. Hogle & Co."

From the time he acquired the Logan and Bryan wire, James Hogle was fascinated by the immediate effect of the news on the prices of stock. Across-the-board fluctuations in the market were directly related to the news items that came across the wire with the quotations. In those days news, national and international, was the controlling force behind the market, and quotations fluctuated wildly with the events of the times. This sensitivity was so acute that the board markers could sometimes tell that something had happened before the news was actually reported. To be a telegrapher in a brokerage house during the twenties was literally to be wired into the pulse of the nation.

Very early on, James began charting the performance of several bonds and stocks against the overall movement of the market. These items were plotted on graphs which listed, among other things, news items, mortgage interest rates, the purchasing power of the dollar, the strength of specific stock groups, inventories, and shipping. He noted and tracked those stocks that bucked trends and those that set them. He sought not only to forecast the market but to identify undervalued stocks. Hogle was always a bargain-hunter, and through his entire career he remained a faithful and meticulous chartist; the two interests went hand in hand.

Zitelle McClellan recalled that most of Hogle's customers smoked pipes, cigars, or cigarettes. The place was always filled with thick clouds of tobacco smoke that settled over everything. The smell of stale tobacco was always in the air and on everyone's clothing. Often the smoke got so thick that the board markers, who stood on a platform several feet above the floor, had red, smoke-irritated eyes that smarted and watered.

Zitelle remembered that some of the men preferred to chew their tobacco, and a number of spittoons were set around the floor of the board room. She remembered too the loud "ping" which reverberated intermittently through the office as the "chewers" spat their bit of plug into one of the brass receptacles.

Zitelle was a Mormon, and the church's strict admonition against tobacco in "The Word of Wisdom" probably made the noxious smoke and spitting particularly offensive to her. Early in her career with the company, she complained to J. C. Johnson, the chief of the bookkeeping department (who had hired her), about the heavy tobacco use, not knowing that he too indulged in the "evil habit." A little later, Johnson brought to her desk a scrap of doggerel verse on the subject:

> Tobacco is a filthy weed, I like it!
> It satisfies my normal need, I like it!

> It makes ya thin, it makes ya lean,
> It takes the hair right off your bean,
> It's the greatest stuff I've ever seen,
> I like it!

Cliff Johnson's silent lecture on tolerance for the habits of others was an important lesson for the young Miss McClellan. It was very typical of Hogle's office manager, who, with both gentle hints and stern lectures, advised and cautioned the employees of their responsibilities to the customers, the firm, and Mr. Hogle. Spittoons notwithstanding, John Clifford Johnson was a man obsessed with appearances. He was never seen without a dark suit and bow tie, and he demanded that the employees dress and act in a proper and dignified manner. He sent home several employees whose attire did not suit his taste and fired at least one board marker whose posture and attitude did not meet his standards.

Johnson's watchful eye was, for the most part, constructive. Occasionally, when the controversial Harry K. Thaw was in town, or when some juicy bit of gossip was circulating, he would take extra care to see that the staff did not engage in idle or potentially damaging whispering. On one occasion, when office talk about a certain employee was getting out of hand, he passed out little wooden carvings of the three monkeys "see no evil, hear no evil, speak no evil." This represented more than a word to the wise; it was understood as a command from the man in the back office. As James A. Hogle himself wrote:

> Getting along with your fellow employees is a matter of give and take. One very important thing to remember is: do not criticize and do not find fault. This applies at home as well as in business. A man can easily form the habit of finding fault with everything, his home, his job, his city, and his country. Try to build a constructive state of mind. If something's wrong fix it, but be positive, never negative. One of the first things we tell a new employee is do not criticize a competitor. If a competitor criticizes you, hire him. Show appreciation! Appreciation is the oil of life. Criticism is like throwing sand in the gears.

It was a simple philosophy, and at J. A. Hogle & Co. it helped to build a cohesive and dedicated staff. The employees knew that bickering and in-fighting would not be tolerated. This contributed to a sense of mutual trust and security, the end result of which was an intense feeling of loyalty, not just to the firm, but to each other and to the Hogle family.

Zitelle McClellan worked for the company until 1929, and she always remembered the firm as a family. On holidays and week-ends the employees were often taken on outings and picnics by the company. Zitelle recalled several trips that everyone took to Eureka, Utah, where they visited the Chief Consolidated mine and feasted on green apple pie at a local cafe. She remembered other trips to Park City, parties at Alta and Brighton, and holiday excursions to Saltair, where they would all splash about during the day and dance in the evening to one of the famous big bands playing at the resort. Some of these events were lavish catered affairs with hors d'oeuvres and Mary Hogle's famous canapes. Over the years the Hogles fre-quently held the company Christmas party, sometimes at the office, sometimes at the Hotel Utah, and occasionally at the Hogle home.

Between 1917 and 1926 the brokerage business expanded rapidly, with twenty-seven employees in Salt Lake and six more in Ogden. The growth of the bond and real estate departments made conditions at 169 intolerable, and in early 1926 the firm moved into new offices on the ground floor of the Kearns Building at 132 South Main — a location that would remain its headquarters for the next forty-four years. The move was made over a weekend, and the new offices were huge compared to 169. Zitelle remembered the high ceilings in the Kearns Building and the ample lighting, both vast improvements over the dim and cramped quarters above Browne's Billiard Hall. During the move the staff discovered that not all of Hogle's investments had been far-sighted. Several remem-bered moving boxes of Imperial Russian war bonds and Kerensky government notes.

The whole Main Street front of No. 132 was taken up by the bond and real estate departments. Behind them was the cashier's cage and the enclosed bookkeeping and accounting areas. The other side of the office was taken up by the board, which displayed quotations from the New York Stock Exchange, the Chicago Exchange, the Chicago Board of Trade, the New York cotton, grain, and sugar exchanges, and active mining stocks on the Salt Lake Exchange. There were two dozen black captain's chairs in front of the board and high glass-topped counters in the center of the room for writing orders. In the back northwest corner of the building was J. A. Hogle's private office and above that, the switchboard operator's alcove.

Few furnishings were brought over from 169, except for the spittoons, the Prince Albert Tobacco tins, the customers, the smoke, and the noise. Zitelle remembered that one of the young women in the office, Clarke Stevenson, had a nervous disposition and would frequently retire to the back of the filing room to escape the constant racket of the ticker tapes and the telegraph.

NAMES FROM A BYGONE ERA

Richard C. (Dick) Andrew first went to work for the firm as a messenger in May of 1926, shortly after the move to the Kearns Building. He too remembered that the noise took some getting used to. He recalled the tile floor at 132, the two-foot-high platform in front of the board, the rows of chairs, and every ten feet, a big brass spittoon. Andrew recalled with a shudder that a certain old mining broker, Joe S——, accidentally spat or sneezed his dentures into a spittoon with a chaw of tobacco. "Old Joe dove across the row of chairs, retrieved the chompers, shook them off and plopped them back in his mouth, then went back to his chair and sat down." He remembered that sometimes the smoke would get so bad that it was hard to see the board. Like Zitelle, Dick Andrew was a Mormon, and he was certain that during his long employment with Hogle he inhaled as much tobacco smoke as if he had been a life-long chain smoker.

During the twenties Andrew would go down to the Salt Lake Exchange as an apprentice to the firm's broker, I. D. Lowe. The Salt Lake Stock Exchange was one of the few open auction exchanges in the country, and the gallery above the floor was often filled with spectators who came to see the show. Andrew remem-

The office and cage of J. A. Hogle & Co. in the Kearns Building, about 1930.

bered the old-time miners and mining brokers from the exchange who sat around the board room at 132 in the afternoon. He remembered men like W. H. Childs, who never took off his felt slouch hat and perpetually chomped on a cigar; Harry Cole, a big boisterous broker; W. H. Clark, a tiny man with fiery hostility toward Cole, and many other old-time brokers and clients: Ralph A. Badger, B. W. Dixon, J. Cortney Lynch, and John Bogrus.

Andrew remembered Hogle's mining associates and customers: Walter Fitch of Eureka's Chief Consolidated; William Dern, brother of Utah's governor and long-time Hogle associate with the Battle Mountain properties in Nevada; James Ivers of Silver King Coalition; Andy Hurley, who had the New Quincy Mining Co.; Mr. Radditz of the Tintic Standard; the MacIntires, who controlled the Mammoth Mining Company; and old George Watson. Watson owned the Alta Merger and Alta Con mines in Little Cottonwood Canyon and held the honorary title Mayor of Alta. Little Cottonwood was usually blocked by snow in the winter and Watson's mines were closed, but during the winter months the stock value of his mines would always double as speculators bet on whether Old George would finally hit the motherlode the coming summer. He never did. When the Alta mines opened again in June the stock would plummet.

Zitelle McClellan shared Dick Andrew's penchant for remembering names. Fifty years after her employment at J. A. Hogle & Co. she would recall with special fondness some of the dedicated men and women who worked for the firm during the twenties. The bookkeepers were Wallace Butterworth, W. R. Chatterton, William James, Ed Parry, L. T. Ellsworth, Del Larsen, and Jack Hollberg. They had to stand all day at two huge desks, four on a side, recording the day's transactions in the giant ledgers. She remembered Maud Thorne, the bookkeeper and cashier who befriended her when she first went to work at Hogle's; Florence Stevenson, who helped to train her at the switchboard; the people

The board room of J. A. Hogle & Co. in the Kearns Building, about 1930.

who worked in the bond department — Alva Lee, Richard Beck, David Carleson, George Dobson, Donald Penney, and Irene Shipp; and the other secretaries and women in the office — Lucile Christensen, Mary Telford, Mary Bertagnole, Peggy Neilson, Clarke Stevenson, and Olga Johnson. She remembered too some of the people in the insurance department — Frank Goeltz, Allen Bradley, George Hurd, and John Hodson. And of course she remembered James A. Hogle:

> Mr. Hogle was always very kind to me. He was always concerned about our well being. He would frequently ask us how we were doing and always said good morning to each of us. He was tactful and gracious and caring and solicitous. After I became his secretary, I took his dictation and typed his correspondence. I worked five full days a week and half a day on Saturday. Saturday mornings I would take down the letters he would write to his son, Jim, who was away at School. He always spoke very softly and it was sometimes hard to hear what he was saying. I once had to move up so close to him to hear what he was saying that he was startled and jumped back in his chair. When Mr. Hogle realized that I couldn't hear him he apologized to me and said he'd try to speak louder. But he was always soft-spoken.
>
> I remember him dictating those letters to his son. He would close his eyes, put his head back, and put his hand up to his forehead and rub it with the tips of his fingers while he was thinking, contemplating what he was going to say. . . . He was a very caring man and was always giving fatherly advice. I remember when young Jim was away at school he took up boxing. I don't think his mother was very pleased but Mr. Hogle wrote his son and told him how much he admired Jack Dempsey and what he had made of his life. I remember particularly him telling his son in one of the letters, "there are two things you should always keep in mind when you're boxing. Don't ever let your opponent know if you're afraid of him. And don't ever let him know if you're hurt."

ECHOES OF ST. PAUL'S

About the time that his son enrolled at St. Paul's, James A. Hogle began to think back on his own educational experience and what it had meant to him. Most of his employees had not had the

The Brighton cabin. Courtesy Sadie Ballard.

opportunity for a good education. Many of the young men who went to work for him had attended high school in Salt Lake, but very few had gone beyond that. Hogle knew that the success of his company would depend on the quality of his employees, and over the years he concocted all sorts of methods to eliminate their educational deficiencies.

Before joining J. A. Hogle & Co., Dick Andrew had worked as a stock boy in the Fulton Fruit Market. Hogle encouraged Andrew to resume his education, and the young man took extension division night courses at the University of Utah in a number of subjects, including commercial law, economics, and banking. The arrangement was a simple one: if an employee passed a course, Hogle would pay for it.

Dick Andrew went to school under Hogle's employee program for ten years. Hogle also paid his tuition at the New York Stock Exchange Institute, the Grain Exchange Institute, and the American Institute of Banking. Dick Andrew was not unique, and a number of other Hogle employees also availed themselves of educational opportunities through the company. In addition, James A. also assisted with their educations at Yale and Princeton several particularly bright and promising young men who never were employed by the firm.

Hogle remembered that some of his most worthwhile lessons at St. Paul's were not taught in the classroom. It was on the playing field that the boys learned the value of hard training, perseverance, and, above all, teamwork. By the late twenties J. A. Hogle & Co. fielded a number of amateur athletic teams. The variety of sports played by the company's employees would shame the athletic departments of many a prep school. The company had several bowling and golf teams and married and single men's baseball teams. The firm promoted in-house athletic tournaments in tennis, bowling, and golf and fielded teams to play other companies from the Salt Lake business community. Hogle himself seldom participated, but Dick Andrew recalls that he went to bat at least once for the

A company party at the Brighton cabin. J. C. Johnson and James A. are seated in the foreground. Courtesy Sadie Ballard.

married men's baseball team. Andrew was pitching, and more out of deference to James A.'s age than his exalted position, he was throwing nice, easy pitches. Hogle became aggravated and told Andrew to throw it to him just as hard as he had the other players. Andrew wound up and hurled a wild pitch which nearly dusted off the boss. Nothing was ever said of the incident.

Hogle was almost fifty when he took up golf, introduced to the game by Alex McCafferty, the pro at the Salt Lake Country Club. Hogle quickly mastered the sport. He never had a very powerful drive, but his short game was excellent. Golf requires study, concentration, and patience — attributes that Hogle possessed in abundance. He also got in plenty of practice, frequently playing five days of the week. It was no wonder that he brought home many trophies from the club tournaments.

The Hogle employees were also encouraged to participate in individual sports and recreation. Like the athletic program at St. Paul's, these were seasonal activities — skiing at the office cabin in Brighton, horseback riding, or sailing on the Great Salt Lake. J. A. Hogle & Co. did not ever manage to launch a rowing crew, however.

Whether or not the sporting events were responsible, the firm prided itself on teamwork. The employees all shared the feeling that they were working together toward a common goal. As with an athletic team, there was a sense of pride and integrity in their shared efforts. When the bottom dropped out of the market in 1929, their company pride and spirit were in part responsible for carrying them through the disaster.

CHAPTER TWENTY-FIVE

Capitalist

THERE WERE MANY ECHOES OF ST. PAUL'S in the professional career of James A. Hogle, not the least of which was a certain Calvinistic strain which had probably come as much from his fellow students as from Dr. Henry Coit. To some degree Hogle believed that his salvation depended on his being a good businessman. For him, creating wealth was not simply a matter of making money, but a moral responsibility, a drive to accomplish something with his life that could be passed on to others. His daughter Katharine remembered him saying, "I'm going to prove that it's possible to be an ethical businessman; that's going to be the meaning of my life." He also told her, "I'm building you children. That's what I'm working for, building you." What he was also building was their capital. When he had first returned from school in the east he was listed in a directory of prominent Utahns, not as a civil or mining engineer, but as "James A. Hogle, Capitalist."

If there is an intellectual tradition or philosophy that most typifies the American capitalist and is most representative of the capitalist ethic behind our civilization, it is probably Calvinism. There are similarities between Calvinism and capitalism, and James A. Hogle had strong strains of both in his makeup. From his grandfather's experience in Ireland, Hogle may have learned at an early age that survival itself is often a matter of having money. From his Presbyterian in-laws, he may have gained an insight into the values of struggle, effort, and saving, and from Uncle Owen learned something of the mysteries of Divine Providence. But James Hogle's notion that he had an ordained duty to make money was one that he acquired while attending St. Paul's.

For him there was never any shame involved in making money. Money was simply the product of hard work, thrift, and common sense. It was something that he created in the same sense that an artist created a painting. He also felt an artistic detachment from his creation which allowed him to be generous in its use.

Hogle never could bring himself to believe that the money he made was actually his; rather, it was a tool that he manipulated for the good of his children and the community. Nor was there ever a tinge of doubt or "Catholic guilt" in Hogle's philosophy to obscure the purity of his motives. As he once said to Katharine, "There are three things in this world that I truly enjoy and they all begin with 'M,' music, mining, and money. I have to admit it. I really enjoy making money." People are usually very good at those things they most enjoy, and James A. Hogle was a veritable Rembrandt in the fine art of making money.

Hogle Investment

James had inherited a number of properties from his father, and during the twenties and thirties he vigorously expanded his real estate holdings. He knew that property values in the West were greatly undervalued and anticipated the day when land would be at a premium. He investigated the possibility of buying land tracts in Los Angeles and Spokane, but he finally decided that he would invest in property in and around Salt Lake City where he was more familiar with the asking price. Very early he acquired a large tract of land near the University, almost 100 acres, then generally known as Popperton Place. The hilly terrain was at the junction of the city's north and east benches, where General Patrick Connor had placed his artillery when the California cavalry was watching over the Mormons. This history would give the neighborhood its name, Federal Heights.

A close friend of Hogle's was a real estate broker named Young, through whom he acquired a 40-acre section on the east bench near the farm, southeast of the mouth of Emigration Canyon. He purchased another 40-acre section on Seventh East, the Peale farm, which had changed hands several times before Hogle bought it.

He was able to pick up the tract at a distressed price following a bank foreclosure. The property was bottom land, with several small lakes and ice ponds, not thought to be worth much at the time.

J. A. Hogle & Co. underwrote a project called the Brighton Drainage District which held 800 acres of property between the city and the lake at 5600 West and North Temple. When the District failed, Hogle had to bail the company out and acquired most of their land. Over the years he continued to acquire adjoining properties to the north and west until his holdings in this extreme western quarter, near the Salt Lake airport, eventually exceeded 3,750 acres.

Hogle continued to purchase properties in Salt Lake's business district, including the Ness Building, just east of the Capitol Theatre on Second South, the American Building, just north of the post office on Main Street, the New York Life Building on the southwest corner of State Street and Second South, and the Axelrad Building north of the Center Theatre on State Street. There were many scattered properties in other sections of the city as well.

During the twenties Frank D. McGregor managed the real estate department, with a staff of five to keep track of the holdings: J. Healy, Bryan Martinson, Thomas L. Davis, Blair Richardson and Ruby Turner. Just as Hogle had anticipated, over the years his property continued to increase in value and Hogle Investment signs began to appear everywhere.

CAPITALIST VENTURES

For all the money he made in the brokerage business, real estate, and investing, Hogle made even more with his third love, mining. When quite young he had come close to striking the motherlode with Colonel Wall at Utah Copper. He had worked hard on that project, and when it slipped through his fingers he had felt a sense of being cheated by Fate. He continued to prospect in the Oquirrh Mountains west of Salt Lake City, sometimes in the company of Joe Lerwill, who operated the Bingham Hotel, and sometimes with Joe Beeson, a geologist, mining engineer, and distant relative of his wife.

But the ground he covered all seemed to have been prospected before, and everything worth finding seemed already to have been found. James turned his attention to the mountains around Eureka and Park City, but those districts too were covered with existing claims and operating mines. Still, he felt that something was being overlooked.

His explorations and trips to Park City and Eureka were profitable nonetheless. His keen eye for geology and passion for mining engineering were appreciated by the mine owners, and he formed close working relationships with men like David Keith, Thomas Kearns, and Walter Fitch — relationships which were of inestimable value in the early days of the brokerage house.

James's on-site mine inspections and geology excursions were also important because occasionally his fieldwork would enable him to identify an undervalued stock. Eureka's Tintic Standard Mine was a property that he recognized as having great potential, and he and more than a few of his customers invested in it.

When the United States entered the Great War in 1917, Hogle looked for ways to assist the war effort. His classmate "Cornie" Vanderbilt had gone down on the *Lusitania*, and James felt a personal as well as an economic obligation. Reasoning that the country would need sulphur for gunpowder, J. A. Hogle & Co. underwrote an issue of a sulphur mine in Cody, Wyoming. The idea was good; the mine was not. The failure of the sulphur company resulted in a $20,000 loss to the firm, and that experience convinced Hogle that the brokerage business and promotion were not compatible. The firm would keep its mining interests and brokerage business entirely separate and would never again promote a speculative venture with which it was directly involved.

Instead of using the firm's money to supply venture capital, Hogle would use his private profits from speculation to increase the capital of the firm. He did encourage his customers to invest in properties in which he himself held blocks of stock, always taking care to inform the customers that he was also an investor or, in some rare cases, a principal. Properties like the Tintic Standard Mine made both Hogle and his customers very happy.

Partnerships and Trusts

When Hogle entered the brokerage business, his at-risk capital investment was $200,000. The majority of this was in real estate, and he was able to live off the earnings of these properties alone. The profits from his investments in stock he was able to put behind the capital of J. A. Hogle & Co., and over the years the capitalization of the firm continued to grow.

During the First World War James A. made small purchases of Liberty Bonds as gifts for his children. He also gave them, from time to time, gifts of stock and money and had them open their own accounts. He encouraged the children to save their allowances and to invest, and as his two boys grew older, he employed them during the summer months as messengers and clerks at the brokerage house and later at the Bingham Prospect Mine. In this way he began preparing them at an early age to take over the brokerage business, investment interests, and mining properties when the time came.

The world-wide influenza epidemic of 1918 and 1919 killed 20 million people, more than 500,000 in the United States. Hogle, J. C. Johnson, and a number of employees were stricken with the flu, and although no one in the company died, many in Salt Lake City did. Hogle became increasingly troubled by thoughts of his own mortality and worried about what might happen to his family if he were suddenly taken. He became obsessed with the fear that all he had been working for would be lost to taxes after his passing. Entire departments of government were busily plotting ways to undo what he had accomplished.

Hogle considered ways to protect his heirs. He began a concentrated study of trusts, reading the probate records of other wealthy industrialists. The study was not a temporary interest. Tax and probate laws would change and he studied every altered clause in the legal codes with all the meticulous scrutiny of a corporation lawyer.

His attorney William Bradley was an old friend of the family who had handled the first James Hogle's legal affairs. During the 1919 flu epidemic Hogle told Bradley that he wanted to divide all his stocks and property with his wife. Bradley pointed out that to do so would weaken the position of the firm, its standing with the banks, its credit, and the safety of the customers' accounts. He suggested that Hogle make his wife a full partner. If he should die she would take over the company and her share of the assets would be fully protected. Hogle agreed to Bradley's suggestion and in 1919 drew up the papers making Mary C. Hogle a full partner. Shortly after this, James opened a separate account for her with shares of Tintic Standard, Walker Brothers' Bank, Scott Hardware Company, and others. From that time on, the partners carried their securities in separate personal accounts, both backing the firm of J. A. Hogle & Co. The capitalization would remain intact.

In 1922 James established irrevocable trusts for his three children. They could not have use of the trusts until they reached the age of twenty-one. When the children came of age, they could each decide if they wanted to become partners, which all of them did, thereby strengthening the capital of the firm substantially.

OLD EMERY OIL

In 1921 James and a number of other investors participated in an attempt to drill a wildcat oil well in Utah's rugged San Rafael Swell. The geology reports looked good, but there were no roads into the area and the difficulties of getting a drill rig to the site were monumental. The disassembled rig, pipe, crane, steam engine, generator, and drilling tools were loaded onto nineteen wagons at Huntington, Utah, on February 13, 1921. The drilling crew carried plows, picks, scrapers, and shovels to build the road into the drilling site as well as the derrick. There was no native lumber suitable for construction, so lumber for the derrick and numerous bridges had to be shipped from Salt Lake City to Price, Utah, by railroad and then transferred to wagons for the sixty-mile trek into the most desolate and rugged country in the West. Numerous gulches and washes had to be bridged before heavy equipment could be brought in. It was a month before the crew finally reached the San Rafael River at Buckhorn Draw, forty-nine miles south of Price. At precisely 4:35 P.M. on March 11, 1921, James A. Hogle and several other men rode the first automobile across a bridge jerry-rigged over the

San Rafael River. It was two more months before all the equipment was in place.

The completion of the derrick was an occasion for celebration. A special train from Salt Lake brought investors and dignitaries to Price, where thirty automobiles waited to take the new oil barons to their well. The festivities surrounding the opening of the Emery Oil Company were in keeping with the magnitude of the enterprise. There were speeches and ribbon-cutting ceremonies and a formal commemorative photographic session — everything in preparation for the gusher that would shower the hundreds of expectant onlookers with glorious black gold. But it was not to be. The well was dry.

THE BINGHAM PROSPECT

Hogle was through with the oil business for good, but not with the financing of mining ventures. In the story of a mine called "The Bingham Prospect" there was more good initiative and engineering to make up for the earlier disappointments.

In the early twenties James A. became what was then known as an "aviation enthusiast." He was one of the very first passengers to fly on a Western Air Express regular commercial flight between Los Angeles and Salt Lake City, the first regularly scheduled airline service in the country. He made several air trips between Salt Lake and Los Angeles, and one particular flight was most memorable.

James had been in Los Angeles visiting Mrs. Copley and investigating real estate possibilities. He decided to return by air and purchased a $90.00 ticket for a flight to Salt Lake City. This was nearly double the price for a comfortable room in a Pullman car on the train, but as things turned out, it was a bargain.

The aircraft was a two-seat, open-cockpit Douglas A-2 biplane that was both passenger plane and mail carrier. The top speed of the craft was 120 miles an hour, and against a strong headwind it could seem to be hardly moving. It took seven hours for the biplane to make the journey, with a brief refueling stop in Las Vegas. The pilot and the single passenger both wore flight jackets, leather helmets, scarves, gloves, and goggles to protect them from the cold, but even so, the prop wash and winds aloft were freezing. There

The "Gusher Celebration" at Old Emery Oil. The arrow points to James A. Hogle.

was no radio or navigation gear aboard, and the pilot had to follow the railroad tracks to stay on course. The aircraft never flew above 8,000 feet, and they had to fly through mountain passes with peaks exceeding 11,000 feet towering around them. It was not a trip for the faint of heart.

As the plane approached the Salt Lake area, the pilot asked his passenger if there was anything he wanted to see from the air. James was freezing and tired, but he asked the pilot to fly over the Bingham mine. He was fascinated by the excavation work in progress at Bingham Canyon and recalled the many days he had spent tramping the area on foot with Professor Kemp and his students a quarter of a century earlier.

Then he asked the pilot to fly a few miles southeast of the Bingham mines. As the plane skimmed the ridges on the eastern slope of the Oquirrh Mountains, Hogle saw an outcropping of mineralization he had never noticed from the ground. He asked the pilot to fly over the ridge again. Hogle was an expert mining engineer and a good amateur geologist. Even from the air there was no mistaking what he had seen.

When the plane landed in Salt Lake City, James called Joe Beeson and told him that he had discovered a potentially rich mineral deposit in the Oquirrhs. He asked Beeson to accompany him to the site to evaluate the property's potential. When they climbed the steep ridge to the outcropping Hogle had seen from the air, Beeson confirmed his suspicions. James located the claim and then quietly began acquiring all the old claims that covered the general area.

The acquisitions did not take long, and within three months he began to sink an incline shaft on the east slope of the Oquirrhs, several hundred feet below the outcropping. They did not have to dig very far before their incline intersected areas of mineralization directly in line with the outcropping above. They followed the mineralized rock until it intersected with the limestone beddings, and here they found their first ore bodies. The plan for developing the mine was a simple one. First they located and mapped the strata and folds of the limestone beddings. Then they made cross cuts in the mine to intersect the mineralized fissures and followed these to the limestone beds. In nearly every case, where the fissures intersected the limestone there was a rich ore deposit. The ore was high-grade lead, zinc, and silver.

It was a great discovery, and the mine was in continuous operation from 1926 until 1931, when depressed metal prices forced suspension of operations. But in those years the Bingham Prospect was a very profitable operation.

James loved to fly, and he continued to prospect by air — although he never saw another outcropping like the one that had led to the founding of the Bingham Prospect. He became an early devotee of aerial photography and mapping and spent many hours poring over aerial photographs of mining districts. Like his stock market charts, they were tools he used to find prospective mining properties. He also studied aerial photographs of the Salt Lake Valley and found that they were very helpful in evaluating and managing his real estate holdings.

James A. Hogle's ability to sort out and analyze information from diverse sources was his special genius. His career was filled with incidents demonstrating a remarkable sense of integration. Everything seemed to have a place, and his special talents and interests all played a role in his success.

CHAPTER TWENTY-SIX

The Crash & the Depression

MARIAN STYLES went to work for J. A. Hogle & Co. in February of 1929, replacing Zitelle McClellan, who had married and was to leave the firm that summer. Jack Lerwill, son of Joe Lerwill, a prospecting associate of Hogle's, also joined the company that year, starting work the second week of October.

It was an exciting time to go to work for a brokerage house. The past three years had witnessed an unprecedented stock market boom, and the market that October was at an all-time high. Prosperity seemed general, and optimism was rampant. President Hoover predicted the end of poverty. *Barron's Weekly* said that the market had never been stronger and Irving Fisher, professor of economics at Hogle's alma mater, Yale, proclaimed that stock prices "had reached a permanently high plateau."

Hogle was one of the very few who saw trouble ahead. As early as 1927, some of his indicators were giving clear notice that there was something wrong. The amount of speculative money in the market coupled with the large volume of margin accounts, was inflating the value of stocks beyond any reasonable expectation. Hogle's charts of the commodities market showed overproduction across the board.

The prices of copper, silver, and zinc — metals the owner of the Bingham Prospect followed very closely — remained high, even though production figures were up. It made no sense in a peacetime economy that production volume and metals prices were rising at the same time. Hogle could be pleased at the large profits his mine was making, but the volume of the metals being mined belied their supposed rarity. An "adjustment" was clearly in the offing.

But there were more disturbing indicators than the price of zinc. Hogle's charts told him that the market was being driven neither by productivity nor demand, but by unrestrained borrowing — a fantasy world having little relationship to economic reality. Professor Fisher was wrong; it couldn't possibly last.

Eight days after the Yale professor made his now-famous statement, the bubble burst. On October 24, 1929, thirteen million shares were traded in a single day of sustained panic now known as "Black Thursday."

In October of 1929 Mary Hogle was recovering in Los Angeles from the effects of her longest fast and the battery of examinations she had undergone at St. Vincent's Hospital. Katharine had been attending Sarah Lawrence College in New York, but was taken out of school to help her mother in Los Angeles. James, Mary, and Katharine were all staying together in a small stucco home when news of the crash reached them. James A. made immediate arrangements to return by train to Salt Lake City.

Joe Copley, Mary's youngest brother, also lived in Los Angeles, and Joe had a car. He was supposed to pick Hogle up and take him to the train early the next morning, but when dawn arrived, Joe was nowhere to be seen. James Hogle paced and fretted as he awaited the arrival of his brother-in-law. Finally, in anger and frustration, he walked to Joe's home, some blocks from where the Hogles were staying. He shouted, then pounded and kicked at the door, until Joe finally dragged himself out of bed. James was furious, not simply because he had missed his train, but because so much depended on him; without him there was no telling what might happen. Long-time employees of Hogle remembered him as a soft-spoken man. Some who worked for him for over twenty years had never heard him raise his voice. The uncharacteristic vehemence came from his sincere belief that he could actually do something about the crash. He wasn't just trying to save his own money; he was fighting to preserve his creation and to rescue his friends from calamity — but he was being thwarted by inexcusable negligence, and his righteous indignation poured out on his hapless brother-in-law. He would eventually recognize that the crash was far greater than even his powers were capable of remedying.

There is some evidence that, in spite of his careful planning and even anticipation of the crash, if he had been present at the brokerage house on October 24 he might have overreacted to the enormity of the crisis. As it was, he was able to carefully plot his strategy on the train ride back to Salt Lake.

Hogle believed in the charts he had carefully prepared and studied since 1917. The evidence that he had meticulously collected over the years had given him a clear picture of the market and he acted accordingly. In the months preceding the crash he sold short on thousands of shares of stock and had to pay the dividends out up through the early months of the crash. He then "covered his shorts," went long and during the next three years purchased thousands of shares of stock at their lowest points in history. Many of these "worthless stocks" that he bought at very reasonable prices were placed in a new trust for the children called The Three Trust, which would prove a major pillar in the financial security of his family. The stocks could do nothing but go up.

Hogle had charted his own way through the shoals of financial disaster, but all about him was wreck and ruin. Black Thursday was only the beginning of the crash; October 28 and 29 were even worse. Over the next few months the market made efforts at recovery, but by April of 1930 it had settled into a steady slide that would not bottom out until the summer of 1932.

Marian Styles, Jack Lerwill, and Dick Andrew remembered Black Thursday and the months which followed. On October 29 Marian wrote more than fifty margin calls an hour while another woman addressed and stamped the envelopes. That evening the entire staff worked straight through the night just trying to keep up with the volume. Dick remembered that through November of 1929 they worked every day from seven in the morning until after midnight. When the worst of it was over and things had settled down, Hogle personally presented each employee with an extra month's salary as a bonus.

Not even the far-sighted James Hogle foresaw the widespread effects of the crash, however, or the severity of the depression which followed. But as prices plummeted, like a house of cards the props went out one by one. The failure of the international commodities market weakened currencies worldwide. Bank runs and failures wiped out the life savings of small and large depositors alike. Agriculture and mineral prices dropped below the point where production could be maintained. Mines were shut down, farms were foreclosed on, industries collapsed, unemployment soared, and the entire world was plunged into ten years of depression.

Hogle had once vowed never again to mix his brokerage and mining businesses, and while he didn't use the firm's capital to finance mining ventures, there was an unexpected link. The Bingham Prospect Mine would provide Hogle with the capital he needed to sustain the brokerage house through the worst of the Depression. It is worth noting that not a single employee of J. A. Hogle & Co. was laid off because of the crash — an accomplishment in which James Hogle took great personal pride.

Hogle's employees were not the only ones to benefit from his farsighted planning and fortunate timing. His largest clients were not just customers but his closest friends. He owed the very existence of his firm to some of these men, and he wasn't about to see them wiped out. Eventually the economy would recover and eventually the brokerage business would pay off again, but not if his best customers were all bankrupt. From October of 1929 through the first few years of the Depression, Hogle carried the undervalued accounts of many customers. It was a gracious act that they would not soon forget, and it earned him the undying gratitude and loyalty of many investors.

Salt Lake City, though economically depressed during the thirties, was not as severely hit by the national calamity as the heavily industrialized cities of the east. Many factors have been cited for this, including the Mormon church's early establishment of bishops' storehouses and the expansion of their in-house welfare system, then called the Church Security Program, to meet the crisis.

It was fitting, somehow, that the son of the saloonkeeper who had helped to end the bitter Gentile–Mormon conflict of the nineteenth century would make a major contribution to the establishment and support of the L.D.S. church's extensive welfare system. J. Reuben Clark, Jr., who would eventually serve the country as ambassador to Mexico and president of the World Bank, was a counselor in the First Presidency of the L.D.S. church. During the Great Depression he approached James Hogle with an outline of the church's plan to establish a welfare granary and manufacturing site in Salt Lake City.

The L.D.S. church had long preached the values of self-reliance, independence, and hard work. The welfare plan as explained by Presiding Bishop Sylvester Q. Cannon was, "to help men and women help themselves, whereby the unemployed church membership could obtain work and thus have no need for private or public charity." J. Reuben Clark expressed the church's viewpoint this way: "The thought that we should get all we can from the government because everybody else is getting it, is unworthy of us as American citizens. It will debauch us . . . . We must be as careful with the government's funds as with our own or with the Church's." Clark stated that "the former policy of giving something for nothing had created precedents which spelled trouble ahead for communities and individuals . . . . The ideal policy is working for what we receive."

Under the church's system, a man was not paid by the hour at a fixed wage, but with foodstuffs, clothing, and other necessities of the church's own manufacture. A cash stipend was also given, but a worker with a family was automatically given more than a single worker. "One gives what one has, one gets what one needs."

Hogle and Clark shared grave concerns about Roosevelt's New Deal and were of a mind on many matters of economics and politics. Hogle suffered sleepless nights fretting over Roosevelt's "socialistic administration" until he resolved his worries with the happy solution of "Finding ways of profiting by it." When the church leader explained the church's welfare program and asked for his help, Hogle immediately agreed to contribute half the price of the purchase of the property for a welfare granary and factory.

Hogle's philanthropy during this period was made possible in part by the successful negotiation of another outstanding deal — his sale of the Bingham Prospect Mine to U.S. Smelting and Refining.

Hogle's Bingham Prospect mines at Lark, Utah, were very rich, and U.S. Smelting had long coveted the property. That company had approached Hogle several times with cash offers, but he had turned them down. Now he saw an opportunity to sell them the Lark mines to mutual advantage. The sale would be sweetened with a generous offer of U.S. Smelting stock. In 1932 U.S. Smelting was at its lowest point in history, having dropped from a high of $72 a share in 1929 to $10 a share in 1932. The company was more than willing to include a block of stock in the purchase of Hogle's mines.

Hogle sold the Bingham Prospect mines to U.S. Smelting for 10,000 shares of common stock, 5,000 shares of preferred stock, and $375,935.98 in cash, and the money and stock were deposited with the Guaranty Trust Company of New York. Over the next fifteen years Hogle was paid more than half a million dollars in dividends alone from the U.S. Smelting stock, which amount was credited to the firm's account. The price of the stock, as Hogle had anticipated, gradually rose to approach its pre-Depression highs. With this additional capital, J. A. Hogle & Co. was as solid and as solvent as any bank in the country. Throughout the turbulent and unsettled thirties, it remained a rock of financial stability, and while other brokerage houses were closing their doors forever, Hogle quietly expanded.

Hogle had belonged to the Chicago Board of Trade since acquiring the Salt Lake office of Logan and Bryan. During the twenties he had joined the New York Curb Exchange and all the other major commodities exchanges. Until 1933 J. A. Hogle & Co. had been the correspondent of Post and Flagg on the New York Stock Exchange. When that firm split into two new firms, E. F. Hutton and E. A. Pierce, the Salt Lake brokerage house became a customer of the latter, which had acquired the northern correspondents of the former firm. In October of that same year Hogle took the big step, purchasing a seat on the New York Stock Exchange.

In early 1934, J. A. Hogle & Co. opened a new office in Beverly Hills, and another in Bakersfield, California, several months later. In 1935 the company opened additional offices in Los Angeles and San Diego, followed by branches in Butte and Missoula, Montana. With the exception of the Beverly Hills office, which was established from scratch, Hogle usually acquired and kept intact the staffs of other firms as he bought them out. It was a method of expansion which ensured both continuity and customers. With the exception of the Los Angeles office, which took some time to develop, all of the branch offices showed a profit within a year of being added to the Hogle family. (Following the old recipe, Hogle would acquire the Los Angeles office of Post and Flagg in early 1941.)

Although Hogle had sold the Bingham Prospect, he was not out of the mining game for long. In 1935 he took over the development of the Diamond & Excelsior Mining Company, which was then owned by the John Hayes Hammond interests. The claims were located several miles up New York Canyon from the old 1880's mining camp of Eureka, Nevada.

Hogle and his superintendents in the project, George Stott and Bill Holt, began a development program in the summer of 1935, and subsequently constructed a chlordizing roasting mill and cyanide plant to process the ore. Hoping, perhaps, that a little of the Bingham Prospect luck would rub off on the new venture, Hogle called his company The Eureka Prospect.

Both his sons, James Edward and George Hollister, would assist with the development of the mine. Jim had completed four years' study in mining engineering at the University of California the previous spring. After a short time working in Globe, Arizona, he went to Eureka to work at the new Prospect. Sherman Hinkley, another young mining engineer, went to work for Hogle at Eureka in September of 1935 and would stay on there until after Christmas of 1936.

In early 1936 George replaced his brother at the mine and Jim began working full time in the brokerage business. This enabled him to fulfill two major goals he had postponed for at least two years. The first was to marry his long-time sweetheart Bonnie Elaine Smith, who he had met at the University of California at the end of his sophomore year. Because Jim's mother was still in Los Angeles recovering from her illness, they decided to have their wedding in the All Saints Cathedral in Beverly Hills, where the Hogles' old family friend Rev. W. W. Fleetwood officiated.

After the reception at the Los Angeles Country Club, the young couple started on their extended honeymoon, which included Santa Barbara and San Francisco, and then went on to Eureka, where George took a game Bonnie down into the mine. She had to

Bonnie Elaine Smith Hogle.

literally slide by the seat of her pants down to the 400-foot level, mostly through the wet and slippery cave system.

In a more civilized fashion, the newlyweds continued on through Salt Lake to Quebec and down through New England, enjoying the marvelous fall colors and finally arriving in New York City on Columbus Day, Jim's father's birthday. After spending that evening with Katharine, who was living in Greenwich Village, they settled down in a small apartment on East 66th Street, and Jim reported to work at the main office of E. A. Pierce & Co., where he was to work for a full year as a trainee in every department of the firm.

Bonnie and Jim returned to Salt Lake City in time to celebrate the birth of their first son, Jim Jr., on August 16, 1937, and Jim became an active partner in J. A. Hogle & Co.

The developing Eureka Prospect milled over 12,000 tons of ore during this two-year period. But the mill was inadequate and the ore reserve much smaller than expected. The return was poor, less than five ounces of silver and a trace of gold per ton. Early on, Sherm Hinkley reported the disappointing results to James A. Hogle personally. But Hogle was not discouraged and said, "Young man, I've made more money in mining than I ever did in the brokerage business." The development would go on.

At about this time, his old friends and partners Joe Beeson and Charles T. Van Winkle brought to Hogle's attention another mining

At the Eureka Prospect mine, George Hogle (*left*) hosts Bonnie and Jim, who visited during their honeymoon in 1936.

prospect, this one in Colorado. Hogle spent two years acquiring controlling interest in the Rico Argentine Mining Company and then financed its development without ever making a public offering of stock. In 1938 he put Van Winkle in charge, and Jim joined this operation as well. In contrast to the Eureka Prospect, Rico began shipping ore within a year of Hogle's acquisition. Both mines, however, would play important roles in the subsequent financial history of the Hogle family.

During the thirties the Salt Lake home offices of Hogle's brokerage and investment companies continued to grow, and more employees were added to the payroll. Even so, Hogle continued his keen interest in the health and well-being of the staff. He always said good morning to everyone in the office and each week he would make the rounds of the office to ask each employee how he was doing, how his family was, and other matters of personal interest. His concern was genuine. The employees never felt that this was small talk, and neither did Hogle. Small talk was trivial; the well-being of his staff was important. If there were real problems, Hogle would invite the employee back to his private office where they could discuss the matter at length. None of this was easy, particularly as his deafness continued to worsen and conversation became difficult for him. But throughout his long career he never abandoned the practice.

Hogle's advice to the younger staff members undoubtedly included the rules for a good marriage that he took great pains to teach to his own children when they reached marriageable age. "Never let a day go by without saying 'I love you'," he instructed, and "Never let the sun go down on a quarrel."

CHAPTER TWENTY-SEVEN

Remembering the Boss

JAMES A. HOGLE'S FIRST ELECTRIC HEARING AID was built by Jack Lerwill shortly after he went to work for the firm in 1929. It was a bulky, cumbersome apparatus, as the battery packs which powered it had to be strapped about Hogle's waist. He went through a number of hearing aids during the thirties and forties, but his progressive hearing loss was always far in advance of technological improvements. For those who knew him only in his final years, the affliction seemed the most notable aspect of his character.

OF BATTERIES

To the man who begrudged spending money on soap and electricity at home, the purchase of batteries was especially irksome, for they seemed to combine the worst aspects of those most hated of wasteful expenditures. Like soap melting away in the tub, the batteries quickly ran down with continual use; like Utah Power and Light, they were electrical. Hogle used his device sparingly — only when he absolutely *had* to hear what was going on. Trivial conversation had always been painful for him anyway. Everything had to have a point and a place in the scheme of things, and useless talk wasted both time and money.

Hogle's procedure for carrying on business meetings with his staff eventually formalized itself into a routine which bordered on ritual. His manipulation of the hearing device was so definite an action that it was remembered as a kind of signal by his employees.

Bert Hickok, who went to work for the firm in 1937, remembered the manner in which his boss conducted business meetings.

> There would be four or five of us sitting around the table and he would pose to us whatever the problem was — usually having to do with the operational end of the business — and then he would turn off his hearing aid and close his eyes and sit back in his chair for five or sometimes ten minutes. Then he would turn his hearing aid back on and ask us what our recommendations were. We would make our suggestions and then he would turn his hearing aid back off again, close his eyes and think about it for awhile. Then he'd turn it on and say, "All right, this is what we're going to do . . . ." And that was it — period.

Like everything else in his life, Hogle recognized that his handicap had a place and once wrote: "A lot of people don't understand what a wonderful blessing deafness can be. For one thing it certainly eliminates a lot of arguments." Bert Hickok concurred: "When he turned that hearing aid off there was nothing more to say. You knew he couldn't hear you."

At some point Hogle discovered that dead batteries, if they were left in the desk drawer for awhile, would mysteriously revive themselves. The revival was very temporary, but he would not throw one away if there was any chance of its briefly coming back to life. His desk drawer was consequently cluttered with batteries, some permanently drained and others patiently awaiting resurrection. But the quick and the dead were not easily distinguished by the severely deaf Mr. Hogle.

Jack Gallivan worked at the *Salt Lake Tribune*, across the street from the Kearns Building. He parked his car in the Kearns Building garage and cut through Hogle's every morning. Mr. Hogle's private office was a room at the rear of the brokerage house, by the back door of the Kearns Building. As the stock market in the east opened two hours ahead of Salt Lake time, Hogle was always in his office by the time the young man came through. Gallivan would wave to Mr. Hogle as he passed by a small window in the office, and frequently Hogle would motion to him to come in.

Through trial and error, Hogle would then begin the process of determining which batteries had rallied. Each time he put a battery into the pack he would look up at Gallivan, who would loudly inquire, "Can you hear me now, Mr. Hogle?" until finally he would light up and say "yes," nodding his head with approval.

Years later an employee, Frank C. Archer, became his official battery tester and purchasing agent. Hogle would catch Archer before he left to go to the Salt Lake Stock Exchange and hand him a sack full of batteries which Archer would take to have tested at Walgreen's Drug on the corner. The dead batteries were replaced, those still showing signs of life kept.

Hogle clipped coupons out of the paper for discounts on batteries and watched the ads for sales. The coupons he clipped were usually discounts of two or three cents a purchase.

Frank Archer remembered that Hogle and a certain elderly salesman of registered securities, George Dobson, had a particularly hard time communicating with each other. Dobson was also deaf and also wore a hearing aid. When both hearing aids were turned on and the two men were in close conversation, the screeching feedback produced by their microphones would occasionally send both men reeling as they struggled with their dials.

Of Alleyways and Fenders

Hogle's deafness resulted in a number of related problems of which he was not fully aware. Like Jack Gallivan, he parked his car in the Kearns Garage behind the building. The narrow alleyway between the Kearns Building and the old Daft Building (now the site of Daynes Jewelry) was barely wide enough to accommodate Hogle's old Packard. He left work every day right after the market closed, and it had become a regular event on Main Street. The loud grating sound of his bumper scraping along the rough granite foundation of the Kearns Building echoed like the groaning screech of some prehistoric beast dying in the alleyway, and everyone on the block knew that Mr. Hogle was going home. He was so punctual that it was claimed that the shopkeepers on Main Street set their clocks by his departure.

Hogle's driving problems were not solely attributable to his deafness, however. He was a notoriously atrocious driver, and employees frequently heard the screech of brakes after the beast in the alley had died. Sometimes there was also the wail of a siren. At the end of the alley, which emptied onto Main Street, was a large, clearly marked sign reading No Left Turn. For more than thirty years, without exception and without fail, Hogle routinely turned left across two lanes of traffic to take the most direct route to South Temple and home. As he seldom wasted his battery power while driving, horns and sirens fell on deaf ears. Ed Whitney, the property manager of Hogle Investment, was the employee saddled with the duty of explaining things to the traffic cops.

Another practice that brought his passengers to the point of white-knuckle terror probably was a result of his deafness. He was in the habit of turning his head around to look at his passengers when he spoke to them, possibly to hear better himself or to read their lips; but for whatever reason, few who had the pleasure of experiencing the trick ever again engaged Hogle in conversation while he was driving. Marian Styles recalled that Mr. Hogle once drove her to the post office to mail a packet of letters. The journey was only three blocks, but the experience was memorable enough that forty years later she shuddered at the thought of it and commented: "I never let that happen again."

His daughter Katharine remembered a time that she and her father were driving down the highway when she suddenly realized that they were on the wrong side of the road. His explanation was classic J. A. Hogle: "I think it's a little smoother over here."

James Edward also remembered his father's driving technique. "He would just pick a spot he was going to go to, and he'd head for it and not let anything interfere with him. Then he'd get there and look for another spot."

Mr. Hogle was one of the city's most prominent citizens and a principal benefactor, but there was a limit to the patience of the Salt Lake City Police Department, both as to the driving habits of Mr. Hogle and the excuses of Mr. Whitney. Finally they had had enough. The police came to the office and approached James E. with a request: "Can't you do anything to get your dad to stop driving?"

James E. studied the problem and came up with a reasoned and convincing argument to present to his father. He took the cost of his father's car, calculated the depreciation on it, the cost of gas, oil, taxes, insurance, and any other expenses incident to its operation. He broke these expenses down by the year, month, week, and day. He then called Tex Boyington, who operated the Salt Lake Yellow Cab Company, and asked him how much it would cost to deliver his father to work every morning and pick him up every afternoon. Boyington's bid was $1.50 a day. When the younger Hogle presented his father with the figures, the issue was settled. "When I showed Dad the total cost of operating his own car against being driven to work he said 'By all means let's do it! I can save some money that way.' "

The ever-thrifty Mr. Hogle saved old envelopes and cards in his desk at the office to use as scratch paper so he wouldn't have to waste good stationery making notes. He kept his own inventory of paper clips, pens, and other office supplies and used pencils until they were impossibly small. Once when the office was being remodeled he chastised an employee for throwing out discarded lumber from an old broom closet. It should be reused somewhere else. Katharine remembered buying her father a dark gray suit in the mid-thirties that he was still wearing ten years later. He ate very frugally as well and seldom took his lunch or dinner at a restaurant. Katharine remembered that he often scrounged around the attic to find birthday and anniversary gifts for friends and relatives, and Frank Archer recalled being handed a broken football and asked to see if he could find a bladder for it, as replacing it would be too expensive.

To the mining engineer who had dug tons of silver ore out of the ground, the notion of carrying little scraps of the metal in his pocket might have seemed absurd. But avoiding spending his money had become a way of life for the man, and one way not to spend it was never to carry any. Almost everyone associated with James Albert Hogle has a story about loaning him pocket change.

When James A. was still driving his car, he continually borrowed change from Marian Styles and J. C. Johnson for the parking meters. The "loans" were not recoverable. When Bert Hickok went to work for the firm as a board marker and stock runner in 1937, he too encountered the "penniless" Mr. Hogle:

> There was a brokerage problem nationally at the time and *Life* magazine came out and took pictures of the Salt Lake Stock Exchange. There was a newsstand on the main floor of the Kearns Building and I had just bought a copy of the magazine when J. A. Hogle came up. He wanted a copy too, but he didn't have any change on him, so he asked me to lend him a dime. I did, of course, and he never paid me back.

Frank Archer recalled a story told him by his father, Frank Archer, Sr.

> My father used to go to the old Grabeteria Restaurant for coffee in the mornings and Mr. Hogle, who by that time was driven down to work, would drop in to buy an apple each day before going to the office. One day my father was at the front counter and had just put his dime down to pay for his coffee when Mr. Hogle came in and grabbed an apple. He then went all through his pockets as my father watched. He looked down, pointed at the counter and said: "Oh there's my dime," then turned and walked out.

His thrift and extremely modest lifestyle gave Hogle a reputation as a penny pincher. But this reputation was accentuated by his deafness, and as he was a naturally introspective man anyway, his increasing withdrawal into himself became something of a trial for those of his tenants who didn't understand his affliction and mistook it for absent-mindedness. Jack Gallivan recalled that Hogle would sometimes be given the rents by tenants of the Scott and Boyd Park buildings when they encountered him on the street. Hogle would occasionally neglect to inform Mr. Whitney that he had received them, and this caused problems between Hogle Investment and tenants who were sometimes dunned by the company's dutiful property manager.

Those who worked for him knew that Hogle was no Silas Marner. He liked to hand the employees their annual Christmas bonuses personally, and these bonuses more than made up for whatever losses they might have sustained as walking coin machines during the year. That the private man contrasted sharply with his cool and reserved exterior is witnessed to by the fact that Hogle carried around in his wallet a list of his office staff's birthdays. His frugality was primarily directed at himself and not others.

Typical of this tendency toward self-denial was his refusal to replace the roof on his South Temple home even though it reportedly leaked like a sieve. Ed Whitney had repeatedly tried to get Hogle to have it repaired, but without success. Hogle's response paraphrased the reply of the old character in the song "Tennessee Traveler," "It only leaks when it rains." Mr. Whitney bided his time until Hogle went out of town on a trip. The minute he left, Whitney had a crew of men at work replacing the roof. But the property manager knew Hogle well and had the roof painted a faded charcoal gray to match the color of its previous decay. So effective was the "antiquing" that Hogle never knew he had a new roof on the home. "All of a sudden it just stopped leaking." The employees of J. A. Hogle & Co. had respect and affection for their boss, and no one ever explained to him the mystery of the self-repairing roof.

THE WORLD ACCORDING TO THE DOW

Hogle spent a great deal of time working on his charts. This activity was not restricted to office hours, and after dinner in the evenings he would frequently retire to his library to study the ever-changing graphs. For Hogle these were indicators that he used to forecast the market, but the charts also recorded the history of the period. Those events which most affected the market stood out as peaks and deep pits in blue, red, and black ink lines across the continuous rolls of paper, a seismograph of stock performance and volume that mapped the passage of history. The charts were, in a way, the "brief chronicles of the times."

The events scribbled across Hogle's charts which most influenced the market represented a cavalcade of mid-century history: England abandons the gold standard; the Banking Act of 1933; the bottom of the Depression; imposed bank holiday; Roosevelt elected; the Securities Act of 1933; the Repeal of Prohibition; Germany cancels its debts; NRA declared unconstitutional; Social Security Bill enacted; Italian–Ethiopian War erupts; the League of Nations collapses; Germany marches into the Rhineland; civil war in Spain; Roosevelt elected to a second term; Chinese–Japanese war erupts anew; Germany annexes Austria; the conference at Munich; Germany invades Czechoslovakia; Italy invades Albania; Germany invades Poland; the invasion of Denmark and Norway; the German breakthrough at Sudan; the fall of France; the Battle of Britain; Germany invades Russia; Roosevelt elected to a third term; and the Japanese attack Pearl Harbor.

Some events, such as the repeal of Prohibition, had only slightly measurable influence on the market. Others, such as the German breakthrough at Sudan, had an immediate and dramatic effect. Some of the market activity seems at first glance contradictory. The outbreak of World War II with the invasion of Poland sent stocks down for only the first two hours of trading. As the day went on, the morning losses were not only recovered but the market went to new heights, buoyed by the assumption that heavy industry was sure to boom and the Depression was at an end.

Some events, such as the attack on Pearl Harbor, did result in substantial declines, but these were not as great as might be thought — perhaps because the country was expecting to be drawn into the war and an attack, somewhere, was generally anticipated.

A very low period in any broker's view of history had to be the winter and spring of 1942, and it didn't take an expert chartist to know that the situation was grim. Nearly every dispatch from the front sent shock waves through the market. Hogle had first started his charting during World War I, when such dispatches seemed to be the driving force behind every movement on the board. Once again the board markers at J. A. Hogle & Co. had a ringside seat on world events, and once again they could frequently sense a breaking news item before its official announcement.

Even a casual market watcher during that dark period could follow the declining fortunes of the war by watching the action on the New York Stock Exchange. The Imperial Japanese Navy had followed up its successful attack on Pearl Harbor with the sinking of the H.M.S. *Rodney* and H.M.S. *Nelson*. Then on January 2 news came from the Philippines that Manila had been captured. The headline in the financial section of the *Times* summed up the situation on Wall Street: "War News Drys up Buyers."

On February 12 the news that, "Jap hordes are threatening Singapore" drove transactions down to a mere 413,000 shares. When the news arrived on February 15 that General Percival had surrendered Singapore, "the Invincible Gibraltar of the East," to General Yamashita, the volume fell to 163,000 shares. Although this came during a half-day Saturday trading session, it was still the smallest aggregate number of shares transferred since Hitler's successes in Russia in 1941.

News of Japanese victories in Burma, Java, and the Dutch East Indies on March 6 pushed leading stocks to new lows as declines ranged from 2 to 7 points. This was the biggest single day's drop since December 9, following the Pearl Harbor attack.

There was a brief rally on St. Patrick's Day, when an overly optimistic report from General Douglas MacArthur on the Philippine situation was released, but more accurate reports and accounts of military disasters on Java and Bataan on March 20 pushed the market down and volume to 274,800 shares, the smallest volume in a full session since June of 1941. On Saturday, March 30, trading slumped to 131,350 shares.

The worst news came the second week of April: on the eighth that the Allied line across Bataan had been breached, then on the tenth that the American/Philippine army had been smashed and 36,850 were facing immediate death or capture. On that day prices hit a four-year low.

On April eleventh news arrived that the British aircraft carrier *Hermes* had been sunk off Ceylon. By April twenty-first the daily volume of stocks traded had dropped to below 240,000 shares. On April twenty-fourth the *Times* reported that the average share of stock had fallen to its lowest level since April of 1933.

On May third the Japanese announced the capture of Mandalay. The one forlorn ray of hope that spring was General Wainwright's spirited, if doomed, defense of the tiny island of Corregidor at the entrance to Manila Bay. When the news came that General Homma had accepted the surrender of Wainwright and more than

7,000 American soldiers on Corregidor, America had truly reached rock bottom.

As a general market strategy, James A. Hogle had always advised that the time to invest was when things were bad. In the spring of 1942 things were very bad indeed, and the brokerage business in particular was anything but good, verging on depression. James A. was given a chance to practice what he preached. The opportunity came with a surprise offer from the Denver firm of Sargeant, Malo and Co.

In the early years, Hogle & Co. and Sargeant, Malo had both been correspondents of Post and Flagg. When that firm had split in two, both became the customers of E. A. Pierce in New York, represented by James E. Hogle. During the past two years the young Hogle had stopped frequently in Denver on his way east to meet with E. A. Pierce. There he would confer with Ray Sargeant, who acted as director of the business.

James E. was familiar with the Denver operation and was acquainted with Mr. Sargeant's two sons, William and Raymond, Jr. The senior Mr. Sargeant had been interested in getting out of the brokerage business for some time, but he knew he could never convince his partner, Mr. Malo. However, the bad business and worse news of 1942 gave Ray Sargeant the leverage he needed, and Mr. Malo agreed to sell the business if a suitable buyer could be found.

In the spring of 1942, Sargeant traveled to Salt Lake City to discuss the potential takeover. James A. and James E. Hogle met with Sargeant and quickly concluded the sale. Ray Sargeant commented on the general business slump and the nature of the times, "I could never be here talking to you about this if times were good because my partner would never agree to sell. When things are at the bottom, he doesn't want 'em."

For James A. nothing could have seemed more opportune. Young Jim suggested as a provision of the sale that William and Ray, Jr., agree to come in with Hogle and participate in the business. Sargeant had hoped for just such an arrangement and the deal was concluded. Ray Sargeant became manager of the Denver office of James A. Hogle & Co., but he was soon drafted into the Navy

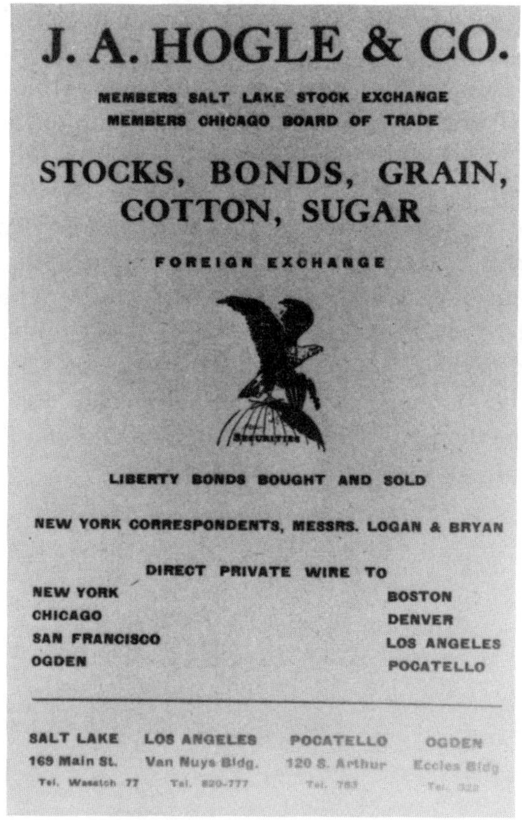

Advertisement for J. A. Hogle & Co. during World War II.

and served in the Pacific through the war. His younger brother, William, took over the Denver operation and was later made a partner of the firm.

The Sargeant, Malo takeover was another timely move, bringing additional customers and valuable employees under the Hogle banner. Moreover, it demonstrated that Hogle's investment philosophy was consistent, whether he was dealing in stocks or brokerage firms.

As the final papers concluding the acquisition were being prepared, news arrived of the great U.S. naval victory at the Battle of Midway. The darkest period of the war was over, and although final victory would take three more years of bloody fighting, the country had turned the corner. The news items on Hogle's charts after that denoted market peaks, not valleys: the Allied invasion of Africa, the fall of the German army at Stalingrad, the fall of Mussolini in Italy, the D-Day invasion, the invasion of the Philippines, V.E. Day, and V.J. Day.

After the Second World War, large institutional buyers moved into the market, and while political disasters and world news would still cause tremors on Wall Street, the sheer volume of business being transacted tended to stabilize the fluctuations. World political events would never again control the market as they had before the war, when the pioneer chartist, James A. Hogle, received his news and stock quotations rattled from the tinny depths of a Prince Albert Tobacco can.

Part V

AFFLICTION, STRUGGLE, & TRIUMPH

CHAPTER TWENTY-EIGHT

Mary Hogle's Travails

DURING THE THIRTIES Mary continued to host her lavish luncheons and dinner parties, sometimes for house guests, sometimes for a new artist in town or a visiting author. She loved to bring people of different interests and backgrounds together, and her parties were major social events, long remembered by all who attended them.

Christmas time, in particular, was a season for parties at the Hogle home. For several days during the season Mary held an open house for her friends and the employees at the office. She rarely went to the Hogle offices herself, so many of the employees remember her chiefly from these gatherings.

Employees recalled that Mary was always lively and vibrant at the affairs and that she took great effort to see that each guest was made to feel especially welcome. James, too, went out of his way to make the guests feel comfortable, often mixing special drinks for particular individuals. As the son of a saloonkeeper, he knew how to mix a good drink — iced bourbon toddies with lemon and honey were a favorite — but he was also acutely aware of the dangers of alcohol and was exceptionally temperate in its use and distribution. Perhaps taking a cue from his father's saloon tokens, he usually dispensed one drink to a customer.

The marriage of Katharine to John Tripp McTernan on July 19, 1939, was a very lavish affair. There were two ceremonies, one at the Cathedral of the Madeleine — McTernan was Catholic — and another at the Hogles' country home at 4224 South Seventh East. The country estate was then known as the Hill Farm. (Years later the property would become known as Old Farm.) The reception which followed went late into the night, and James E. recalled

James A. and Mary C. Hogle in Mexico City, about 1936.

that his father was more liberal that evening than usual in his distribution of the Champagne. Indeed, several of the guests were "well lubricated" by the evening's close. But the marriage of an only daughter was the most special of special occasions, and on this one evening at least, an exception to the rule was allowed; no one remembered going away wanting.

Another memorable social event at the farm was a party held on the afternoon of September 7, 1940. The farm had been greatly improved since Hogle acquired it. The little lakes were populated with swans, geese, and wild ducks. The idyllic and heavily wooded estate — which could easily have passed for the setting of his poem, "An Island in Arcady" — seemed particularly appropriate for the occasion, the Hogles' thirtieth wedding anniversary.

More than 150 guests were invited to the country home that day. A dozen of Mary's close friends, all members of her sewing club, assisted in receiving and serving. They included Miss Daisy

Raybould, Mrs. Roger L. Strobel, Mrs. Dean F. Brayton, Mrs. Daniel Alexander, Mrs. Percival Perkins, and Mrs. Sarah Boggs.

The home was decorated with a profusion of garden blooms. In the large dining room there were arrays of pale pink gladioli, in the living room arrangements of yellow roses, and on the tables, set about in the wooded grounds and gardens, were bright sprays of golden marigolds. The society page of the paper commented that "the event was as elegant and festive a party as was ever held in the valley."

For those who knew Mrs. Hogle only through her social activities or her parties, her life seemed the picture of contentment. There was certainly nothing to indicate that anything might be wrong. She was also very active in the community, and few outside the family knew the torment she suffered.

During the thirties, Mary continued to work through her Foundation for the betterment of society at large and needy individuals in particular. She revised, expanded and updated her pamphlet *Foods That Alkalinize and Heal* and collected testimonials in support of carrot juice and her dietary theories. She traveled and lectured on health and nutrition and became active in the American Society for the Prevention of Cancer. She was also active on the boards of numerous charitable and community organizations, continuing to contribute her time and money in support of the Art Barn, the YWCA, the Pi Phi sorority at the "U," the National Recreation Society, the Association of University Women, and the Episcopal church.

In the late thirties she took an increasingly active role in various peace organizations that were desperately trying to prevent another global war. The military build-up throughout the world was ominous, and Mary threw herself energetically into the campaign for peace. In 1938 her efforts for that cause were outlined in an article written by a colleague, Gladys Hobbs. The story gives a clear picture of Mary Hogle's activities prior to the outbreak of the war.

Salt Lake Woman Invited on Peace Tour

Enlisted in the cause of peace as a young child, and an active worker since then, Mrs. James A. Hogle has received an invitation to join the "Flying Caravan" to South America by the People's Mandate Committee.

In Los Angeles to attend the regional convention of the Soroptimist Club, Mrs. Hogle received a letter from The People's Mandate Committee in Washington, urging her to join the Caravan. The Caravan leaves from Miami on October 30th. With other members of the Caravan, Mrs. Hogle will be received by President Roosevelt and Secretary of State Cordell Hull on October 28th. She also will confer with Mrs. Roosevelt prior to her departure.

The Caravan will visit 20 countries in Central and South America. The purpose of the Caravan is to urge the ratification of treaties made at the International Peace Conference last year.

Coincidentally, Mrs. Hogle was presenting a resolution urging the American Federation of Soroptimist Clubs to become affiliated with the National Peace Conference when her invitation from the Mandate Committee came.

Mrs Hogle's father enlisted in General Grant's Army during the Civil War. He was captured and held prisoner by the Con-

The Copley family, about 1935. *Left to right*, Edward, Anna Woodward Copley, George, Mary C., and Joe.

federacy. The horror of his experience made an indelible impression on her as a child and it was this that later led to her activities in the cause of peace.

She was one of the earliest members of the Woman's League for Peace and Freedom, the organization which sponsored the People's Mandate Committee. She was also an officer and leader of the Foreign Policy Forum.

Mrs. Hogle is a charter member of the Utah Council for the Prevention of War and a member of the National Council for the Prevention of War and the Utah Peace Council.

Mary Hogle did not accept the invitation to join the Flying Caravan, however. Her reasons for turning down the informal diplomatic mission are not known, but it seems likely that her husband dissuaded her. Within a year Germany had invaded Poland and the war she had worked so long and hard to prevent was under way.

The invasion of Poland in September of 1939 and the fall of France the following spring divided the American peace movement. The isolationist "America Firsters" wanted peace at any cost. They saw the European conflict as just another manifestation of ancient and irresolvable Old World conflicts having nothing to do with the United States and best left alone. Others, Mary Hogle included, began to see that appeasing tyrants like Hitler and Mussolini did nothing but encourage their further aggression.

Although she never lost her abhorrence of war and continued to serve the Women's League for Peace and Freedom, by 1940 she also served on the Committee to Defend America by Aiding the Allies. There was nothing inconsistent in her divided allegiance. Whatever her emotional attachment to the peace movement, she also had a practical side and knew that there were times when action had to be taken.

The outbreak of the conflict was particularly troubling to Mary, however. She had spent much of her adult life preaching and campaigning against war, and she began to feel that no one had listened to her, that her warnings had gone unheeded, that her efforts had been in vain. Swept along by events, she felt helpless. All her work for peace had come to nothing. For the gentle woman who could be moved to tears over the maltreatment of a dray horse, the slaughter now taking place on the battlefields was too much to bear, and Mary became profoundly depressed over the world situation.

Although the war in Europe may have been the immediate cause of her despair, the family knew that she had suffered serious attacks of depression before. Mary's personal antidote for the problem seems to have been activity. She tried to bury herself in the work of the Mary C. Hogle Foundation. During much of 1940 and early 1941, she traveled and gave lectures on health and diet and continued to distribute her pamphlets. Then, on April 20, came yet another blow. She was staying in Los Angeles when she got the news and immediately wrote her husband for help:

My Dear Jim:

This morning — we received by way of the Foundation a letter from the Federal Trade Commission asking for a copy of the Foundation Pamphlet and any information we can submit as to the reasons for and methods of conducting the foundation. So I presume that the long-expected investigation is about to begin [with the end] of suppressing the pamphlet.

A year ago Mr. Grant spoke to me of this very eventuality and begged me to examine the feasibility of protecting myself against an attack by this very body. He took me to call on the lawyers, Driscol and L'Bourgeois who had devised a method of protecting people through a trust estate.

It seems a terrible pity that a program such as I have outlined, that has saved so many from the fate predicted by doctors, should have to succumb, just through lack of protection of a perfectly legitimate sort. I asked you at least twice to look into the matter but I don't believe that you were impressed with the importance of it.

I am writing in great haste to ask you and Mr. Bradley, to whom I am sending a copy of this letter, to find out at once if there [is anything] to prevent my forming a trust estate for the sole purpose of defending this, my life work.

You will see by the enclosed report that the receipts for the past week were seventy dollars which is, of course, the highest yet. Seattle, San Diego, Tucson and Kansas City have been ahead of Los Angeles but Mr. Grant says that his orders are growing since I appeared on the scene.

I had the most wonderful welcome at the health food stores in Santa Monica on Thursday, and the Woman at Westwood

Anna Woodward Copley, Mary Hogle's mother, in a photograph labeled "Los Angeles — 1932."

said she needed me out there to encourage some of the despairing ones.

Dr. Walker at Long Beach is dispensing seven hundred quarts of juice a day and is just waiting for your consent before buying ten thousand of my pamphlets AT COST! Southern California will tell the whole world . . . .

There is an amendment that I need to make in the discussion on surgery. See if you don't think it's advisable. It could be stamped in red. It is this: "There are experienced doctors in every community that can be called in consultation with regard to surgery for the removal of tumours. Their decision is usually based on years of experience." Seems to me that that should be enough to [appease] the A.M.A.

I do need advice so badly and not a soul here to give it to me. I hate to bother you with one thing more than you already have, but I guess we are going to have to face this problem right away.

The offer of Dr. Walker in Long Beach to purchase 10,000 copies of the pamphlet "at cost" was much more generous than it may appear at first glance. Ames Bagley, who had worked closely with Mrs. Hogle on the pamphlet and who had compiled much of the background research for the work, recalled:

Mary Hogle never intended that the pamphlet would show a profit. It was subsidized all the way. We'd send out the pamphlet for twenty-five cents but it cost us thirty-five cents to print. Our price never covered the cost of publication let alone the administrative cost or research that went behind it . . . . There was never a debit entry made on the orders. If someone wrote us for the pamphlet, we'd send it and if they paid us later, fine. The offer to buy 10,000 at cost was probably the best deal we ever made.

The letter indicates the widespread recognition that Mary Hogle enjoyed in the fields of health and nutrition before the war. She autographed thousands of the pamphlets for faithful believers of her program, but the impending investigation of her work overshadowed any sense of personal triumph.

The Federal Trade Commission's inquiry was in response to complaints that they had received from medical doctors who believed that the pamphlet's claims for carrot juice and vitamin A would dissuade patients with tumors from opting for surgery. The Foundation had received letters from time to time that had accused Mrs. Hogle of peddling quackery. Mary had, from the earliest editions of the pamphlet, encouraged her readers to seek professional help. Each of the editions published over the previous ten years had cautioned cancer patients to seek early professional care, and each had outlined conventional methods of treatment. But each new edition also contained a longer list of testimonials from people who claimed complete nonsurgical cures.

Nutrition and Quackery

Mary C. Hogle was not alone in advocating cancer prevention through nutrition. Through the thirties both the popular press and the scientific journals contained frequent articles on the probable relationship of diet to cancer. It should be noted that a majority of the scientists of that period believed that cancer and diet were related. Mary and her collaborator Ames Bagley compiled this information, and each edition of her pamphlet contained data from the latest studies. Mary was a tireless campaigner for research into the relationship between diet and cancer, and throughout the thirties she privately funded, published, and distributed studies in nutrition and lectured extensively on the subject.

But her "theories" were strongly opposed by the medical establishment of her day, which genuinely regarded nutritionist approaches as the very worst sort of quackery — and some of them were just that. Dietary fads of all kinds — vitamin elixirs, folk remedies, secret herbal formulas, special cleansing diets, and even starvation — were promoted by various self-styled nutritionists as cures for cancer. The medical profession rightly fought the dietary quacks with all the means at their disposal. Unfortunately, the campaign was equally successful against serious researchers into the actual role of nutrition in the development of cancer.

Quackery has thrived in all areas of medicine for centuries, but in the area of cancer treatment — where the medical profession offered little or no hope — charlatans abounded. The history of quackery and the history of cancer research are intimately linked. What was most lacking in modern scientific methodology was the one thing that the cancer patient wanted most — hope. The scientific method and modern medical practice, with their emphasis on objective clinical approaches, were fine when they were dealing with problems for which they had both a cause and a treatment. Cancer was incurable, and the cold truth of such a diagnosis was hard to accept. Denial, anger, frustration, and suspicion are part and parcel of the reaction to the disease. It wasn't simple ignorance or gullibility that drove cancer patients to the quacks; it was human nature. Desperation turned the afflicted to "Magnetic" and "Electric" treatments, to faith healers, to the peddlers of worthless nostrums and secret elixirs.

Dangerous frauds preyed upon the gullible public well into the twentieth century. It was not until the passage of the Pure Food and Drug Act of 1906 and the subsequent creation of its enforcement arm, the Food and Drug Administration, that any progress was made against the nationwide scandal of medical quackery.

But the problem was not restricted to the peddlers of bottled medicine or mechanical cures. There were also traveling lecturers and self-degreed "professors" who toured the health circuit preaching their own personal secrets of long life, health, happiness, and sexual potency — and who made a good living lecturing and selling their books. The scientific community was as appalled by the pseudo-scientists as by the medical quacks. Indeed, the general feeling was that these new witch doctors threatened the very foundations of modern science, and that if something weren't done to curtail the false prophets, the world would be plunged back into the superstitious medical practices of the Dark Ages.

The FDA was ill-suited to taking on the special problem of the traveling lecturer. There were First Amendment rights of free speech involved that were clearly beyond the scope of the Pure Food and Drug Act. Through the first three decades of the century the "health circuit lecturers" peddled their theories unhindered. But free speech has its limits, and the abuses of some of these health preachers were horrific. One man, a Dr. Kaadt, told diabetics to throw away their insulin, and at least twelve who took his advice died. The medical messiahs often augmented their dietary theories with strong doses of fundamentalist religion to further protect themselves under the First Amendment.

The scientific and medical communities increasingly adopted a strategy of discrediting the preachers with information and lecture campaigns of their own warning the public to avoid "Unproved Theories." "Unproved" became the new watchword in the battle against health quackery. The American Medical Association and other professional groups lobbied Congress to strengthen existing laws to address the problem. During the thirties the Federal Trade Commission, which already had power to enjoin the distribution of false advertising, was given new teeth to stop the interstate distribution of false medical and nutritional theories, and the U.S. postal authorities were enlisted in the effort. A new Inquisition was taking place, and it was directed against a new kind of heretic — anyone who preached medical theories outside the prevailing and accepted scientific views.

On the face of it, this was all well and good, but the scientific method depends upon strict and exacting observations and measurements. The scientific instrumentation of the day was inadequate to the task of supplying the needed tests and proofs. Even a casual review of the court cases from the late thirties and forties reveals that a number of terms, including "unproved," "unprovable," "unsound," and "unknown," were becoming synonymous with "false."

Biochemists in nutrition research found themselves in a kind of no man's land. In fact, their techniques and instruments could only follow the digestive and nutritive processes so far. Theories abounded concerning the role that particular compounds and molecules might play in the development of cancer at the subcellular level, but the evidence was beyond the range of the available technology. The attitude of the American Medical Association toward nutrition-based cancer theories was clear. During the thirties a common medical adage was "Doctors deal in facts." Those engaged in the lucrative "health food industries" portrayed the attitude of the AMA as self-serving. Their own attitude toward the subject was no less so.

The dangers of nutritionist quackery were great, and society had to protect itself from those who bilked the public and endangered the lives of thousands while wrapping themselves in the protective cloak of the First Amendment. As more regulatory laws were enacted, the scope of legal authority broadened. What started as a campaign against scientific ignorance became a self-righteous battle to preserve the medical and scientific status quo. The entire field of nutrition sciences became suspect, and one of the results of this campaign was to drive competent researchers from the field altogether.

For those who remained, funding was exceptionally hard to come by. Dietary science became a minor area of study on college campuses, often relegated to the backwater of home economics departments. And efforts to discredit the field did not stop there. Some researchers and advocates of nutritional approaches to cancer prevention or dietary therapy became the targets of governmental investigation and prosecution — Mary C. Hogle among them.

Through the late thirties and forties, the *Journal of the American Medical Association* kept track of the quacks, and the government's success in prosecuting them, in a column entitled "Bureau of Investigations." In January of 1940 they reported the successful prosecution for mail fraud of a man whose prescription for long life was a diet of carrot juice, orange juice, alfalfa sprouts, and eggs. The man had touted the vitamin content of his diet as a preventive against the onset of cancer. The journal applauded his prosecution and conviction and quoted from the trial record: "No amount of chemical elements will prevent or cure serious conditions such as cancer." This was the AMA's approved canon and creed on the subject.

The medical and governmental bias that gave funding preference to diagnosis and cure over cancer prevention research can be dated to policy decisions made in the late thirties: There were promising new areas of cancer research to be explored and new disciplines were opening up. Radiation and chemotherapy were in their earliest phase. New and better surgical tools and procedures were being developed. The new techniques, diagnostic tools, surgical devices, therapeutic compounds, and radioactive elements were our front-line weapons in the newly declared "War on Cancer." These weapons were expensive and funding was limited. The choices that were made seemed logical at the time. The nutrition field was — to a large extent — abandoned to the amateurs.

The diligent researcher undertaking a historical re-examination of the early work on diet and its relationship to cancer should approach the Indicus Medicus with a divining rod in one hand. Some of the best-known advocates of prevention through diet were quacks or borderline quacks. Some of the best researchers in the field held views which supported the very worst of the charlatans. The English surgeon Sir William Arbuthnot Lane said: "I will never have cancer and what I am doing any man can do." He claimed that cancer was primarily caused by diet, and he was famous for his statement that "there is only one disease, deficient drainage." Dr. Horace Packard said that "all disease [is] the result of loss of immunity and that immunity depends chiefly upon vitamins found in foods." Alfred W. McCann believed that there was a direct relationship between known causes of constipation and some causes of cancer. Benjamin Gaylord Hauser touted the vitamin content of fruit juices for protection against disease. G. E. Harter, creator of "the defensive diet" claimed that all disease was the result of "the habitual and continued eating of the wrong foods at the wrong times in the wrong combinations." Dr. J. H. Tilden supported Harter's theories to the point that food itself became for him the root of all evil, and so he prescribed starvation diets as a cancer cure. Sorting out the quacks from the scientists was not easy.

Mary Hogle was not a laboratory researcher. Rather, she was a person with a respectable scientific background who became an indefatigable reader in the current major scientific literature — a synthesizer and interpreter of the laboratory findings of others. Scholarship of all kinds has traditionally depended upon the work of field researchers, who discover the "facts," and interpreters, who create a meaningful context within which the laboratory findings can benefit society.

Mary Hogle was an independently wealthy woman who came to believe in the relationship of diet to cancer. She was a dietary theorist and patron of the health sciences who sponsored, compiled, and published research which supported her own theories. She was a "doer" and not the sort of person to wait forty years for final proof if humanity could be served now. Mary's life's work became to gather the best scientific information she could find and distribute it to the general public where it could do some good.

As one who had herself been victimized by some of the most famous quacks of the period, including the famous Dr. Tilden, at worst she could be accused of the fallacy of "special pleading." In Mary's ardor to find evidence which supported her theories she violated the most basic principle of the scientific method, objectivity (a principle which has been adhered to imperfectly by even the best of scientists). Some of her views on nutrition were indeed in error, and some of the sources she quoted were perhaps not the best of

those she had read. But unlike the "health practitioners" who bilked
the public for millions of dollars in worthless remedies, Mary was
not motivated by financial gain, but by a true desire to help "suffering humanity." Although she was a strong advocate of vitamins —
particularly vitamin A in cancer prevention — she was not a pro-
ponent of vitamin supplements, preparations, or tonics and recommended instead the consumption of foods rich in essential elements.
Her own favorite was carrots, and she was widely known simply as
the Carrot Juice Lady.

Through the Mary C. Hogle Foundation she distributed funds
to the needy as well as to community health organizations, hospitals, and a number of research foundations, including the American Society for the Prevention of Cancer and — after the organization's goals had changed — the American Cancer Society.

For all her altruism, there were certain similarities between
Mary's materials and those of practitioners whose interest in cancer
prevention was motivated solely by greed. Because her pamphlets
were directed at the general public, they contained conclusions
rather than research data or tables compiled from laboratory experiments. Some information was drawn from personal experience or
was otherwise anecdotal. There were many personal testimonials
and endorsements as well — the very kind of "evidence" made
popular by the patent medicine trade and so detested by both research scientists and the AMA — and it is unlikely that this anecdotal material would ever stand for real case studies. Mary clearly
relied heavily on the research of others, and one of her principal
sources was a research scientist and statistician with the Franklin
Institute, Dr. Frederick Hoffman.

In 1937 Hoffman published *Cancer and Diet, With Facts and
Observations on Related Subjects*. The text was divided into four
parts. The first reviewed the historical development of dietary
theories on cancer arranged in periods from 1777 to 1935. The
second dealt with the modern diet. Hoffman correlated various
food consumption statistics from modern countries with the incidence of cancer and demonstrated that increased consumption of
fat and cholesterol increases the frequency of cancer. In the third
section Hoffman offered his own theories on cancer metabolism and

causation. He claimed that tumor origin depends on nutritional factors both qualitative and quantitative. He also placed specific blame for some cancers on the increase of carcinogenic toxins in the environment of modern urbanized societies — identifying specific substances such as lead, arsenic, and tobacco as being carcinogenic. He also believed that modern food processing techniques and preservatives were in part responsible for the increase in cancer deaths in modern industrialized countries. (Hoffman cited a number of studies which claimed that vitamins helped protect against cancer, but his own statistical work showed no such relationship. He believed that increased vitamin intake might even *cause* cancer.) The fourth section of his book consisted entirely of statistical tables compiled from various countries, relating aspects of diet to cancer.

Hoffman believed that his extensive historical research, statistical tables, and careful analysis would lay the groundwork for further scientific studies on diet and cancer. In 1937, the *New England Journal of Medicine* reviewed Hoffman's work, and while praising his data collection had little praise for the thrust of his argument: "While he feels that a definite relation exists between cancer and diet, he does not claim to have found the exact answer. Much of the evidence is contradictory as for instance the fact that reliable workers have taken a stand both for and against certain factors in the diet. After careful study of the book, the reviewer feels the answer is not yet proved."

The kind of proof that the *New England Journal of Medicine* wanted could not be forthcoming. Statistical tables proved nothing, and it would be more than thirty years before the biochemists would have the tools to demonstrate the links suggested by Hoffman's data. Hoffman's "unproved" theories counted little more than those of Gaylord Hauser and the rest. If the work of men like Frederick Hoffman could be so easily dismissed, then it was little wonder that the study of diet and cancer was — for all intents and purposes — abandoned.

Mary Hogle was a firm believer in Dr. Hoffman's research, and she frequently quoted his work. Unlike Hoffman, however, Mary was convinced that cellular immunity was linked to certain vitamins, especially vitamin A. Mary was sensitive to the opinions of the medical profession and knew too that her theories were well outside established treatment and medical practice. She was willing to include in her pamphlet any number of cautionary warnings, but she was not willing to give up her belief in the relationship of cancer to diet.

More than any of her many other interests and projects, Mary considered health and nutrition her life's work and cancer prevention, rather than cure, the one true solution for that disease. Now that cause was being threatened, and there was more than a little desperation in the letter she wrote to her husband about the Federal Trade Commission's investigation of her work.

Mary implied in her letter that James A. had neglected to have their attorney, William M. Bradley, look into the matter of the pamphlet and any problems that might arise with the FTC. But James had, in fact, given Mr. Bradley a copy of the pamphlet and had instructed him to look into the matter thoroughly. Bradley did what any good attorney would do under the circumstances. He sought the expert advice of a medical doctor and asked him to evaluate the material contained in Mary's publication. Apparently the doctor, whose name is unknown, informed Bradley that Mary's dietary theories were unsound. Bradley then advised Hogle that before the FTC moved to suppress the pamphlet, it would be wiser for the sake of the firm, the Foundation, and the partnership to voluntarily suspend publication.

Hogle had not taken any action in the matter earlier since there hadn't seemed to be any concerted effort on the part of the government to investigate the Foundation or Mary's publication. Now that an investigation seemed certain, it was time to tell Mary of his decision.

Their marriage had always been one of continuous compromise. Although they often disagreed and even argued on many matters, from household finance to politics, they had not had a dispute before in which mutual accommodation was not possible.

The decision of her husband, on the advice of Mr. Bradley, to suspend publication of *Foods That Alkalinize and Heal* was not a matter in which accommodation was possible. This new setback followed closely upon the collapse of her peace efforts, and Mary felt particularly adamant that her work in health and nutrition continue. Her husband felt equally strongly that Bradley was right. The dispute which must have followed went unrecorded. In the end, however, James A. prevailed. The pamphlet had gone through eight revised editions with a worldwide distribution in excess of 200,000 copies. The eighth would be the last. For many years thereafter, the Foundation continued to distribute the pamphlet to those who wrote specifically requesting it, but no additional revisions or printings were undertaken.

CHAPTER TWENTY-NINE

A Private War

NO LIFE OF SUBSTANCE AND MEANING is free of suffering, struggle, disappointment, and failure. Strength of character is not a quality built on continuous good fortune. Through the forties, the Hogles had more than their share of hardship and affliction, and for Mary the times were particularly trying.

America's entry into the war following the attack on Pearl Harbor had been a severe blow, and during those early war years Mary was deeply depressed. She believed so strongly in her work and her many projects that she began to see a conspiracy behind the coincidental collapse of her most passionately held causes. There seemed no shortage of possible conspiratorial culprits. Certainly the government was to blame through the FTC, but during the war Mary also suspected the all-seeing FBI and the self-serving meddlers in the AMA. Although she may have felt that her primary antagonist was the government, her suspicions also fell on her neighbors and even her husband, whose advisors, at least, tended to side with those who were against her.

Mary's bouts with depression and periodic withdrawal from the world alternated with periods of intense activity. She had always been a doer, and in spite of her personal state, she struggled to accomplish things, whatever the obstacles, no matter how great her anguish and frustration, no matter who was, or seemed to be, against her.

As she had during World War I, Mary entertained and instructed soldiers stationed at nearby Fort Douglas and Kearns Field. She became active in the Republican Party and was elected president of the Federation of Women's Republican Clubs. She worked for the League of Women Voters, the Salt Lake chapter of the Silver Star Legion, the Woman's Christian Temperance Union, and the Reading Room for the Blind. She expanded her work with the YWCA and became increasingly active in the National Recreation Association. The remarkable thing about Mary during the war years was that in spite of her personal feelings of failure, disappointment, and depression, she continued to have an enormous effect on those around her and the community at large. In January of 1943 the *Salt Lake Tribune* reported on one of the many awards she garnered in those trying times. The story was entitled "Mary C. Hogle Wins Honors for Utah" and read in part:

> Devotion to an ideal . . . greater recreational facilities for kids . . . all kinds of them . . . brought national recognition Thursday to a Salt Lake woman who has geared her life to promoting the interests of humanity.
>
> She is Mrs. James A. Hogle . . . who believes the world owes kids happy childhoods. She works at her belief by fostering recreational centers and facilities. Now her good works have

George, James A., Mary, and Jim Hogle at the Brighton cabin, about 1940.

returned dividends, for her name has just been inscribed on the roll of honor of the National Recreation Society.

The announcement was made by Major George W. Braden, western field director for the organization, on his annual visit of inspection to Salt Lake City. Mrs. Hogle's life-long work earned her [the honor].

Playgrounds and Recreational Centers, she says, can reduce delinquency. She works with other association members in fostering playgrounds, athletic fields, baseball diamonds, tennis courts, skating rinks and other centers.

She has worked for the establishment of playgrounds for Negro children and other underprivileged groups as well as for boys and girls more apt to get their fair share of good things in this world.

During the depression days she worked with groups to secure jobs for youth. Although she has been prominent in women's club life and civic affairs, her interest always has centered around the ideal of service.

When Mary wasn't working, she was fighting her recurrent bouts of depression. For a time she played duplicate bridge with her friends the Rayboulds and Harriet MacClosky, but she found the game unsuited to her temperament and wrote, "It is utterly dull and loses all the fun of playing because the gambling element is so lacking."

For some years a Mrs. Pidge had worked at the Hogles' home as a live-in cook and housekeeper. When she left in August of 1943, Mary appropriated her room for her own purposes. On September 19, in a revealing letter to her children, she wrote of the room and of her battle with depression.

> I can't tell you how cosy it is up here under the tall lamp at night and by the south window by day. Now I understand why I have been late to every function for so long. It is because I can't tear myself away from this room, lined not only with every comfort, but with my favorite pictures and books . . . . Now I have inherited not only the comfort but the cooking, and worse than that, the cleaning of this great house.
>
> . . . You will be glad to hear that I have got hold of myself to the extent of being able to listen to the music that comes in over the radio; so "Pa" is having an orgy of sweet sounds as well as news broadcasts. He should have relegated me to the back,

upstairs room long ago and had his accustomed freedom, but if he thought of it, he didn't suggest it. He had been told, Ed said, that the way to get me back to a normal state of mind was to let me have my way in everything. Finally, when the one who balked me at every turn disappeared, I came to.

Today Mrs. Boggs' landlady happened to remember a wonderful notice that the L.D.S. Women had in their *Relief Society Magazine* about me way back in March. If I had known about it then, it would have ended my torture in regard to what people thought of me and what they might do to the family in consequence. . . . Why couldn't someone have told me about it or sent us a copy of the magazine. Aunt Amelia said, "There I told you so! There is no one who doesn't think well of you."

The notice in the *Relief Society Magazine* of the L.D.S. church was an editorial comment on Mary's award from the National Recreation Society, and the editor affirmed the Society's assent to the prestigious award, saying in part, "Mrs. Hogle deserves this high honor. Thousands of Utah children and young people have been blessed with opportunities for happiness and progress through her boundless kindness."

A Legacy of Service

Mary's continuous social and charitable activities had a profound influence on her three children, and during the forties and early fifties their own contributions and organizational involvements closely paralleled her own.

As a child Katharine had watched and even participated in her mother's community activities. Once, dressed as a clown, she toured offices and poker games to collect funds for a new YWCA home for working women.

At Rowland Hall School and St. Mark's Cathedral she developed a friendship with Bishop Moulton which resonated through her youth and her planning for life: The Bishop had a profound consideration for people — all people. At the Bishop's School in La Jolla, California, it was Bishop Moulton who presided over Katharine's graduation ceremony in 1928 and gave her the prize in English — ironically, according to Katharine, as she had not inherited her mother's gift of expression.

Following her parents' suggestions, Katharine had gone to the Bishop's School and then to Sarah Lawrence College, hoping to fulfill their goals for her. Privately the young girl hated to leave her beloved Rowland Hall School in Salt Lake and her friends. When she finished college she went on to take her master's degree in the social sciences at Columbia University in 1938. She met John McTernan while she was doing intern work at the National Labor Relations Board in Washington, where she "was paid a mighty $90 a month." They married, and John gave his support to Katharine as she pursued her interests and activities, which he shared. (He wanted her to be a good cook, too — but, according to Katharine herself, "that remained a dream.")

Katharine was influenced by her mother's example as a teacher and believed that through teaching she could extend her knowledge of the world about her and would be able to better follow her father's suggestion that she take up social work. She taught economics at the University of California at Berkeley and at the California Labor School (1941–45). When her two daughters, Kathleen McTernan and Deborah Copley McTernan, were born, she gave up teaching in order to devote full time to them. They seemed to her to be celebrity beauties straight from heaven and gave her a feeling of love for everything and everybody on earth. She saw so much of her mother in her older daughter as she grew; she even expressed herself in Mary Hogle's inimitable style. "Kathy was poetic and expressive. Deborah was the wit."

When the children began school, Katharine took time to become active in community work. The "social work" suggested by her father came to mean social involvement. In 1939, she joined a long and difficult legislative campaign on behalf of small farmers and agricultural laborers. During World War II she joined in a civil defense program and a committee that engaged in education on the dangers of Nazism. After that war she devoted herself to working for peace, eventually joining the Women's International League for Peace and Freedom of which her mother was a co-founder.

She also followed her lifelong interest in Native Americans by developing community support for assistance in a variety of programs related to the development of employment, youth counseling, health services, land rights, human rights, and environmental protection.

Katharine believed that her parents' guidance and examples gave her confidence and a sense of having done the "right things." She noted, however, that they often wished she had chosen different paths in her teaching and "social work." Her father did allow in one of their many talks that she had "a right to challenge the way things are — even the constitutionality of certain laws. After all," he said, "I have always been against the income tax."

Mary's elder son, Jim (James Edward) was influenced by both parents and became a dedicated "doer." During the forties, he followed his mother's example by directing or serving on the boards of numerous community, church, and charitable organizations, including the Vestry of St. Mark's Church (1941), the Victory Fund Committee (1942), the War Finance Committee (1943–45), the Community Chest as chairman (1947), and from 1948 to 1950, the Salt Lake Board of Education. As had his mother, he took an active interest in the support of the arts, and he was the founder of the Utah Opera Society. He supported Rowland Hall School and served as chairman of the school's board of directors. In 1945 he accepted a position on the board of St. Mark's Hospital, a post he would hold for twenty-five years. In 1950 he founded the Utah Zoological Society, which oversaw the operation of Hogle Zoo. (Jim's eldest son, James E. Hogle, Jr., would continue the tradition, assuming the chairmanship of the society twenty-seven years later.)

Not all of James E.'s activities were inspired by his mother, however. He would serve for twelve years on the board of Westminster College. Jim's father felt so strongly about the great value of his education at St. Paul's School that he thought there should be an equally fine preparatory school for boys in Salt Lake City. He suggested to Jim that he discuss the matter with Bishop Richard Watson, which he did — a discussion which resulted in the founding of St. Mark's School (which some years later merged with Rowland Hall).

James A. was pleased with his elder son's accomplishments in the brokerage business. His protégé served several terms as president of the Salt Lake Stock Exchange. He was elected a governor of the National Association of Stock Exchange Firms, serving three three-year terms, and was a governor of the New York Stock Exchange. Jim continued his civic activities for many years.

Mary's younger son, George Hollister, was probably closest to his mother in temperament. She profoundly influenced his attitudes toward life, and he seemed to have inherited from her a keen interest in health sciences and a profound abhorrence of war. But until 1941, George had followed closely in his father's footsteps. He had attended both St. Paul's and the Sheffield Scientific School at Yale. He had even joined his father's old fraternity, the St. Elmo Society.

But when George began his studies at Yale his interest and inclination was to study health, medicine, and nutrition. Initially he enrolled in a course of biochemistry at "Sheff." When he told James A. of the course of study he was beginning, his father's reaction surprised him. "Why would you want to do that?" he asked. He then explained to his obviously confused son that the family business was in stocks and mining, not in health, medicine, or biochemistry.

George's older brother was already studying for a degree in mining engineering at the University of California. Perhaps, his father suggested, it would be better if George went into something which complemented his brother's education, something like metallurgy. The suggestion was, of course, taken, and George received his degree from Yale in metallurgy.

For a time it seemed that George would follow the career his father had planned for him. With his brother he worked at the Eureka Prospect Mine in Nevada and later, like Jim, he joined the family firm, became a member of the New York Stock Exchange, and represented J. A. Hogle & Co. on the Floor of that exchange for several years. But his personal tendencies toward his mother's interests were strong. Circumstance and personal belief would drastically alter the career of the youngest Hogle.

George had several pacifist friends, including Bayard Rustin (a co-founder with George Hauser of CORE), and he also became interested in the Society of Friends (the Quakers). No doubt under their influence, as well as his mother's, he himself became a sincere pacifist. When the war came, he applied for and received Conscientious Objector status from the Draft Board. His career as a stock broker ended abruptly. During most of the war, George served his alternative service working in a malaria research program at the Massachusetts General Hospital. Here the young Hogle's interest in medicine was reawakened.

Following the war George received another interesting communication from his father. Now that he was free, his father said, George should return home to take care of his ailing mother. The suggestion came as a complete surprise to George. He had already made plans for the immediate future; he had volunteered to accompany a party of Quakers to Germany to assist in the post-war relief effort there. The suggestion that George should drop everything and nurse his mother was perhaps prompted by the elder Hogle's experience of caring for his own father during his last illness and a concession to George's interest in health. But it was also an indication of the elder Hogle's own inability to deal with his wife's periodic bouts with severe depression.

George informed his father of his decision to pursue his own career. He offered later to return to his father the substantial interest he had been given in the family firm, but James A. rejected the offer and said that his son should continue to participate as a capital partner. It was then that George finally decided to go into medicine. Even though he was a graduate engineer, Columbia's College of Physicians and Surgeons accepted him, and he received his MD there, interning at Presbyterian Hospital in New York City. (He later did postgraduate work in psychiatry in London and at the great Jungian school in Switzerland. After having taught and practiced in the Palo Alto area for more than thirty years, he was made president of the Jungian Society.)

In December of 1945, George returned briefly to Salt Lake. In stark contrast to the gay Christmas activities of the pre-war years, the Christmas of 1945 was bleak. There was no tree, no festive parties, not even a wreath to mark the holiday season.

The United Nations was only two months old that December, and a poster commemorating the founding had been printed which displayed the flags of all the member nations. George cut the small colorful flags from two of the posters, pasted them together, and then used them to decorate a small tree at the Hogle home. Mary was deeply moved by her son's touching gesture, and it seemed to lift her sagging spirits. George had intuitively found a partial remedy for his mother's depression. Symbolically, at least, the little tree represented a ray of hope, a shared understanding between the mother and her son, and a reaffirmation of Mary Hogle's lifelong quest for peace.

James A. very seldom gave his wife presents, even on those occasions when gift-giving is customarily prescribed. Ames Bagley remembered a birthday party given for Mrs. Hogle in the forties where Mary asked her husband why he hadn't given her a gift. Hogle laughed and said, "My dear, how can I possibly select a present for you? You give yourself presents every day." For the woman who, indeed, seemed to have everything, gift selection was a knotty problem better left alone. But far from being insensitive to sentiment, James A., like his son, recognized the superiority of the small gesture over the lavish gift.

During one of Mary's episodes of depression in the late forties James sought to lift his wife's spirits with just such a gesture. He wrote a fellow Yale alumnus, Edward Weeks, who was a senior editor of the *Atlantic Monthly*.

Dear Mr. Weeks,

The enclosed verses were originally written to my fiancée in 1910 but have been much altered. The last line since a recent illness of hers. So far as I know they have not been seen by anyone, except our three children and the woman who typed them.

The *Atlantic* is the only monthly we subscribe to now that publishes poetry. That is the reason I am sending the verses to you, knowing that my wife will see them if you use them — in which case all I ask is that my initials, J.A.H. be attached. She would understand while my business friends would only scoff at my sentiment or deride my effort.

At school when I played football, red head Julian Day and Reginald Kauffman would have been surprised at my intrusion into the *Horae Scholasticae*. Day is living in London and Kauffman is gone. . . . Henry Canby, a classmate at Sheff would never understand, I am sure, how a seemingly successful stock broker could write verses you might publish and no doubt would be right.

I was interested in your "St. Nicholas" article in the last *Atlantic.* . . . I dislike the same books you do, which gives me the courage to inflict you with this.

You are a busy man and if the verses are not suitable, don't take the time to reply; just return them and this letter to me in the enclosed, self-addressed, stamped envelope.

Yours very truly,
James A. Hogle

Hogle's reticence to reveal himself as a closet post-Romantic poet is understandable. Certainly his office manager, the tough-minded Cliff Johnson, would have found it hard to belief that the man in the back office could possibly be working on anything except his charts. But the private intellectual life of the west's foremost financial analyst was a far cry from the expectations of those who knew him only in business circles.

"An Island in Arcady" had undergone hundreds of changes over the years. Although its scansion remained regular iambic pentameter, the entire structure of the poem had been substantially altered by continuous revision. The 1949 version was more conventional than its 1910 counterpart, in both its imagery and its sparser use of slant rhyme. The rhyme scheme itself remained unconventional and, as the numerous versions indicate, random. What is most significant, however, is the altered intent of the poem as expressed in the last four lines. Like George's U.N. Christmas tree, the theme of the work had become "peace."

AN ISLAND IN ARCADY

An azure lake, font of a mountain stream
    Enfolds an Isle, all clad in purest green.
Kissed only by the rain upon its face,
    Its crystal shadow casts a fond embrace;
Each passing cloud enshrined this sacred place,
    A vision on earth of heavenly grace.

When first, from the merging stream I gazed
    Across its cedar crown and willow strand,

Saw mirror'd in shadow, high peaks upraised,
    Like watchful spirits sent to guard this land,
Then with thrill entranced, as in a dream,
    Loved I forever more this Isle and Stream.

And so, like this, one day I found thee, dear,
    Swept not in life's deep flow, but led to dream,
And laugh or scoff at fate, yet love to fear,
    So little had life's action been thy scene
To rouse thy slumbering spirit from its dream
    And teach thy fearful heart a love serene.

And then some happy days gave light to me
    To see what lay beneath that pure and pale face,
And bring to pass through love what had to be
    To reach thy heart, that in this worldly space
Thy life should round itself in all its grace —
    Gain real peace — and win the final race.

The poem was probably too sentimental for the *Atlantic Monthly* editors of 1949, and they returned it without comment. But for James Hogle the sentiment was real and was as sincere an expression of his devotion as the original had been forty years earlier.

CHAPTER THIRTY

The Renaissance Man

JAMES A. HOGLE had spent his entire career building something which could be passed on to his posterity. His own frugality would ensure that the bulk of his capital would remain intact for the benefit of his children. His attitude toward that capital is especially evident in the management of his large real estate holdings.

He had been slowly bringing Jim (James E.) along, grooming him to take over the family business when the time came. In the early forties his son had a number of responsibilities with the firm, including working with the real estate department. Mr. Richardson, the property manager, informed the younger Hogle on one occasion of an offer from Safeway Food Stores to purchase the old South Temple home built by the first James Hogle. This home had been given to the three Hogle children by their grandmother but was managed by the real estate department along with the other family holdings. Jim assumed that the decision to dispose of the property was his prerogative. The old home had fallen into disrepair over the years, and the offer from Safeway seemed a handsome price, so he directed Mr. Richardson to sell.

When James A. learned that his father's home was being sold he became most upset. He didn't berate his son for the mistake, but his displeasure was evident. "How in the world could this have happened?" he asked. His dismay was not sentimental. The elder Hogle knew that the property would become much more valuable as time passed. It was to the forward-looking Hogle "A key corner on South Temple," and however run-down the property might have seemed at the time, its value could do nothing but increase. "Well," he finally remarked to his son, "We can take the money and use it in the market. Maybe we can make up the loss that way."

Whenever Hogle saw an under-priced piece of property, he bought it. But the acquisitions were seldom made with the intent of turning the property over later for a profit. In fact, when Hogle bought real estate properties, he never intended to sell them. By the mid-forties he had two dozen or so parcels in Salt Lake, among them a large piece on the southwest corner of First South and Second East. That property was occupied by some old shacks on Second East, an auto body shop and lot on First South and, directly on the corner, a dilapidated beer parlor. This establishment was something of an embarrassment to the family as it was kitty corner from St. Mark's Cathedral.

William Nightingale, the president of Mountain Fuel Supply Company, wanted to acquire the land for the company's headquarters building and had asked Hogle several times if he was willing to sell it. The answer had always been "No."

Nightingale approached the younger Hogle and told him of the fine building that Mountain Fuel wanted to build on the property and that the company was willing to pay a handsome price. The property was appraised at $125,000, and Nightingale offered to pay $250,000. To Jim this seemed an incredibly good price for an old beer parlor and body shop, and he informed his father of the generous offer. But once again his father was anything but enthusiastic. He told his son that however fabulous the present offer seemed, if his children kept the property, some years down the road it would be worth many times Nightingale's offer. But, after discussing the matter with the property manager and comparing the prices that commercial lots were then selling for, Jim recommended that the property be sold to Mountain Fuel Supply, and it was. Once again James A. invested the money in the market to "Make up the loss." Thirty years later, a similar downtown lot would sell for ten times the price and the elder Hogle was again proven right.

One odd parcel of Hogle property, on 17th South just west of Foothill Boulevard, was a large residential piece that had remained undeveloped. Representatives of Salt Lake's Jewish community approached Hogle and asked him what he was planning to do with the property. He replied that he had no particular use in mind for it and was informed that the Jewish community was interested in the lot as a site for their social center. "Well in that case," Hogle told them, "You can have it. I'll be happy to give it to you." Hogle's generosity in the matter was perhaps motivated by the fact that some of his best customers and closest friends were Jewish. It was perhaps also meant as a strong statement to the less open minded of his staff as to what the boss thought of their anti-Semitism. But then, too, Hogle contributed generously to many religious organizations. He donated land to the L.D.S. church for ward houses; money, stock, and land to the Episcopal church of Utah; and he made numerous cash donations to various church-operated schools and hospitals in the Salt Lake area. His philanthropy in the religious sphere was nothing if not ecumenical. He

Jim and Bonnie Hogle and Jodie Taylor, their long-time houseman and gardener, feed rare Siberian tigers born at Hogle Zoo.

Duck hunters Jim and James A., about 1943.

had always believed that his capitalism was linked to social and spiritual responsibility, and if a collection plate was being passed he always seemed to be on the spot.

During this period his own religious views were undergoing unexpected transformations. Although he remained throughout his life a faithful member of Saint Mark's Episcopal Cathedral, he became increasingly interested in eastern and mystical religions. His unlikely interest in the subject had been sparked by his son George, who had sent his father various texts on the subject. Yet another turn was his sudden interest in philosophy and literature. As unlikely was his simultaneous broad and intensive reading in the sciences: anthropology, archeology, astronomy, applied and theoretical nuclear physics.

His spiritual, and coincidentally intellectual, rebirth during the mid- to late 1940's can be traced to an accident which substantially altered both his working routine and his entire outlook on life. Like the rain barrel incident of his childhood the "bad accident," as he frequently referred to it, involved freezing water and ice. It marked such an abrupt turn in Hogle's life that he dated much of what followed from the episode.

His Uncle Owen had frequently taken him duck hunting in his youth. Through much of his life, weekends in the late fall were spent on the marshes around the Great Salt Lake. These hunting expeditions were gentlemanly affairs. The duck clubs he belonged to were some of the most exclusive in the country. The memberships were as much matters of inheritance and social standing as of financial wherewithal.

The weather in the early fall of 1944 had been mild. There had been several snow flurries in the valley during November, but these were small storms and there was no significant accumulation of snow. The last week of the month had been sunny, and early December, though crisp, was clear. On Saturday afternoon, December 9, Hogle and a companion were in a duck blind after a long day of hunting when a sudden rainstorm swept across the Great Salt Lake. The blinds could only be reached by boat, and the hunters quickly loaded their small craft and set off for the clubhouse some miles distant. The engine stalled, and try as he might, Hogle was unable to re-start it. The two men tried to row back to the clubhouse, but the choppy water and a brisk wind kept the boat off course. At dusk the storm turned to freezing rain and sleet. The men struggled against wave, rain, and wind before finally reaching the clubhouse some hours after dark, soaking wet, frozen, and exhausted.

Hogle was suffering from exposure. He later described to Paul N. Dann, an old friend and classmate, his ordeal on the lake and its effect on his career. "That night something happened to the circulation and nerves in my legs and feet. I thought at first I was having a stroke, but fortunately it was not that. . . . I am taking it easy now and only come down [to work] for two or three hours in the morning. My older son, Jim, has taken over the management of the business."

For many months after the incident, Hogle complained of numbness in his legs and extremities. He found himself easily tired and annoyed by the routines of the office which had once been second nature to him. He had been planning for quite some time on turning the business over to his son, but the accident on the lake brought that day sooner than expected. Although he retained his position as head of the firm and remained the unquestioned authority in all matters of its operation, it was now James E. Hogle who shouldered most of the burden. James A. Hogle was now sixty-nine years old, and Jim was thirty-three.

The Man of Letters

Relieved of much of the operational responsibility, the elder Hogle began to take over a larger share of the firm's correspondence. Always a conscientious letter writer, he now found he had the time to write to some of the customers at length about their investments. He also extended his correspondence with his relatives and old schoolmates from St. Paul's, Yale, and Columbia. He became increasingly active in the alumni associations of those schools and worked on various drives soliciting funds in their behalf. His free time in the afternoons was now dedicated to study and reading.

> One reason I do a lot of reading now is that I formed the habit as a young boy. I did a lot of reading in boarding school and not much at college but a great deal over the next 11 years until I got married. Now I again have the time since my partial retirement from business.
>
> I became interested in reading oriental and mystical philosophies from trying to derive benefit of their breathing exercises, of which they are adept, informed and expert. George got

me interested in them and that is how I began reading their religious philosophy. Lately my reading has had entirely to do with methods in Tibet. Eventually I intend to read Chinese and Indian literature as well.

Hogle's deafness, always a problem, had since the late thirties become a major obstacle to making new acquaintances. By the late forties he complained: "My hearing is so bad recently, that I can't hear at times even locally. . . . My deafness probably has most to do with my withdrawal from social life."

The difficulties with his hearing aids and their irksome batteries made normal conversation tedious. In all business matters Hogle was therefore terse and to the point. In his letters, however, he could be expansive. This is most evident in his letters to one of the firm's clients, a retired U.S. Army Colonel, George F. Murrell, and in his lengthy correspondence with Lois Crozier, his future daughter-in-law.

Hogle's association with Col. Murrell had started as a purely professional one between a broker and his client, but gradually the two men found that they had more in common than the stock market. Col. Murrell was living in Ojai, California, at the time, so their association was primarily one of correspondence. In the ten years following Hogle's accident, the two men would exchange more than 1,200 letters.

Colonel Murrell was an expressive person, an attorney by training and education, inclined to write comments and asides in his letters. In one of these he happened to quote a short passage which Hogle recognized as being from Byron. The Colonel must have been startled to receive back from his stock broker a scholarly epistle on the poet.

In the flurry of letters which followed, the two men exchanged their opinions on and mutual admiration for poetry. They also found that they shared an appreciation for Shakespeare, Goldsmith, and Emerson. Their political views too were equally conservative, and during the late forties both men were devoted listeners to the radio broadcasts of the archconservative commentator Fulton J. Lewis.

Although the first topic of discussion was always the market or the economy, Hogle and his pen pal frequently digressed to other subjects. His long suppressed and closely guarded interest in poetry, literature, and philosophy had finally found expression. Hogle wrote to Murrell that, "It is a great satisfaction to me to have found someone with whom I can discuss such matters." Other than his secretary, Marian Styles, who typed the letters, the people in the office had no inkling of Hogle's intellectual renaissance.

Much of the men's correspondence concerned contemporary political matters, most particularly the situation in the Soviet Union. Hogle had followed developments in Russia, with considerable disgust, since his 1910 visit. He had once handled the sale of Imperial Russian war bonds and later bonds of Kerenski's anti-Soviet government. American policy toward the Soviet Union was frequently mentioned in the letters, and the subject would eventually spark a sharp disagreement between Hogle and Murrell. But the primary topic of the epistolary asides was philosophy. The men exchanged philosophical essays and personal notes and observations on various philosophers, both modern and ancient.

Excerpts from the letters trace the breadth and depth of Hogle's studious interests during the period and his growing friendship with the Colonel. In January of 1948 he described for Murrell what he was searching for in philosophy and once again dated his spiritual quest to the incident on the lake:

> I am not satisfied with practical philosophy, I want spiritual help as well. . . . When I was a young man I read everything of Emerson that I could find and got much help and inspiration from his splendid writings. As I grew older I became absorbed in business and practical affairs. But since my accident four years ago I have had lots of time to think and then you came into my life and that, together with the reading my son, George, started me on, has changed my whole attitude toward life.

Hogle had spent much of 1947 and early '48 studying the works of the Dutch rationalist philosopher Baruch Spinoza. He read Will Durant's *The Story of Philosophy* and several books on oriental philosophy sent by George. By March of '48 his private studies had settled into a routine: "I have gotten in the habit of setting aside a definite time every day for contemplation and serious reading and fortunately I am so placed that I can have an hour and a half to two hours every day after lunch for this purpose. I find that the more I read and study the more contented I am and I am less disturbed by things that used to upset me." His routine usually included "breathing exercises as an aid to my meditation." These exercises were also a form of self-therapy. He found that they not only relaxed him but helped clear his mind before periods of intense study as well. The little distractions that had always been so annoying to him he would not allow to interfere with his meditation, and he wrote Murrell:

> All my life I have been bothered emotionally more by little things than I have by the big things. Perhaps I will be a philosopher when I realize that little things are little things and big things are big!
> You will recall our conversation . . . my mentioning that important things did not bother me as much as little things and cited some trifles that upset me. My talking to you must have had some influence. In fact for the first time in my life I know what Catholics accomplish through "Confession."

But Hogle was not seeking absolution, and his personal struggle was not simply against distraction. What he wanted was considerably more than isolation from the annoyances of the outside world. What Hogle wanted was to remake himself:

> Meditation to me means concentration and deep thinking. . . . I am not satisfied to simply stand still but look for improvement in my thinking and my condition. I will not be satisfied [with meditation] until I get it.
> Most active people, I suppose, want to change things and what most of us do not realize is that perhaps it is ourselves who need changing and that adapting oneself to conditions as they exist is better, on the whole, than trying to change things to suit each individual's desires. . . . My reading and studying go on constantly. I have just finished a book my son, George, sent to me called *The Source of Civilization* by Gerald Heard. His thesis is that the solution of our problems, both collective and personal, is the realization of our being but a part of the whole, instead of individual units, selfish and self centered.

Hogle's desire to change himself focused on what he felt were his bad habits. "Habits," he wrote, "create memory, and a human being is the sum total of his habits. . . . What is desirable is that we supplant good habits for bad habits . . . strength for weakness, concentration for mental laziness."

His stratagem for self-improvement was meticulous, well thought out, and diligently pursued. He was greatly influenced by his reading of Spinoza, Gerald Heard, Edith Hamilton, Arnold Toynbee, Aldous Huxley, and others. Hogle's great talent had always been in his ability to synthesize information from a variety of sources. The personal philosophy he eventually espoused was less original than an artful combination of all he had been reading. By 1948 he was confident enough to put into his own words some of the discoveries he had made over the last four years of study, spelling them out in some detail for Lois Crozier.

Lois had first come to Salt Lake in 1946 under the auspices of the YWCA to establish a student foundation at the University of Utah. Mary Hogle had become acquainted with her through her work with the Y and had introduced her to her husband, who, in turn, would later introduce her to her future husband, George. James A. and Lois Crozier quickly found that they shared a number of intellectual interests and similar views. After her return to the east in 1948, the two began exchanging lengthy epistles on a variety of topics, primarily philosophical in nature. In February of 1948 Hogle wrote Lois a long letter on Spinoza which is an indication of his ardor toward his studies. But the letter also outlined Hogle's own evolving philosophy.

> I am now finishing Spinoza for the third time — some of it I have read five times. . . . If you read Spinoza don't try to ferret out his meaning when he begins to rationalize, but read on, for some of it, is the greatest philosophy ever written and most of it is inspiring. For the first time he has given me the basis upon which I can form an idea of God. . . . All my life I could never conceive of Him. In fact my ideas were so nebulous that it was difficult for me to be devout. . . . After my accident four years ago, I began reading Philosophy and religious writings but it was not until I read Spinoza that I began to get something tangible and satisfactory.

I had already gotten the idea that a human being had somewhat the same relationship to the universe that a cell in the body had to the whole human being in which it was contained. Every cell's function is to cooperate and work for the welfare of the whole living organization of which it is a part, its environment. The cell therefore must have some kind of direction, or intelligence, but if it had awareness it would only know intuitively of the mind which really controlled or directed it.

The cell is only aware of the environment in which it exists. That brings to mind the subconscious, my idea of which I will try to interpret for you after I tell you of the conception I have gained from Spinoza . . . of the relationship of the cell to the body, the organism to the world and the human being to the universe.

Each human being is a part of the universe, the same as each cell is a part of the human body. God in an infinite way is the intelligence and the creative force who rules the universe with infinite wisdom, similar to the way our mind and intelligence, in its insignificant way regulates and directs its little sphere.

Most individuals have but a few short years with which to develop their intelligence, whereas the universe has, so far as we know, an infinite period of time with which to develop its nature and intelligence. Spinoza takes the stand that God's perfection is infinite in time and in space. We are a part of this cosmic intelligence and in our infinitely small way add to its progress or the contrary. Therefore, that part of us must be immortal. Spiritual concepts such as these can not be proven by logic or pure reason but they are the kinds of ideas one feels so strongly that they involve something beyond normal experience.

I believe we are made up of three parts, The Superconscious, or spiritual part, the conscious reasoning, or mental part, and the material body, which is at least partially powered or regulated by what we call the subconscious. It is through the superconscious that we have contact with the soul of God.

Astronomy has shown us that the Universe appears to transcend our earth in an infinite way. Where does nature get its force?, its laws? What is the creative force behind it all?

Is it not logical to believe that the universe requires an intelligence proportionately as great to guide and control its existence? I have come to believe that this is the mind, the intelligence and creative force of God. This "Soul of the Universe" is the Spirit humans have intuitively imagined as the Holy Ghost and it is this part of God that we intuitively feel through our soul. This is what I have tried to express to you before when I have used the expression "spiritual contact with reality" or as Spinoza expresses it, "Our contact with perfection."

In the spring and summer of 1948 Hogle reread *Sartor Resartus*, Edith Hamilton's "Witness to Truth," and essays by Carrol, Kunkle, Adler, Freud, and Jung on psychotherapy. In 1949 he read a book by Chandler on mysticism and began rereading the essays of Emerson. Not all of Hogle's reading was profound, however. He frequently mentioned plays by Shaw, and in October of 1949 he wrote to Murrell: "When I was young I tried several times to read Dickens but could never get interested in him. Last week I picked up a volume of the *Pickwick Papers* and began reading about the breach of promise suit. I haven't had so many good laughs out of a book since I read *Tom Jones*."

Hogle's intensive reading opened up a new life. He even seemed to regret some of the time he had spent making his fortune:

> It seems a pity that most of us have to grow old before we realize that many of the activities of youth are either useless or harmful. It has only been in the last three years that I have begun to understand a little of what life really means.
>
> It is not easy to compare different periods of one's life, but I think I can say without any reservations that I have gotten more out of life the last three years than at any time in my 74 years . . . [though] there are still vital questions that I have not been able to solve. . . . I am starting off my 75th year with confidence and contentment.
>
> I consider thinking the principal phase of our being, our thoughts are what we are. . . . We are occupied all our waking hours with some kind of thinking and most of it is useless or harmful, such as worry or fear. I have found that the valuable factors are imagination, reasoning and concentration. The lack of any one of these three is a great handicap. . . . It has taken me a lifetime to find some of this out.

Although Hogle and Murrell had a great deal in common, they did not agree on everything. Murrell was fond of Shelley and Keats, while Hogle much preferred Coleridge and Byron. Murrell frequently quoted the Roman poets, while Hogle preferred the Greeks: "The only latin poet with whom I am familiar is Virgil. I have read little of Horace. . . . I am much more familiar with the Greek Poets. I have always felt the Greeks [were greater] than the Romans. . . . Pindar, the comedian; Herodotus, the seer; Xenophon, the historian; and the dramatists, Aeschylus, Sophocles and Euripides. The Greeks are more accessible to the modern mind."

Hogle had also been greatly influenced by the reading George had sent him, much of which was philosophically pacifistic. As early as 1947 he had written, "I am beginning to think that George has the right idea, that there is more to be gained by peaceful means than by force or violence." He had also been struggling to understand his daughter Katharine's decidedly progressive political philosophy. Their political differences had, in fact, strained the relationship between father and daughter for some time: "My daughter and I have the same ends in view but differ absolutely on how to go about accomplishing those ends. She told me a short time ago that she thought her ideas were coming closer to mine and I have no doubt that some day we will be reconciled."

But Hogle was changing as well, and although he remained a conservative Republican, there was a most unexpected liberal drift in some of his political opinions. Though not in any way leftist, these opinions sparked a long debate with his friend the Colonel.

During 1951 and '52 Hogle had focused his reading on Hindu and Buddhist philosophy, in the spring reading the *Bhagavad Gita* and *Upanishads* and other texts translated from the Sanscrit. In a letter to Murrell he again mentioned Gerald Heard's book and said in part that, "A significant fact is that India is one of the oldest civilizations in the world. Gerald Heard attributes it to their philosophy of peace and takes the position that nations that have resorted to war eventually destroy themselves." Murrell, a military man at heart, was not comfortable with this thought, or for that matter with any of the eastern religions Hogle had been studying, and he finally revealed to Hogle his own opinion of their world view: "I have always thought the religions of the far east with their strong tone of pacifism are wrong. Animals which do not protect themselves soon perish. . . . India is a shining example. . . . The negative religion of India is a failure, because even in religion there must be positive action."

Hogle was not about to argue the case for pacificism with Col. George Murrell, U.S. Army, retired. But there was something gently chiding in his reply. "It is not an easy subject for the western mind to understand." He pointed out to Murrell that "Some of the best philosophy we have was written by Shakespeare or left us by poets such as Goldsmith." Retired army officer philosophers weren't mentioned, and Hogle closed the letter with a quote from Byron which gently countered the Colonel's truculent positivism.

> I live not in myself, but become a
> Portion of all that surrounds me; and to me
> High mountains are a feeling, but the hum
> Of human cities torture: I can see
> Nothing to loathe in nature, save to be
> A link reluctant in a fleshly chain,
> Classed among creatures, when the soul can flee,
> And with the sky, the peak, the heaving plain
> Or ocean, or the stars, mingle, and not in vain.

The discussion of eastern religion and pacifism was not immediately taken up again. But shortly after the exchange Hogle gave Murrell his opinion of the conflict then raging in Korea: "Yesterday, Edward R. Murrow reported that our air force and bombers had killed 16,000 Chinese and North Koreans in two days. It seems a pity that in this day and age we have to resort to such a slaughter. I believe that the large majority of the American people are not in sympathy with what is going on and they certainly don't want to be led into China."

In a number of earlier letters Col. Murrell had argued that "The law of nature is survival of the fittest" and had equated that fitness with military strength. "Nature abhors the weakling," he wrote, "Each creature must support himself." Several weeks after the exchange on eastern philosophy Hogle returned to the theme and revealed his true feelings on the subjects of nature, ecology, and pacifism: "Of late years my reading and study have led me to believe that cooperation is the real law of nature and that most of our troubles, among nations as well as individuals, arise from the breaking of this law. I believe this extends right down to animal life as well. If one doesn't practice union with his fellow man, he is apt to be obsessed by fear . . . [and fear] leads to aggression."

Murrell, of course, was not of the same mind, but he did not press Hogle on this theory and for the moment, at least, the matter was dropped. But Hogle continued to mention in his letters the appalling waste of military spending and to point out the need for more efficiency in the procurement system. What he was driving at was finally brought home in an exchange that took place in the spring of 1952. Murrell had written Hogle that, "Force is the only language the Communists understand, [a force] greater than theirs." But perhaps remembering Hogle's comments on the need to curb military spending, he added that it was "a mistake to simply out-spend the Russians." The door having been cracked open, Hogle walked in, and his reply would have surprised many of his conservative acquaintances:

> After reading your remarks about spending money to lick Communism, I feel more strongly than ever that we are wasting a lot of money. In some ways, it does more harm than good, especially from a psychological standpoint. All through my childhood there was a fight against the Mormon people and whether it was justified or not, Mormons thought it was persecution and retaliated in kind. After the Gentiles got control of the [City] government, it began to die out.
>
> There is a great element of fear in Russia. It is just as much a sign of weakness as pain is a danger signal physically. We have got to keep strong but the more we leave them alone, the sooner they will work out their internal revolution.

The theme was clear. Hogle — the religiously dedicated capitalist, the same man who thirty years earlier had bought and sold anti-Soviet bonds, who opposed communism as much as any member of the right — had come to the conclusion that the outside pressure on the Soviet Union was in some way responsible for the Communists' hold on Russia, and that the fierce opposition to the Russian Revolution in Europe and the U.S. had, in part, been responsible for the Communists' equally fierce attitude toward the West. Hogle believed that without that mutual hostility the Communist state might have "withered away," to be replaced by something less odious.

But perhaps more significant than the thought itself was the time in which it was written. The period of the early fifties was dominated by anti-communist hysteria. McCarthyism was at its height. Politicians who were thought to be "soft on communism" were being driven from office. Hogle's advice to "leave them alone" was clearly out of step with the right wing of the Republican Party as represented by Senator Joseph McCarthy. The behavior of McCarthy and his followers had disturbed Hogle for some time, and he became increasingly disaffected with their tactics. How far he had come in three short years is indicated in a letter he wrote to Murrell in 1953: "I only listen regularly now to Edward R. Murrow. He is not only intelligent and well informed, but is about as fair as one can be in times like these."

By the spring of 1953, Fulton J. Lewis, the conservative commentator Hogle had once listened to religiously, had been turned off.

CHAPTER THIRTY-ONE

Speculations with Uncle Bert

ALBERT T. COPLEY WAS MARY HOGLE'S FIRST COUSIN, but out of respect for his eighty-four years he was more commonly known to the family by the honorary title "Uncle Bert." Bert was an old-time mining engineer who had received his training in the Cripple Creek District of Colorado in the eighties and nineties. He had worked for the Hogles from time to time, performing various odd jobs at the mines in Nevada and around the Hogles' country home in Salt Lake. Uncle Bert, though very frail, was proud of his longevity. He claimed, in fact, to be the oldest Copley who had ever lived. Bert had a cheerful disposition and an exceptionally keen mind. He and his wife Poldie were special favorites of all the Hogle family.

After Bert moved permanently to California in 1950, James A. began corresponding with him regularly. The two men exchanged letters about mining developments in Eureka and passed on family tidbits. Like Colonel George Murrell, Copley had political beliefs compatible with Hogle's: "I am a died in the wool conservative, but Irish enough to hate any compromise that weakens a stand for principle."

Hogle subscribed to several mining and technical journals, and occasionally he would send interesting articles along to Mary's eighty-four-year-old cousin. In February of 1951 he sent Bert an issue of *Scientific American* and received back an enthusiastic letter of thanks saying how he had "devoured every word of it." Hogle wrote back to Bert saying, "I did not know before that you were interested in modern science. . . . I would like to hear more from you along these lines." Bert, who had previously described himself in his letters as "Just an Old Desert Rat," wrote, revealing a Bert Copley that Hogle was unfamiliar with: "Most anything that sheds light on the riddle of our existence, and the causes for it, is of great interest to me. . . . The reasoning of all thinkers who have delved into philosophy stimulates our sciences. . . . I am interested in all phases of science and research."

Fifty-five years earlier, James Hogle had been elected an officer of the Scientific Club at St. Paul's. He had heard lectures on X-rays and radiation by distinguished physicists of the day and had studied the light from distant stars through telescopes. He had heard lectures on Darwin and Malthus and had glimpsed the mysteries of the infant science of anthropology. As his son George and Lois Crozier stimulated his interest in philosophy, and Col. Murrell had sparked his renewed interest in poetry and literature, Bert Copley would rekindle Hogle's interest in the sciences.

Over the next four years the two men exchanged weekly letters on a variety of eclectic and sometimes bizarre subjects of special interest to them. Usually the topic for discussion was drawn from articles in the current scientific journals they exchanged. In March of 1951 Bert sent James an article on astronomy by Frederick Hoyle and James sent Bert one on quantum physics by Max Born. James described his studies to date:

> I got interested in Hindu Philosophy through a book George gave me to read on Yogi practice. Soon after, I read a wonderful book by Geraldine Coster on the similarity of modern psychiatry and ancient Hindu Philosophy.
>
> I then [took up] breathing exercises worked out over the last three thousand years by the Hindus and later the Buddhists and Tibetans. . . . One doesn't have to subscribe to their other beliefs to get real benefit out of their spirituality.

In the spring and summer of 1951 the correspondents took up the debate between the quantum physicists and Einstein, and for some months their letters touched on the merits of the opposing theories. Copley, whose religious views were "Hopefully Agnostic," was clearly in the camp of the quantum physicists. Hogle sided with Einstein's Grand Unified Theory, more for religious and aesthetic than scientific reasons, and wrote to Copley early in the exchange:

> Hindu Philosophy has it that there is but one ultimate substance from which the Universe and even the intelligence of God evolves. [The theories] in physics and chemistry concerning the singular nature of the atom, space and time suggest they are approaching a metaphysical situation which the purely mechanical theory of life doesn't adequately explain. If there is one ultimate substance of which all atoms are made up then, from a metaphysical standpoint, why can't one consider force and mass and time as part of this substance, which from a religious standpoint should embrace the intelligence of the Universe itself, which we call God.
>
> Unless you are familiar with this modern Philosophy [theoretical physics], which resembles the Hindu and is somewhat like the Greek, the subject may not appeal to you.

Copley's reply was sufficiently detailed to convince Hogle that the old man was indeed familiar with the subject:

> Oppenheimer too was struck with the similarity between some Hindu philosophy and modern theories regarding the Universe; so much so, in fact, that he studied Sanscrit so as to be able to read some of the Veda in the original. Einstein also said that some of the old Hindu Philosophy was strikingly in line with modern scientific thought about physics.
>
> . . . However, while they may have hit upon some truths through pure thought and reasoning they just as certainly failed in other areas. . . .
>
> In my opinion, the origin of Religion is the attempt of man to ascribe some author to the events he could not understand, and his fear of such a being, fear to the extent that questioning the truth of his superstitions was taboo.
>
> . . . I do not have the least belief in anything occult and I steer clear of anything too nebulous. I feel that everything must conform to some natural law and that the only reason for superstition is ignorance on our part.

In the same letter Copley expressed his belief that the universe was much older than the 3.5 billion years then observable. He believed in the expanding universe theory and said "New stars are being born today and others are blowing up . . . creating the very elements that make life possible." He also pointed out that when he had been in college sixty years earlier they still taught the theory of the universal "ether."

Hogle did not believe that his own carefully constructed religious view was at all "superstitious." Nor did he believe that Bert's scientific views were necessarily antagonistic to religious philosophy and wrote back, "Your scientific references about astronomy and other matters interest me greatly. . . . Regarding your agnostic views, they may be unorthodox but are not anti-religious."

That spring and summer they exchanged articles and notes on the recently invented "electronic digital computing machines," on archeological digs in Peru and Mexico, and on oceanographic surveys of the Pacific Ocean floor. Copley was also a naturalist, and he wrote extensively on animal behavior, much of it drawn from his sixty-odd years of experience as a "desert rat." On August 30, Copley sent Frederick Hoyle's latest book, *The Nature of the Universe*, and added his own observations: "Hoyle's idea of the probability of other satellites of other suns having living creatures is something I have contended for many years. I can easily imagine that such creatures might have had longer evolution, or more rapid, and thus have arrived at a state of intelligence so far beyond our grade that we would consider them gods."

James's interest in science was keen, and through Bert's letters he stayed current on scientific matters. But Hogle frequently let Copley know that his interest in science in no way affected his religious beliefs or his preference for philosophy. For all his study in eastern religions, he remained a Christian and a faithful member of St. Mark's Cathedral. In a letter to Murrell, he wrote, "Much of my reading and studying has been in Hindu and Chinese Literature and I am glad to say that while I find it inspiring and helpful, it has not changed my basic belief in Christianity. In some ways, it has explained Christianity to me."

Hogle repeatedly tried to persuade his agnostic old cousin that there was more to life than was dreamed of in his sciences:

> A few years ago, I felt about the same as you do and was more interested in what science could do for man than religion or ethics. Then two people came into my life who got me started on another track.

I think our George was the first one, but about the same time I got to know well one of our best customers who lived in California. I used to read philosophy as a young man, especially Emerson, and of course, some Greek Philosophy. Then my California friend got me started again on Aristotle. I read all of Will Durant's book, *The Story of Philosophy* and then read of Spinoza's life and his principal writings, then dipped back in Greek Philosophy and finally that of India and China.

I am not belittling science and the physical comforts it has brought to the human race, but I doubt whether that alone has increased our happiness, whereas one can demonstrate every day in one's own life that the [teachings of great philosophers] if followed, can bring happiness and contentment. When you think of the influence Christ has had on the human race and compare it with the great historical heroes or the scientific geniuses, I think one is justified in believing that there is a force for good in the world and that it is the human race that craves improvement.

Copley remained unconvinced. He disliked priests of any kind and enumerated for Hogle the misery brought upon the world by "Holy Wars" and religious fanatics. Copley was a dedicated skeptic and moreover had little use for the life hereafter:

Ethical teaching and writing has, as you say, done much for the world . . . but the ethical view does not change the inherited instincts [of man] and that is why the world doesn't improve much toward the golden rule. Thus wars will be a normal part of "civilization" for many generations to come.

Personally, and for those I love, I am not interested in a hereafter, either as an entity of some sort, or as an attenuated gas. As I told my mother, who was deeply religious, "I felt that where she went, I would go, but I saw no future for me that was not shared by every living thing from the single cell on up." I suppose I'm a mutation, for I am the only one on either side of the family for the past few generations that has not inherited a tendency to believe in the supernatural.

I am intensely interested in facts — I would like to be sure of just what makes the wheels go around and what started them and when, if ever, they will stop. But I can not accept what is known now as being much more than "a preponderance of evidence."

Of the mental ability of humans in general, I have poor opinion. I feel sure that if I had superior speaking ability and a large enough bank account, I could start a new religion and secure a large following like Joseph Smith or Mrs. Eddy, or, with a little more effort, Mohammed. I could so inflame the people that I could start a war in most countries, even if the whole idea I was promulgating was absurd. The point I am trying to make is that ethics are fine and are much to be desired . . . but people will follow a Hitler, a Stalin or a Mussolini as faithfully as a Christ, a Moses or the Pope.

So I am interested in research in anthropology, biology, physics, astronomy and chemistry, hoping for more evidence as to the why of things and how they came to be as they are, if indeed they are as they seem to be. . . . I can not believe that philosophy changes the instincts [of man] more than a dash of cream changes a cup of coffee.

Copley's agnosticism and Hogle's spiritualism were subjects of continuous debate throughout their long correspondence. Hogle found nothing in science to negate his own beliefs and neither did Copley. Science was a neutral ground where they sparred in amicable opposition. The subjects they discussed were far-ranging and, at times, prophetic.

In the fall of 1951 the two speculated on the future of atomic energy and expressed grave concerns over the problems of disposing of nuclear wastes. They also discussed air pollution, water pollution, and overpopulation and their effects on the environment. Copley believed that rationality, problem-solving, and intelligence were not the exclusive traits of human beings, and he wrote Hogle of his own observation of tool-making behavior in chimpanzees and the cooperative hunting methods used by coyotes and wolves. In physics Copley speculated that protons and neutrons were in fact compound elements made up of subatomic particles yet to be discovered. They discussed the possibility that mass extinctions in the past had been brought about through catastrophic events such as multiple volcanic eruptions which obscured the sun, changed the climate, and brought on the ice ages. Copley speculated that the same thing might happen following a nuclear war.

In 1952 Copley wrote more letters touching on matters of particle physics, including the search for neutrinos and gravitons. Of the search for mesons he wrote: "How will it ever be possible to measure a particle whose life lasts only the tenth to fifteenth power of a second?" They exchanged articles on astronomy, ecology, psychiatry, and the search for a cancer cure. They discussed recent discoveries in Africa of pre-human hominids and the breakthroughs in radiocarbon dating. Various speculations were broached, including heart and embryo transplants, and the breeder reactor.

Not all of their speculations have yet been proven correct, though many have. Copley for some time believed in a scientific basis for "thought transference," ESP, and racial memory. He also believed that there had to be something to all the flying saucer sightings reported in the popular press that year and felt that the government was covering up the evidence. Extraterrestrial life was a subject that he was most fond of, and he wrote that radio-astronomy would soon prove him right.

Both men shared a belief that space travel was just around the corner. This notion was further supported by a mutual relative, Dr. Dinsmore Alters, an astronomer with the Los Angeles Planetarium, who spent much of his time at the Palomar Observatory. Dr. Alters' mother was Jeanette Copley Alters, an aunt of both Mary Hogle and Bert Copley.

Dr. Alters gave public lectures at the planetarium on a number of interesting technical subjects, and Bert frequently sent copies along to Hogle. Alters lectured on the feasibility of launching artificial satellites in the immediate future, on the problems of interplanetary travel, weightlessness and navigation, of landing a man on the moon and the building of a permanent manned observatory there by the end of the century. During one of Hogle's trips to California, Bert arranged for him to meet Alters.

Dinsmore Alters was a true visionary. His pioneering work, and that of a handful of other scientists, would eventually take man off the planet, while the majority of the scientists at the time regarded such matters as the most fantastic fiction. But Hogle and Copley respected Dr. Alters' work and anticipated the events with relish. On several occasions Hogle expressed to his son Jim his hope that he would live long enough to see the space age. Dr. Alters' proposals seemed so feasible, in fact, that Hogle expected the launching of an artificial satellite at any time. He would not have been pleased to know that the feat would be first accomplished by the U.S.S.R.

Hogle's correspondence with Bert Copley was not exclusively about science or philosophy. Many of the letters were concerned with family matters, the stock market, and politics. Nor was the information exclusive to Bert. Frequently Hogle's letters to George Murrell or his son George would contain the same paragraphs. Hogle would often pass Copley's speculations on to the others and often enough would sent Murrell or Copley recent communications from the other man. Hogle's close circle of friends shared information and ideas openly. The circle was, in a way, an informal correspondence school with a very broad and undefined curriculum.

The regular commencement ceremonies of Westminster College were held on June 8, 1950. James A. and Mary C. Hogle were in attendance, both to be honored on the occasion. In a speech delivered to the assembled graduates and faculty, Westminster president Dr. H. W. Reherd sketched the life of James A. Hogle and revealed that he had served on the College's board of trustees for thirty years: "In accepting election in 1920 as a Trustee of this College, Mr. Hogle, you stated that you considered it a greater honor than being elected Director of any bank. You have served Westminster continuously for thirty years, not only giving us the benefit of your wise counsel, but giving most generously for the support and expansion of the College." James A. had been consulted outside of the regular board meetings, and his membership was not publicly known.

In his speech President Reherd also recognized Mary's contributions: "In honoring you, Mr. Hogle, we wish to pay special tribute to your wife, Mary Copley Hogle . . . a prominent leader in many worthwhile public movements. She has been a most helpful partner of yours for many years and by your own testimony, you owe to her your spirit of unselfish philanthropy."

President Reherd closed his address by saying, "It is with much appreciation for your services to the entire community that I present you, James Albert Hogle [with] the Honorary Degree, Doctor of Laws."

It was most fitting that James Hogle received his doctorate at this time. Although it was an honorary award given for his philanthropic and community service efforts in Salt Lake City, it could just as easily have been a doctorate of philosophy for the five years of independent study that he had just completed.

CHAPTER THIRTY-TWO

Epistles & Lamentations

JAMES HOGLE'S CORRESPONDENCE was never confined exclusively to intellectual or business matters. He was the undisputed patriarch of a large extended family, and their well-being was his paramount concern. As his charts had chronicled, in shorthand form, the history of the nation, his letters recorded, in detail, the changing history of the family. His patriarchal position gave him a unique perspective on nearly everything that affected the Clan. Through the forties and early fifties he acted as a kind of information clearinghouse for his relatives. Every bout with illness or accident was passed along. Every notice of marriage, birth, or death was sent to family members with typically efficient dispatch. He naturally became the personal confidant of many relatives who turned to him for both help and advice.

James A. was never overbearing or dictatorial, and no subject seemed too great, too trivial, or too personal to broach with him. Whether it was advice to his grandson Holly at St. Paul's on the importance of learning the correct wrist action in rowing, to his brother-in-law George Copley on estate planning, or to his son George on romantic matters, he was equally accessible.

The employees at J. A. Hogle & Co. were part of his extended family, and they too regarded him as a fatherly sage. The younger employees, in particular, frequently sought his counsel and guidance. He was so often asked for advice that he prepared several lectures for his young employees which he delivered at a number of the company offices. Although some elements from his study of eastern religions can be discerned, for the most part the advice was down-to-earth and practical:

It is difficult to condense the experience of a lifetime into a short talk like this. What I will try to do is give you the things I know are so — what I have learned in my 76 years of life.

There are three things that are necessary for financial success:

1. Get the study habit. Of course it is best to develop this in school or college. But if you did not do so there, then rest assured it can be acquired later.

2. Get the work habit. If a man will study and work and has any ability at all, then there is only one other thing necessary for his material success and that is:

3. The saving habit. The first two habits will assure a living for himself and his family, but if he is unable to save he can not take advantage of opportunities that may come along.

It is most important to find agreeable work. It is a grave mistake for a man to work at a job he does not enjoy. It is much the same with reading books: If you do not enjoy them, you will not get much out of them. So get a job that is agreeable and then adjust yourself to your associates. Getting along with others is a matter of give and take. Adjust yourself to your surroundings. Don't try to make others conform to you.

One of the most important things to remember is don't criticize and do not go about finding fault with others. Build a constructive state of mind. Try to be positive, never negative. Show appreciation. Appreciation is the oil of life. Criticism is like throwing sand in the gears.

Have patience. Patience has as much to do with a man's success as anything else. It is certainly the most important thing in speculative investing. It is more important than nerve. It is more important than capability. The good things in life and business do not come easily. A man to be successful must stick with things and see them through. Imagination is a fine thing. Resolution is a fine thing. But if you haven't the patience and energy to carry things through, you will fail.

The most important thing I have to tell you about is "Thinking." You should take a few minutes off every day to think. Make it the same time every day. Think out your problems, your business problems, your problems at home or with your life or health. Ask yourself, what am I? What am I here for? What is life? I believe that you will gradually find that the more you think about your situation, the more you will realize that there is a power within you stronger than your own thoughts. There is something within each of us that is stronger than we are. Find it and use it. Learn to think; learn to plan; learn to control your thoughts; learn to control your emotions; learn to control your habits. You alone are responsible for your success. No one else can do this for you. . . . There are those who believe that success is a matter of luck, but I tell you a successful man makes his own luck.

Hogle's role as confidant and advisor was not confined to members of the family or the firm. The sons of his friends, neighbors, and business associates also sought and received the benefit of his counsel, as did community and religious leaders. He served on fund-raising committees for St. Paul's School, Rowland Hall School, Westminster College, Yale and Columbia Universities and the University of Utah. His counsel and advice were clearly worth listening to.

But James's chief interest had always been in the protection of his immediate family, his own children and their offspring. Throughout his life he also maintained close ties with his wife's siblings as well as his cousins on the Gilmore side of the family — the Steeles, the Mantors, the Weeds, and the Wyncoops. He helped manage some of their stock portfolios and faithfully kept the promise he had made to his own father to look after his aunts. He helped support them through their lives and assisted in the support of several of his cousins as well. The health and well-being of all were closely monitored in his family correspondence, as was the state of his own health and the gradual deterioration of Mary's.

During the late forties, Mary continued to battle episodes of severe depression. Her struggle was a profoundly personal one, her anguish compounded by her flat refusal to seek professional help. The accusations of her peddling quackery with her carrot juice pamphlet and her long fight for her nutritional and dietary theories had turned her against the medical profession. She was not about to give herself over to the very people who she perceived as being at the root of her problems.

Nor was Mary going to have anyone think that she was not competent to solve her own emotional difficulties, least of all some medical doctor, or worse, a psychiatrist. There was a stubborn integrity in her insistence on fighting it out by herself, but that insistence assured that her battle would be a lonely one. It was a tragic illness and her suffering was at times intense. During the attacks, her moods revealed a wide range of emotions, from feelings of utter hopelessness to fear and anger. On occasion her anger boiled to the surface in outbursts against her husband, close friends, and children.

It was ironical that at this time her son George decided to take up the study of medicine. George's interest in health had been sparked by his mother very early on, but it was not until the late forties that it began to take a definite direction when he was accepted by the medical school at Columbia University. An even greater irony was that her refusal to seek outside help was directly responsible for another turn in the career of her second son. George's desire to understand his own parents better, particularly his mother, would eventually lead him into the field of psychiatry. What could not be done for his own mother would be translated into helping other similarly distressed families.

How Mary felt about her son going into medicine at all must be wondered at. She may have thought at first that he was joining the ranks of her persecutors. She was particularly fragile in the summer of 1950 and even insisted that George stay in Salt Lake rather than return to Columbia. Her desire to keep George at home was less an attempt to thwart his medical career than simply a desire for his company. George, through no real fault of his own, had been away from home for the better part of the previous eight years — in alternative service during the war, then working in Germany with the Quakers for two years before his enrollment at Columbia. It is the natural course of things, as the biblical admonition goes, "that a man should leave his mother and father," but although an unshakeable tenet of the Divine plan, that separation is always painful. It was an irrefutable fact that Mary's children had all grown up and were living lives of their own. Some causes of her depression would be understood by any parent.

It is clear that Mary's behavior was dictated by her depression. She was normally intensely interested in her children and everything about their families. It is also clear that she did not harbor any actual animosity toward George for entering medical school. When the summer spell passed, the true nature of their relationship was revealed in their letters. George wrote to her of the classes he was taking, and she read with keen interest his detailed notes on various subjects, particularly biochemistry, which she had studied at the University of Kansas when the science was in its infancy.

Mary Hogle's melancholia was periodic in nature and varied both in duration and intensity. During one of her worst episodes she seldom left her room and lay in bed for days at a time staring at the ceiling. Her husband tried repeatedly to draw her out but was overwhelmed by the depth of her depression. He would go up to her bedside in the afternoons, sit by her side and hold her hand silently for hours. He felt utterly helpless and didn't know what to do. Gradually the spell ended and she was up and about to the relief of everyone.

Mary's physical health had also been declining for some time, and bouts with sickness compounded her struggle against depres-

Mary and James enjoying themselves at the Hogle farm on Seventh East.

The Hogles' fortieth wedding anniversary celebration in 1950. This light-hearted photograph was used as the basis for an oil portrait.

sion. On the evening of August 23, 1950, she was attending a dinner party at the Salt Lake Country Club; after dinner she slipped on the polished floor and broke her right arm just above the wrist. The break did not appear serious. Her arm was set at the hospital, a wrist cast and sling were put on, and she was sent home.

In the days that followed, the pain in her arm worsened and Mary found it almost impossible to sleep. She was admitted into the hospital for X-rays. As if to verify her opinion of the medical profession, the X-rays showed that the break was indeed a bad one and, even worse, that the arm had been improperly set. Resetting the arm entailed rebreaking it and encasing the entire lower arm in a heavy cast. Her response to the incident is expressed in a single-word postscript to a letter written to her close friends Francis and Katharine Crosby: "Doctors!"

The accident coincidentally brought the entire family together for the Hogles' fortieth wedding anniversary, and in spite of her broken arm, Mary was in good spirits at the celebration. But her recovery was very slow. At Christmas James wrote to his relatives, "Mary doesn't seem to be as active as in former years on account of her hand which is still almost helpless, although the swelling is about gone."

Mary's physical ailments were not confined to her arm. She suffered from a variety of complaints, and her family encouraged her to get a thorough medical examination. She would have nothing to do with it, and no amount of coaxing was going to change her mind.

After Christmas she felt well enough to visit her daughter Katharine in Los Angeles for several weeks. James accompanied her and took the opportunity to visit George Murrell and the L.A. offices of J. A. Hogle & Co. Mary stayed on until the first week in February, returning to Salt Lake in better health than she had been in for years. Though the weather that month was bitterly cold, with temperatures dropping well below zero, her spirits remained high.

By mid-March, however, Mary began to complain again of digestive upsets, pains, and dizziness. Her family tried to get her to see a doctor, but without success. At the end of the month she went to a private clinic near Bridal Veil, Oregon, to undergo six weeks of special treatments.

The regimen at Mrs. Reynolds' Health School was part dietary and part religious. Prayer and fasting were included in the treatment, and the amount of benefit gained appeared to depend to some degree on the amount of faith one had in it. For the first three weeks Mary's condition improved dramatically, but by the fourth week she began to complain of symptoms again and her mood turned gloomy. She left the clinic in May, taking with her Eloise Page, a young woman who became for her both nurse and close friend. Most of May and June were spent at the home of her brother George in Auburn, California. There she regained her strength and, with the help of Miss Page, her sagging spirits lifted.

While Mary was staying at her brother's home in California, James Hogle and her son Jim flew back east to join George at their respective class reunions at St. Paul's. It was Hogle's fifty-sixth anniversary year, Jim's twentieth, and George's nineteenth. A third generation of Hogles would soon be enrolled in the school. The trip had been in the works since January, and it proved to be an especially rewarding one. Hogle met his old friends and classmates Richard Graff, Sanford Stoddard, Jimmy Gray, Reddy Littell, Holkins Palmer, Haskel Derby, and Parker Straw. They reminisced about the years when they had all lived together on the top floor of Old Upper. They toured the school's enlarged facilities and, as half a century earlier, the class of '95 was "bunked" in one of the dormi-

James A. stands second from the right in this photograph of the roommates at the fifty-fifth anniversary of the Fifth Form, St. Paul's Class of 1895.

tories. Hogle wrote, "My trip east was the most interesting I have ever taken and in many ways, was the most enjoyable. My class reunion at Concord was especially fine. . . . There were eight members of my graduating class there. I am only sorry that we didn't have more time to recall the old days when we were boys together at the school."

Shortly after Hogle returned from the reunion, Mary came home from California. She had lost some weight and James believed that her time at the clinic must have done her some good. But her symptoms did not entirely disappear, and though she remained emotionally up through the early summer, her physical complaints were very real.

On Sunday evening, July 22, Mary began hemorrhaging. Her condition was now obviously too serious to be treated with dietary remedies. She would have to go to a doctor. She was admitted to the hospital the following morning and operated on for the removal of a tumor that afternoon. This time things seemed to go well. The operation was termed a complete success, and although she suffered a good deal during the following week, she made a rapid recovery.

By the second week of August, Hogle could report to the family that "Mary's physical health and spirits are better now than in some time. . . . It is surprising the way in which she has recovered. She has not been as active or vigorous for several years." Hogle attributed her progress to Miss Page, who came to Salt Lake from her home in Montana to assist in Mary's recuperation. Her positive attitude and continuous encouragement kept Mary from lapsing into another depression. By October 1 Hogle could write: "Mary has completely recovered and is more her old self. Saturday she went up to Brighton for a visit . . . . Yesterday I joined them [at the office cabin] partly to see the autumn foliage and partly for the visit. It was a wonderful occasion."

The autumn display that year was spectacular. The scrub oak along the floor of Big Cottonwood Canyon was intensely red, and the groves of aspen trees above the Brighton Bowl were a shimmering yellow. Mary wrote to her brother George that she could "hardly remember a more beautiful fall."

On Sunday morning, New Year's Day of 1952, Mary Hogle

suddenly became violently ill. A doctor was called in and diagnosed the flu. But Mary's condition worsened during the day, and she complained of severe pain throughout the night. On Monday she was admitted to St. Mark's Hospital, where it was discovered that she was suffering from a gall bladder attack. She was operated on the following morning in a long and complicated procedure. The gall duct was affected and fifteen stones were removed during the operation.

Recovery from this, her second major surgery in less than five months, would be painful and slow. Mary spent almost four weeks in the hospital and did not go home until January 26. Once again Eloise Page had come to care for her, and by February 25 she seemed completely recovered. Her husband wrote to the family, "Her color is good, and I am certain that she is stronger and in better health than she has been for many years."

On the afternoon of March 15, 1952, Mary Hogle went downtown to her hair dresser. After having her permanent, she walked to her husband's office close by. It was immediately obvious that something was seriously wrong. She had difficulty walking, her speech seemed impaired, and she complained of pain in her hips. Her husband initially thought that "They had someway injured her in drying her hair." Over the next two weeks her condition continued to worsen, and James wrote to the family of the latest misfortune:

> It soon became apparent that her left side was affected. . . . Dr. Lindem could not tell at first what seemed to be the matter. But Friday night he had a brain specialist examine her and Sunday they told Jim that either a tumor had developed on the right side of the brain or a blood clot had formed. At any rate they said they could do nothing, except give her the best of care and await developments.
>
> She sat up three times yesterday and is able to write a little with her right hand. All her old worrying has disappeared and except when she moves about, she suffers no pain.

James wrote to Katharine and George, informing them that their mother was going downhill, and they immediately flew to Salt Lake to see her. She was lying in bed, eyes open, unblinking. There was no response and medically nothing could be done. In addition, their experience of Mary's previous episodes of withdrawal from the world, coupled with the hopes of the immediate family, masked the truth of her condition and the grim reality of her inexorable slide.

Mary's condition seemed much the same day after day. Finally James insisted that the children return to their own homes. There had been some signs of improvement, and if there was any change for the worse, he would call them. He explained the situation to Mary's brother George:

> Katharine returned to Los Angeles on Sunday, George left Monday noon for New York. Jim and I both urged them to go, partly because there is nothing they can do here, and partly because Mary's condition was improved. She is in bed all the time but we have secured a hospital bed in which she can sit up. She doesn't talk but seems to understand what we say.
>
> We have an especially good woman here and with three nurses and Mrs. Thompson and Jim's help, everything is being done that can be done.

James A. Hogle had always dated the beginning of spring in the Salt Lake Valley on April 15. In a number of letters over the years he had mentioned the date's significance. Years earlier he had set April 15 as the date of maturation of the Three Trust for his children and once wrote to Katharine: "I would rather you came here after Easter than before April 1st. The best time is after April 15th when the fruit trees begin to bloom." The year before he had written to George Murrell: "If you feel like coming up here this spring, I hope you will come in late April or early May. Our pleasant spring weather begins here about the 15th of April, at which time the trees usually leaf out and we have a month of delightful weather. It is the loveliest time of the whole year." To Dr. Elton Littell he once wrote: "Do come to Salt Lake this Spring. Arrive after April 15th when the blossoms are in Bloom. It is the best season to visit the city."

In fact, the fruit trees are not in bloom every year on April 15. In some years the blossoms have all fallen by that date, and in other years the buds have yet to open. Why he believed that the trees were in bloom every year on April 15 is uncertain. It is possible that it was on that date in 1909 that he took Mary Copley to Ensign Peak above the city and proposed to her. Mary had often recalled to her daughter that the trees were in bloom that day.

No trees were in bloom on Tuesday, April 15, 1952. The winter had been unusually hard and had lasted through March. The largest snowstorm of the year had occurred in mid-March, breaking all records, and the week of April 13 would also set new records for precipitation, this time in the form of rain. Nationwide there were devastating floods, the country's midsection being hit particularly hard, and President Truman flew over the flooded Midwest to see the devastation first-hand.

In northern Utah on April 14 a huge downpour added to the already high spring runoff; the storm sewers could not handle the volume, and throughout the city manholes had pushed aside their covers and were gushing water. By evening Main Street was a lake. On the morning of April 15 the skies were still overcast, but it had started to clear by mid-morning. At 10:15 A.M., Mary Copley Hogle died quietly. After a life of struggle and accomplishment, her time of doing was over.

The news of Mary's death saddened the entire city. As the *Salt Lake Evening Telegram* editorialized:

> The death of Mary Hogle, wife of the well known financier, will bring many expressions of sorrow and at the same time many heartfelt tributes to the memory of a woman who in her lifetime did so much for this community and for humanity in general.
>
> . . . Mrs. Hogle was a leader in civic and cultural affairs. Her interests were so wide and varied, ranging from the Hogle Zoological Gardens, which she founded with her husband, to the Y.W.C.A., which she also helped to found, that it is impossible in a brief editorial to enumerate them all.
>
> Mrs. Hogle was interested in anything that had to do with education, health, recreation, music, the arts — in fact anything that might lead to human betterment. She supported all kinds of charitable activity. In her lifetime we think it is safe to say that her compassionate interest in doing for others touched the lives of many thousands. . . .

She had a great resentment for injustice. And a great compassion for those in trouble. But she wasn't one to just sympathize. She did something about it — and the community benefited greatly thereby. . . .

The *Salt Lake Tribune* editorial read, in part:

She was a leader in numerous civic, religious and educational organizations and a contributor to many important causes. . . . There are hundreds who will remember Mrs. Hogle with deep gratitude because of her aid in time of need or trouble.

She was grateful herself that she had the means to help. But her giving was more than charity. She gave of herself. Her giving had charm and grace. It was the act of a friend.

Mrs. Hogle saw the person who needed help as an individual, not as a statistic. . . . She received all with compassion and gave encouragement.

A useful, wonderful career has ended. But it will live in memory. Mary C. Hogle did great good for many. The *Tribune* adds its voice to the chorus of the many who sorrow.

The Mormon church–owned *Deseret News* also editorialized on Mary's death:

The passing of Mary C. Hogle ends the mortal life of a most beloved benefactress, but her friendship to all men will long live as an inspiration to the people she reached.

Throughout her life, this great humanitarian placed an accent on people. She was cultured, erudite, and remarkably well read and well informed in all fields, yet her true interests were not with things or ideas but with people.

The real greatness in the life of Mrs. Hogle, even over and above the many civic and religious causes which she served with leadership and financial contribution, lies in the multitude of inconspicuous, unrecorded, generally unseen but surely not unappreciated personal assistances to individuals. The young student, the aspiring author or musician, those bereaved, the sick, the discouraged, all have known her help.

She gave more than just encouragement. She opened ways to solve personal problems and emergencies. She established the Mary C. Hogle Foundation to coordinate a program of service. But no one can systematize a prompt and responsive labor of love. Her compassion knew no office hours.

Through the years, the Foundation served its useful purpose with meeting and reading facilities. It was a haven to the lonely and others in need, and its contributions reached its zenith during the dark and discouraging depression years, further tribute to Mrs. Hogle's true spirit of service.

She was a loving mother and her family is a credit to this community. With that family and her many friends we share the sorrow of this hour and the pride in knowing a life so rich in giving.

Those she had helped over the years had not forgotten Mary's kindness and generosity. Hundreds of letters and telegrams of condolence poured in. Dozens of churches and community organizations passed resolutions of sympathy. The loss was deeply felt, and Mary Hogle would be sorely missed. James expressed amazement at the outpouring of sympathy from the community and wrote, "I can not remember a single woman who has ever been mourned and honored here as has Mary. It is truly remarkable."

Back in 1929, when Mary believed she was dying of cancer, she had written in a letter to her young son James Edward, then at St. Paul's, a short postscript which twenty-three years later could still serve as a last behest. She wrote, "The ones that are your own flesh and blood are the ones that care. I am praying that you four, three men and a woman, will stand by each other through thick and thin. You are capable of doing anything if you do."

The Hogle and Copley families gathered in Salt Lake City for Mary's funeral, which was held at St. Mark's Cathedral on Friday, April 18, 1952. As her son George left home, he happened to pick up a scrap of wood from an old box that was going to be burned. With his pocket knife he devised a small cross. This he gave to the mortuary personnel and instructed them to place it in his mother's coffin. It was just the kind of little gesture his mother would have most appreciated.

CHAPTER THIRTY-THREE

The Legacies of Mary Hogle

MARY C. HOGLE LEFT TO HER FAMILY, and to the community as well, a legacy of service which continued to inspire decades after her death. The Copley tradition of caring and "doing" had been passed on to her children. The many projects and causes she embraced, the Zoological Gardens, the YWCA, Rowland Hall School, Westminster College, St. Mark's Cathedral, and the many arts organizations, continued to receive the patronage of the Hogle family through memorial funds and donations made in her name. Nor did the general public soon forget Mrs. Hogle. Thirty years after her death, the Hogles were still receiving requests for her pamphlet *Foods That Alkalinize and Heal.*

Mary believed strongly in cancer prevention. She had at one time insisted that the health and nutrition program outlined in her little booklet was her life's work. In 1941, the Federal Trade Commission, the attorneys, and the medical establishment had apparently succeeded in suppressing her theories. In the more than forty years which followed that suppression, the American Cancer Society and modern medical science searched in vain for a cancer cure.

In May of 1986, the *New England Journal of Medicine* published an article by researchers John C. Bailar III and Elaine M. Smith reviewing the progress made against cancer from 1950 through 1982, the most recent year for which complete data were then available. The study analyzed mortality data, site-specific mortality data, incidence, and survival data for the common types of cancer over the period. Their findings were alarming:

> The main conclusion we draw is that some 35 years of intense effort focused largely on improved treatment must be

judged a qualified failure. Results have not been what they were intended and expected to be. We think that there could be much current value in a comprehensive, consolidated objective review of the technical reasons for this failure. . . . Why were hopes so high, what went wrong, and can future hopes be built on more realistic expectations? Why is cancer the only major cause of death for which age-adjusted mortality rates are still increasing?

. . . It is time for an open debate to take stock of past achievements and to consider what level of funds should be invested in what kinds of future efforts.

. . . We are losing the war against cancer, notwithstanding the progress against several uncommon forms of the disease, improvements in palliation and extension of the productive years of life. A shift in research emphasis, from research on treatment to research on prevention, seems necessary if substantial progress is to be forthcoming.

Over the last forty years, upward of $500 million has been spent on cancer research. The American scientific establishment has always held the firm belief that given enough time, effort, and money — most especially money — it could find the cure for anything. At the end of World War II, the *New England Journal of Medicine* expressed the prevailing opinion of cancer researchers with the statement that "the limiting factor in cancer research is money." It now appears that time, effort, and money have been spent in a generally futile effort. While notable progress has been made in diagnosis and treatment, age-adjusted mortality rates continue to rise. The search for a cure has led nowhere.

Bailar and Smith call for "a comprehensive, . . . objective review of the technical reasons for this failure." But an objective review of the historical record will show that the failure was not a technical one. Much of the failure was of policy: medical, governmental, and scientific.

The medical and governmental bias which gave funding preference to cancer diagnosis and cure research over cancer prevention research can be dated to policy decisions made more than forty years ago. It is no mere coincidence that the American Society for the Prevention of Cancer became the American Cancer Society at that time. Governmental policy — dictated by the powerful medical lobby — was not only setting the goals but predicting the conclusions to be found as well.

It is easy to see now that that policy was a mistake. It was not so easy to see then, with the new areas of cancer research and new weapons in the "War on Cancer" to be exploited. Entire new disciplines were opening up. Radiation and chemotherapy were in their earliest phase. New and better surgical tools and procedures were being developed. These new techniques, diagnostic tools, surgical devices, therapeutic compounds, and radioactive elements were the costly front-line weapons.

It is difficult to find solid research information on diet and cancer from 1941 to 1980. This is explainable in part by the understandable phenomenon that qualified scientists in research fields do not generally flock to the investigation of discredited theories in unfundable or taboo disciplines. The blame must be placed at the door of the medical profession and the government that helped to discredit nutrition and dietary theories.

In fairness to the medical and scientific community of the thirties, these errors were less the result of poor science than of primitive scientific instrumentation and the lack of comprehensive data. The work of dietary theorists like Mary Hogle and researchers such as Frederick Hoffman was undertaken before the invention of the electron microscope, before the discovery of the double helix structure of the DNA molecule, and before the advent of the computer, which has made possible the analysis of vast amounts of complex demographic and statistical data. Biochemistry — the very heart of modern nutrition science — was in its infancy. Given the tools then at their disposal, it is impressive that the early workers hit upon anything worthwhile. What they accomplished and what happened to their work provides a sad commentary on the politics of cancer research in this country and serves as a lesson to those who would impose policy restraints on research, public discussion, or inquiry. If there is a lesson in this story, it is that major breakthroughs in medical science seldom come about through blind acceptance of existing dogma. Desirable scientific results simply cannot be legislated.

The vindication of Frederick Hoffman and Mary Hogle was

long in coming. Hoffman's extensive work on diet and cancer — published in 1937 — was not followed up by any other major studies for more than thirty years. It was not until May of 1983 that the National Cancer Institute in Washington, D.C., published its findings, "That diet may be responsible for 60 percent of all cancers among women and 40 percent among men." That same year, the National Research Council of the National Academy of Sciences and the National Cancer Society published a joint report of their findings on the links between diet and cancer, stressing some of the same points that Hoffman's discredited text had forty-six years earlier. Hoffman's speculation on the role of cholesterol as a carcinogen was later confirmed in other studies, as were many of his observations on carcinogens in the environment and in food additives. The joint study also contained some vindication of Mary Hogle's long-forgotten pamphlet, including data on the importance of roughage in the diet to prevent certain intestinal and colon cancers. As in Mary's diet, the study cautioned against the excessive use of salt, sugar, and coffee. As had Mary's diet, it recommended the elimination of fat from the diet and encouraged the consumption of whole grains, fresh fruits, and vegetables.

But it was Mary's claim that carrot juice *prevented* cancer that had got her in trouble with the FTC and the AMA. Mary had explained in the pamphlet that it wasn't the carrots per se that prevented cancer but the beta carotene that the carrots contained. Mary did not claim that if you ate carrots you would never have cancer. What she did claim was that they "helped prevent cancer." This assertion, flatly debunked by the medical establishment of the day, was the primary reason that the FTC began its investigation of her foundation in 1941 and the reason that Hogle's attorney advised suspending the publication of her pamphlet.

In September of 1983, the scholarly journal *Science* published an article by Dr. Bruce Ames, chairman of the department of biochemistry at the University of California, Berkeley. The results would not have surprised Mary Hogle: "Beta Carotene has been shown to be a powerful anti-oxidant . . . and may offer some protection against cancer." Dr. Ames had come to the same conclusion that Mary Hogle had reached decades earlier. Other studies by the biochemistry department of Johns Hopkins University, by the Mayo Clinic, and by the National Research Council of Canada provided the same conclusion. According to the Canadian study, "Beta Carotene may exert a genuine protective effect against the onset of cancer."

Cancer prevention and diet was suddenly back in vogue. Other studies linking diet to cancer and dozens showing the importance of beta carotene in helping to prevent cancer were published. In 1985 the *Periodical Index* listed more than eighty such articles; in 1986 there were more than one hundred. Mary Hogle was right all along.

The most remarkable of these articles appeared in the *New England Journal of Medicine* in November of 1986. This study by Dr. Marilyn Menkes, Dr. George W. Comstock, et al., claims that 80 percent of all cancers are related to environmental factors, the most important being diet. It stresses — as Hoffman's study had decades earlier — that fat and cholesterol consumption are directly related to the incidence of cancer. As did Hoffman's study, it calls for more research into diet and its relationship to cancer. But most interesting are the findings that vitamin A and beta carotene in the diet "helped prevent certain types of cancer" and were even of some value in cancer treatment. This from the same medical journal that forty-five years earlier had labeled Hoffman's work "unproven" and dismissed the notion that vitamins had any value as a cancer inhibitor or treatment. In 1940 the AMA had applauded the prosecution of those who said vitamin A helped prevent cancer with the flat statement that "No amount of chemical elements will prevent or cure serious diseases such as cancer."

By 1987, the medical establishment had finally come to recognize research conclusions remarkably similar to those of Frederick Hoffman and had come to embrace the principal tenets of Mary Hogle's booklet. It is arguable whether Mary Hogle arrived at her conclusions through the scientific method or through intuition, but her firm belief in their efficacy is still historically arresting. It is intriguing to speculate on what might have come from early extensive research into Mary C. Hogle's theories and Frederick Hoffman's research — and disturbing to speculate on how many lives might have been saved.

An ounce of bitter truth contains a pound of irony. Mary Hogle never knew the truth of her own theories. She died thirty years before the evidence was available to vindicate her work. But an even sadder irony was that although her theories on diet and cancer prevention were decades ahead of medical science, this knowledge was not sufficient to save her own life. The death certificate signed by Dr. Martin Lindem left no doubt as to the cause of her passing: "Multiple metastatic sarcoma, cerebral and general." Mary Hogle had died of cancer.

CHAPTER THIRTY-FOUR

James Albert Hogle — The Last Years

DURING MOST OF THE WINTER AND EARLY SPRING OF 1952, Mary's health had completely occupied James Hogle. Now that she was gone, he plunged back into his work, his reading, and his correspondence. If anything, he became more active than he had been since his accident on the lake eight years earlier. His work and study were therapeutic and helped keep his mind from his sorrow.

Mining had always been one of Hogle's special loves. It was one of the "Three M's," and throughout his long career he continued to be deeply involved in the industry. His interest in mining had been the cornerstone of his brokerage business, but it was the practical problems of mining engineering that fascinated him most. He loved all aspects of the profession, but particularly the puzzles of mining geology, which he studied with the same intensity as philosophy and literature. In the summer of 1952 he began to focus his energies on developments at the Rico Argentine Mine in Colorado and his properties in Eureka, Nevada.

The Eureka mining district had a long and colorful history. A number of rich strikes had been found in the 1880's, but the ore bodies were scattered in pockets over a wide geographic area. Over the next seventy years, the mines went through periods of sporadic boom and bust as rich deposits appeared and disappeared with baffling regularity. Many large mines had operated in the area, but their histories were marked by the same pattern of alternating success and ruin. The problem was that the discovery of rich deposits encouraged the investors to enlarge their operations well beyond the localized ore bodies. The time and expense involved in excavating worthless rock was frequently greater than the profits extracted.

Many a mining company put all its profits back into the ground.

With the acquisition of the Eureka Prospect and John Hayes Hammond's Diamond Excelsior Mine in the thirties, Hogle began focusing his attention in the area. In the late thirties both his sons had worked at Eureka with Hogle's mining engineer, Sherm Hinkley. New shafts were opened throughout the forties, and while ore was shipped, most of the work was in locating, surveying, and acquiring adjacent claims. Hogle was certain that substantial ore bodies would eventually be found in the area, but he was intimately familiar with the history of the district and moved cautiously.

Hogle described his search for the hidden pockets of buried treasure as "intensely absorbing." He studied the assay reports in detail and pored over the geological maps. Hogle wrote to a friend: "The geology is very complicated. In fact, I have never thoroughly understood it, but I have always been impressed by the widespread mineralization."

As with everything else in his career, the treasure hunting involved months of careful study and analysis and years of perseverance. In November of 1949 he had written to one of the stockholders:

> At the present time, no actual mining is being done at the Consolidated Eureka. The development program, which was started two years ago, did not prove successful, but enough geological information was secured that we felt justified in doing other work.
>
> However, before spending any more money, we decided it would be advisable to have a careful geological examination made of the old ore bodies and of the new work done during the past two years, so as to learn where it would be advisable to continue.

Hogle received a good deal of assay and survey assistance from the U.S. Geological Survey. After months of preparation, Consolidated Eureka began deep diamond drilling at selected locations on the property. This work too was in the nature of a survey. The preliminary results were disappointing, but Hogle was not discouraged in the least. He was certain the ore was there.

In December of 1950 an ore discovery was made in the Diamond Tunnel at Eureka. The ore body produced 144 tons which averaged 12.7 percent lead, 30 ounces of silver, and .27 ounces of gold per ton. It was a good strike, but like earlier deposits it was quickly exhausted. Two years later, Hogle was still studying the geology and having drilling samples taken at Eureka.

It wasn't until June of 1952 that Sherm Hinkley and Hogle decided to resume mining. They believed they had finally solved the complicated puzzle, and Hogle was ready to take the gamble. During that summer he acquired six additional claims and by September was gearing up to reopen the mine. It was an expensive proposition. A five-inch compressed-air line had to be entirely replaced. New timbering was stockpiled and new machinery ordered. Hogle had no illusions about the formidable obstacles they faced and was preparing for a long campaign.

To finance the operations, Hogle drew $28,546 from the family-held Bonneville on the Hill Corporation in the form of a loan to Consolidated Eureka. He undertook the exploration phase without assessing the minority stockholders. He also assumed financial responsibility for management, office space, accounting, and stock transference. Hogle was bearing the lion's share of the financial risk for the development of Consolidated Eureka Mining Company.

But bearing risk was not the sole responsibility of the private sector. At the beginning of World War II the Defense Department's Minerals Exploration Administration had been established to provide interest-free loans to assist in the location and development of strategic metals. Although philosophically he might have had reservations about receiving government assistance, James was not one to look a gift horse in the mouth, and on April 18, 1953, he applied for government funds to continue the exploration.

The government geologists were suitably impressed with work already completed at Eureka, and on October 26, 1953, Hogle signed a contract under which the government agreed to participate in the rehabilitation of several old shafts and drifts and in the opening of extensive new cross-cuts at the Diamond Mine. The new development commenced on November first, and during the next eight months the government's share came to $24,956. In the last week of July 1954, commercially mineable ore was finally located in one of the cross-cuts. It was not the rich strike that Hogle had anticipated, but it provided inducement for continuing the search. Now that ore had been found, Hogle canceled the government contract.

In August Consolidated Eureka shipped 267 tons of dry ore to the smelter. After freight, smelter costs, and government royalties had been deducted, the company netted $44,266. As with earlier finds, the discovery was tantalizing, if not substantial. Hogle would continue to search for additional mineralized areas.

While Hogle's attention was focused on the search for precious metals in Nevada, a mining development of an entirely different sort was about to take southern Utah by storm. On October 31, 1952, Dr. John Dunning, dean of engineering at Columbia University, visited with Hogle at his offices in Salt Lake City. Hogle served on an alumni committee that was raising $16 million for the engineering school, and Dunning's visit was to confer on the progress of the drive. But Dunning had other matters on his mind besides fund-raising. "While he was talking to Jim and me," said Hogle, "he pulled a cube of uranium metal from a case he was carrying. It was two inches square and he said it represented the fuel power of 6,000 tons of coal! If you think of what that might mean for shipping and power plants, you can realize the possibilities."

For Hogle, the immediate opportunity was not in mining uranium but in taking advantage of other mineral needs created by the nuclear development. The Rico Argentine in Colorado was primarily a lead, zinc, and silver mine, and the profitability of its operations was tied to price fluctuations in the metals market. At the end of World War II a substantial drop in the price of metals had forced its temporary closure, although Rico did continue to ship ore and pay dividends through the worst of the slump.

But Rico also had large deposits of iron pyrite, which was needed by the nuclear industry to process uranium ore. In the months following the visit of Dean Dunning, Hogle and his associates at Rico studied ways to take advantage of the coming nuclear age. By November of 1953, Rico Argentine was preparing to supply the emerging atomic industry: "Rico is investigating the situation and already we have been approached to furnish pyrite for a sulfuric acid plant. This acid is required for the reduction of uranium ore and there is now a demand in the Rico territory for over 100 tons a day."

Although Hogle anticipated the importance of the nuclear industry, he was completely surprised by the uranium rush and boom which was developing. Nothing quite like it had been seen in the west for over half a century. It was the very kind of old-fashioned rush that his father had witnessed at Gregory's Gulch, Alder Gulch, Helena, and Leesburg, with prospectors flooding into southern Utah seeking instant riches. Disputes over claims and actual incidents of claim-jumping soon had many of the prospectors wearing side arms. Moab, Utah, which was at the very center of the uranium strikes in the southeastern corner of the state, was transformed overnight into a wild west boom camp, complete with suppliers, grubstakers, saloon keepers, gamblers, prostitutes, and instant millionaires. As in Gregory's Gulch a hundred years before, gunfights were not uncommon. It was something out of another era, and the similarity to those bygone days was not lost on James A. Hogle:

> Salt Lake has become the focus of this extraordinary Uranium Boom. It is different from the Goldfield Boom of 1906, although there seems to be the same national interest. In that boom, the development work was costly for nearly every undertaking. Whereas, this boom resembles a placer strike out of the 19th century.
> It is something which has not happened in mining in this century, perhaps since the California Gold Rush of '49. Then, one or two men with a shovel and a sluice box or pan could make a living or in some cases a fortune without any investment. Somewhat the same thing has happened here in uranium mining.

The uranium boom brought about a corresponding boom in the penny stock market which was without precedent. For the next three years, the Salt Lake Stock Exchange was a mecca for speculators. Many of Hogle's customers were eager to get into uranium stocks and wrote to him for advice. Although J. A. Hogle & Co. was the oldest mining brokerage house in the Intermountain West and handled uranium stocks as part of its regular service, he personally tried to dissuade his customers from engaging in the wild speculation:

> How long this boom is going to last is problematical but the mining of the ore itself is just getting started and will bring an important new industry into this area. However, we are not recommending the purchase of any uranium stocks at this time. . . .
>
> You have no doubt read about what is going on here. Our local situation is rather unique as Salt Lake has become the focus of this extraordinary uranium boom. There have been several articles in national magazines. This last week, *Business Week* had an article about the Salt Lake Exchange and a few days ago *Life* sent their photographer in to take pictures of the crowd that assembles every morning in our office. . . .
>
> . . . Regarding the uranium boom, of course it can not keep pace with the last few weeks, but it is an entirely new industry which will last as long as there is a demand for the metal. We have left the mining end of it alone for the same reason that we did not go into oil stocks in Canada a few years ago, the reason being that the market was all out of line with the real values. . . .
>
> . . . There are some important uranium developments here in Utah but most of the prospects are being held at too high a price. . . .
>
> . . . The uranium boom here is almost as bad as the Goldfield Boom of 1906. It is absurd the way some of the stocks have advanced and, of course, the outcome will be disastrous in the end. I will let you know later how Rico is going to try to take advantage of it by building an acid plant, as the company has several million tons of iron pyrites available. . . .

As the number of worthless penny stocks increased, Hogle's initial caution turned to skepticism. Those who were wise enough to have followed his early counsel were safely vested in other areas: "We are not now, nor have we in the past, recommended the purchase of uranium stocks. At one time it was reported that there were 600 producers on the Colorado Plateau. I doubt now if there were ever more than 150 mines in the area that were actually producing ore at any one time."

CHEMICALS
OILS AND AVIATIONS
INDUSTRIALS

Hogle's interest in mining and mineral development was not confined to the search for underground deposits. He had frequently told his son Jim that "perhaps the greatest mineral storehouse in the country was the Great Salt Lake." It was a long-held belief of his that some day a process would be developed to extract the minerals from the briny waters. It had been sixty-five years since he had witnessed his Uncle Owen's rescue of the drunken passenger who fell from the deck of the steamer *General Garfield* into the bitter waters of the lake. Perhaps that experience had something to do with his conviction that the lake would one day be mined. But even if it didn't, there is something historically arresting in his personal certainty of the lake's mining future. His father and his Uncle Owen must have described to him the placer operations at Pikes Peak, Helena, and Loon Creek, where water was used to separate the dirt from the gold-bearing gravels. For thousands upon thousands of years the spring runoffs had been doing much the same thing to the mineral-rich mountains of the Great Basin, dissolving rock, exposing the underlying ore bodies, and eventually depositing tons of mineral silts in Utah's dead sea. When the lake level was particularly low and the mineral concentrations high, he firmly believed the lake water would be "mineable." As with his prophetic belief in space travel, the extraction of minerals from the lake would one day become a reality.

Cousin Archie

Uncle Owen was frequently on Hogle's mind in the early fifties, but not because of his close association with the frothy brine. In June of 1951, he received via the Ogden office a letter from a first cousin he had never met, Archie Owen Gilmore.

Archie was the eldest child of Hogle's uncle Albert. The other offspring were Anna, Mary, Lucile, and Jimmy. Jimmy, who died in infancy, had been named for Hogle's father. Hogle's second

The Big Board at J. A. Hogle & Co. in a photograph taken on November 20, 1958, for *Life* magazine. Sadie Ballard is the head board marker, at left. Tom Ivers stands at center right, talking to a customer. Courtesy Sadie Ballard.

name came from Albert Gilmore, Archie's second name from Uncle Owen. In the matter of namesakes, at least, the families had once been very close.

Archie first joined the Army in 1909 and later served as a first lieutenant in World War I. He had spent most of the next twenty years in and out of the Army and the National Guard. In 1951 he was living at the Elks Club in Albuquerque, New Mexico. His letter was a request for James A. to help him get his army pension, which had been tied up in red tape for several years. For James there must have been something hauntingly familiar about the correspondence. Fifty years earlier he had tried, unsuccessfully, to help Uncle Owen get his pension for his Civil War service.

It was obvious that Archie was in some financial straits. In his letter he also mentioned that his daughter Gloria was getting married. James wrote back to his long-lost cousin that he would be happy to help him solve his pension problems and mailed along a check as a wedding present for Archie's daughter.

Archie's younger sisters, Mary Wynkoop, Anna Martin, and Lucile Robinson, had corresponded with James for several years, but when they heard that their brother Archie had written him requesting his help, Anna and Mary became incensed. Anna wrote a letter strongly advising that James "Not get further involved with Archie," and Mary wrote a long letter explaining why.

> When I got back from my vacation I found things very normal here — A.O.G. was at it again only this time he had broken out in a new spot. Anna has asked me to verify her advice. . . . A.O.G. has never broken into civilian life. He has lived beyond his means and is critical of those who try to save. I had little chance to save myself as my pay usually went to him to keep mother from knowing what a heel her first born and best loved child was. . . .

Mary Wynkoop's antagonism toward her older brother was of long standing. It was compounded by loans she had made to him that were never repaid. She wrote, "No matter how much is sent, it will be spent before you blink your eyes and it is spent with a flourish. . . . That repayment line is a huge laugh. At the end of the proposed expiration date a new and more terrible emergency will arise. . . ."

But Mary's chief complaint against Archie was not that he was a moocher but that he was "just like Uncle Henry." What that meant she made very clear to her cousin:

> In regard to Uncle Henry. . . . For years he had not touched liquor and Mother let me go to California with him. I was about 13 years old and that was the time we made the visit to Salt Lake City. After depositing me with Aunt Anna and Aunt Mary, Uncle Henry returned to Utah. He must have bent his arm there many times for when he got back to California, he was on a protracted spree.
>
> He and I were put on a train and headed back to Lebanon. I'll never forget that terrifying experience. It took us two weeks to get home, stopping in cities all along the way to have convivial sessions with brother Elks. He would wander away, Brother Elks would round him up put us on another train — and in the next city, all would be done over again. After three days in New Orleans I was a wreck and broke down and cried, asking him if he felt no responsibility for his brother's child. I dogged his footsteps and since he couldn't take me into a bar, he must have become sober enough for this to penetrate, for he went to a barber shop and got the works. Then we took the first train home. It was about four years later that Uncle Henry started drinking again and from then on nothing could make him stop. This experience has left its mark on me and I can not help it if I'm a little resentful.

Mary Wynkoop's bitter resentment of Uncle Henry she projected onto her older brother Archie, who was also a Brother Elk and who, when he wasn't living at an Elks Club, was frequently in Veterans' Administration hospitals around the country. Mary contended that his periods of hospitalization were to take "the cure" for his addiction.

At first James was inclined to follow Mary and Anna's advice, but the more he learned about Cousin Archie, the less severe was his judgment. Archie was not abstemious when it came to alcohol, but neither was he "just like Uncle Henry," as Mary had claimed. As a young man Archie had nursed Henry during his last illness, as James had nursed his father. For Archie this task was a particularly painful experience as Henry had gone blind before succumbing to his alcoholism. Archie later recalled that ordeal to James and commented that "it probably saved me from a similar fate." Nor was Mary accurate in her appraisal of Archie's health problems, as he suffered from heart disease and acute bronchial asthma.

Archie, in fact, had been sent to New Mexico from a V.A. hospital in Lexington, Kentucky, in the hope that the dry desert climate would benefit his condition. He later moved to a hospital in Prescott, Arizona, and then to a military hospital at Camp White, Oregon.

Mary Wynkoop well knew James's position as the clearinghouse of all family information. In her letter of warning about Archie she asked him not to pass on any of it to "a certain relative in California, who has an uncanny way of finding out and emphasizing the worst in the families of all her kin." Mary did not have to mention the relative's name. James knew Edna Weed well. Her tongue was legendary. Cousin Edna was as caustic as Cousin Elsie was sweet, but James recognized and appreciated Edna's wit. While most of the family avoided her, he carried on a long, friendly correspondence with her. Nor would Mary's or Anna's strident warnings stop him from beginning a long and friendly correspondence with Archie Owen Gilmore. James treated all his kin with equal consideration, and neither gossip nor family squabbles seemed to affect his personal relationships with individual members of his extensive clan.

The letters exchanged by the new-found cousins were open and chatty and soon became a regular part of Hogle's weekly correspondence. Most of them dealt with Archie's pension and health problems, but they also touched on matters concerning the family. Archie's mother, Nancy Gilmore, was still alive in her late eighties, and the letters usually contained updates on her health. Many also included reminiscences about the family. Archie recalled meeting James's father as a boy and remembered too that his own father and Uncle Henry used to receive mail from the west under the name of "Hogle." He recalled visiting their mutual cousins the Steeles and the Weeds in Denver and the Mantors in California. Both men remembered Uncle Owen fondly. James wrote Archie of the fishing and hunting trips he took with Owen as a boy and of the influence Owen had had on his life. Archie frequently wrote James of his own fishing trips, of various techniques he used on bass, crappie, and walleyed pike, of special flies he had developed and his favorite fishing spots.

Against Mary Wynkoop's advice, James sent Archie periodic gifts of money, often unsolicited. Several letters included the following postscript: "I am enclosing a check for you as a gift in memory of Uncle Owen. I hope you get some good fishing with it and keep well." James's thoughtful manner insured that Archie's feelings would not be hurt and that his self-esteem would remain intact.

The letters to Archie Owen Gilmore spanned the period from August of 1951 to June of 1954. James had frequently invited Archie to visit him in Salt Lake City, but health problems had repeatedly prevented the two cousins from actually meeting. Finally, in late May of 1954, the arrangements for the visit were completed. Archie would arrive on June eighth. That morning, Hogle was at home expecting a call from the railroad station to pick Archie up when Western Union delivered the following telegram: "Archie died in Oregon yesterday, Mary Wynkoop." In a follow-up letter she explained what had occurred: "Archie passed away on Monday [June 7th]. He had his bag packed for the trip when he had a sudden attack of asthma. . . . He was taken to the hospital in Portland. He felt better and left the hospital against the advice of the doctors. Back at his hotel he had another attack and was returned to the hospital by ambulance, where he had the fatal heart attack. . . ."

Archie's sudden death came as a great shock to James. Although he had never actually met the man, he had grown to know him during their three-year correspondence. Archie's death was a profound loss to his aged mother, Nancy Gilmore. Her health declined rapidly during the next six months, and she passed away the first week of December 1954. Nancy was the last Gilmore relative of his father's generation, and James wrote his cousins Mary Wynkoop, Anna Martin, and Lucile Robinson long letters of tribute and condolence.

James continued to take a keen interest in all members of the family — no matter how distant the relationship. In August of

1953 he received a letter from cousin Edna informing him of the coming marriage of Edna's grandson, Patrick Owen Neil:

> Patrick asked me to give him the picture I had of Grandfather [Patrick Gilmore], his great, great grandfather. I told him I had given it to you. He seemed to be very disappointed so I told him I would ask you to give it back to me. Anyway, since he is the only one in the family who has the two names, Patrick and Owen, I thought he should have it.
>
> The reason he wants it is to show to Delores, the girl he is going to marry. She has a lot of relatives and family means a lot to them. Pat has so few relatives, just you, brother Jim, Elsie, Mary Wynkoop and Jimmy Martin, that he wants them to know he has them. Goodness knows what he thinks they suspect!

But James was unable to find the snapshot of Patrick Gilmore, so he had two duplicates made of the large portrait of Patrick which had once hung over the mantlepiece in his fathers' home and sent one each to Edna and her grandson. As he had for Archie's daughter

Jim and his father, about 1953.

Gloria, James also sent a sum of money as a wedding present to the future wife of his second cousin twice removed. Edna was delighted with the portraits and wrote thanking James for them and for the unexpected gift he had sent Delores. Edna also mentioned her continuing battle with heart disease.

Finale

James's own health had been generally good in the years 1952 through '54, but when he visited Katharine in California for Christmas, he complained of digestive upsets, which he attributed to their softened water, and mentioned other symptoms that worried his daughter. His own eating habits had always been simple, but since his wife's death the simple meals had become increasingly spartan. The list of items that upset his stomach had grown long. His brother-in-law Ed Copley and his wife Maud had moved in to help James with the cooking and housekeeping, but he generally preferred to prepare his own meals and usually took them alone. Maud was also in failing health, so much of Ed's time was spent in caring for her.

James's health problems were annoying, but he seldom let them interrupt his established routine. He continued to work at the office in the mornings and followed the progress of Consolidated Eureka closely. In February assay reports from the mine indicated that they were finally closing in on a rich ore deposit. Rumors of the strike had already caused Consolidated Eureka stock to skyrocket. It was no time to slow down. On January 12 he wrote to George Murrell, describing his daily schedule: "From the time I leave here before noon until I sit down to dinner at six o'clock, and except for a short nap after lunch, every minute of my time is occupied. Then in the evening I continue my reading and my studying."

James's stomach and digestive problems continued to bother him through the early spring of 1955. On the recommendation of his doctor he radically altered his diet and began taking injections of vitamin B-12 to boost his sagging blood count. The vitamin treatments and dietary changes appear to have brought him some relief. In April he wrote to Katharine about his improved health, but he included advice and wishes for her future that were somewhat out of keeping with the optimistic tone of the beginning of the letter:

> I am sure you will be interested to know that I have conquered my health problems which began to develop last December and culminated in an acute attack of colitis in March. Acids and acid fruits were the chief cause, and too much food of the wrong variety, especially the rough foods caused the distress.
>
> I have to be very careful now in my eating and work and recreation. Living as simply as I do gives me a wonderful appetite and I probably never enjoyed food as much as I do now — also life itself.
>
> I thought this would be an opportune time to give you the personal facts about myself. I know you will take good care of the children and hope you will also live in a way to keep well yourself and will continue with eagerness the work you are doing.

James Hogle was seventy-nine years old. He had lived a long, productive, and prosperous life. Increasingly his letters digressed to the subject of his mortality. These were not morbid or fatalistic comments, but deeply personal and spiritual observations — summations of his life's experience and expressions of gratitude to his friends. Many have the tone of fond farewell, and the same phrases turn up again and again. As he wrote George Murrell that spring,

> I was an only child and learned early to amuse myself with reading and being alone. I have only been lonesome two or three times in my life. Of late years I have been especially thankful for my remembrance of life and peace of mind.
>
> When I was a young man, I only had one or two close or intimate good friends at the same time, but after I went into business I did not make any more close friends until you came into my life.
>
> I have given you these details because I want to take this occasion to tell you how much our friendship has meant to me, as well as how much I have enjoyed it.

In late May of 1955 Sherm Hinkley and the miners at Eureka finally made the big strike. The ore deposit, located in fissures in the bottom of Jumbo Cave in the Diamond Mine, was one of the richest strikes in the area since the 1880's. Hogle's faith, hard work, and perseverance had paid off once again. Though the size of the deposit was unknown, there was no question that the mine was now a moneymaker, as James wrote: "The strike is so strong and big and rich that I wouldn't have the slightest doubt in tapping it 400 ft. deeper. Drifting on the Diamond Fault or north from the Jumbo Cave this summer should be exciting."

While James's primary attention was fixed on Jumbo Cave in Eureka, his immediate family were garnering successes of their own, as he wrote on June 8:

> Jim and Bonnie left for the east this morning to attend the graduation of their oldest boy at St. Paul's School, Concord. Jim is now 18 and is going to go to Stanford. Holly [Hugh], 16, will be in the 4th form next year, having completed 2 years. They will see George and Lois while there. George will finish his internship at Presbyterian Hospital the end of this month and is going back to London for another year's study in September. He is going to come here for a short visit before he goes abroad.

James looked forward to his son's visit with much anticipation, and hardly a letter was mailed to the family that summer that did not mention George's trip to Salt Lake in August. He arrived as scheduled on August 16. While their meeting was warm and friendly, George, who had not seen his father in over a year, was alarmed at his appearance. His father looked pale and weak and seemed to have lost weight. He asked him if he was all right and how he'd been feeling. James told his son that he didn't have much energy anymore and felt fatigued. When George asked if he'd been to the doctor, his father told him that he had and that his "hemoglobin was down."

George knew that a lowered hemoglobin count was one of the things that might indicate the presence of cancer and asked his father if the doctor had examined him. James replied that he hadn't. George was stunned that the doctor had failed to examine his father after receiving the results of the blood test. He told him that he had to have a thorough examination, and James suggested that since George was now a doctor perhaps he himself would perform it. The unanticipated suggestion surprised the young doctor, but he told his father that he would be honored to perform the service.

George Hogle knew that doctors weren't supposed to examine their next of kin, as objectivity is crucial in making any medical diagnosis. But George felt that James's personal doctor might already have made a mistake, and so he prepared to examine his father, in part to relieve his own fears.

The examination started well. The heartbeat was regular and fine, but when George got to the abdomen he found two large masses and stifled the impulse to say, "Oh, my God, no!" After the examination was completed and James had dressed, George told his father that he had an inflammation of the transverse colon and that if it wasn't taken care of, it could create a blockage. He would have to have an operation. James Hogle thanked his son and shook his hand. He then opened his wallet and handed George a twenty-dollar bill, saying, "I think you should have this for a very professional job." George accepted and said, "Thank you, Dad." It was George Hogle's first private fee.

In 1955, telling someone he had cancer was tantamount to pronouncing the death sentence. Neither the medical profession nor the public of that period spoke openly of the disease for which there was no cure.

A number of vague euphemisms were used to describe symptoms and, generally, unless the patient demanded to be told the truth, an unspoken conspiracy of silence prevailed. James A. Hogle was unusually well versed on the subject, however. Not only had his wife died of cancer, but James had exchanged with Bert Copley dozens of articles on the disease from the foremost medical and scientific journals of the day. It is almost certain that he was aware of his true condition.

But in a very practical way, James had been preparing for his own death for many years. The spiritual and religious reading that had so absorbed him for the last decade was directed toward this one absolute and unavoidable reality. He had frequently written of the comfort his studies had given him, and he was now resigned to the natural course of things.

James Albert Hogle signing his will on August 26, 1955, in a photograph taken by his son George.

Then too, he was seventy-nine and had lived a long and extraordinarily productive life. He had seen to the education of his children and had followed with pride the beginnings of their careers. He had lived long enough to see and to know all nine of his grandchildren: Katharine's daughters, Kathleen and Deborah McTernan; the four boys of James E. and Bonnie, James E., Jr., Hugh H., Donald M., and Owen C.; and George and Lois's three children, Allan C., Stephen C., and Frances.

For more than thirty years too, he had been preparing his will. He had spent years studying the wills of various industrialists to learn how to save as much of his life's work for his posterity as he could.

At precisely 9:58 A.M. on the morning of August 26, 1955, James A. Hogle signed the final amendment to the document. George Hogle recorded the event with his camera. It was the last photograph of his father ever taken.

James checked into LDS Hospital some days before the sched-uled operation to undergo tests and prepare for the ordeal. The hospital routine was very boring for him, and on several occasions

Katharine Hogle Cole.

he called a taxi and went to the office. He was there the morning before the scheduled surgery. Several employees remembered him shaking hands with them, thinking to themselves that Mr. Hogle was saying goodbye. Perhaps he was. The letters written during those short trips to the office have an unmistakeable tone, echoing the farewells he had written several months earlier. To his friend George Murrell he wrote:

> Miss Styles wrote you about my check-up. They found an inflammatory constriction in the middle of my colon, which necessitates an operation. . . . I would like to take this occasion to tell you how much I have appreciated and enjoyed your friendship and letters, with the hope that they will both continue as long as I retain my faculties. I hope that you will continue to have a happy and interesting long life.

To the eighty-six-year-old Bert Copley he wrote: "Since I wrote you last, I have been to the hospital for a complete check-up. George is here having completed his internship at Presbyterian Hospital and I wanted him to look me over while he was here. He found an inflammatory constriction in the middle of the colon which necessitates an operation: So if you do not hear from me you will know the reason." The letter closed with the same farewell paragraph as that to George Murrell. When Copley read the letter to his wife Poldi, she said, "He's dying and is saying goodbye."

The operation was performed on Tuesday, September 1, 1955. George Hogle was permitted to observe the entire procedure. When they opened James up they found the colon cancer and removed it, but they also found metastasis of the liver, for which nothing could be done. He would survive the operation, but it was only a matter of time.

While James was in recovery, his son George went to Jack Lerwill, who kept the books for the family and the firm. He asked him to account all of the family holdings and come up with a figure for their worth. The Hogles were, of course, worth many millions of dollars. George took the figure to his father to show him what he had built in his life. He tried to control his emotions, but his eyes welled up with tears, and there was no disguising his grief.

James E. Hogle.

Clearly, James already suspected that his illness was terminal. He told Katharine and Jim that he wanted nothing else done to prolong his life. George believed that the progress of the liver cancer would be slow and that his father would live for many months. Indeed, he did seem to be quite recovered from the operation within a week and even sat up in bed and had a martini with Katharine. But within two weeks peritonitis had set in, and he declined rapidly until death ended the ordeal on the evening of September fourteenth. During an afternoon visit the day before, he had said to Jim, "I have no fear of death."

In his last full letter to George Murrell, Hogle had quoted a passage from Aldous Huxley, a quotation most out of tone with the rest of the letter. In retrospect, after James's death, it seemed to Murrell that he had been attempting to convey to his friend a final summation of his life.

For in so far, as we are not dependent upon temperament or fortune's accident, happiness, goodness and creativeness, are the products of an individual's philosophy of life. As we believe, so we are. And what we believe depends upon what we have been taught — by our parents and schoolmasters, by the books

Dr. George H. Hogle.

and newspapers we read, by traditions clearly formulated or unspoken, or the economic, political and ecclesiastical organizations to which we belong.

If there is to be genuine human progress, happiness, goodness and creativeness must be maintained by individuals of successive generations and throughout the whole span of lives that are by nature, unprogressive, and in the teeth of circumstance that must often be unfavorable.

Fortune did indeed smile upon James A. Hogle, but his success was no accident. The strong traditions of his family were deeply ingrained in him. From Patrick Gilmore, James Hogle, and Uncle Owen he had acquired a strong desire to succeed, from his mother the drive to excel. James and Owen Hogle were practical men, and from them he got his keen insight into the ways of the world. But he learned much more from these two vital, adventurous, life-loving characters than how to beat the odds. In a very real way, they taught him how men should live. From Bishop Tuttle and Henry and Joseph Coit came Hogle's strong ethical convictions. From his classmates and instructors at St. Paul's came his capitalism and political conservatism. From men such as James F. Kemp and Billie Craig he acquired the crucial skills which would serve him through his professional life.

Although the early influences on James A. Hogle can be traced throughout his career, he never became static and always remained open to new influences and ideas. Mary C. Hogle had an enormous impact on his life. She was the contrast and counterpoint of his existence, and to Mary can be given much of the credit for James's personal growth. At the very end of his life, George Murrell, Bert Copley, and especially his son George contributed to the final picture. It was George who first introduced his father to eastern philosophy and helped to broaden his spiritual horizons, which in the end brought him peace.

There was a complexity to James Hogle that was not often seen or even suspected by his business associates. His love of poetry, literature, opera, and philosophy were very private passions, unknown to most of his employees and colleagues. All of these elements, influences, interests, and convictions combined in him in such a weave that success was inevitable. His life was the sum and consummation of all who had gone before and all he had learned in the process of living. James A. Hogle could well have served as a paradigm of Aldous Huxley's well-led life.

Afterword

Within each of us burns a flame of atavistic curiosity. The desire to know from whence we came begs for satisfaction. Genealogists have constructed complex family trees, but for most of us the only way to know our ancestors is to know ourselves. Within our genes their biologic legacy lives on, and to each of us they have bequeathed a planet changed for their having been here.

This book is a microcosmic record of a few lives. But it is a beginning. And for our family it shall become a torch to be passed from generation to generation so that those who are to come may reach back across the span of years and touch the wrinkled faces of their kin.

The flame of the Gilmore family has burned with many essences. Loyalty, generosity, and integrity are redolent in its vapors. Whether coded in the genes or passed down by example and tradition, these three endowments are the hallmark of the Gilmore legacy.

As the torch is passed, the influence of parent upon child will assure the survival of our ancestors.

Epitaph from a Scottish Gravestone

"The whole earth is the tomb of heroic men, and their story is not graven only on the stone over their clay — but abides everywhere without visible symbol woven into the fabric of other men's lives."

Who shall pick up the torch?

Hugh H. Hogle, M.D.

[503]

GILMORES, HOGLES AND KINGS

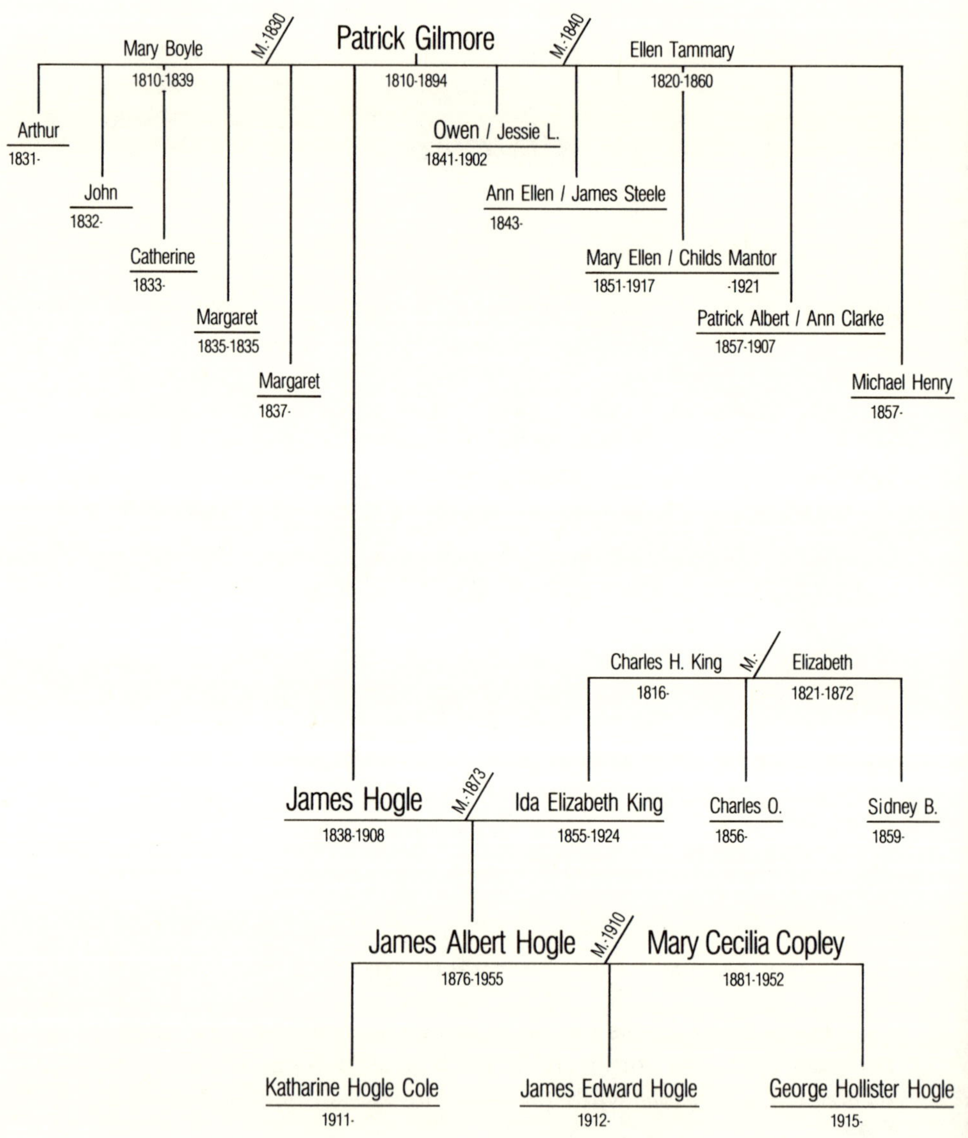

COPLEYS, HOLLISTERS AND WOODWARDS

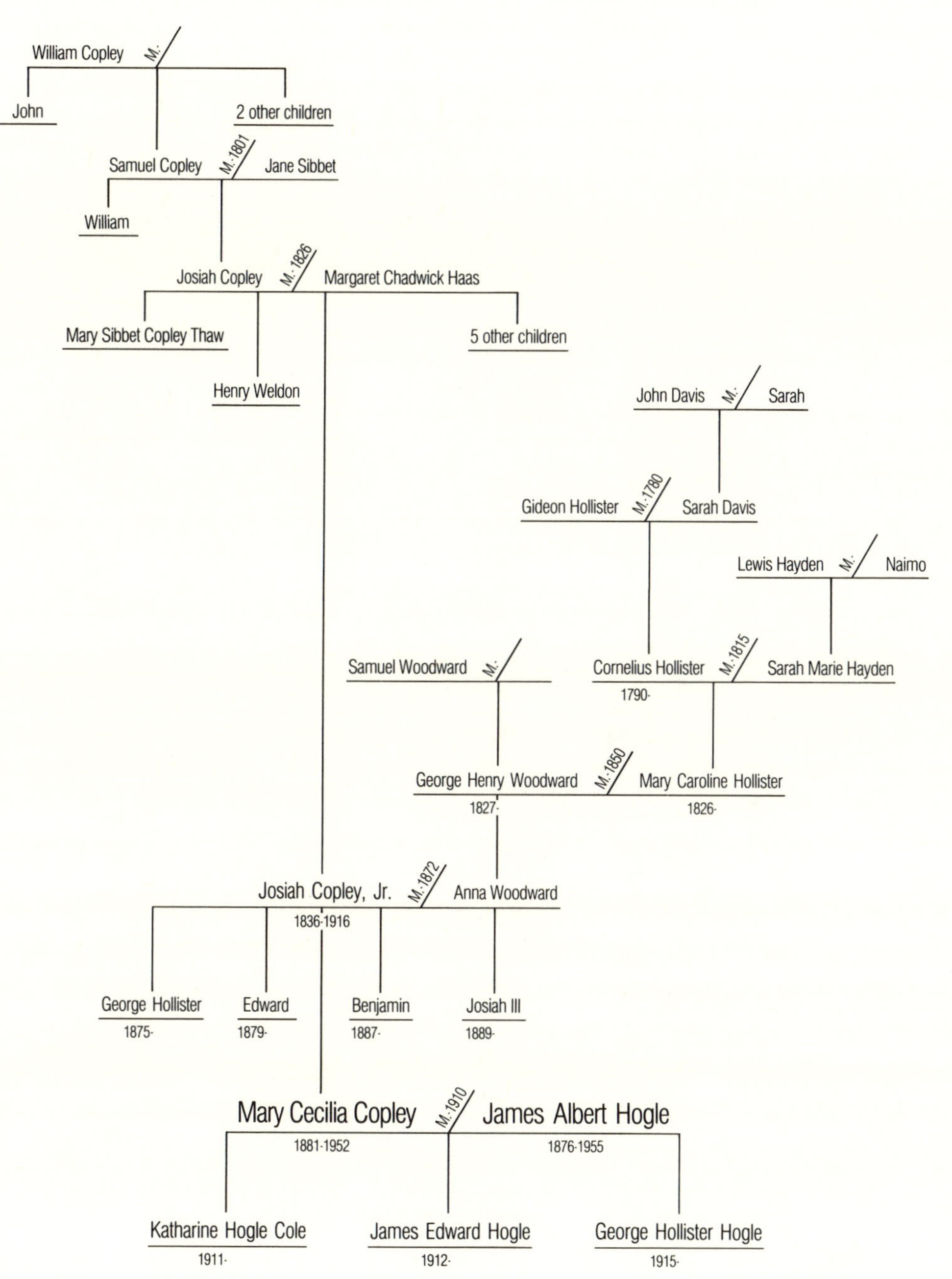

GEORGE H. HOGLE AND KATHARINE HOGLE COLE FAMILIES

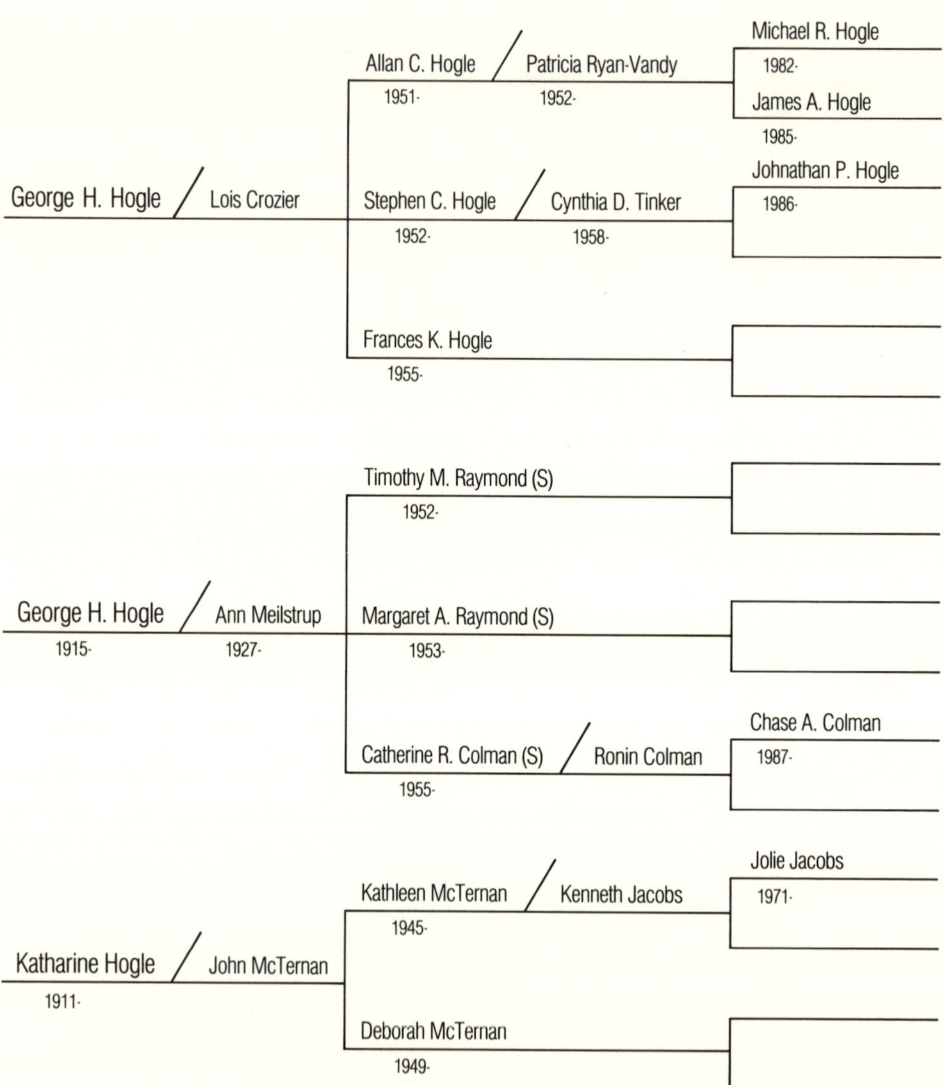

NOTE: A - Adopted

    S - Stepchild

SMITHS AND RICHES

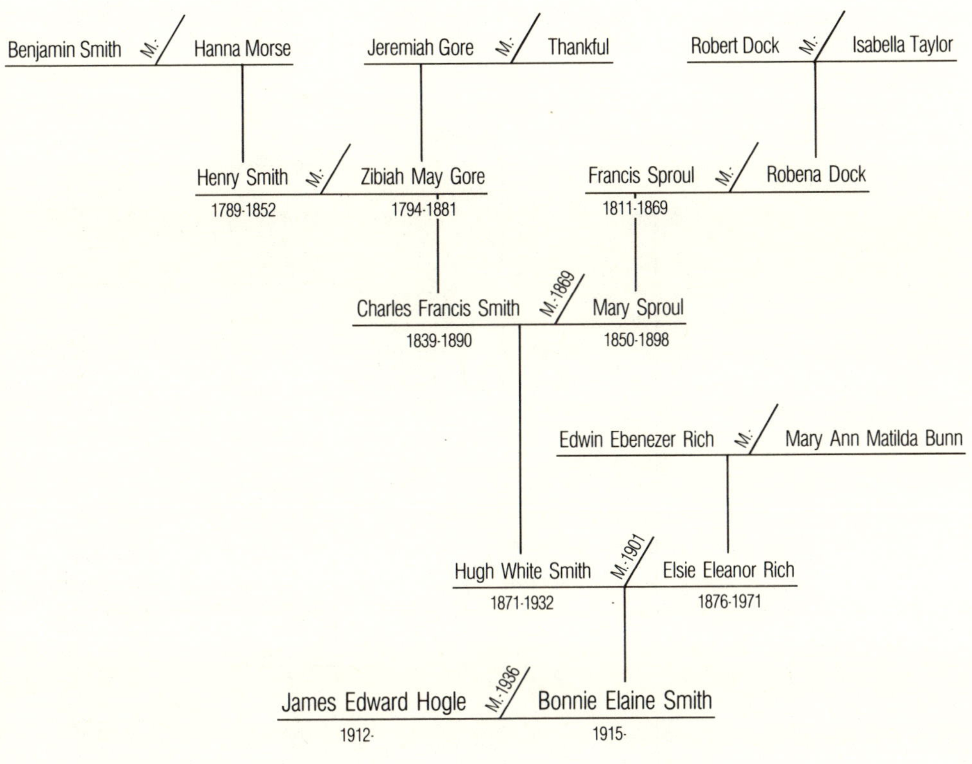

JAMES E. HOGLE FAMILY

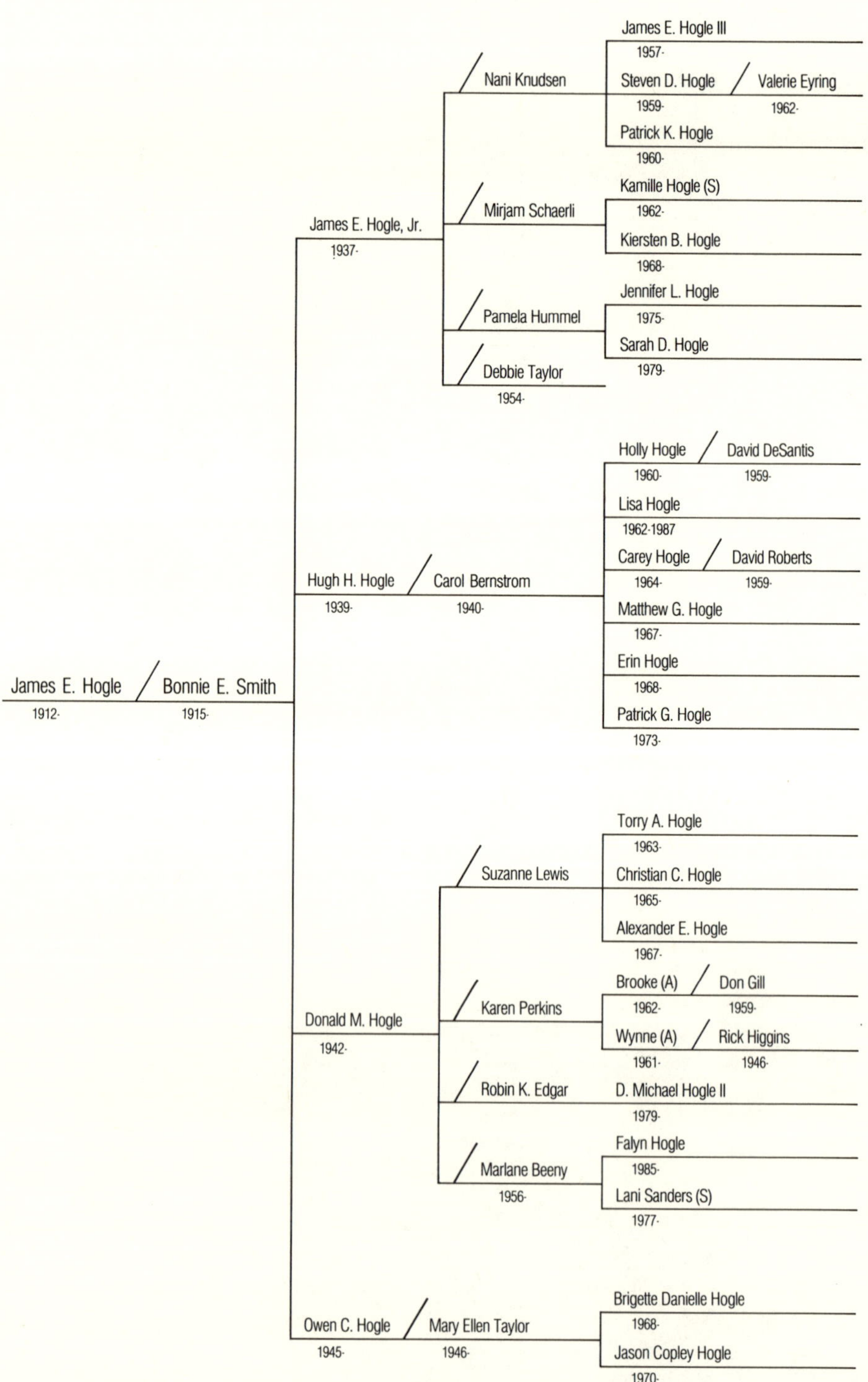

GRANDCHILDREN AND GREAT–GRANDCHILDREN OF JAMES E. AND BONNIE S. HOGLE

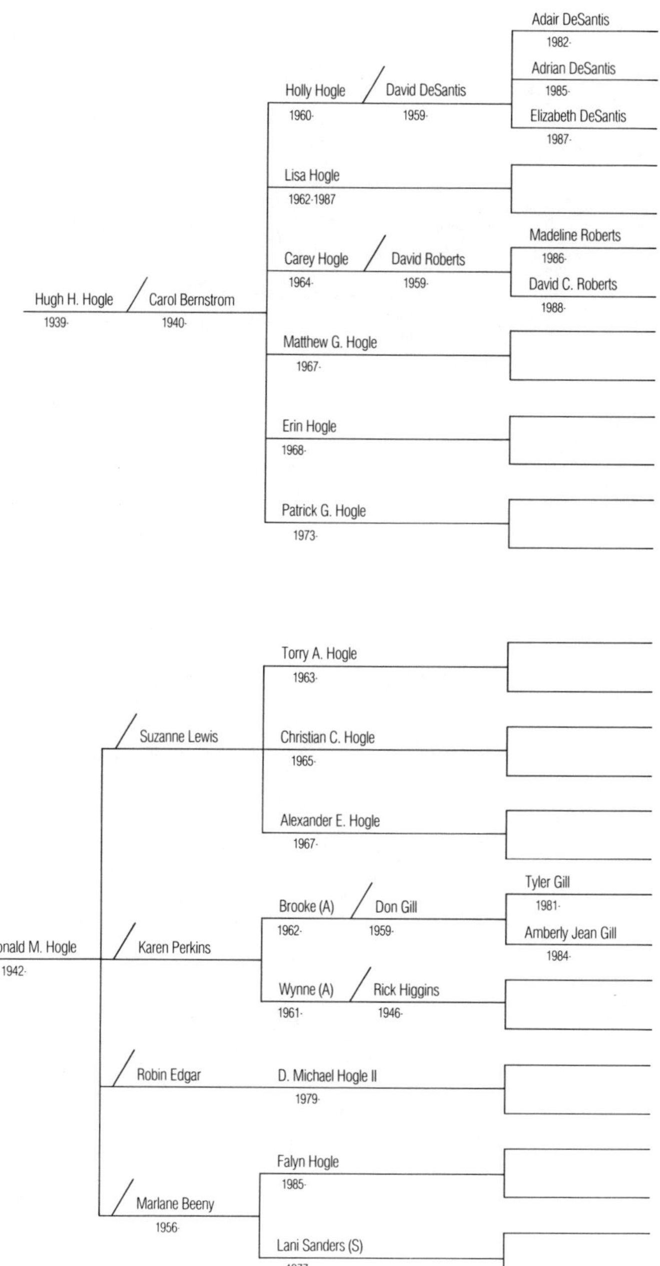

Acknowledgments

No volume of this size and complexity could be written without the contributions of many people. *The Hogles* is a family history, and it is safe to assume that it could not have been written at all without the continuous assistance of the Hogle family. Moreover, the project from the beginning was the brainchild of James E. Hogle. It had long been his wish that the story of his family should be recorded in as much detail as possible before the memories of the past and the principal characters are forgotten. Unfortunately, much of the early history of the family was already lost and the oral family history obscured by misinformation. There was the added wrinkle of the change of identity and the questions which naturally arose from that significant event. It took more than two years of extensive research and hundreds of hours of taped interviews to build the record to its present state. It has been a long haul. It could not have been accomplished without the patience and thoughtful encouragement of James E. Hogle and the keen insight of his charming and truly brilliant wife, Bonnie.

The author is grateful to Katharine Hogle Cole and Dr. George H. Hogle, who gave generously of their time and hospitality in helping to fill in the story of their parents, and to James E. Hogle, Jr., Dr. Hugh H. Hogle, Donald M. Hogle, and Owen C. Hogle for their suggestions and assistance over the duration of the project.

The author is indebted to the former employees of J. A. Hogle & Co. and Hogle Investment for their recollections — particularly to Zitelle McClellan Snarr and Marian Styles, James A. Hogle's personal secretaries, whose close association with their boss provided details available from no other sources. Other employees interviewed included Richard C. Andrew, Frank Archer, Sadie Ballard, Bert Hickok, Sherm Hinkley, and Jack Lerwill. Much of the information on the Mary C. Hogle Foundation was supplied by Ames Bagley, who worked closely with Mary Hogle on her many health and educational projects. Details of the founding of Hogle Zoological Gardens were taken from interviews and materials provided by Zoo Director Lamar Farnsworth.

The author is grateful to the office staff of Hogle Associates and Hogle Insurance, particularly to Rosalie Bywater and Barbara Miller, who searched files, typed letters of inquiry, and answered hundreds of questions over four years of close association. The author also wishes to thank Milton Moon, Gordon Bader, Ted Whitney, and Shauna Marcroft for their help, and for putting up with considerable office disruption while the research was being compiled.

Many friends and associates of the Hogle family were also interviewed, including John W. Gallivan, James Ivers III, Clarence Bamberger, and Given A. "Skip" Light. Valuable information was provided by O. N. Malmquist, Ted Speros, Olive Burt, and Jack Goodman, who created the drawing of the saloon building found on page 125 of the text.

A special note of thanks goes to David L. Freed, who donated the Hogle Brothers' Saloon token which became a motif for the dust jacket, and to Mike Nelson of Bailey-Montague & Associates, who executed the jacket design. Information on the saloon token was provided by Harry Campbell. Some materials and photographs were donated by Mary Ann Tanselle, daughter of Mary Wynkoop and great-granddaughter of Patrick Gilmore. Other photographs were contributed by Sadie Ballard, Owen C. Hogle, George H. Hogle, and Katharine Hogle Cole.

The author acknowledges the considerable help provided by the professional staffs of the Montana Historical Society, the Utah State Historical Society, the Idaho State Historical Society, the Genealogical Society of Utah, and the Salt Lake City Library System. These agencies are invaluable public resources.

The author is indebted to Richard D. Sawyer, Executive Director of the Alumni Association of St. Paul's School, for his research into James A.'s academic career and for copying issues of the *Horae Scholasticae*; Katie Moore for her microfilm research and help in compiling the Bibliography; Edward J. McDonough for his many suggestions and for his editorial assistance with the first draft of the manuscript; Roger J. McDonough for his astute if not always cheerfully received criticism; John D. Banchero for the use of his computer when the author's machine gave out, and Helen Banchero for her technical wizardry.

A good deal of credit goes to Trudy McMurrin, who took on the herculean task of editing a huge and difficult manuscript and who brought the book to completion.

Finally, I thank my wife Ronni, who lived with the Hogle Archive for the better part of three years, compiled and designed the genealogical tables, and worked on countless research, reference, and genealogical problems from the very beginning of the project. And I thank my children, Molly Bridget and Roger John. Without the help and understanding of my family, *The Hogles* could not have been written.

Notes & Sources

ABBREVIATIONS

C&C	Salt Lake City & County Archives, Salt Lake City, UT.
CH	Colorado Historical Society, Denver, CO.
CR	Sexton's Records, Salt Lake City Cemetery, Salt Lake City, UT.
FD	Fort Douglas Military Museum Library, Salt Lake City, UT.
GHH	George Hollister Hogle, Interviews and Correspondence.
GS	Genealogical Society of Utah, Salt Lake City, UT.
HA	Hogle Family Archive, Hogle Associates Office, 220 Kearns Building, Salt Lake City, UT.
IH	Idaho State Historical Society, Boise, ID.
IlH	Illinois Historical Society, Springfield, IL.
KH	Katharine Hogle Cole, Interviews and Correspondence.
JAH	James Albert Hogle, Business and Personal Correspondence.
JEH	James Edward Hogle, Interviews and Correspondence.
MiHi	Montana Historical Society Library, Helena, MT.
SaL	Salt Lake City Public Library, Salt Lake City, UT.
SCT	Third District Court Records, Salt Lake City, UT.
UH	Utah State Historical Society, Salt Lake City, UT.
UU	Marriott Library, University of Utah, Salt Lake City, UT.

THE HOGLES was written from extensive personal interviews and original research in addition to documents and materials in the Hogle Family Archive.

In the spring of 1985, a stack of unconsolidated papers, business records, and memorabilia was discovered under a pile of debris in a dilapidated shed at the Salt Lake, Garfield and Western Railroad yards. This material included ledgers, business and legal papers, letters, and other documents relating to the Hogle, Gilmore, King, and Copley families, dating from the 1870's to 1940. Much of the material was too water-damaged and weathered to be salvaged, but approximately 2,000 documents were eventually recovered. These were cleaned, sorted, filed, and indexed and now comprise the Hogle Family Archive. In addition to this collection, material was drawn from the business and personal correspondence (1940–55) of James A. Hogle and other papers on file at Hogle offices in the Kearns Building in downtown Salt Lake City. Published sources — newspapers, periodicals, and public collections — are cited for the interested reader in the text or in the notes and bibliography.

[513]

Early drafts of the manuscript were heavily footnoted. But since the purpose of this project was a book for the general reader rather than the historian or specialist, I have contented myself with citing chapter sources here and refer the researcher to the selected bibliography. Sources cited in the text are not repeated in the notes. Some documents and letters have been altered slightly for the sake of readability.

Part I. ORIGINS

Primary source materials for Part I were drawn from the Hogle Archive, the collected letters of James A. Hogle, and interviews with James E. Hogle, George H. Hogle, and Katharine Hogle Cole. Extensive research was conducted at the Genealogical Society of Utah, the Montana Historical Society Library, the Idaho State Historical Society, and the Utah State Historical Society.

Genealogical information on the Gilmore family was provided by the firm of D. Fitzpatrick & Co., Dublin, Ireland. Information on the Gilmore family in Illinois came from materials on loan from the Illinois and Iroquois County Historical Societies, including microfilm of Illinois newspapers, periodicals, and government records.

CHAPTERS 1, 2, & 3

Documents. Tithe Composition Applotments for Co. Armagh; Townlands of Ireland; church records and tax rolls for Armagh; Index to Indentures of Ireland; Canadian and American census records, 1840–80 (GS). Iroquois Co. Mortality Tables; Cemetery Records of L'Erable, IL; Reports of Iroquois Co. Board of Supervisors, 1857–60; *Iroquois Co. Republican* (IlH). John Conner Diary; N. P. Langford Papers; Luke Voorhees Memoirs; Joseph C. Walker File; Helen and W. F. Sanders Papers; Al Noyes Papers and Notes; Register of the Vote, Virginia City, MT, Oct. 24, 1863; Directory of Virginia City, 1865; Helena Directory, 1865 (MiHi).

Published Sources. Chapter 1: MacLysaght, pp. 236–37; Ranelagh; *Handbook on Irish Genealogy.* Chapter 2: Hafen, "C. W. Post Diary," pp. 28–32, "Patterson Diary," p. 66; Hall, pp. 173, 187–90, 270; Morison, p. 232; Voorhees, pp. 7–8, 31; Willison, pp. 57–59, 62–63, 110. Catton, *Picture Hist.*, p. 537; Catton, *Terrible Swift Sword*, pp. 8, 55; Dimsdale, pp. 94–101; Stuart, pp. 255–72; Tuttle, pp. 121, 124, 129–31; Voorhees, pp. 7, 8, 31 (MiHi).

Newspapers. Chapter 2: *Iroquois County Republican*, Mar. 17, 1859; *Cherry Creek News*, Dec. 10, 1858; *Bloomington Pantagraph*, Mar. 8, Apr. 15, May 1, May 9, May 20, 1859 (IlH). *Rocky Mountain News*, May 16, June 10, 1859 (CH). Chapter 3: *Rocky Mountain News*, Apr. 19–24, 1863 (CH). *Montana Post*, Apr.–June, 1865 (MiHi).

CHAPTER 4

This chapter is primarily based on research conducted at MiHi during the summer of 1985. The Keene trial was an important event in early Helena, and there are several accounts in the pioneer diaries and early papers. The most complete is found in the *Montana Post*, which Dimsdale quotes in *Vigilantes of Montana*. Additional details were taken from papers in HA, interviews with Hogle family members, and material from the MiHi manuscript collection.

Material on Owen Hogle is from HA, with additional information from IlH and Hogle family interviews.

Documents. Wyncoop Letters to JAH; Owen Hogle Discharge Papers; Nathan Thompson Deposition, 1909; Edward Rafferty Letter, 1909 (HA). (These last two documents are reproduced in the text of Chapter 9.) Also helpful were the guest, receipt, and register records of the International Hotel, Helena (Box 9); Business Directory of Montana, published by *The Montana Post*, 1866 (MiHi). Iroquois Co. Census, 1860; Mortality Schedules of Illinois, 1860 (IlH).

Published Sources. Voorhees, pp. 43–45; Dimsdale, pp. 166–73; Shoup; Tuttle, pp. 141–42, 232–37. Tuttle page references are to the published original, available in MiHi and SaL.

Newspapers. The Montana Post, Nov. 5, 1864, Mar. 10, Dec. 1, 1866 (MiHi); *Deseret News*, June–Aug. and Oct. 5, 1864, May 1865; *The Helena Herald*, July 26, 1866 (UH).

CHAPTER 5

Primary sources were researched in the spring of 1985 at IH and include interviews and research conducted in Salmon and Challis, Idaho, in the fall of that year. Additional information was taken from documents, letters, and legal papers in HA and interviews with Hogle family members. *The Idaho Statesman* provided solid information on Oro Grande in 1869–70, as did *The New Northwest* (UU). Also helpful were interviews with James Ivers III and John W. Gallivan.

Documents. U.S. Forest Service Information Packet on "Moyer Grave," Salmon, ID, 1985. Note: The location given for the grave is correct, but the Forest Service had no detailed information on the actual Loon Creek Incident and placed the events leading up to it in Yellowjacket some years later. George Shoup places the incident in Leesburg. Idaho Census, Lemhi Co., 1870, p. 24; Interview with James Horton, *Challis Silver Messenger*, Mar.–Apr. 1908 (HA). Manuscript and biography files, IH, for W. B. Emery, George Shoup, Alva P. Challis, Frank Hagenbarth, Pat Doody, and John David Wood.

Published Sources. Kirkpatrick, pp. 44–65; Yarber, p. 166; "Leesburg Discovered," in *Idaho Yesterdays Magazine* (n.d.).

Newspapers. The Idaho Statesman, "Oro Grande Notes," Sept. 1870–Jan. 1871 (IH). *The New Northwest*, Sept. 1870–Mar. 1871 (UU). *Challis Silver Messenger*, Mar.–Apr. 1908; *Salmon Idaho Recorder*, Mar.–Apr. 1908 (IH, HA).

CHAPTERS 6 & 7

Most of the material for these chapters came from research conducted at UH in the winter of 1985–86. Extensive use was made of the *Salt Lake Tribune* and *Deseret News* microfilm collections and the Polk City Directories. Material on the King family was researched at GS and in the records of St. Mark's Episcopal Cathedral (SM). Interviews with Hogle family members were also used.

Documents. Material from diaries and reminiscences of Alexander Majors, Alexander Toponce, Luke Voorhees, Bishop Daniel S. Tuttle (MiHi). Enos A. Wall File; Marcus Daly File (UH). Records of the Utah Expedition; Gen. Patrick E. Connor File (FD). Baptism, Marriage & Death Records (SM, CR). Third District Ct. Records (C&C).

Published Sources. Chapter 6: Tullidge, chs. 7 and 8, for details of early Gentile–Mormon trading and Stansbury Expedition, also, pp. 39–40, 53, 278, 281, 328; Whitney, Vols. I and II, on Gentiles in early Utah; Dwyer, chs. 1–4, esp. pp. 64, 65, 75; Morison, p. 309; Malmquist, pp. 21–53; Toponce, pp. 20–25; *Utah Historical Quarterly* (Winter 1968), pp. 40–43, 70–95. Chapter 7: "This Is Alta," Alta File (UH); Tullidge, ch. 8; Whitney, pp. 552–56, 722–30; Malmquist; Dwyer, pp. 86–93; Toponce, 155–58; Yarber, pp. 36, 125, 141, 171.

Newspapers. Chapter 6: *Salt Lake Tribune,* Dec. 26–29, 1872 (UH). Chapter 7: *Salt Lake Tribune,* July 26–28, Oct. 12, 1872; Nov. 11, 1876; Feb. 13, Mar. 17, Oct. 17, 1877; Oct. 18, 1879 (UH).

CHAPTERS 8, 9, & 10

Material on Owen Hogle is from documents in HA and interviews with Hogle family members. Much of this latter information came in turn from James E. Hogle's conversations with Owen's close friend Lena Wagener Wilson, daughter of Henry Wagener. Additional material was drawn from the letters of JAH to Mary Gilmore Wyncoop, Molly Mantor, and Archie Owen Gilmore. Invaluable information was supplied by Mary Anne Tanselle, a daughter of Mary Wyncoop. Saloon records and newspaper clippings were also very helpful, as were Salt Lake City records, licenses, and other documents in C&C.

Published Sources. Chapter 8: Polk City Directories, 1879–86; Custer Co., ID, Census, 1880; Gittins; Toponce, pp. 171–75; Fisher; Yarber; Dwyer, pp. 94–99. Chapters 9 & 10: Shoup; Runyon; Shoebotham; Tullidge; Whitney, 674–79, 722–30; Polk City Directories, 1880–1902 (UH).

Newspapers. Chapter 8: *Yankee Fork Herald,* June and July and Oct. 18, 1879; *Salt Lake Tribune,* Feb. and May 9, 1882; Aug. 25–26, 1883. Chapters 9 & 10: *Salt Lake Tribune,* Oct. 22, 1888 — May 7–12, 1889; *Salmon Idaho Recorder,* week of Mar. 20, 1908; *Deseret News,* Aug. 17, 1859 — May 12, 1889.

CHAPTERS 11, 12, & 13

Source materials for these chapters are found in HA, including deeds, depositions, contracts and other legal documents, letters, record books, ledgers, receipts, and memorabilia. Interviews with JEH and GHH were important in setting this information in context.

Documents. Historical Sketches of the Clark–Hoagland Families, p. 8 (IlH). Anti-Saloon League pamphlet; Polk City Directories, 1890–1917 (UH). Nathan Thompson Deposition; Ed Rafferty Letter (HA). Illinois Census, 1900 (GS).

Published Sources. Whitney, pp. 610–15; Morison, pp. 104–6.

Newspapers. *Salt Lake Tribune,* Apr. 28, 1894, Sept. 7, 1902, Mar. 8–16, 1908; *Salt Lake Herald,* Mar. 16, 1908 (UH). *Salt Lake Telegram,* Mar. 16–17, 1908, July 3, 1911 (UU). *Salmon Idaho Recorder,* Mar. 1908; *Challis Silver Messenger,* Mar. 1908 (HA, IH).

Part II. JAMES ALBERT HOGLE

Chapters on the early life of James A. Hogle were written from letters, documents, and other materials in HA and interviews with KH, JEH, and

GHH. Material was also drawn from the business and personal correspondence (1940–55) of JAH and from other papers on file at the Hogle Associates offices.

CHAPTERS 14 & 15

Documents. Ida E. Hogle File, Letters, 1890–1900; JAH Autobiographical Essay and School papers and lessons; Owen Hogle Files; JAH Letters to Archie Owen Gilmore, Mary Wyncoop (HA). Polk Directories, 1876–90; Great Salt Lake and Salt Lake City Pamphlet Files; Lithographs of Salt Lake City (UH).

Published Sources. Tullidge; Whitney; Shoebotham.

Newspapers. New York Times, Aug. 31–July 1, 1892.

CHAPTERS 16 & 17

Material on James A. Hogle's school days at St. Paul's is drawn primarily from his business and personal correspondence, 1940–55. The author is indebted to Richard D. Sawyer, Executive Director of the Alumni Association of St. Paul's, for helping to research James A.'s academic career and for copying issues of the *Horae Scholasticae,* 1892–96. Background material on the history of St. Paul's is from the *Horae Scholasticae* and from August Heckscher's excellent history. Some details were supplied through interviews with JEH and GHH.

Documents. Ida E. Hogle File, Letters, 1890–1900; JAH School papers and lessons and Letters to Dr. Elton Littell, James Gray, Holkins Palmer, Richard Graff, George Murrell, Parker Straw, and Alumni Association correspondence, 1947–55 (HA).

Published Sources: Heckscher, pp. 8–10, 25–26, 98–103, 112–15, 120–39.

CHAPTER 18

Material for this chapter drawn from the business and personal correspondence of JAH (1940–55) and from interviews with Hogle family members.

Documents. JAH Letters to George Murrell, Dr. Elton Littell, Paul N. Dann, Edward Skinner, Marcus Daly; also JAH Autobiographical Essay (HA).

Published Sources. Shoebotham.

Newspapers. New York Times, June 25–30, 1899. *Salt Lake Tribune,* Nov. 3, 1946.

CHAPTER 19

The details of James A. Hogle's trip to Russia are drawn from a packet of letters uncovered at a shed at the Salt Lake, Garfield and Western Railroad yards in 1985. The letters, addressed to Mary Copley, cover the entire trip from February to July 1910. Other sources include JAH Autobiographical Essay, interviews with KH, and *Salt Lake Tribune,* Nov. 3, 1946.

Part III. MARY CECILIA COPLEY

Most of the material for this section was taken from documents on file in HA and interviews with Hogle family members.

CHAPTER 20

Documents. Genealogical information on the Copley and Sibbet families is from the Copley–Thaw Family History and the Letters and writings of Mary

C. Hogle; see also History of the Appleby Manor Memorial Chapel (HA). Information on the Woodward and Hollister families was found at GS. Civil War material is from the writings of Josiah Copley and the Letters of Josiah Copley, Jr. (HA).

Published Sources. Catton, *Picture Hist.*, pp. 418–43, 500–5; Long, pp. 114–15, 297–307, 408–15.

Chapter 21

Compiled exclusively from materials in HA. Mary C. Hogle wrote several versions of "Say 'No' to Fate." The one which appears in this volume was rewritten slightly for readability; some sections were augmented by the author with material from Mary's letters.

Chapters 22 & 23

Interviews with KH, GHH, JEH, and Ames Bagley, and materials from HA and SM. The newspaper clipping file at the Hogle Zoological Gardens was the primary source of information on the founding of the zoo; also see the Zoo File at UH.

Part IV. J. A. HOGLE & CO.
Part V. AFFLICTION, STRUGGLE, & TRIUMPH

Chapters on the business career of James A. Hogle are based on interviews with former employees of J. A. Hogle & Co. and with Hogle family members. HA documents and JAH correspondence files were also used. Material on Mary C. Hogle comes primarily from interviews with family members. Some of her correspondence is on file, but most of the records of the Mary C. Hogle Foundation have been lost.

Chapter 24

Interviews with Zitelle McClellan Snarr, Marian Styles, Richard C. Andrew, and Ames Bagley.

Chapter 25

Interviews with KH, GHH, and JEH, and documents in HA as cited in the text.

Chapter 26

Interviews with Marian Styles, Jack Lerwill, Ames Bagley, and Hogle family members. See Pamphlet File, LDS Church Security [Welfare] System, UH; also JAH Letters and documents and Autobiographical Essay (HA).

Chapter 27

Interviews with Bert Hickok, John W. Gallivan, Skip Light, Marian Styles, Frank Archer, Ed Whitney, Rosalie Bywater, and Gordon Bader. War and market history from *Salt Lake Tribune*, December 1941 to July 1942.

Chapter 28

Interviews with Ames Bagley, Marian Styles, KH, GHH, JEH, and letters of Mary C. Hogle (HA).

Published Sources. Young, pp. 13–37, 76–79, 158–89, 333–59; Barrett, pp. 100–22, 176, 186; Hoffman, pp. 7–27, 55–117, 128–45, 299–381, 478–90, 573–79, 605–7, 655–64.

CHAPTERS 29 & 30

Interviews with JEH, GHH, KH, and Marian Styles; also JAH Letters to Paul N. Dann, George Murrell, Lois Crozier, and KH, in HA.

CHAPTERS 31, 32, & 33

Documents on file in HA were used extensively in writing the chapters on the final illness of Mary C. Hogle. These included medical reports and various letters of JAH; also, interviews with KH, JEH, GHH; JAH Letters to James Gray, Dr. Elton Littell, George Copley, Bert Copley, as cited in the text. See also *Science* (Sept. 1983) and *The New England Journal of Medicine* (May and Nov. 1986).

Newspapers. Salt Lake Evening Telegram, Apr. 15–16, 1952; *Salt Lake Tribune*, Apr. 16–17, 1952; *Deseret News*, Apr. 16, 18, 1952.

CHAPTER 34

Interviews with KH, JEH, GHH, and Marian Styles; also JAH Letters to Archie Owen Gilmore, Mary Wyncoop, Edna Weed, George Murrell, George Copley, and Bert Copley.

Selected Bibliography

The abbreviations appearing at the beginning of the Notes and Sources section are utilized here as well to identify the locations of documents, manuscripts, letters, and rare or out-of-print books. An attempt has been made to identify current editions of books the author consulted in earlier forms in the various archives.

DOCUMENTS

Cemetery Records, Salt Lake City, 1860–1930 (CR).

Census Records: Canada, 1830–60 (GS); Colorado, 1860, 1870, 1900, 1910 (GS); Lemhi and Custer Counties, Idaho, 1870, 1880, 1910 (IH, GS); Illinois, 1850, 1860, 1870, 1880, 1900 (GS); Indiana, 1870, 1880, 1910 (GS); Montana, 1870, 1880, 1910 (MiHi, GS); Utah, 1870, 1880–1920 (GS).

City Licenses, Salt Lake City, 1860–1918 (C&C).

Directories: Denver, CO, 1860 (CH); Helena, MT, 1864–70 (MiHi); Salt Lake City, UT, 1880–1940 (UH); Virginia City, MT, 1863–65 (MiHi).

Langford, Nathan P., Papers (MiHi).

Mortality Schedules, Illinois, 1860 (IlH).

Mortality Tables, Iroquois Co., IL, 1860 (IlH).

Moyer Grave, U.S. Forest Service Pamphlet, Place Names of Idaho File (IH).

Parish Records: Marriages, Baptisms, Burials, St. Mark's Cathedral, 1869–1955 (SM).

Poll Census, Virginia City, MT, Doc. 1997 (MiHi).

Registers, International Hotel, Virginia City/Helena, MT (MiHi).

Saloon Records, 1885–1908 (HA).

Third District Court Records, Salt Lake City, 1887, 1889, 1900, 1902 (SCT).

Thompson, Nathan, Deposition Taken Dec. 9, 1909 (HA).

Tithe Composition Applotments, Co. Armagh, Ireland (GS).

Townlands of Ireland (GS).

Manuscripts & Letters

Autobiographical Sketches, Biographical Notes, and Diaries: X Beidler, John Conner, G. Julius Germain, Alexander Majors, William F. Sanders, Luke Voorhees, Joseph C. Walker (MiHi); Marcus Daly, George Hearst, Thomas Kearns, Alexander Toponce, Enos A. Wall (UH); Alva Challis, Frank Hagenbarth, James Hayden, A. A. Mayfield, George Shoup, John David Wood (IH).

Historical Sketches of Clark–Hoagland Families, Iroquois County (IL) Historical Society (IlH).

Hogle Family, Collected Correspondence (HA):

James Hogle, 1880–1907;
Ida E. Hogle, 1880–1920;
James Albert Hogle, 1883–1910;
Mary C. Hogle, 1909–52;
Owen Hogle (Letters to), 1889–1901.

Hogle, James Albert, Business and Personal Correspondence, 1940–55 (HA).

Hogle, James Edward, Selected Correspondence with Various Family Members, 1955–80 (HA).

Hogle, Mary C. "Say 'No' to Fate." Unpublished Autobiographical Sketch in Several Drafts (HA).

Pamphlet Files, by Topic: Alta, UT; Anti-Saloon League; Great Salt Lake; Hogle Zoo; Police Report, 1876 (UH). Bonanza, ID; Challis, ID; Leesburg Pioneers; Oro Grande, ID; Salmon City, ID (IH). Alder Gulch, MT; Helena, MT; Montana Vigilantes (MiHi).

Books and Pamphlets

Adams, Ramon F. *Burs Under the Saddle*. Norman: Univ. of Oklahoma Press, 1964.

————. *Six-Guns and Saddle Leather*. Norman: Univ. of Oklahoma Press, 1969.

Bailey, Robert G. *River of No Return: The Great Salmon River of Idaho*. Lewiston, ID: Bailey, Blake Printing Co., 1935.

Bailyn, Bernard, David Brion Davis, David Herbert Donald, et al. *The Great Republic: A History of the American People*. Boston: Little, Brown, 1977.

Barrett, Stephen, and Gilda Knight, eds. *Health Robbers*. Philadelphia: George F. Stickley, Co., 1969.

Barsness, Larry. *Gold Camp; Alder Gulch and Virginia City, Montana*. New York: Hastings House, 1962.

Baucus, Jean. *Gold in the Gulch*. Helena, MT: Bar Wineglass Publications, 1981.

Birney, Hoffman. *Vigilantes*. Philadelphia: Penn. Publishing, 1929. (MiHi)

Blankenship, Russell, and Alfred A. Knopf, eds. *And There Were Men*. New York: 1942.

Boller, Henry A. *Among the Indians: Four Years on the Upper Missouri, 1858–1862*. 1868. Reprint. Milo M. Quaife, ed. Lincoln: Univ. of Nebraska Press, 1972.

Bruffy, George A. *Eighty-one Years in the West*. Butte, MT: 1925. (MiHi)

Burdick, Usher L. *Tales From Buffalo Land*. Baltimore: North Bros., 1940. (CI)

Campbell, William C. *From the Queries of Last Chance Gulch: A Long History*. Helena, MT: 1951. (MiHi)

Catton, Bruce. *The Coming Fury*. The Centennial History of the Civil War, Vol. I. New York: Doubleday, 1961.

————. *Terrible Swift Sword*. The Centennial History of the Civil War, Vol. II. New York: Doubleday, 1963.

————. *Never Call Retreat*. The Centennial History of the Civil War, Vol. III. New York: Doubleday, 1965.

————. *American Heritage Picture History of the Civil War*. New York: Outlet Books, 1964.

Clampitt, W. *Echoes from the Rocky Mountains*. Chicago: 1888. (MiHi, UH)

Connolly, Christopher P. *The Devil Learns to Vote*. New York: 1938. (MiHi, UH)

Contributions to the Historical Society of Montana, Vol. V. Helena, MT: Independent Publishing Co., 1904. (MiHi)

Copley–Thaw Family History. Pennsylvania: Privately published, ca. 1898. (HA)

Dimsdale, Thomas J. *Vigilantes of Montana*. 1864; edition includes notes by Al Noyes. Reprint. Norman: Univ. of Oklahoma Press, 1985. (SaL)

Dwyer, Robert Joseph. *The Gentile Comes to Utah*. Salt Lake City: Western Epics, 1971. (UH)

Esshom, Frank. *Pioneers and Prominent Men of Utah*. Salt Lake City: Utah Pioneer Book Publishing, 1913. (SaL)

Fisher, Vardis. *Idaho Lore*. Caldwell, ID: Caxton, 1939. (IH)

Gittins, H. Leigh. *Idaho's Gold Road*. Moscow, ID: Univ. of Idaho Press, 1976.

Hafen, LeRoy R., ed. *Overland Routes to the Gold Fields; From Contemporary Diaries*. Southwest Historical Series, Vol. XI. Glendale, CA: The Arthur H. Clark Co., 1942. (CH, MiHi, SaL)

Hall, Frank, for the Rocky Mountain Historical Company. *History of the State of Colorado*, Vol. I. Chicago: The Blakely Printing Co., 1889. (CH)

Handbook on Irish Genealogy: How to Trace Your Ancestors and Relatives in Ireland. Dublin: Heraldic Artists, Ltd., 1980.

Harte, Bret. *Tales of the Gold Rush*. Introduction by Oscar Lewis. New York: The Heritage Press, 1944. (IH, UH)

Heckscher, August. *St. Paul's: The Life of a New England School*. New York: Charles Scribner's Sons, 1980.

Hoffman, Frederick L. *Cancer and Diet*. Baltimore: Waverly Press, 1937. (Univ. of CT Medical Lib.)

Hogle, Mary C. *Foods That Alkalinize and Heal*. Salt Lake City: Mary C. Hogle Fd., 8 eds., 1932–40.

Hunter, George. *Reminiscences of an Old Timer*. San Francisco: 1887. (MiHi)

522 *Selected Bibliography*

Hutchens, John K. *One Man's Montana*. Philadelphia: Lippincott, 1964.

Kirkpatrick, Orion. *History of the Leesburg Pioneers*. Salt Lake City: 1936. (IH)

Long, E. B., and Barbara Long. *The Civil War Day by Day: An Almanac, 1861–1865*. New York: Doubleday, 1971.

Lyman, George D. *The Saga of the Comstock Lode; Boom Days in Virginia City*. New York: Charles Scribner's Sons, 1951. (SaL)

McClure, A. K. *Three Thousand Miles Through the Rocky Mountains*. Philadelphia: 1869. (MiHi)

MacLysaght, Edward. *Irish Families; Their Names, Arms and Origins*. Illustrated by Myra Maguire. Dublin: Allen Figgs and Co., Ltd., 1957.

Mather, Ruth E., and F. E. Boswell. *Hanging the Sheriff: A Biography of Henry Plummer*. University of Utah Publications in the American West, Vol. 21. Salt Lake City: Univ. of Utah Press, 1987.

Malmquist, O. N. *The First Hundred Years: A History of the Salt Lake Tribune, 1871–1971*. Salt Lake City: Utah State Historical Society, 1971. (UH)

Monaghan, Jay. *Civil War on the Western Border, Eighteen Fifty–four to Eighteen Sixty–five*. 1955. Reprint. Lincoln: Univ. of Nebraska Press, 1984.

Morison, Samuel Eliot. *The Oxford History of the American People, Vol. II, 1789–1887*. London: The New English Library, Ltd., 1965.

Munson, Judge Lyman E. "Reminiscences of Montana," in *Journal of American History*. New Haven, CT: 1907. (MiHi)

Pace, Dick, and Sidney Cosens. *Golden Gulch*. Butte, MT: 1962. (MiHi, SaL)

Peltier, Jerome, ed. *Banditti of the Rockies*. Berkeley, CA: Ross, 1964.

Ranelagh, John O'Beirne. *A Short History of Ireland*. London: Cambridge Univ. Press, 1983.

Robertson, Ruth Winder. "Mining," "Ghost Towns of Utah," "This Is Alta." Three essays bound together. Alta, UT: 1972. (UH)

Runyon, Damon. *More Guys and Dolls; Thirty-four of the Best Short Stories*. Introduction by Clark Kinnaird. Philadelphia and New York: Lippincott, 1951.

Salisbury, Jane, and Albert Salisbury. *Here Rolled the Covered Wagons*. 1948. Reprint. Np: Midwest Old Settlers, nd. (MiHi)

Sanders, Helen, and William H. Bertsche, Jr., eds. *X Beidler: Vigilante*. Foreword by A. B. Guthrie, Jr. Norman: Univ. of Oklahoma Press, 1957. (UH)

Shoebotham, H. Minar. *Anaconda: Life of Marcus Daly — The Copper King*. Harrisburg, PA: The Stackpole Co., 1956. (UH, SaL)

Shoup, Col. George. *History of Lemhi County*. Salmon, ID: *Salmon Idaho Recorder*, 1940. (IH)

Smith, Alson Jesse. *Brother Van*. New York: Ca. 1922. (MiHi)

Stone, Arthur. *Following Old Trails*. Missoula, MT: 1913. (MiHi)

Strahorn, Carrie Adell. *Fifteen Thousand Miles by Stage*. (UH)

Stuart, Granville. *Prospecting for Gold: From Dogtown to Virginia City, 1852–1864*. Edited by Paul C. Phillips. Glendale, CA: Arthur H. Clark Co., 1925. (Originally published under the title *Forty Years on the Frontier as Seen in the Journals and Reminiscences of Granville Stuart, Gold Miner, Trader, Merchant, Rancher and Politician*, Vol. I.) (MiHi)

Thane, Eric. *High Border Country*. New York: Duell, Sloan, & Pearce, 1942.

Thomas, D. K. *Wild Life in the Rocky Mountains*. 1917.

Toponce, Alexander. *Reminiscences of Alexander Toponce*. Ogden, UT: Privately published, 1923. (UH)

Trimble, William J. *The Mining Advance into the Inland Empire: A Comparative Study of the Beginnings of the Mining Industry in Idaho and Montana, Eastern Washington and Oregon and the Southern Interior of British Columbia, and of Institutions and Laws Based Upon That Industry*. 1914. Reprint. New York: Johnson Reprints, nd.

Tullidge, Edward W. *History of Salt Lake City*. By Authority of the City Council under the Supervision of a Committee Appointed by the Council and the Author; Revising Committee, John R. Winder, Chairman. Salt Lake City: Star Printing Company, 1886. (UH, SaL)

Tuttle, Daniel S. *Missionary to the Mountain West: The Reminiscences of Episcopal Bishop Daniel S. Tuttle, 1866–1886*. 1906. Reprint. Foreword by Brigham D. Madsen. Salt Lake City: Univ. of Utah Press, 1987.

Voorhees, Luke. *Personal Recollections of Pioneer Life on the Plains of the Great West*. Cheyenne, WY: 1920. (MiHi)

Whitney, Orson F. *History of Utah . . . in Four Volumes*. Salt Lake City: George Q. Cannon & Sons, Publishers, 1892–1904. (UH, SaL)

Willison, George F. *Here They Dug the Gold: Colorado's Gold Rush, 1859–1869*. 1943. Reprint. Glorieta, NM: Rio Grande Press, 1986.

Wood, J. D. *Reminiscence*. Salt Lake City: 1902. (IH)

Yarber, Esther. *Land of the Yankee Fork*. 1963. Reprint. Salt Lake City: Publisher's Press, 1970. (IH)

Young, James Harvey. *Medical Messiahs: A Social History of Medical Quackery in Twentieth-Century America*. Princeton, NJ: Princeton University Press, 1967.

NEWSPAPERS, BY DEPOSITORY

Colorado Historical Society:
Cherry Creek News, Denver, CO.
Rocky Mountain News, Denver, CO.

Idaho State Historical Society:
The Challis Silver Messenger, Challis, ID.
The Idaho Statesman, Boise, ID.
The Salmon Idaho Recorder, Salmon City, ID.
The Yankee Fork Herald, Challis, ID.

Illinois Historical Society:
The Bloomington Pantagraph, Bloomington, IL.
Iroquois Republican, West Middleport, IL.

Montana State Historical Society:
The Montana Post, Virginia City/Helena, MT.
The Helena Herald, Helena, MT.

St. Paul's School, Concord, NH:
Horae Scholasticae.

University of Utah Marriott Library:
  The New Northwest, Deer Lodge, MT.
  The New York Times, New York City, NY.
  The Rocky Mountain News, Denver, CO.
  The Salt Lake Telegram, Salt Lake City, UT.
  The Union Vedette, Fort Douglas, UT Terr.
Utah State Historical Society:
  The Deseret News. Salt Lake City, UT.
  Park City Record. Park City, UT.
  The Salt Lake Herald. Salt Lake City, UT.
  The Salt Lake Tribune. Salt Lake City, UT.

The Hogles was edited and the production supervised by Trudy McMurrin.

The book was designed and set in hot metal Intertype Baskerville
by Donald M. Henriksen.

McMurrin and Henriksen were assisted by the following suppliers,
all of Salt Lake City:

Disk correction and additional typing: Jeoffrey R. McAllister

Jacket design and mechanicals and genealogical charts:
Bailey-Montague & Associates

Printing: Publishers Press

Binding: Mountain States Bindery